OTHELLO

EDITED BY
JULIE HANKEY

CAMBRIDGE
UNIVERSITY PRESS

PUBLISHED BY THE PRESS SYNDICATE OF THE UNIVERSITY OF CAMBRIDGE
The Pitt Building, Trumpington Street, Cambridge, United Kingdom

CAMBRIDGE UNIVERSITY PRESS
The Edinburgh Building, Cambridge, CB2 2RU, UK
40 West 20th Street, New York, NY 10011–4211, USA
477 Williamstown Road, Port Melbourne, VIC 3207, Australia
Ruiz de Alarcón 13, 28014 Madrid, Spain
Dock House, The Waterfront, Cape Town 8001, South Africa

http://www.cambridge.org

First published 2005

Printed in the United Kingdom at the University Press, Cambridge

Typefaces EhrhardtMT 10/12.5 pt. and FormataCond   *System* LATEX 2$_\varepsilon$ [TB]

A catalogue record for this book is available from the British Library

Library of Congress Cataloguing in Publication data
Shakespeare, William, 1564–1616.
Othello / edited by Julie Hankey – 2nd edn.
p.   cm. – (Shakespeare in production)
Includes bibliographical references and index.
ISBN 0 521 83458 9 – ISBN 0 521 54236 7 (pbk)
1. Othello (Fictitious character) – Drama.   2. Shakespeare, William, 1564–1616. Othello –
Criticism, Textual.   3. Shakespeare, William, 1564–1616 – Stage history.   I. Hankey, Julie.
II. Title.
PR2829.A2H36   2005
822.3′3 – dc22   2004054031

ISBN-13 978 0 521 83458 2 (hardback)
ISBN-10 0 521 83458 9 (hardback)
ISBN-13 978 0 521 54236 4 (paperback)
ISBN-10 0 521 54236 7 (paperback)

The publisher has used its best endeavours to ensure that the URLs for external websites
referred to in this book are correct and active at the time of going to press. However, the
publisher has no responsibility for the websites and can make no guarantee that a site will
remain live or that the content is or will remain appropriate.

CONTENTS

ILLUSTRATIONS

SERIES EDITORS' PREFACE

It is no longer necessary to stress that the text of a play is only its starting-point, and that only in production is its potential realised and capable of being appreciated fully. Since the coming-of-age of Theatre Studies as an academic discipline, we now understand that even Shakespeare is only one collaborator in the creation and infinite recreation of his play upon the stage. And just as we now agree that no play is complete until it is produced, so we have become interested in the way in which plays often produced – and pre-eminently the plays of the national Bard, William Shakespeare – acquire a life history of their own, after they leave the hands of their first maker.

Since the eighteenth century Shakespeare has become a cultural construct: sometimes the guarantor of nationhood, heritage and the status quo, sometimes seized and transformed to be its critic and antidote. This latter role has been particularly evident in countries where Shakespeare has to be translated. The irony is that while his status as national icon grows in the English-speaking world, his language is both lost and renewed, so that for good or ill, Shakespeare can be made to seem more urgently 'relevant' than in England or America, and may become the one dissenting voice that the censors mistake as harmless.

'Shakespeare in Production' gives the reader, the student and the scholar a comprehensive dossier of materials – eye-witness accounts, contemporary criticism, promptbook marginalia, stage business, cuts, additions and rewritings – from which to construct an understanding of the many meanings that the plays have carried down the ages and across the world. These materials are organised alongside the New Cambridge Shakespeare text of the play, line by line and scene by scene, while a substantial introduction in each volume offers a guide to their interpretation. One may trace an argument about, for example, the many ways of playing Queen Gertrude, or the political transmutations of the text of *Henry V*; or take a scene, an act, or a whole play, and work out how it has succeeded or failed in presentation over four hundred years.

For, despite our insistence that the plays are endlessly made and remade by history, Shakespeare is not a blank, scribbled upon by the age. Theatre history charts changes, but also registers something in spite of those changes. Some productions work and others do not. Two interpretations may be entirely different, and yet both will bring the play to life. Why? Without setting out to give absolute answers, the history of a play in the theatre can often show where the energy and shape of it lie, what has made it tick, through many permutations. In this way theatre history can find common ground with literary criticism. Both will find suggestive directions in the introductions to these volumes, while the commentaries provide raw material for readers to recreate the living experience of theatre, and become their own eye-witness.

J. S. Bratton
Julie Hankey

ABBREVIATIONS

A	*Athenaeum*
Bell	*Bell's Edition of Shakespeare's plays*, ed. Francis Gentleman, vol. 1. *Othello*, as Performed at the Theatre Royal Drury Lane. Regulated from the Prompt-Book . . . by Mr Hopkins, Prompter, London, 1774
BM	*Blackwood's Magazine*
C	*Century*
Carroll	Janet Barton Carroll, 'A Promptbook Study of Margaret Webster's Production of Othello', PhD dissertation, Louisiana State University, 1977
Cumberland	Cumberland edition. *Othello, a Tragedy*. Printed from the Acting Copy with Remarks by D-G [George Daniel]. (Issued as part of *Cumberland's British Theatre*, vol. 11), 1829
DT	*Daily Telegraph*
EIM	*English Illustrated Magazine*
EN	*Evening News*
ES	*Evening Standard*
FT	*Financial Times*
G	*Guardian*
Hazlitt	William Hazlitt, *The Complete Works of William Hazlitt*, ed. P. P. Howe, 21 vols., London and Toronto, 1930–4, vols. v and xviii
I	*Independent*
IHT	*International Herald Tribune*
ILN	*Illustrated London News*
IoS	*Independent on Sunday*
L	*Listener*
LI	*Life International*
LM	*Lippincott's Magazine*
LR	*Literary Review*
Mason	E. T. Mason, *The Othello of Tommaso Salvini*, New York: Putnam's, 1890

MG	*Manchester Guardian*
MM	*Macmillan's Magazine*
MoS	*Mail on Sunday*
MS	*Morning Star*
NS	*New Statesman*
NS and N	*New Statesman and National*
NYT	*New York Times*
O	*Observer*
Ottley	Henry Ottley, *Fechter's Version of Othello Critically Analysed*, London, 1861
P and P	*Plays and Players*
PQ	*Philological Quarterly*
S	*Spectator*
SB	*Shakespeare Bulletin*
Sh. S	*Shakespeare Survey*
Sprague	A. C. Sprague, *Shakespeare and the Actors: The Stage Business in His Plays (1660–1905)*, Cambridge, MA: Harvard University Press, 1945
SQ	*Shakespeare Quarterly*
ST	*Sunday Times*
STel	*Sunday Telegraph*
T	*The Times*
TB	*Temple Bar*
TJ	*Theatrical Journal*
TLS	*Times Literary Supplement*
TO	*Time Out*
TQ	*Theatre Quarterly*
Variorum	Horace Howard Furness, *Othello: A New Variorum Edition of Shakespeare*, Philadelphia, 1886, vol. VI
F1	The first Folio, published in 1623
OED	*Oxford English Dictionary*
Q1	The first quarto, published in 1622
Q2	The second quarto, published in 1630
RSC	Royal Shakespeare Company
WP	*Washington Post*

PRODUCTIONS

Location is London unless otherwise noted.

Date	Actor(s)/Director	Theatre/medium
?1603–18	Richard Burbage	Globe/Blackfriars
1618–42	Ellyaerdt Swanston	Globe/Blackfriars
	Joseph Taylor: Iago	
1660–9	Nicholas Burt	The Cockpit, Drury Lane
	Walter Clun (died 1664): Iago	The Bridges Street Theatre (from
	Michael Mohun (after 1664): Iago	1663)
?1674–82	Charles Hart	The Theatre Royal (hereafter
	Michael Mohun: Iago	Drury Lane)
1682–1709	Thomas Betterton	Drury Lane
	Samuel Sandford: Iago (until 1702)	
1710–27	Barton Booth	Drury Lane
1720–51	James Quin	Lincoln's Inn Fields
	Colley Cibber: Iago	
1734–77	Charles Macklin: Iago	Haymarket
1745–6	David Garrick (3 performances)	Drury Lane
1747–75	Spranger Barry	Drury Lane (Barry was at the
	Macklin, Garrick, Ryan, Bensley:	Smock Alley Theatre, Dublin,
	Iago	1744–6)
	Susanna Cibber: Desdemona	
1771–94	Robert Bensley: Iago	Covent Garden
1780–5	John Henderson: Iago	Covent Garden
1785–1805	J. P. Kemble	Drury Lane
	Sarah Siddons: Desdemona	
	Charles Kemble: Cassio	
1792	Francois-Joseph Talma in Ducis's	Théâtre-Français
	transl./version	
1803	G. F. Cooke: Iago	Covent Garden

Date	Actor(s)/Director	Theatre/medium
1814–33	Edmund Kean J. B. Booth, W. C. Macready, Edwin Forrest: Iago	Drury Lane
1816–51	W. C. Macready George Vandenhoff, C. M. Young: Iago Fanny Kemble, Helena Faucit: Desdemona	Covent Garden
1827–8	Edmund Kean Macready: Iago	Théâtre Favert, Paris
1829	Joanny in Alfred de Vigny's translation Mlle Mars: Desdemona	La Comédie Française
1833, 1858, 1865	Ira Aldridge Ellen Tree, Madge Kendal: Desdemona	Covent Garden, Lyceum, Haymarket
1826–71	Edwin Forrest	The Bowery, New York Drury Lane (1836)
1834, 1836	*Othello Travestie: an operatic burlesque*, by Maurice G. Dowling	The Liver Theatre (Liverpool); The Strand
1837–72	Samuel Phelps	Haymarket Sadlers Wells (1844–61)
1848	Gustavus Vaughan Brooke	Olympic Theatre Queens' Theatre, Melbourne (1855)
1856	Charles Dillon	Lyceum
1861–2	Charles Fechter/John Ryder (alternating Othello and Iago)	The Princess's Theatre
1860–9	Edwin Booth	Winter Garden, New York; Booth's Theatre, New York (1869–73)
1875, 1884	Tommaso Salvini	Drury Lane; Covent Garden
1876	Henry Irving Isabel Bateman: Desdemona	Lyceum
1881	Henry Irving/Edwin Booth (alternating Othello and Iago) Ellen Terry: Desdemona	Lyceum

Date	Actor(s)/Director	Theatre/medium
1881	Ernesto Rossi	Booth's Theatre, New York(in 1876 Rossi did extracts from *Othello* at Drury Lane)
1886–1921	Frank Benson	Shakespeare Memorial Theatre (hereafter Stratford)
1889	*Otello* by Verdi	Covent Garden (English debut)
1898	Ellen Terry: Desdemona Frank Cooper: Othello	Grand Theatre, Fulham
1902	Johnston Forbes-Robertson	Lyric
1907, 1908, 1911	Oscar Asche Alfred Brydone: Iago	His Majesty's Theatre
1907	Ermete Novelli	Lyric Theatre, New York
1910	Giovanni Grasso	Lyric
1912	Herbert Beerbohm Tree Laurence Irving: Iago Phyllis Neilson-Terry: Desdemona	His Majesty's Theatre
1921, 1948, 1949	Godfrey Tearle	Court Theatre (1921); Stratford
1922, 1927, 1943	Baliol Holloway (alternating Othello/Iago with Abraham Sofaer, 1943)	Stratford
1924	Ion Swinley	Old Vic
1929	H. K. Ayliffe (director)	Birmingham Repertory
1930	Paul Robeson Peggy Ashcroft: Desdemona Sybil Thorndyke: Emilia	The Savoy Theatre
1930, 1932	Wilfred Walter George Hayes: Iago (1930) Ralph Richardson: Iago (1932)	Stratford (1930) Old Vic (1932)
1931	Edmund Willard	Arts Theatre
1932	Ernest Milton	St James's
1935	Abraham Sofaer Maurice Evans: Iago	Old Vic
1938	Ralph Richardson Laurence Olivier: Iago Tyrone Guthrie (director)	Old Vic

Date	Actor(s)/Director	Theatre/medium
1940, 1944	Donald Wolfit	Kingsway (1940)
		Scala (1944)
1942, 1947	Frederic Valk	The New Theatre (1942)
	Bernard Miles: Iago (1942)	Savoy (1947)
	Donald Wolfit: Iago (1947)	
1943	Paul Robeson	Shubert Theatre, New York
	José Ferrer: Iago	
	Uta Hagen: Desdemona	
	Margaret Webster (director)	
1947	Jack Hawkins	Piccadilly
	Anthony Quayle: Iago	
1950, 1952,	Anthony Quayle	Stratford (and on tour in
1954		Australia)
1951	Orson Welles	St James's
1952, 1956	Orson Welles	Film (1952, USA
	Michael MacLiammoir: Iago	1956, UK)
	Suzanne Cloutier: Desdemona	
	Fay Compton: Emilia	
1953, 1957	Earle Hyman	Jan Hus Auditorium, New York
		(1953)
		Shakespeare Festival, Stratford,
		Connecticut (1957)
1956	Richard Burton/John Neville	Old Vic
	(alternating Othello and Iago)	
1959	Paul Robeson	Stratford
1964	Laurence Olivier	Old Vic
	Frank Finlay: Iago	
	Maggie Smith: Desdemona	
	John Dexter (director)	
1964	James Earl Jones	The New York Shakespeare
		Festival, Central Park; The
		Martinique
1965	Olivier/Finlay/Smith	Film of 1964 Old Vic production
	Stuart Burge (director)	
1968	*Not Now, Sweet Desdemona*, by	Makarere University College
	Murray Carlin	
1970–1	*Catch My Soul* (Rock musical version	The Roundhouse
	of *Othello*)	

Date	Actor(s)/Director	Theatre/medium
1971, 1972	Brewster Mason	Stratford (1971)
	Emrys James: Iago	Aldwych (1972)
	Lisa Harrow: Desdemona	
	Elizabeth Spriggs: Emilia	
	John Barton (director)	
1971	Bruce Purchase	Mermaid Theatre
	Bernard Miles: Iago	
1972	*An Othello*, by Charles Marowitz	Open Space Theatre
1979, 1980	Donald Sinden	Stratford (1979)
	Bob Peck: Iago	Aldwych (1980)
	Ronald Eyre (director)	
1980	Paul Scofield	The National Theatre
	Michael Bryant: Iago	
	Felicity Kendal: Desdemona	
	Yvonne Bryceland: Emilia	
	Peter Hall (director)	
1981	Anthony Hopkins	Television film: BBC (available on
	Bob Hoskins: Iago	video)
	Penelope Wilton: Desdemona	
	Jonathan Miller (director)	
1982	James Earl Jones	Winter Garden, New York
	Christopher Plummer: Iago	
1985, 1986	Ben Kingsley	Stratford (1985)
	David Suchet: Iago	Barbican (1986)
	Terry Hands (director)	
1987	John Kani	The Market Theatre,
	Richard Haines: Iago	Johannesberg, South Africa
	Joanna Weinberg: Desdemona	
	Janet Suzman (director)	
1988	Kani/Haines/Weinberg (as above)	Television film: ITV/Channel 4
	Janet Suzman (director)	(available on video)
1989	Willard White	The Other Place, Stratford
	Ian McKellen: Iago	
	Imogen Stubbs: Desdemona	
	Zoë Wanamaker: Emilia	
	Trevor Nunn (director)	

Date	Actor(s)/Director	Theatre/medium
1990	White/McKellen/Stubbs/Wanamaker (as above) Trevor Nunn (director)	Television film: BBC (available on video)
1990	Avery Brooks	Folger Shakespeare Library, Washington DC
	Andre Braugher: Iago Franchelle Stewart-Dorn: Emilia Hal Scott (director)	
1995	Laurence Fishburne Kenneth Branagh: Iago Irene Jacob: Desdemona Anna Patrick: Emilia Oliver Parker (director)	. Film
1996, 1998	*Casting Othello*, by Caleen Sinnette Jennings	Washington Summer Theatre Festival (1996) Folger Shakespeare Theatre, Washington DC (1998)
1997	Patrick Stewart Ron Canada: Iago Patrice Johnson: Desdemona Franchelle Stewart-Dorn: Emilia Jude Kelly (director)	The Shakespeare Theatre, Washington DC
1997	David Harewood Simon Russell Beale: Iago Claire Skinner: Desdemona Maureen Beattie: Emilia Sam Mendes (director)	The National Theatre
1999	Ray Fearon Richard McCabe: Iago Zoë Waites: Dsdemona Rachel Joyce: Emilia Michael Attenborough (director)	Stratford
2001	*Othello* adapted by Andrew Davies Eamonn Walker Christopher Ecclestone: Ben Jago Keeley Hawes: Dessie	Television film: LWT (available on video)

INTRODUCTION

Over the last twenty years or so, *Othello* has leapt into focus as a play for
our times. Its story of 'us and them' (or rather 'him'), of brute racism and
misogyny, of miscegenation, sexual anxiety and domestic violence – all this
seems, with uncanny prescience, to speak directly to us now. At certain
moments and places and with certain actors (e.g. in 1943 in the USA with
Robeson; in apartheid South Africa with John Kani) the racism within the
play has resonated so loudly with the racism outside, that the fit between the
seventeenth and the twentieth centuries has seemed complete. 'Well, I ask
you', wrote Janet Suzman, who directed John Kani, 'is there a subject on
earth which Shakespeare hasn't thought of first? It is as if he is toying with
the theory of apartheid four hundred years before the policy was cooked
up.'[1]

It is often maintained in this way that Shakespeare overturns the racist
stereotypes of his day. It is pointed out that the stage Moors that preceded
Othello[2] would have led audiences to expect a lecherous, crafty, cruel, vengeful braggart; that the opening ribaldry of Iago and Roderigo plays to these
expectations, and that Othello undercuts them as soon as he appears.[3] We are
reminded that the play's 'demi-devil' is not the black Othello, but the white
Iago. Writing in 1987, the same year as Suzman's production, the South
African critic Martin Orkin was convinced that it was precisely because of
this that the play was never taught in South African high schools – that
Shakespeare was being censored as an anti-racist before his time.[4]

But on second thoughts, other resonances jangle. As Edward Pechter
points out, *Othello* 'remains . . . a strange play, lodged in a past whose beliefs
and assumptions are not easily accommodated to our own'.[5] Half-way across

1 Suzman, 'Parables', p. 279.
2 For example, Muly Hamet in George Peele's *The Battle of Alcazar* (1588), Eleazar
 in the anonymous *Lust's Dominion* (circa 1600), or Shakespeare's own Aaron in
 Titus Andronicus (circa 1592).
3 I argued in this way in the first edition of this work.
4 Orkin, 'Othello and the "Plain Face" of Racism', p. 184. Suzman reports that there
 was no copy of the play at the University of the Witwatersrand bookshop: ' "not a
 play often called for here" ', said the assistant ('Parables', p. 274).
5 Pechter, *Interpretive Traditions*, p. 3.

I

the world, also in 1987, Ben Okri was sitting in the Barbican Theatre in London, watching Ben Kingsley as Othello and David Suchet as Iago in Terry Hands's production for the Royal Shakespeare Company. He was, he tells us, 'practically the only black person in the audience', and he found himself overwhelmed by a lonely empathy with Othello, another black man isolated in a white world. 'It hurts', he wrote, 'to watch Othello as a black man.'

'As a black man' – that's the point. Okri's hurt was bound up with his conviction that none of the white people around him were hurting as much: 'two centuries of Othello committing murder and suicide on the stage has not produced any significant change in attitude towards black people.' And yet, he asks, how could it have been different: 'How can white people imagine themselves in Othello's predicament?' Okri's question comes from a political, post-colonial perspective. The 'predicament' he refers to is not personal or moral. It is the black man's place in history. Othello's 'colour, his otherness', Okri insists, 'must imply a specific history in white society.' But Shakespeare has made him into a creature who 'throws no shadows', whose 'colour is empty of history': 'Othello is a character with only one road leading out of him, but none lead into him.'

The reason that 'it hurts to watch Othello as a black man' lies in the man's political emasculation: 'There he is', writes Okri, 'a man of royal birth, taken as a slave, and he has no bitterness. He doesn't possess an ounce of anger, or even a sense of injustice.' Shakespeare has given him nobility, but even that is tainted, says Okri: 'When white people speak so highly of a black man's nobility they are usually referring to his impotence. It is Othello's neutrality and social impotence that really frightens me.'

Okri never quite accuses Shakespeare of racism, though he comes close: 'It is possible', he writes, 'that Shakespeare, as a white man, could not fully concede Othello an equal status of humanity.' He is torn between his pain at what is missing from the man, and a recognition that Othello is neverthe-less a powerful, haunting presence: someone who 'will not vanish from our dreams'.[6] A decade or so later the Ghanaian-born actor Hugh Quarshie was less circumspect. In September 1998, he gave a lecture at the University of Alabama in which he explained why, against the hopes of colleagues, he had no wish to play the role of Othello. He had come to feel that the play did not merely expose racism, but was itself racist.

Quarshie and Okri are in agreement on many points, but their perspectives are different. Okri is concerned with history, Quarshie – naturally, as an actor – with psychology. While Okri sees political displacement in Othello's

6 Okri, 'Meditations', *West Africa*, 23 and 30 March 1987.

furious jealousy, Quarshie sees racist theories of 'character.' He quotes from one of Shakespeare's sources, the *Geographical Historie of Africa* by John Leo, known as Leo Africanus, published in London in 1600: 'No nation in the world is so subject unto jealousie, for they will rather leese their lives, then put up any disgrace in the behalfe of their women.' And he could have quoted further: 'Most honest people they are, and destitute of fraud and guile', 'very proud and high-minded, and woonderfully addicted unto wrath . . . Their wits are but meane, and they are so credulous, that they will beleeve matters impossible, which are told them.'[7]

'From a perfomance point of view', writes Quarshie, 'the main difficulty about playing Othello is getting plausibly from the magnanimous and dignified warrior of the first half to the obsessive, homicidal, gibbering wreck of the second half.' It all happens too quickly, he feels, and is only credible within a culture that figures the black man as naturally gullible, jealous and emotionally extreme. Quarshie's fear is that 'that figure still occupies the same space in the imagination of modern theatre-goers as it did among Shakespeare's contemporaries':[8]

> if a black actor plays Othello does he not risk making racial stereotypes seem
> legitimate and even true? . . . does he not encourage the white way . . . of
> looking at black men [as] . . . over-emotional, excitable and unstable, thereby
> vindicating Iago's statement, 'These Moors are changeable in their wills.'

At which point he concludes that 'of all the parts in the canon, perhaps Othello is the one which should most definitely not be played by a black actor.'[9]

A whole library of criticism and a whole history of stage performance has laboured over the transition that Quarshie so briskly dismisses. From time to time, as we shall see, white actors in blackface have negotiated it without appearing to 'explain' the feat in terms of Othello's blackness. But Quarshie has a point with black actors. In his essay, 'Shakespeare and the Ethnic Question', Sukanta Chaudhuri notes that 'Othello's jealousy bears a singular violence or aggression that, in performance, almost compulsively assimilates itself to his Moorish features.'[10] Faced with 'the real thing', critics often slip into making false connections of that kind. Margaret Webster, for example, who directed Paul Robeson in 1943, said that 'all the elements of the action fall automatically into place, as they do not when he is merely played in blackface . . . the simplicity of the noble Moor, caught in the toils of villainy, no

7 Quoted by Honigmann, *Othello*, p. 4.
8 Quarshie, 'Second Thoughts', pp. 7, 11.
9 Ibid., p. 5.   10 Chaudhuri, 'The Ethnic Question', p. 180.

longer strains belief when Paul Robeson gives it the very image of nature'.[11] This 'image of nature' is not Robeson's acting, but his appearance. This on its own, it seems, signals 'simplicity' – a double-edged word, like 'innocence.' Olivier's 'image' was not 'of nature', of course, but to many at the time he was amazingly close ('unfurling pink palms and all' as Suzman drily put it)[12] – close enough to trigger the same racist assumptions. Quarshie quotes Norman Sanders and Ken Tynan, for example: Sanders approving Olivier for depicting 'a primitive man . . . relapsing into barbarism'; and Tynan, impressed by the actor's climactic moment of atavism (see commentary, 3.3.461–3).[13]

Is this 'primitivism' written into the play by Shakespeare? Acted into it by the performer? Or read into it by the viewer? Between these three, there is room for slippage. But for the modern black actor, the viewers are enough – never mind Shakespeare. In 1997, David Harewood, the Othello in a production directed by Sam Mendes, worried whether people would think '"Oh, he's just another crazy black man."' His way through the problem, he said, was to show 'the how of Othello's downfall – what Iago's doing to this man, rather than what's happening to him'.[14] As a strategy, this focuses attention on process, rather than on spectacle, and brings us closer to the long tradition, in both performance and criticism, of sympathy for Othello. Quarshie is certain that Othello's gullibility is the tragic flaw 'least likely to engage sympathetic understanding'.[15] But there was a revealing moment during Sam Mendes's 'public dialogue' session on the play which took place in Salzburg where the production opened before moving to London's National Theatre. One of the participants asked with genuine concern in his decorous English: '"Tell me please, I am having more moments of sympathy for Othello than for Desdemona. Should I see a psychiatrist?"'[16]

Sympathy is precisely what marks most of the theatre history of *Othello*. Not, perhaps, the kind of sympathy that Ben Okri had in mind – a historical understanding of Othello's 'predicament', or as he expresses it elsewhere in his piece, of 'the nightmare that history has made real'.[17] But something closer, narrower, more personal. In fact, so intense has been the sympathetic engagement of audiences, that it has spawned a mass of anecdotes about people fainting, calling out, warning the characters, and threatening Iago. It is as though *Othello* bursts the limit between reality and fiction more readily than Shakespeare's other tragedies. In 1825, when the American actor Edwin

11 Quoted by Cowhig, 'Blacks in English Renaissance Drama', p. 22.

12 Suzman, 'Parables', p. 276.   13 Quarshie, 'Second Thoughts', pp. 16, 17.

14 *I*, 16 September 1997.   15 Quarshie, 'Second Thoughts', p. 14.

16 *I*, 16 September 1997.   17 Okri, 'Meditations', *West Africa*, 23 March 1987.

Forrest played Iago to Edmund Kean's Othello, a man in the front row was heard to say, 'You damn'd lying scoundrel, I would like to get hold of you after this show is over and wring your infernal neck.'[18] Margaret Webster heard a girl in the audience whispering to herself over and over again 'Oh God, don't let him kill her . . . don't let him kill her . . . '[19] On the whole, it's the women who cry out for Desdemona and the men who offer to fight Iago. As for the soldier on guard duty at a Baltimore theatre in 1822, it was presumably some potent combination of his profession and his racism that made him shout, as Stendhal reported: ' "It will never be said in my presence a confounded Negro has killed a white woman" '. Whereupon he shot the white actor of Othello and broke his arm.[20] Wife-murder, it seems, should at least observe the colour bar.

Othello during the early seventeenth century

The earliest recorded performance of *Othello* was on 1 November 1604, at the court of James I, but the first performance has usually been put between 1603 and 1604, with the Arden editor, E. A. J. Honigmann, arguing for somewhere between 1600 and 1601. No text of the play was printed in Shakespeare's life time. The first quarto (Q1) was published in 1622 and the first Folio in 1623. The most striking difference between the two, among many thousands of variant readings, is that only the Folio text contains Desdemona's willow song (4.3) and Emilia's later reference to it just before she dies. Emilia's 'feminist' speech (4.3.82–99), and Othello's Pontic Sea passage (3.3.454–61) are also absent from the quarto. These are generally assumed to be omissions in the quarto, rather than additions to the Folio, perhaps for the purposes of compression and speed – common theatrical reasons, as we shall see. But the omission of Desdemona's song remains puzzling, and it is in trying to explain it that Honigmann arrives at his earlier date.

He notices a similarity in casting patterns in *Twelfth Night* (1600–1) and *Othello*, particularly in the gulls Roderigo and Aguecheek and their gull-masters, Iago and Toby Belch ('Put money in thy purse' (1.3.330) and 'Send for money, knight' respectively (2.3.205)). He also sees a likeness between the heroines, Desdemona and Viola, and between these and Ophelia (1600) – all patient, gentle, ill-used women who can sing. Or rather, Viola seems to have been intended to sing: 'I can sing / And speak to him in many sorts of music' she says in 1.3, but she never does. Honigmann surmises that her

---

18 Alger, *Edwin Forrest*, I, p. 477.
19 Quoted by Carroll from Webster, *Without Tears*, p. 66.
20 Quoted by Pechter in *Interpretive Traditions*, p. 12.

boy-actor's voice broke some time in 1600–1, and that this explains what appears to be an awkward transfer of the song 'Come away, come away, death' at 2.4 to Feste. Desdemona, so the argument goes, suffered the loss of her song for the same reason and therefore at about the same time.[21]

Either way, 1600–1 or 1603–4, it was a period when tragedies were being written about middle-class English husbands and wives, rather than kings and queens, about adultery and murder in the home rather than in castles. Dekker's *Patient Grissil* (1599–1600), Heywood's *A Woman Killed with Kindness* (1602–3), and the anonymous *A Warning for Fair Women* (1599) are among the plays of this kind, the last of which, according to Honigmann, had a direct influence on Shakespeare's *Othello*.[22] It is true that neither the exotic Othello nor Desdemona quite fit the genre, but the whole movement of the play is away from the wide perspective of warring Turks and Christians, towards the tight focus of this particular marriage, narrowing at last to a few square feet of bed.

The play also owes much to comedy – how much, is evident from the kind of impatient snort that goes up when the tragedy fails: ' "And all that for a pocket- handkerchief!" (E tutto questo per un fazzoletto!) was the Italian lady's comment when she saw the play', wrote Herman Merivale in 1902.[23] If the Othello fails to convince, the handkerchief trick stands exposed as an essentially comic device, and the tragedy can quickly degenerate into farce. The trickster Iago, Honigmann thinks, is a descendant of the 'intriguing slave of classical comedy', the 'universal adviser, "friend", and joker' of Terence and Plautus.[24] He is also (like Richard III) a relative of the Vice[25] from the old morality plays, delighting in his own wickedness and that of his good friends, the audience. Iago's vernacular ('Blest fig's end . . . Blest pudding' (2.1.238–40)), his audience-addressing soliloquies, his cynical assumption of virtue, and his control over the plot – these are all attributes of the Vice.

As it happens, there is some evidence that the original Iago was played by a comedian. Writing in 1694, Charles Gildon says he had it 'from very good hands that the person that acted Iago was in much esteem for a comedian'.[26] If this actor was John Lowin, as has been conjectured,[27] then his other parts were Falstaff, Jonson's Sir Epicure Mammon, and a number of blunt-speaking, 'honest' soldier types. It seems therefore that Othello may always have been hard pressed to preserve his tragic dignity. The first actor to play

21 See Honigmann, *Othello*, Appendix 1.   22 Ibid., p. 74.
23 Merivale, *Bar, Stage*, p. 148.   24 Ibid., p. 75.
25 Bernard Spivak, *Allegory of Evil*, second chapter passim, esp. pp. 57–9.
26 Gildon, 'Some Reflections', p. 68.
27 Baldwin, *Organisation and Personnel*, p. 248.

him was the chief tragedian of his day, Richard Burbage, who according to Richard Flecknoe's epitaph on him, also excelled as Hamlet, Lear, 'and more beside.' Flecknoe describes Burbage's Othello only as 'the Greved Moor',[28] so there is little to go on. 'Greved' is a hint. 'Cruel' or 'noble' would have scanned just as well. Perhaps already pity was the point, rather than judgement either way.

Shakespeare's source and what he did with it

Shakespeare's main source for the play is a tale from *Gli Hecatommithi* by Giovanni Battista Giraldi Cinthio (1566),[29] about a Moor (never named), who is deceived by his Ensign (not named either) into believing that his wife, Disdemona (so spelt), has been unfaithful to him with his Corporal (also nameless). As Cinthio tells it, the narrative moves in a straight line. The Ensign plants suspicion in the Moor's mind and the Moor falls into a melancholy. He loses his temper with Disdemona once, but on the whole he holds himself in suspense, moving patiently from one piece of 'evidence' to the next, doggedly returning to Iago for more 'proof.' Only when he is convinced does he give way to murderous frenzy, after which he is never 'unprovided', as Othello is, by returning love. On the contrary, he eagerly accepts his Ensign's plan that together they should batter Disdemona to death with a sand-filled stocking, break her skull, and pull the ceiling down over her bed to make it look like an accident.

Shakespeare's Iago similarly offers reasons and 'evidence' for Desdemona's supposed adultery, but the effect on the Moor is much more chaotic than in Cinthio. 'Evidence' exacerbates rather than causes his crisis. It is disputable how long it takes him to feel the poison during Iago's first conversation with him in 3.3, but immediately after Iago's exit his imagination leaps ahead to the very worst: 'She's gone; I am abused, and my relief / Must be to loathe her . . .' (269–70). Before he even thinks of 'proof' in the next encounter with Iago, he feels himself betrayed, Cassio's kisses on her lips, his occupation gone. And the mere mention of the handkerchief is enough, without any further check, to make him formally swear vengeance and withdraw 'To furnish me with some swift means of death / For the fair devil' (478–9).

Iago's tale of Cassio's dream and his erotic insinuations before the epileptic fit in the next act do not occur in Cinthio. Each of these moments provoke Othello to his utmost pitch (the vow of vengeance, and the fit itself) and

---

28 For Flecknoe's elegy, see Nagler, *Source Book*, p. 127.
29 See Honigmann, *Othello*, Appendix 3.

each climax *precedes* the unfolding of what to Cinthio's Moor would be the deciding 'evidence': Desdemona's loss of the handkerchief, and the sight of it in the hands of Cassio's friend, Bianca. Both in themselves, and in their timing these Shakespearean additions reverse the overall tendency of Cinthio's narrative. Shakespeare's Othello cannot cope with evidence. In a curious moment before the fit, he even has to be reminded of the handkerchief. And, as if it scarcely mattered, Shakespeare omits one of Cinthio's most 'evidential' incidents, in which his Moor returns home unexpectedly one day, and surprises the Corporal (i.e. Cassio) at his back door trying to return Disdemona's handkerchief.

Of course it is not evidence that works on Othello in the first place. It has to do with his intense feeling for Desdemona, something that critics have struggled to define. Helen Gardner thought it was 'joy' and that it was intrinsically bewildering: 'great joy bewilders, leaving the heart apt to doubt the reality of its joy.' Great sex bewilders too. In Othello's speech of greeting to Desdemona on Cyprus (2.1.175ff., 'It gives me wonder great as my content . . .') Stephen Greenblatt hears an erotic intensity which 'may express gratified desire, but, as the repeated invocation of death suggests, may equally express the longing for a final release from desire, from the dangerous violence, the sense of extremes . . .' Michael Neill follows the idea further, into the murk of voyeuristic obsession – something, he argues, which Iago and the play both create and discover in us and in Othello: 'a technique that works close to the unstable ground of consciousness itself'.[30]

Critics can argue, but actors must decide: how to make Othello's reversal plausible without time and evidence? Will a leap do it? Or a creep? Many actors have tried gradualism, but ultimately the precipice cannot be avoided. On the other hand, those who go for the leap have to convince an audience of certain paradoxes. *Othello* commentators find themselves reaching for the kind of extremes and opposites that, in 1621, Robert Burton described in lovers generally: 'though they be . . . rapt beyond themselves for joy; yet . . . love is a plague, a torture, a hell.' Take this, from the *Guardian* in 1713: 'The most extravagant love . . . is nearest the strongest hatred'; or this from Stendhal in 1824: 'all great passions are fearful and superstitious'.[31] In a piece extolling the Othello of James Earl Jones in 1982, the reviewer Walter Kerr lamented that 'most productions, and most performances of the title role, are so entirely concerned with making us believe, step by step by step,

---

30 Gardner, 'The Noble Moor', p. 171; Greenblatt, *Self-Fashioning*, p. 243; Neill, 'Unproper Beds', p. 395.
31 Burton, *Anatomy*, Part 3, Sec. 2, Mem. 3; *The Guardian*, no. 37, 23 April 1713; Stendhal, *Rossini*, p. 228.

in the Moor's distrust of his wife that they quite forget his love for his wife. But these two co-exist.'[32]

This 'love' is a variable concept. It has moved sharply up and down the scale of idealism, both in literary criticism and in the theatre. The mid-to-late nineteenth-century American tragedian Edwin Booth, for example, at 'Damn her lewd minx! O, damn her, damn her!' (3.3.476), advised repeating 'damn her' four times, so as to say 'the first savagely, the second less so, melt with the third, and choke with tears at the fourth.' At 'O curse of marriage, / That we can call these delicate creatures ours / And not their appetites' (271–2), he laid his hand on his heart at the word 'appetites', so as to de-physicalise the word.[33] On the other hand, in a production at the Mermaid in 1971 which sought to demonstrate that the play was 'all about sex, about bed' (*T*, 8 September 1971) Bruce Purchase spoke the line 'The fountain from the which my current runs / Or else dries up' (4.2.58–9), looking straight at Desdemona's crotch (see commentary). Whatever the nature of Othello's love, Kerr's point is the futility of 'step by step by step' and (as he says in the same review) the 'enormous practical value' that Othello's instability and contradictions have for the play's performance: 'It's never very interesting just to watch a man become more and more gullible from 9 o'clock, say, till 11. If there's no yes-and-no, no tug-and-pull going on inside him, the single-minded advance of the narrative becomes monotonous; and he in turn turns into little more than a fool.'

Othello's colour and what it meant

There has been debate about the shade of Othello's skin: black or olive? north or west African? negroid or not? The objection to a black negroid Othello arose fairly late in the day with Lamb and Coleridge. As we shall see, it sprang from their own prejudices and, in Coleridge's case, from the mistaken assumption that Shakespeare knew of such men only as slaves.[34] It is true that the slaving voyages of Sir John Hawkins in the 1560s, and others, had brought increasing numbers of west African slaves to England – so much so that Elizabeth I issued two edicts of deportation on the gounds that they were consuming the provision intended for the English 'in these times of dearth'.[35] But, equally, the traveller's tales popular at the time described

---

32 *NYT*, 14 February 1982.
33 One of the notes supplied by Booth to Furness, to be inserted among the annotations to his *New Variorum* edition of *Othello* (1886).
34 Coleridge, *On Shakespeare*, see p. 187.
35 See Jones, *Elizabethan Image*, p. 21, for a fuller extract from one of these edicts.

African societies and individuals of many colours and kinds, including kings and nobles, scholars and merchants. A man 'of royal seige' who was also black would have been nothing extraordinary, and on the stage, even less so. According to Eldred Jones, 'regardless of what the more informed writers may have said about the different colours of Africans, only their blackness seems to have registered firmly in the minds of audiences and playwrights alike'.[36]

The theatre did have its 'tawney' or 'white' Moors, like the Prince of Morocco in the *Merchant of Venice*, and the light-skinned Abdilmalec, Muly Hamet's 'good' uncle in *The Battle of Alcazar*. But most stage Moors were devils, and their colour proclaimed them so. As G. K. Hunter's essay 'Othello and Colour Prejudice' has shown, in religious literature, in the medieval romances, in pictorial tradition, in mummers' plays, masques and processions, all the devils, infidels, Saracens, Turks, pagans and bogeymen, were black. The fact that there were white villains as well did not detract from the force of blackness as a symbol. Its prime significance was moral and religious rather than racial or geographical. The first *OED* meaning of 'Moor' is in fact 'Mahomedan', and terminology was so vague at the time that, in use, 'Moor' meant no more than someone living in 'that outer circuit of non-Christian lands where the saving grace of Jerusalem is weakest in its whitening power'.[37] The taking of Cyprus by the Turks (the dispersal of their fleet in *Othello* is Shakespeare's invention) led directly to the great battle of Lepanto in 1571, which was still regarded twenty years later (in the words of one contemporary) as 'the Halleluia of Christendom and the wellaway of Turkey'.[38] James I wrote a poem on the subject,[39] and in 1603 Richard Knolles published a vivid account of it in his *Generall Historie of the Turks*, a probable source for Shakespeare (if the 1603–4 date for *Othello* is right). Anyone in the early seventeenth century going to a play about a Moor which touched on the wars between Venice and the Turks would have expected no 'whitening power' at all.

Furthermore, Shakespeare, juggling with categories, makes a point of this colour coding. The Duke commends Othello to Brabantio in ironic terms: 'If virtue no delighted beauty lack / Your son-in-law is far more fair than black' (1.3.285–6). Desdemona 'saw Othello's visage in his mind' – meaning that there at least he was white. Othello himself is obsessed with Desdemona's whiteness ('that whiter skin of hers than snow . . .' (5.2.4)) and

36 Jones, *Othello's Countrymen*, p. 39.
37 Hunter, 'Othello and Colour Prejudice', p. 41.
38 Quoted by Hunter, 'Elizabethans and Foreigners', p. 25.
39 See Emrys Jones, '*Othello, Lepanto* and the Cyprus Wars', *Sh.S* 21, pp. 47–52.

with its contrast to the blackness of her supposed adultery, which in turn is symbolised by his own blackness ('Her name, that was as fresh / As Dian's visage, is now begrimed and black / As mine own face' (3.3.387–9)). In view of this – quite apart from the 'black ram' / 'thick-lips' / 'sooty bosom' jibes of Iago, Roderigo and Brabantio (1.1.89, 67, 1.2.70) – it would seem theatrically inept to make Othello only a little bit black.

We know that the representation of blackness was well established and thoroughgoing before, during and after Shakespeare's lifetime. Vizards, long black velvet gloves and leggings of black leather had been used for masques and processions earlier in the sixteenth century. Painting with burnt cork and oil replaced these in the seventeenth. There is some evidence that woolly hair and thick lips were also attempted. The accounts of the Office of Revels record payments for 'corled hed sculles of blacke laune' for characters representing Africans, and Eldred Jones cites Massinger's *The Parliament of Love* in which Beaupré, disguised as a Moor, is described as 'the handsomest / I ere saw of her country, she hath neither / Thick lips nor rough corled hair (1a.92b–4a).[40]

Burbage, then, would probably have painted himself as black as possible. On the projecting stage at the open-air Globe theatre, the 'scenery' was the magnificently carved and painted architecture of the stage and building itself. From some angles, he would have stood out against a background of faces, listening to his tale in the afternoon light as visibly as the Senators at 1.3. Any number of Brabantios and Desdemonas in the audience would have pressed Othello to tell the story of his life, and have listened with as rapt attention. And if Desdemona's choice was scandalous, it was probably not unheard of. Robert Burton, in *The Anatomy of Melancholy*, even gave it the authority of mythology: 'a black man is a pearl in a fair woman's eye,' he wrote, 'and is as acceptable as lame Vulcan was to Venus'.[41] At the end of the century, Charles Gildon defended Shakespeare, saying that 'even here at home ladies that have not wanted white adorers have indulged their amorous dalliances with their sable lovers, without any of Othello's qualifications. . . '.[42] He might have pointed to Aphra Behn's novel *Oroonoko* (1688, dramatised in 1695 by Thomas Southerne) and her loving descriptions of its eponymous black hero – a figure who shares many of Othello's 'qualifications.'

So that although he was strange, Othello wouldn't necessarily have seemed monstrous. In fact the perception of the grotesque in Othello's behaviour,

---

40 Jones, *Othello's Countrymen*; for masks, leggings and paint, see pp. 33–5, and for rough hair, see p. 123.
41 Burton, *Anatomy*, Part 3, Sec. 2, Mem. 2, Subs. 2.
42 See Vickers, *Heritage*, 11, p. 75.

which some equate with racism in Shakespeare, may to some extent be a modern phenomenon. In her book *Othello, a Contextual History*, Virginia Vaughan quotes from Thomas Wright's *The Passions of the Minde in Generale*, published in 1601, and expanded in 1604. In it, Wright talks about

> Inordinate passions . . . [which] neither observe time nor place: but upon every occasion would be leaping into action, importuning execution. Let a man be praying or studying . . . and very often he shal feele a headlesse Passion to rush in upon him, importuning him even then to leave all, and prosecute revenge . . . or some other unbridled desire.[43]

Wright is not talking about black men. Nor is Robert Burton when he describes, specifically, the jealous man, who will 'rave, roar, and lay about him like a mad man, thump her sides, drag her about perchance . . . mandring, gazing, listening, affrighted . . . ; why did she smile, why did she pity him, commend him? why did she drink twice to such a man? why did she offer to kiss, to dance? etc. a whore, a whore, an arrant whore'.[44]

Wright and Burton do not completely close the gap between a black Othello and a white seventeenth-century Englishman. Neither writer talks specifically about gullibility or bare-handed murder. But those are not the only things that make Othello grotesque to us. The actual spectacle of a man losing control, roaring for blood, screaming 'a whore, a whore, an arrant whore' (or words to that effect) suggests, at least to theatre-going, middle-class audiences, something un-English, abnormal, 'foreign', and it partly explains the charge of caricature which sounds through much contemporary criticism of the play. Such criticism is not invalidated by historical contextualisation. A play is its perception at any given time.

But where the context is part of the story, as here, certain points are worth making. We know nothing of Othello's costume before the Restoration, but it is perhaps significant that from then until the last quarter of the eighteenth century – except for a brief and unsuccessful experiment by Garrick – Othello wore an English general's uniform, sometimes even with a white-powdered wig. Nothing very exotic was attempted before the nineteenth century. The oriental robes and jewellery of that period and in the twentieth century mark the distance travelled since then between Othello and his portrayers.

Lastly, in all the discussion about racial difference, it would be wrong to overlook how much the situation itself simply moved people. There is an

---

43 See Vaughan, *A Contextual History*, p. 78.
44 Burton, *Anatomy*, Part 3, Sec. 3, Mem. 2.

eloquent fragment found in an extract from a letter written in September 1610 by a certain Henry Jackson, a member of Corpus Christi Collge, Oxford. Writing in Latin, he speaks of the King's Men playing at Oxford, and of the tragedies which, 'acted with propriety and fitness . . . moved the audience to tears'.[45] One of these was *Othello* and he describes the terrible last scene when 'the celebrated Desdemona, slayn in our presence by her husband, although she pleaded her case very effectively throughout, yet moved us more after she was dead, when, lying in her bed, she entreated the pity of the spectators by her very countenance.' There is shock in the phrase 'in our presence' but there is no mention of Othello's blackness. He is simply a 'husband', and she (though a boy, 'she' enough) his victim. Unlike many Desdemonas of later periods, she seems to have been spirited in her defence, and the ending was tragic as much on her account as on Othello's.

Othello after Burbage's death

Burbage died in 1618, and his elegist mourned not only him, but 'a world of characters', Othello included. Nevertheless, the play stayed alive. James Wright, in *Historia Histrionica* (1699), records that the part of Othello went to an actor called Ellyaerdt Swanston, and that Iago was taken by Joseph Taylor, whom we know to have succeeded Burbage as Hamlet.[46] Little is known of Swanston except that as D'Ambois in *Bussy d'Ambois*, he is described as 'the stateliest, gravest, and commanding [sic] soul that eye ever beheld'; and in another place he is 'a brave roaring fellow [that] would make the house shake again'.[47] Both qualities would fit, as far as they go. The actor of Hamlet playing Iago is more interesting, for it suggests that Iago was no longer the comedian's role (two other actors, Pollard and Robinson, were the comedians, says Wright), but clearly thought of as fit for a major actor of range and subtlety. Indeed, the play now begins to show its potential as a duel between equals. The great scene in which Othello and Iago act alone, 3.3, was becoming separately admired. John Ford in *Love's Sacrifice* (printed 1633) modelled his 3.2 and 3.3 very closely on it; and in his commonplace book, Abraham Wright, vicar of Oakham, Rutlandshire, remarked in 1637 that the play was 'very good . . . both for lines and plot . . . Act 3, the scene between Iago and Othello, and the first scene of the fourth act, between

45 I use the translation in *The Riverside Shakespeare* (1974), Appendix B, no. 33.
46 Wright, *Historia Histrionica*, p. 406.
47 Quoted from Edmund Gayton, *Festivous Notes on Don Quixote* (1654), in Baldwin, *Organisation and Personnel*, p. 182.

the same shew admirably the villainous humour of Iago when he persuades Othello to his jealousy'.[48]

The vicar mentions the play's 'lines', but he is clearly interested in the drama rather than the poetry. He was probably fairly typical. As we shall see, from the eighteenth century onwards *Othello* has always been cut for the stage, sometimes drastically. Particular cuts have reflected the taste of particular periods – the taste for the heroic for example, or for sexual discretion. But as well as these, there is always a desire for speed and compression. The main omissions from the first quarto have been mentioned. These were restored in later quartos (Q2 was published in 1630), which during the Restoration period carry the legend 'as acted at the theatre royal' on their title pages. But other cuts suggest that poetic or discursive passages, and small moments of quiet pathos were considered expendable. The nub of the play seems increasingly during the seventeenth century to have been the interaction between Othello and Iago, and at the end of the century even Thomas Rymer, the play's earliest and most flamboyant detractor, had to admit that their great scene alone together, 3.3, was known as 'the top scene that raises *Othello* above all other Tragedies in our theatres'.[49]

In 1642 Parliament closed down the theatres, and until 1660 when the monarchy was restored all performances were clandestine, actors and audiences running the risk of being raided by the militia. Perhaps *Othello* was one of those secretly played, for when the theatres reopened, it and the three Falstaff plays were the only pieces by Shakespeare to be instantly in the repertory of the newly titled King's Men.[50]

Othello during the Restoration

In 1660, so as to gain control over the rapid growth of new companies, Charles II confined the acting of plays to the King's Men, under the management of Thomas Killigrew, and the Duke's Men, under William Davenant. Between them they divided out the existing repertory, Killigrew keeping the four Shakespeare plays already mentioned and *Julius Caesar*, while Davenant took his choice of the rest. Davenant was the first adaptor and 'improver' of Shakespeare, and it was therefore a near thing for *Othello* at this moment.

48 Furnivall, ed., *The Shakespeare Allusion-Book*, prints comparable passages from Ford and Shakespeare in parallel columns, I, pp. 379–81; for Abraham Wright see ibid., p. 411.
49 Rymer, *Short View*, p. 149.
50 Furnivall, *Shakespeare Allusion-Book*, I, p. 322.

In the event, it was to be the only one of Shakespeare's tragedies that was never adapted.

Under the new dispensation there were two innovations: scenery and actresses. Now, where the facade of the tiring-house had been, with its doors of entrance, there was a painted backcloth, in front of which, trundling in from each side along grooves in the floor and in overhead beams, was a series of painted shutters. These were brought together to meet in the middle, while corresponding pairs stood at the sides as wings. Actors could be 'discovered' as the shutters were opened to reveal the next scene behind them, or they could make their exits and entrances through doors that were now downstage in the proscenium arch, over each of which was a box or balcony. Roderigo would have banged on one of these doors, and brought Brabantio out immediately above it. In the Restoration theatre the main acting area was out in front of the proscenium, where the actors could catch the added light from the candles in the auditorium (never snuffed), and where, according to one young actor of the 1690s, Colley Cibber, the voice could be heard by 'the most distant ear' and 'the minutest motion of a feature could best be seen'.[51]

The second innovation was the actress. In fact it was as Desdemona that the first professional actress appeared on the stage after the Restoration. Towards the end of 1660 Thomas Jordan wrote a prologue which, with triumphant suggestiveness, announces '*the first woman that came to act on the stage in the tragedy call'd* The Moor of Venice':

> The woman plays today, mistake me not,
> No man in gown or page in petty-coat; . . .
> In this reforming age
> We have intents to civilize the stage . . .
> For (to speak truth) men act, that are between
> Forty and fifty wenches of fifteen;
> With bone so large, and nerve so imcomplyant,
> When you call Desdemona, enter Giant.[52]

The prologue makes fun of the old custom of using men to play women, but we know from John Downes, the book-keeper to Davenant's company, that they did it very persuasively. He even said of one such actor, Kynaston, that 'it has since been disputable among the judicious whether any woman that succeeded him so sensibly touched the audience as he'.[53] In fact, the Desdemona that so moved 'a very pretty lady' sitting near Pepys on

---

51 Cibber, *Apology*, p. 225.
52 See Furnivall, *Shakespeare Allusion-Book*, II, p. 87.
53 Downes, *Roscius Anglicanus*, p. 19.

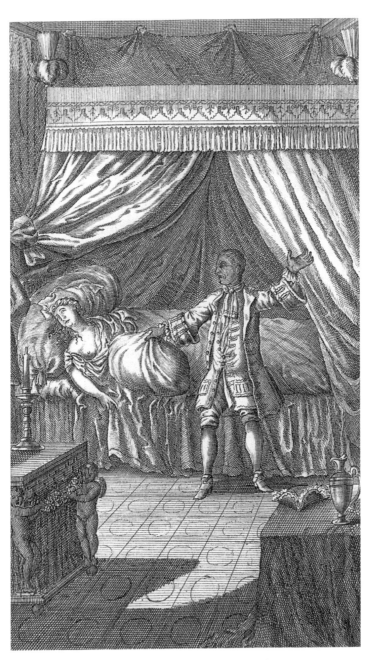

1 The frontispiece to Nicholas Rowe's edition of *Othello* (1709).

11 October 1660 that she 'called out to see Desdimona smothered' must have been male, since it is not – as he tells us – until 3 January 1661 that he has his first sight of a woman on the stage.

This question of whether boys (and men) can adequately represent women recalls the question over the casting of Othello. The Restoration stage exploited the innovation unashamedly. As Richard Steele complained in the *Tatler*, no. 134: 'Adulteries are wrought up to such a height upon the stage, that they are almost put into execution before the actors can get behind the scenes.' *Othello* did certainly attract this kind of treatment, for Aphra Behn, in her preface to *The Lucky Chance or an Alderman's Bargain*, defended herself against the charge of indecency by pointing to other respected plays: 'In *Valentinian*, see . . . Valentinian all loose and ruffled a moment after the rape . . . and a thousand others, the Moor of Venice in many places . . .'[54] It could be argued that casting real women at that time concentrated minds on sex, just as casting real black actors has concentrated minds on race. A little later, in about 1710 or 1711, a correspondent to the *Tatler* or the *Spectator* noted that in the last scene, when Desdemona asks her husband to come to bed 'a general tittering went round the room or stage [members of the audience occupied the stage], that had they all been letchers of sixty odd, they could not have given greater indications of satisfaction in a brutal way'.[55] The engraved frontispieces to Nicholas Rowe's 1709 edition of Shakespeare are generally thought to represent stage practice, and the one for *Othello* shows the smothered Desdemona with one breast prominently exposed.

But having said that, what information we have about the acting is not especially suggestive. Aphra Behn cited *Othello* precisely because it was not considered lewd. The first Restoration cast of *Othello* strongly suggests the continuance of tradition. Nicholas Burt as Othello, Walter Clun as Iago, Michael Mohun replacing him at least by 1664 when Clun died, and Charles Hart as Cassio later replacing Burt as Othello[56] – all these actors had been 'bred up' as boys, says James Wright, in the company at Blackfriars (Shakespeare's indoor winter theatre at Blackfriars), where they had taken the women's parts.[57] They would certainly have seen the last generation of actors, Swanston and Taylor, in *Othello*, and one or more of them may even have played Desdemona. Whatever they did, John Downes tells us that, although tastes were changing, some of Charles Hart's old parts, including Othello, could fill the house 'as at a New Play'. The new taste was for the

---

54 Quoted in Rosenberg, *Masks*, p. 17.   55 Lillie, *Letters*, I, p. 256.
56 For these castings see Pepys, 11 October 1660 and 6 February 1669. For Hart as Othello see Downes, *Roscius Anglicanus*, p. 16.
57 Wright, *Historia Histrionica*, p. 404.

heroic – fashionable with the theatre's court patrons whose exile in France had accustomed them to the stately decorums of French tragedy. This was Hart's strong point. It was said of his Alexander that he carried himself 'with such grandeur and agreeable Majesty, that one of the court [said] . . . that Hart might teach any king on earth how to comport himself'. Othello's royal blood would have been one of the most important things about him.

Of Mohun's Iago we know frustratingly little: 'Oh, Mohun, Mohun' an 'eminent' poet is said to have exclaimed of him, 'thou little man of mettle, if I should write a hundred plays, I'd write a part for thy mouth.' His parts tended to be dour: Cassius in *Julius Caesar* (to Hart's Brutus), Volpone, Face in *The Alchemist*, Melantius in *The Maid's Tragedy*.[58] He was often styled 'Major', having risen to that rank in the wars. Olivier gives us an insight into what army life does for the actor of Iago: 'though I played Iago many years ago, I didn't understand the part till I'd been in service during the war. I think when someone gets a half-stripe more than you your soul can get bitten.'[59] In fact the Civil Wars, in which all the old actors fought, says Wright,[60] would have coloured the play as a whole. Everyone in the theatre would have understood the precariousness of peace on Cyprus, 'in a town of war / Yet wild, the people's hearts brimful of fear' (2.3.194–5).

The printed texts 'as acted at the Theatre Royal' show no significant changes from the earliest texts, but there is one, from the Smock Alley Theatre in Dublin, which shows contemporary play-house cuts. Marvin Rosenberg describes it in *The Masks of Othello*,[61] and shows that it foreshadows later tastes. Its cuts are not nearly as deep as those made towards the end of the eighteenth century or the even deeper ones in the nineteenth, but they suggest that Othello was being acted more loftily – that is, with a greater sense of what is proper to a tragic hero. In it, Othello does not suggest, for example, that housewives might make a skillet of his helm (1.3.268); nor does he exclaim 'Exchange me for a goat / When I shall turn the business of my soul . . .' (3.3.182–5). His first ignoble act – 'Set on thy wife to observe' – is excised, so too is his first, too immediate, sense of betrayal: 'She's gone, I am abused, and my relief / Must be to loathe her.' Once Iago's poison has begun to work in him, he does not say that he would have been happy if the 'general camp . . . had tasted her sweet body, / So I had nothing known' (242, 269–70, 346–8). Nor is his farewell to arms so prolonged and climactic. Perhaps it was felt to be too extravagant, as Rosenberg suggests. But the age loved high-sounding pomp. It could be that, since it hadn't yet acquired

58 Downes, *Roscius Anglicanus*, pp. 16, 17.
59 'The Great Sir Laurence', *Life International*, 18 May 1964.
60 Wright, *Historia Histrionica*, p. 409.   61 Rosenberg, *Masks*, pp. 20–7.

the status of a set-speech, the first three lines of farewell were considered enough. In the 'brothel scene' (4.2) the lines in which Othello recollects his old love ('But there where I have garnered up my heart, / Where either I must live or bear no life', 56–7) are cut. Towards his end he does not demean himself by asking to be whipped by devils and washed in steep-down gulfs of liquid fire, nor does he speak of himself as one who 'Drops tears as fast as the Arabian trees / Their medicinable gum' (52.275–8, 346–7). The other cuts noted by Rosenberg are dealt with in the commentary, but although Rosenberg says that what emerges is an Othello 'closer to Decorum's image of a hero', a great deal of undecorous material is left.

What is more obvious is the curtailment of Desdemona's part. Just as Othello's homely skillet image is cut, so is her picture of domestic life when she begs for Cassio's reinstatement: 'Why, this is not a boon; / 'Tis as I should entreat you wear your gloves, / Or feed on nourishing dishes' (3.3.76–8) and so on. Cut too is her wifely moment after Othello's outburst over the handkerchief, when she comforts herself with her aching-finger comparison (3.4.140–2). But saddest of all, much of her willow-song scene is gone, including the song itself. It was a vulnerable moment as we have seen from the first quarto. As Stark Young, a twentieth-century theatre-critic, observed: no play of Shakespeare's has more tender motifs and exchanges, or a more exact domestic prose and literalness of detail, more surprising lyric immediacy; and yet none is so objective, remote and complete, so classic in its clarity . . .'[62] These cuts to Desdemona's part shift the play towards the 'remote' and 'classic.' In so doing, they make way for the grand, majestic Othellos that succeed each other from then on, up to the end of the eighteenth century.

It was a period that required tragedy to avoid what it called 'meanness' at all costs. For example, when in 1666 Pepys read the play, he wrote in his diary (20 August) that whereas he had until then always thought it a 'mighty good play', he now found it 'a mean thing'. What altered his taste, he says, was his having lately read a new play, *The Adventures of Five Hours*, a tragi-comedy by Sir Samuel Tuke. This play now reads like a stately piece of verbal choreography. All the sentiments belong to a race of courtly people whose dialogue is an alternation of well-turned verse monologues. There is none of *Othello*'s snatched, broken dialogue of half-lines, written for an audience rather than a reader. Steele understood the difference well enough: 'whoever reads in his closet this admirable scene [the handkerchief scene] will find he cannot, except he has as warm an imagination as Shakespeare himself, find any but dry, incoherent and broken sentences'.[63]

---

62 Young, *Immortal Shadows*, p. 234.   63 Steele, *Tatler*, no. 167 (2 May 1710).

Pepys's sense of Shakespeare's meanness was also at the heart of Thomas Rymer's celebrated attack on the play in 1693. When Desdemona says in language that could scarcely be simpler 'What shall I do to win my lord again?' (4.2.148), Rymer explodes. Here, it seems, is a chance for something elevated, in keeping with Desdemona's station. But everywhere, thinks Rymer, 'there is nothing in the noble Desdemona that is not below any country chamber maid with us'. Rymer's point is that although being a Venetian noblewoman may not in fact prevent a girl from being simple, poetry has no business with facts: 'history and *fact* in particular cases of John at Oaks, or John of Styles, are no warrant or direction for a poet'. Poetry must reflect something more 'general and abstracted, . . . the reason and nature of things' where soldiers behave as soldiers should, noblewomen like noblewomen and so on. An Iago may have existed in history but 'the Poet is not without huge labour and preparation to expose the Monster; and after shew divine vengeance executed upon him.' Shakespeare is far too casual about Iago. The same goes for Othello. Not only is Shakespeare's general a 'Blackamoor' who 'with us . . . might rise to be Trumpeter . . .', but the author compounds the fault by giving him language and scenes, such as the eavesdropping episode in 4.1, which 'I would not expect to find . . . acted nearer than Southwark Fair'. As for Iago's intrigue, Rymer's scorn plays straight into the modern analysis of Shakespeare as racist: 'Had it been Desdemona's garter, the sagacious Moor might have smelt a rat; but a handkerchief is so remote a trifle, no Booby on this side Mauritania could make any consequence of it.'

All this notwithstanding, the exasperated Rymer had to admit that *Othello*, unimproved, was said 'to bear the Bell away',[64] and it wasn't until the end of the eighteenth century, with the performances in Paris of Ducis's translation, that his ideas were met in the theatre. Nevertheless, his neo-classical assumptions about the dignity of heroes, the villainy of villains and so on, did affect the play, both its text and its performance.

In 1682 dwindling audiences caused the two companies of Killigrew and Davenant to merge, and soon after that Hart retired. Thomas Betterton succeeded him, and such was his authority as an actor that he remained undisputed head of the profession for the next thirty years.

Betterton's Othello and Sandford's Iago

One of the reasons for *Othello*'s outstanding reputation in the theatre was that it showcased the heroic actor's range by driving him to opposing extremes – and in the process, it could be said, that it highlighted the very thing that

64 Rymer, *Short View* (in order), pp. 158, 134, 160, 134, 157, 155, 160, 131.

has now become Quarshie's racially loaded 'emotional instability.' In the eighteenth century, the sense that Othello's love is fatally close to hate, and that he himself is the object of both compassion and horror, was taken for granted. Innocent of the coming battle for and against Othello (and Shakespeare) the correspondent to *The Guardian*, no. 37 (23 April 1713), could say that Othello is 'furious in both these extremes':

> His love is tempestuous and mingled with a wildness peculiar to his character which seems artfully to prepare for the change which is to follow. How savage, yet how ardent is that expression of the raptures of his heart, when looking after Desdemona as she withdraws he breaks out 'Excellent wretch! Perdition catch my soul, / But I do love thee! and when I love thee not, / Chaos is come again [3.3.90–2].'

It was this part, therefore, that gave Thomas Betterton his greatest triumph, according to Colley Cibber, for 'in Othello he excelled himself'.[65] And Steele, in the same *Guardian* essay, expands: he 'betrayed in his gesture such a variety and vicissitude of passions as would admonish a Man to be afraid of his own heart, and perfectly convince him that it is to stab it to admit that worst of daggers, Jealousy'.

Among the variety and vicissitude, however, what stands out from Cibber's picture of him is the quality of danger. Betterton's voice 'gave more spirit to terror than to the softer passions . . . The Rage and Jealousy of *Othello* became him better than the sighs and Tenderness of Castalio' (in Otway's *The Orphan*). He had 'a commanding mien of majesty, which . . . the curled Darlings of his time ever wanted something to be equal masters of'. And yet, beside this, one must set Steele's softer memories of 'the wonderful agony which [Betterton] appeared in when he examined the circumstances of the handkerchief . . . the mixture of love that intruded upon his mind upon the innocent answers Desdemona makes'.[66]

The system of type-casting that prevailed right up to the end of the nineteenth century made it easier for Othello to sustain this heroic position. According to the system, Iago could never be the threat to Othello that he would later become. Villains had to be nastily, not fascinatingly, villainous, and a good stage villain paid heavily for his success: 'when an Iago is meditating revenge and mischief', wrote Cibber, 'though art and nature may be equally strong in the actor, the spectator is shy of his applause, lest he should in some sort be looked upon as an aider or an abettor of the wickedness in view'.[67] Rymer talks of 'the mops and mows, the grimace and grins, and

---

65 Cibber, *Apology*, p. 69.   66 Ibid.; Steele, *Tatler*, no. 167 (2 May 1710).
67 Cibber, *Apology*, p. 79.

gesticulation' in 3.3 when Iago opens his attack on Othello.[68] Samuel Sandford, Betterton's Iago, was a specialist in the type. Whenever 'there was a hateful or mischievous person' to be played, wrote Cibber, 'Sandford was sure to have no competition for it', for he had 'a low and crooked person' and 'such bodily defects were too strong to be admitted into great or amiable characters'. According to custom, he would have worn a 'black periwig' and an 'old red coat' as though, says Cibber, we should 'suppose it unnatural that a murder should be thoroughly committed out of [them]'.[69]

It is perhaps not surprising therefore, that no chief tragedian before Irving, two centuries later, chose to make his reputation as Iago rather than as Othello.

Barton Booth's Othello

Betterton died in 1710, and was succeeded by Barton Booth as chief tragedian. At about the same time, in 1710 or 1711, it happens that two of Othello's least heroic moments were cut, and disappeared for at least a hundred and fifty years: the fit and the eavesdropping scene (4.1). The critic who first remarked on the omissions says that the trance 'being a thing not strained but very natural . . . did once give great satisfaction', and he speaks of the eavesdropping scene simply as something necessary to the plot.[70] Whether the cut was made at Booth's instigation is not known, but it is suggestive that Colley Cibber describes him as an actor who nursed his dignity. He had 'too solemn a regard to harmony' when he spoke, and 'seemed to think nothing valuable that was not tragically great or marvellous'.[71]

Colley's son, Theophilus (also an actor), described Booth as having 'the deportment of a nobleman, and so well became the Star and Garter he seemed born to it; and would have made as good a figure in the drawing room as on the stage.' A 'drawing-room' seems a far cry from the battlefield – but then Booth's distinguishing characteristic as Othello was pathos rather than terror. Theophilus even talks of tears: 'the heartbreaking anguish of his jealousy which would have drawn tears from the most obdurate'[72] and another contemporary said that he had 'seen all men susceptible of the tender passions in tears.'[73]

These tears are new, and to go with them is a new emphasis on Othello's 'sweetness.' Colley Cibber had described Betterton as 'more manly than

68 Rymer, *Short View*, p. 149.   69 Cibber, *Apology*, pp. 77, 78.
70 Lillie, *Letters*, I, pp. 255–6.   71 Cibber, *Apology*, pp. 314, 313.
72 Theophilus Cibber, 'Barton Booth', pp. 45–6, 50.
73 Victor, *History*, II, p. 13.

sweet',[74] but Booth, according to Theophilus, had a 'manly sweetness', and a 'comeliness which charmed those who sat near him'. His 'attitudes', Theophilus continues, 'were all picturesque', borrowed very often from painting and statuary; and 'the tones of his voice were all musical'. And yet, says Theophilus, 'all his grief, though most feelingly expressed, was never beneath the hero: when he wept, his tears broke from him perforce. He never whindled, whined, or blubbered.'[75]

Beside him was Colley Cibber's Iago, a ludicrous figure, it was said, who in 3.3 'shrugs up his shoulders, shakes his noddle, and with a fawning motion of his hands, drawls out' his words – 'from which gestures, and drawling manner of speaking, Othello must be supposed a fool, a stock, if he does not see through him'.[76] The actor and bookseller Thomas Davies (in whose shop Boswell was first introduced to Dr Johnson), complained that he wore 'the mask of honesty so loosely that Othello who is not drawn a fool, must have seen the villain through his thin disguises'.[77] But audiences seem to have been able to look with selective eyes. Certainly no one did feel that Booth's Othello was a fool or a stock. Though he retired relatively young, in 1728, his Othello remained unsurpassed for the next two decades.

Garrick's failure as Othello

After Booth's death, tragic acting developed a particular style consisting of 'deliberate articulation, distinct use of pausing, solemn significance of looks, and . . . [a] composed air and gravity of . . . motion'.[78] The arch proponent of this school of acting was James Quin, whose Othello is less interesting than the indignation it provoked in the actor–dramatist Samuel Foote: 'Sure never has there been a character more generally misunderstood, both by audience and actor, than this before us, to mistake the most tender-hearted, compassionate, humane man, for a cruel, bloody, and obdurate savage.'[79] The word 'savage' is arresting. Is it a reference to Othello's origins? Does it mean that the moment Othello's tenderness is forgotten, his origins are remembered?

In the early 1740s, there arrived in London a young man, David Garrick who, almost at a stroke, overturned Quin's method. Garrick's 'easy and famil-iar, yet forcible'[80] voice and manner were a revelation, and his Richard III

74 Cibber, *Apology*, p. 69.
75 Theophilus Cibber, 'Barton Booth', pp. 45, 51, 44, 50.
76 *Grub Street Journal*, 31 October 1734.   77 Davies, *Miscellanies*, III, p. 440.
78 Hill, *Prompter*, p. 96.   79 Foote, *Treatise*, pp. 33–4.
80 Davies, *Memoirs*, I, p. 40.

was the talk of the town. This was followed by a variety of successes in both comic and tragic roles, but when it came to Othello, the magic failed. Othello, it seems, occupied a Garrick-proof place of its own. In no other part did it matter that Garrick was neither tall, nobly handsome, nor possessed of a musical voice. But in this part, wrote William Cooke, 'independent of taste and judgement, there is a demand of figure and tones of voice perhaps superior to any in the whole range of drama'.[81]

Garrick had his moments, but no one paid him the usual compliment that he was 'the very man'. His mistake was to reinvent 'the very man'. He wore a turban, for example. Quin ridiculed this by remarking loudly enough for a large part of the audience to hear: 'Why does not he bring the tea-kettle and lamp?'[82] (The reference was to a small black boy in a plumed turban holding a kettle in Hogarth's series *A Harlot's Progress*). More significantly, he restored the fit. This was applauded (to the disgust of a fellow actor, Charles Macklin),[83] but it did not catch on. Garrick's whole conception of the part, it seems, ran counter to heroic convention. Henry Aston felt obliged to advise him against 'little wincings and gesticulations of the body' in the jealous scenes, as being 'much below' Othello's jealousy: 'they were fitter for a man under the impression of fear, or on whom some bodily torture was inflicting, than one labouring under the emotions of such tumultuous passions . . .'[84] Bodily torture and panic are the very things that modern actors try to convey, especially before the fit (see commentary); but Garrick, for once, was out of tune with his audience.

There is an interesting clue to all this. When the Frenchman the Abbé Morellet asked Garrick why he thought Shakespeare had made Othello black, Garrick had an answer which anticipates later ideas about the essential African-ness of Othello's passion:

> His answer was that Shakespeare had shown us white men jealous in other pieces, but that their jealousy had limits, and was not so terrible; that in the part of Othello he had wished to paint that passion in all its violence, and that is why he chose an African in whose veins circulated fire instead of blood and whose true or imaginary character could excuse all boldness of expression and all exaggerations of passion.[85]

Garrick played Othello three times in London, on 7 March 1745, two days later, and on 20 June 1746. There was a flurry of expectation at the end of his career that he would revive *Othello*, but in fact he never played it again.

81 Cooke, *Memoirs*, p. 113.   82 Murphy, *Life*, p. 70.
83 Kirkman, *Memoirs*, II, p. 260.   84 Boaden, *Correspondence*, I, p. 30.
85 Hedgecock, *Cosmopolitan Actor*, footnote on p. 341.

Spranger Barry and 'pathetic sensibility'

The 'very man' was the Irishman, Spranger Barry, 'a fine figure', writes Arthur Murphy, an actor–playwright and one of Garrick's biographers: 'full six feet high, well made . . . graceful in his movements, and certainly one of the handsomest men in Europe'.[86] Barry was an instrument, like Booth, made for Othello as he was conceived at the time:

> the harmony of his voice and the manly beauty of his person, spoke him alike the hero and the lover [wrote Wiliam Cooke], and those who before doubted of the part's consistency in forming a mutual passion between such characters as the black Othello and the fair Desdemona, were now convinced of his propriety. They saw from Barry's predominant and fascinating manner, that mere colour could not be a barrier to affection.[87]

The idea that Othello's colour could be such a barrier is new and had perhaps arisen with Quin. Barry's Othello, brimming with 'tenderness, love, grief, and pity', effectively laid it to rest.[88]

Barry was like Booth, only more so. Booth made Betterton's heroism 'sweet' and 'comely'; Barry was sweeter and comelier still. 'Indeed', wrote Davies, 'the same heartrending feelings which charmed the audience in Othello diffused themselves through all Barry's acting, when the softer passions predominated, in Jaffier, Castalio [in Otway's *Venice Preserved* and *The Orphan*, respectively], Romeo . . .' The list could hardly be more telling. Once Colley Cibber had described Betterton's style as fitter for 'the rage and jealousy of Othello . . . than the sighs and tenderness of Castalio'. Now Othello is added to that family of softer characters that suited Betterton least. From being 'the hero', Othello has now become 'the-hero-and-the-lover'. And yet so pervasive was the shift that Cibber himself, with all his memories, was swept away, preferring Barry's Othello, says Davies, 'to the performances of Betterton and Booth in that part'.[89]

Barry was, in fact, capable of a fine rage. John Bernard describes his gathering fury just before 'I'll tear her all to pieces' (3.3.432): 'you could observe the muscles stiffening, the veins distending, and the red blood boiling through his dark skin . . .'[90] And yet Murphy maintained that even in the most raging moments 'his voice was harmony in uproar'.[91] According to William Cooke, Barry's speciality was 'the blended passages of *rage* and *heartfelt affection* (such as in several passages of Othello)'.[92] Once again, the extremes of the

86 Murphy, *Life*, p. 76.   87 Cooke, *Memoirs*, p. 155.
88 Foote, *Treatise*, p. 35.   89 Davies, *Memoirs*, II, pp. 240, 239.
90 Bernard, *Retrospections*, I, p. 17.   91 Murphy, *Life*, p. 76.
92 Cooke, *Memoirs*, p. 158.

part, far from being a problem, were an opportunity. Whoever succeeds as Othello, wrote John Bernard, 'achieves the loftiest flight of Shakespeare's genius, and bodies forth the *chef d'œuvre* of the British stage': 'Othello, containing in itself all the highest and most opposite elements of tragic character requires greater abilities to do it justice than any or all of Shakespeare's other conceptions.' Barry neither softened his raging moments in the light of his tender passions, nor brutalised his softer moments in the light of his savagery. In fact Bernard illustrates his enthusiasm for Barry just exactly at the two outer limits of his performance: the first at the point before he bursts out with 'I'll tear her all to pieces', and the second at 'away, away, away!' in the 'brothel scene' so-called (4.2.40), which he spoke 'falteringly, and gushed into tears' (see commentary).

Audiences were charmed. Bernard reports that at the height of Barry's rage 'the females . . . used invariably to shriek, while those with stouter nerves grew uproarious in admiration'. For his own part, he says, 'I remember that the thrill it gave me took my sleep the entire night.'[93]

A glimpse of Desdemona

And what of Desdemona during all this time, not heard of since the curtailment of her part and the lecherous tittering during her last scene in 1710–11? Not much, is the answer. It is as though the heroism of Othello required her silence and submission to become right and natural. Here is John Hill in his *Treatise on the Art of Playing* (1750). Othello's murder of Desdemona, he says, is 'one of the most brutal things done by the hero of a play that we have an instance of', yet 'what can we expect of a worthy man convinced of his beloved wife's pretended adultery, but death and punishment?' At the vow of vengeance 'how natural, how excusable does all this fury appear . . . we could scarce have accused him of sinking into brutality had Desdemona fallen by his hand at the instant'. Shakespeare positively reconciles us to the murder, he says, 'by making him even tender and affectionate in the instant he is about to do it'.[94] Opinions of this kind were to have a long history – as late as 1955 Helen Gardner could still write that the murder has 'wonderful tragic rightness'.[95]

But in spite of this, Barry's Desdemona, Susannah Maria Cibber (wife of Theophilus) did stir the critics to some reaction. Part of the reason may have been that she was so aptly and interestingly ill-treated by Theophilus in real life. She acted with Barry when he first made his reputation as Othello, and was his match in 'passion of the tender kind', says Davies, excelling 'in the

---

93 See Bernard, *Retrospections*, I, pp. 17–18.
94 Hill, *The Actor*, pp. 142, 145.   95 Gardner, 'The Noble Moor', p. 175.

expression of love, grief, tenderness'. 'Happy it was', he continues, 'for the frequenters of the theatre when these two genuine children of nature united their charms . . . Mrs Cibber might be styled indeed the daughter or sister of Mr Garrick [from the parts she played, e.g. Cordelia], but could only be the mistress or wife of Barry [e.g. Juliet, Desdemona].'[96] Just as Barry was the quintessential 'lover', so was Mrs Cibber. John Hill thought she had 'a heart better formed for tenderness than any other woman who ever attempted it, and perhaps in real life more deserves the name of lover than any body of her sex ever did'.[97]

The rescue of Iago by Macklin and Garrick

Meanwhile Iago was also being rescued, in his case from ridicule. Charles Macklin was an idiosyncratic actor, a celebrated Shylock, and, according to Davies, gave, in 1744, the first 'proper outline of Iago' that the public had seen 'this century'.[98] William Cooke, an early biographer of Macklin, praised 'above all his soliloquies [which] were so much the natural workings of real character as to demand the profoundest attention'.[99] And another early biographer noted that instead of wearing the mask loosely like Cibber, he 'wrought with great judgement and propriety upon Othello's openness of temper and warmth of heart'. One moment in particular was his 'subtle affectation of chagrin at Othello's boisterous treatment of him, and his blunt method of expression in order to recall the Moor's calmer reason, and to plant the dagger still deeper in his heart'.[100]

It was obviously a temptation then, as now, for Iago to upstage Othello. We hear from Foote (grateful no doubt, since he had played Othello to Macklin's Iago) that Macklin understood his subordinate position as a 'dependant . . . nay perhaps a domestic' and gave Iago a 'distant obsequious behaviour', never attempting to obtain 'more consequence, or a higher regard than the author has thought fit to allow him; from his modest and decent deportment, you are always taught that he has a superior, both in quality and character, on the stage'.[101] The agreement in Foote's mind between the social class of Iago and the regard owing to the actor is typical of the period, and it helps us to understand how strongly the noble rank of the Moor was a presumption in favour of his noble heart.

Garrick, on the other hand, as chief tragedian of the day, was less content to play second fiddle. Having conceded Barry's superiority as Othello, he 'took care' wrote Murphy, 'not to let himself down' in the part of Iago: 'the

96 Davies, *Memoirs*, II, pp. 241–2.   97 Hill, *The Actor*, p. 116.
98 Davies, *Miscellanies*, III, p. 441.   99 Cooke, *Memoirs*, p. 407.
100 Kirkman, *Memoirs*, I, pp. 302, 303.   101 Foote, *Treatise*, pp. 37–8, 39.

several modes of mind that so strongly mark Iago's villainy, were wonderfully expressed; and by consequence the attention of the public was equally divided between the two great performers'.[102] He gave the soliloquy at 2.3.40, 'If I can fasten but one cup upon him', in Macklin's way, 'delivering plainly and without ornament, a speech in which we have been used to see a world of unnatural contortion of face and absurd by-play'.[103] But at the same time he appears to have been inventive. John Hill unfortunately gives us no examples, but he says that Macklin as Shylock and Garrick as Iago were notable 'in expressing to the audience such sentiments as are not delivered in the play, yet are not only agreeable to, but necessary to be understood of the character they represent under the situation in which it is they do it'. Shakespeare, he feels, would have been grateful to both these performers in those parts.[104]

The text during the third quarter of the eighteenth century

Garrick's early audiences were said by Thomas Davies to have a 'more refined and elegant taste' than those of Barton Booth – a taste that 'began to disrelish the coarse language and address of a lover [he is talking about Polydore in Otway's play *The Orphan*] who, in the midst of his courtship, tells the lady "that her soft tender limbs are made for yielding"'.[105] Given this, it is remarkable how much of the text of *Othello* was allowed to stand. It is at this point in the story, at about the middle of the eighteenth century, that we begin to have a more exact idea of the text used in the theatres.

Until now the printed texts 'as acted' have not differed materially from the earliest editions, and we know them to be suspect theatrically because they do not record the 'whole scenes left out, and [the] others barbarously mangled' that the letter-writer to the *Tatler* or *Spectator* complained of in about 1710 or 1711. He specified two major cuts, but they were only two, he said, 'amongst the rest'[106] so that when we come to an edition dated 1755 (suspected by Rosenberg to be a misprint for 1760)[107] which makes other omissions, it is possible that these were already traditional. The bulk of these cuts seems to have been made in order to shorten and concentrate the action. The first forty lines of 2.1, for example, where Montano and two gentlemen describe the storm, are cut. The clown is dropped. Bianca disappears completely. And now the entire willow-song scene, shortened in the Smock

102 Murphy, *Life*, p. 112.   103 Hill, *The Actor*, p. 282.
104 Ibid., p. 249.   105 Davies, *Memoirs*, 1, p. 50.
106 Lillie, *Letters*, 1, p. 255.   107 Rosenberg, 'Refinement of *Othello*'.

Alley version, disappears. James Boaden, the biographer of the tragic actress Sarah Siddons, called this omission a 'barbarous mutilation' and put it down to 'the rage of the English for action [which] in its wild impatience throws away a thousand delicate and essential touches of character'.[108] That the ruling motive was speed and action is probably true, for even in Othello's part lines were lost which would perfectly have suited their conception of him. They cut the eavesdropping scene to avoid anything ridiculous. But by cutting as far as Othello's 'Get me some poison, Iago' (4.1.192), they missed 'O, the world hath not a sweeter creature' and everything down to 'O Iago, the pity of it, Iago!'

Cutting the fit was also to preserve heroic propriety, and other smaller cuts in this edition can be traced to that cause as well. For example, Othello does not say 'Exchange me for a goat . . .', nor does Iago suggest that Desdemona may 'make, unmake, do what she list' with Othello (2.3.13). But there is so much else which Iago is allowed to say about him, and which Othello says about himself, that it is hard to take such censorship seriously. Othello still calls on housewives to make a skillet of his helm if he falls short in his duty; still instructs Iago to set his wife on to observe Desdemona; still talks of himself as being declined into the vale of years; still imagines that he would have been happy if the whole camp had tasted her sweet body 'so I had nothing known' – all cuts made in the Smock Alley version. Similarly, Desdemona is allowed her homely touches, her gloves and nourishing dishes, and her aching finger.

Nor is decency a serious object. True, some of Iago's most carnal passages in 2.1 are cut: for example, his talk about the blood being 'made dull with the act of sport', and the need for certain 'conveniences' to freshen the appetite, without which Desdemona will 'heave the gorge, disrelish and abhor the Moor' (217–22). A little later there is another cut when Iago talks of 'mutualities' marshalling the way to 'the master and main exercise', the 'incorporate conclusion' (246–8). One wonders how old such cuts were. In *The Guardian* of 23 April 1713, John Hughes, who calls himself an old man, describes taking his 'female wards' to see 'the old tragedy of *Othello*'. He says he had the play by heart and therefore occupied himself with watching the faces of the 'young folks', who to his 'secret satisfaction' were all finally 'betrayed into tears'. Would he have made *Othello* his choice if he knew it to contain lines such as these, or would it not have occurred to him to worry? After all, there remains enough to have caused blushes even in the middle of the century. Iago still warns Brabantio that an old black ram is tupping his white ewe; the exchanges at the beginning of 4.1 about being

108 Boaden, *Siddons*, II, p. 156.

naked in bed 'An hour or more, not meaning any harm' are still there. Iago still summons up in Othello's mind pictures of Desdemona being 'topped', of her and Cassio bolstering, as he puts it, and the whole of his dream, with plucking kisses and Cassio's thigh laid across his own, is intact (3.3.397–400, 414–27).

A little later, decency does seem to have been an object. In 1774 Bell's collected edition of Shakespeare's plays, 'as acted' at the Theatres Royal, was published, edited by Francis Gentleman. Clearly some general rationalising of the text has been going on. An idiosyncratic phrase like 'Yet do I hold it very stuff o'the conscience' (1.2.2) becomes the blandly comprehensible 'yet do I hold it base and infamous'. Iago's cryptic ambiguity, 'I am not what I am' (1.1.66) becomes 'I am not what I seem.' Similarly Brabantio's preoccupation with witchcraft in 1.2 is curtailed (see commentary at 64–76). Othello's fantastic imagination is also a little diminished. Where he talks in 1.3 of 'antres vast and deserts idle', and so on to the 'Anthropophagi, and men whose heads / Do grow beneath their shoulders', there appears instead a passage first found in an acting edition of 1770, and which survived in all editions until John Philip Kemble restored the original in 1804 (see commentary 1.3.137–44). In it the strangeness that so enchanted Desdemona is exchanged for a plain exposition of the hardships of a military campaign.

But most significant, in view of the cuts that were to be made later on in the eighteenth century and with increasing efficiency during the nineteenth, is the tidying away of indecencies. In Bell's edition Iago's long exposition of his theory that love is really a 'lust of the blood and a permission of the will' (1.3.326) is gone, together with his idea that Desdemona will soon be sated with Othello's body. Admittedly Gentleman notes that Iago is prolix,[109] but the omissions conveniently dispose of his licentiousness. Again, Iago is not allowed to say to Othello at 3.3: 'Would you, the supervisor, grossly gape on? / Behold her topped?' (396–7). He stops short at 'Behold her – ' leaving Othello and the audience to imagine the unspeakable. And whereas plucking kisses up by the roots was still acceptable, the thigh was too much. Those particular lines about being naked in bed at the beginning of 4.1 are out, and if Gentleman had had his way, everything up to 'Get me some poison' would have gone: 'it would save delicacy a blush or two and be in that sense an improvement'. Within a short period his wish was realised, and Act 4 began with that line in John Philip Kemble's text and for most nineteenth-century performances. In fact Gentleman's comments are usually prophetic. He is in duty bound to print what was said on the stage, so the whole of Iago's speech in 3.3 about the difficulty of catching Desdemona and Cassio in the

---

109 Bell, footnotes on pp. 153, 169.

act is in – 'It is impossible you should see this, / Were they as prime as goats, as hot as monkeys' and so on. But in a note Gentleman remarks 'We wish the greater part of his speech were omitted. Nothing material would be lost and delicacy would be better sustained.' The passage survived a little longer, but when Macready came to prepare one of his promptbooks, probably in 1843, he struck out the lines from as far back as 399, 'Damn them then, / If ever mortal eyes do see them bolster.'

Neo-classicism: John Philip Kemble's acting and text

It was in this gathering atmosphere of embarrassment at its very subject matter that actors from now on approached the play. Spranger Barry died in 1777, and the only person who was not negligible in the part between then and the advent of Edmund Kean's Othello in 1814 was John Philip Kemble, who first performed it at Drury Lane on 8 March 1785. The arrival of Kemble and his sister Sarah Siddons on the London stage marked a change from Garrick's familiarity towards a more statuesque style. Physically Kemble was out of the same mould as Barry – tall, handsome and dignified, 'the very still-life and statuary of the stage', Hazlitt called him.[110] His speciality, however, was noble Romans rather than lovers – Coriolanus rather than Romeo. That hybrid, the hero-and-the-lover, suffered an amputation at his hands, and the result was, 'with all his fine conception, correct reading and noble person, too cold'.[111] Othello's unpredictability had gone. Kemble was all-of-a-piece, in the best neo-classical manner. James Boaden, his biographer and a Kemble devotee, said that he was

> grand and awful and pathetic, but he was European: there seemed to be philosophy in his bearing; there was reason in his rage . . . one of the sublimest things in the language, the professional farewell of Othello, came rather coldly from him . . . It was, at most, only a part very finely played.[112]

Boaden's complaint that Kemble's Othello was European does not, I think, mean that Boaden saw much significance in Othello as an African. It was in fact fairly common for commentators to see Othello as a bit – not very – foreign. The article written in Barton Booth's day already quoted from the *Guardian* (23 April 1713) ends with a story about a Spanish nobleman who treats his wife rather as Othello does Desdemona; it was reprinted in the *New Universal Magazine*, November 1751. Othello was in their minds probably no more foreign than a southern European.

---

110 Hazlitt, v, p. 304.   111 Robson, *Playgoer*, pp. 8–9.
112 Boaden, *Kemble*, i, pp. 256–7.

In 1789 Kemble began publishing his Shakespearean texts, a task which was finally completed in his collected edition of 1815. *Othello* first came out in 1804,[113] and as well as incorporating the cuts in Bell's edition, this one makes a few more which show which way the wind was blowing. Francis Gentleman had used italics for the lewd parts of Iago's summonses to Brabantio in the first scene – the black ram, the Barbary horse, and the beast with two backs – to indicate his disapproval: 'though usually spoken', he says in a textual note, 'for decency's sake' they should be omitted. Kemble does just that – though, surprisingly, he keeps the beast with two backs. There are other small cuts along these lines (noted in the commentary), the most telling being his omission of Desdemona's midnight entrance just after Othello quells the brawl in Cyprus, and the whole of the first section of 4.1 immediately before the fit. Othello's resolution to kill Desdemona comes across therefore as a continuation of his anger in the handkerchief scene, rather than as a result also of newly awakened erotic imaginings – something which even Bell's version preserves a sense of. As for Desdemona's entrance, perhaps Kemble thought it too obvious a reminder of their marriage bed. Most nineteenth-century performances followed his example here, confirming one's suspicions by cutting all of Iago's earlier references to the wedding night, to Othello's making the night wanton, and to their sheets.

Plainly Kemble's cuts still leave a lot, and it is odd that he should mind certain lines and not others. Certainly people were not then as ready to blush as the Victorians, and Kemble did not set himself up to take a moral lead. To an enraged correspondent of the *Monthly Mirror* (January 1808) his cuts fell far short of what was needed:

> as it is at present altered for the stage, we contend that it can never be played without committing such a violence on the modesty and decency of the house as is altogether intolerable . . . *Othello* is indeed the most replenished brothel of the vilest 'goats and monkeys' of Shakespeare's brain. For the sake of morality first, and next, for the sake of the beauties of this piece, it should be brought to its purgation.

Modern *Othello* criticism, remarks Edward Pechter, makes a 'thriving enterprise' of expounding the play's erotic fascination.[114] It seems we have nothing on 1808.

In the circumstances, it's no wonder that Kemble played the part coldly. He would have needed every inch of his famous dignity. Besides, Kemble

---

113 See Odell, *Betterton to Irving*, II, p. 51. The only copy available to me is dated 1814.
114 Pechter, *Interpretive Traditions*, p. 19.

being grand was a pleasure in itself: 'he might stand on the stage for an hour together and not weary us, but there we should be gazing at him as at a fine piece of Grecian sculpture – and dreaming of great ages and magnificent characters all the time' (*Champion*, 25 May 1817). There were other elegant things to look at too. In 1792 an enlarged Drury Lane – newly decorated in blue velvet, with 'silver columns of antique forms', and lighted by candles in 'cutglass lustres'[115] – needed new scenery. Kemble commissioned William Capon, an enthusiast for the now fashionable Gothic architecture, to execute seven sets of scenes: for example, 'six chamber wings of the . . . [Gothic] order, for general use in our English plays – very elaborately studied from actual remains', 'six wings representing ancient English streets . . . selected on account of their picturesque beauty'. These were stock scenes 'for general use',[116] and Kemble, amateur scholar that he was, would not have minded using Capon's English streets for Cyprus, or his English Gothic in Desdemona's bedchamber. When Kemble became manager of Covent Garden in 1803, *Bell's Weekly Messenger* (19 February 1804) reported that the stage arrangements were a lesson in 'tidyness, snugness and elegance': 'Macbeth and King Henry do not sit upon the same throne, Juliet has her own bier . . . while Desdemona has her own bed and damask curtains.'

Desdemona and Iago during the last quarter of the eighteenth century

Beside these aesthetic compensations the play itself was beginning to offer possibilities beyond the role of Othello. As has been noted, Desdemona – and for that matter, Emilia – had never attracted much comment. Francis Gentleman dismisses them, saying that 'in representation we expect nothing of the two characters of Desdemona and Emilia, but delicacy of appearance, and tender expression in the former, and a smart degree of virago spirit in the latter'.[117] Emilia did in fact manage to make some impact, especially at 'A halter pardon him! And hell gnaw his bones!' (see commentary 4.2.129–43). Boaden describes the typical Emilia boasting 'How she used to get six *rounds* of applause . . . and HOW she beat the gentle Desdemona (perhaps Mrs Siddons) to a dead standstill by this overstrained and vulgar violence.'[118] But Boaden's patronising tone tells its own story.

As for Desdemona, Sarah Siddons transformed her. The *London Magazine* of March 1785 actually opened its review with her Desdemona, saying that she 'established an interest and importance to that character which it

---

115 Oulton, *Theatres of London*, II, p. 138.   116 Boaden, *Kemble*, II, p. 102.
117 Bell, footnote on p. 175.   118 Boaden, *Siddons*, I, pp. 73–4 and footnote.

never possessed before. The most successful of her predecessors fall short of her in every scene.' Physically she was the reverse of what was expected and yet, says her biographer, Boaden, she seemed to '*lower* the figure of the lovely being who had been so towering in Euphrasia or terrific in Lady Macbeth'. All the same, her Desdemona was no shrinking girl–wife, but a warm and passionate woman. She made her plea to follow Othello to the wars with a 'generous warmth' that 'delighted' Boaden.[119] Similarly her greeting of Othello on Cyprus was 'full of passion', wrote the critic for the *London Magazine*, March 1785. In her way, she was as much 'the lover' as Mrs Cibber, though no one would have thought of calling her anyone's mistress. The high-waisted flowing gowns and simpler, unpowdered hair with which she displaced the stiff stays, wide hoops and piled-up head-dresses seem in themselves to make the distinction.

One of her best moments, wrote Boaden, was at 4.2.30, where she says 'Upon my knees, what doth your speech import?' Here she showed 'a deep concern that Othello should so grossly err, a feeling that subdued all petulance at being unjustly accused.'[120] This sense of Desdemona's moral strength, of her representing goodness and courage in a vicious world, is new. It was amplified, a generation later, in the writings and performance of the actress Helena Faucit (whose London debut was in 1836, a year before Queen Victoria's accession). Faucit's Desdemona was praised, as Siddons's had been, for giving the part its 'due weight' and restoring the balance of the play.[121] But whether she was able to convey as much as she felt is doubtful. Macready, her Othello, was convinced that the role was a lost cause: 'there is absolutely nothing to be done with it', he told Fanny Kemble, 'nothing'.[122]

Nevertheless, Faucit's essay on Desdemona is extraordinary – a ferocious attack on Othello on Desdemona's behalf, and the first such (as far as I know). Others would become indignant because Othello makes a fool of himself. Faucit is indignant because he wrongs Desdemona. At a time when Othello's nobleness was taken for granted, Faucit passionately disagreed: 'Had Othello been really the "noble Moor", as "true of mind" as Desdemona thought him . . . he would have crushed the insolent traducer [Iago] . . . beneath his heel in bitterest contempt.' As it is, 'The spark scarcely touches the tinder before it is aflame . . . All the love, all the devoted self-sacrifice of Desdemona, all sense of what is due to her and to himself, is forgotten.' 'Well may Emilia exclaim of him, "O gull! O dolt!" He sees nothing but what he is primed to see; in all things else "as ignorant as dirt".'[123]

119 Boaden, *Siddons*, II, pp. 154, 155.   120 Boaden, *Kemble*, I, p. 260.
121 Faucit, *Female Characters*, p. 50.   122 Kemble, *Records*, III, p. 380.
123 Faucit, *Female Characters*, pp. 62, 61–2, 77.

Iago too was beginning to change. Before this period, actors had never been praised for realising the intellect, still less the humour of Iago. Samuel Johnson had commended Shakespeare for never allowing the character to 'steal upon esteem'.[124] The greatest compliment Gentleman could offer Macklin was that he got the 'involuntary applause of as many curses in Iago as in Shylock'. Villainy was not to be offset, even if it meant, as Gentleman observed of Iago, that the character must from sheer length 'pall on an audience'.[125] But just as they did with Richard III (whose career Iago often follows closely), one or two actors and critics began now to hint at something new – an intellectual delight in power.[126] Here's Hazlitt, clearly beguiled by the glamour of a man who

> plots the ruin of his friends as an exercise in ingenuity, and stabs men in the dark to prevent ennui . . . He is an amateur of tragedy in real life and instead of employing his invention in imaginary characters . . . he takes the bolder and more desperate course of setting up his plot at home, casts the principal parts among his nearest friends and connections, and rehearses it in downright earnest with steady nerves and unabated resolution.

All the same, Hazlitt was not quite ready for the implications of this. Iago was not, after all, like Richard, surrounded by ciphers. Othello still cramped his style. So that when Edmund Kean experimented with a 'lighthearted monster, a careless, cordial, comfortable villain', Hazlitt, though dazzled at first, was soon critical: 'Mr Kean's Iago is, we suspect, too much in the sun', he wrote not long after his first rapturous review; Iago's sky should be 'murky', illuminated by 'flashes of lightning . . . which make the darkness more terrible'.[127]

Between the sun and the darkness, the old Iago lingered, neither Kean's nor Hazlitt's, but something closer to a pantomime villain: 'setting his wits at a child', wrote Lamb scornfully, 'and winking all the while at other children who are mightily pleased at being let into the secret'.[128] G. F. Cooke, an actor whose face and voice were made for sneering, was the most popular in this line. Kean, in fact, knew the score. In 1833, though he was billed to swap the parts of Othello and Iago with William Charles Macready, he never did. He stuck to Othello, and is reported to have warned a young actor 'not to

---

124 Johnson, *On Shakespeare*, p. 143.
125 Gentleman in *Dramatic Censor*, p. 153, and *Bell*, footnote on p. 154.
126 See Lamb, *Works*, II, pp. 133–4, on Robert Bensley, and Boaden, *Siddons*, II, pp. 27–30, on John Henderson.
127 Hazlitt, V, pp. 215, 190, 215.   128 Lamb, *Works*, II, pp. 133–4.

From a Painting by E.F. Lambert.   Lithographed by Dow & Mundey, 40 Threadneedle St.

Mr. KEAN,

AS OTHELLO.

2 Edmund Kean 'as if he had been abruptly stabbed' (see commentary at 3.3.166ff.).

peril the sympathies of the audiences as Iago, while he can assuredly possess them wholly by only a moderate picture of Othello'.[129]

Edmund Kean and the Romantic view of *Othello*

John Philip Kemble and Edmund Kean stood on opposite sides of a divide that split society in those revolutionary times. Kemble was tall, statuesque, patrician. Kean was short, mercurial, a man of the people. A correspondent

129 Wood, *Recollections*, pp. 379–80.

to *Blackwood's Magazine* (March 1818), said that Kemble was to Kean what 'as a poet, Racine is to Shakespeare', and that 'in giving us the perfection of nature instead of the perfection of art, Mr Kean has displaced a fine thing to substitute a finer.' Kean did in fact calculate his effects very precisely, but he aimed more to conceal his artifice.

Kean's interpretation of Othello altered in feeling and in certain details over the years, but it was in about 1817 that his performance reached the ideal of the period as expounded by the Romantic critics. Hazlitt wrote that 'anyone who had not seen him in the third act of Othello (and seen him near) cannot have an idea of perfect tragic acting'.[130] The importance of seeing him 'near' is a reference to the huge enlargements that both theatres underwent after the fires of 1808 (Covent Garden) and 1809 (Drury Lane). There were many complaints at the time about not being able to see or hear, and about the exaggerations that actors were forced to adopt. But the need to see Kean 'near' also signals a change in the criticism and playing of Othello, a new inwardness, a new preoccupation with Othello's soul, rather than with his passions.

Now Othello's grandeur no longer had to do with courtly Stars and Garters, but with 'the heaving of the sea in a storm', or the idea of 'a majestic serpent wounded, writhing in its pain, stung to madness. . .'.[131] Nor was he the lover like Barry, the handsomest man in Europe. Kean was short, his voice harsh. But Stendhal reported 'unfathomable depths of love . . . in Othello's exclamation: "Amen, amen, with all my soul" ';[132] and *Blackwood's Magazine* (March 1818) said that 'his whole soul seems to cling to the being on whom he gazes – his eye swims – his voice melts and trembles . . . and when at last he speaks, the words fall from his lips as if *they* were the smallest part of what he would express'. The hero, the lover, rage, pathos, these are things spoken of separately by eighteenth-century critics; the task of the actor was to display them in all their distinctiveness. Now the distinctions are less insisted on, all differences are caught up in what Hazlitt called 'that noble tide of deep and sustained passion, impetuous, but majestic . . . which raises our admiration and pity of the lofty-minded Moor'.[133]

Kean's own development in the part from 1814 to 1817 illustrates this change. *The Times* for 14 May 1814 describes him in the speech beginning 'What sense had I of her stolen hours of lust?' (3.3.339). He started calmly, having 'dropped his arms and relaxed insensibly into a gesture . . . of utter exhaustion'. Gradually 'the slight mention of his connubial endearments seemed to be stealing a delicious tranquility over his mind'. But suddenly, at the sound of Cassio's name ('I found not Cassio's kisses on her lips'), 'the

---

130 Hazlitt, v, p. 357.   131 Ibid., pp. 339, 338.
132 Stendhal, *Rossini*, p. 219 (footnote).   133 Hazlitt, v, p. 189.

whole fierceness of his nature was roused; he sprang from the ground and cried the passage with a wild and grinning desperation'. Kean was notorious for these thrilling transitions. The house 'paused like the actor, and in a moment after gave him one general thunder of applause'.

But Hazlitt thought the whole conception wrong. Violence belonged in parts such as the black Zanga, an Iago-like figure in Young's *The Revenge*, which is a play based on *Othello*, but with the colours of the hero and villain reversed – 'in conformity to our prejudices', Hazlitt interestingly remarks. Here Kean showed 'all the wild impetuosity of barbarous revenge, the glowing energy of the untamed children of the sun, whose blood drinks up the radiance of fiercer skies . . . his quivering visage, his violent gestures, his hollow pauses, his abrupt transitions were all in character'. But this mere 'boiling of the blood', says Hazlitt, is not right 'in the lofty-minded and generous Moor'.[134]

Kean did in fact break with tradition and use light brown for Othello instead of black, so as not to obscure his features. But Hazlitt was looking for a complete change of spirit: 'Othello is tall', he wrote, 'but that is nothing; he was black, but that is nothing. But he was not fierce, and that is everything.' Kean lacked what he termed 'imagination, that faculty which contemplates events and broods over feelings with a certain calmness and grandeur'. It was not the strength of emotion as such that Hazlitt minded, but its 'sharp, slight angular transitions'. Kean was 'too wedgy and determined'.[135]

On 27 October 1817, Hazlitt in *The Times* announced the crucial change. Now instead of 'the energy of passion', Kean showed 'the agony of soul'.[136] In contrast with Barry's jealousy, which had been 'finely smothered', according to Murphy, but which had 'at length . . . burst out with an amazing wildness of rage',[137] Kean's was held at smothering point. One of his most famous gestures literally illustrates this: 'his joined uplifted hands, the palms being upwards, were lowered upon his head, as if to keep his poor brain from bursting'; as if, wrote another critic 'to crush a fevered brain, which threatened to burst out into a volcano'.[138] Hazlitt speaks of 'the involuntary swelling of the veins of the forehead' – but he stops there.[139] Barry's swelling veins, it will be remembered, were merely the 'preparation for the volcanic outburst' (see commentary at 3.3.432). Even on 'blood, blood, blood' (452), Kean spoke 'in a suppressed and muffled voice'.[140]

134 Ibid., pp. 226–7, 271–2.
135 Ibid., pp. 271, 272, 271, 339.   136 Ibid., XVIII, p. 263.
137 *The London Chronicle: or Universal Evening Post*, 7 March 1757.
138 Lewes, *Actors*, p. 152; Ottley, p. 32.   139 Hazlitt, XVIII, p. 263.
140 Robinson, *Diary*, I, p. 225.

All this meant an intensification of emotion beyond any actor so far described. At the same time Kean was not maudlin. According to George Lewes, his pathos was tragic because it was 'impersonal'.[141] When the actor George Vandenhoff tried to define Kean's 'master-quality' he said that it lay 'in intensity', and added – 'in the power of abstraction'.[142] Kean possessed a quality peculiarly admired by the Romantic critics and poets. He could make particular words suggest regions beyond their immediate scope: 'we feel that the utterer is thinking of the past and the future while speaking of the instant', wrote Keats (*Champion*, 21 December 1817; see commentary at 1.2.59). His genius was to expand beyond the instant and at the same time to sharpen it past bearing. Crabb Robinson said of the farewell: 'I could hardly keep from crying; it was pure feeling.' 'We never saw anything that so completely held us suspended and heartstricken', wrote Leigh Hunt of the whole performance. 'Old men', reported Lewes, 'leaned their heads upon their arms and fairly sobbed.'[143]

But some people, brought up in Kemble's 'stately declamatory school'[144] as Lewes called it, could never get used to him. 'I have absolutely *studied* his famous Othello', wrote William Robson, 'to try to like him; but his person and carriage in it were mean and contemptible, his judgement was poor, his pathos weak, his passion violent extravagant and unnatural: he was not Othello' – 'nothing but a little vixenish black girl in short petticoats', he wrote elsewhere, referring to Kean's knee-length tunic.[145] Nor did Kean always please even his admirers. Lewes admitted that there was much in his Othello that was 'spasmodic, slovenly, false.' He failed in passages that were not 'sustained by a strong emotion', so that the 'long simple narrative' of his address to the senate was 'the kind of speech he could not manage at all'. Indeed his first two acts, except for the greeting of Desdemona, which was given with 'passionate fervour', were 'irritating and disappointing'.[146]

And just as Kean needed strong emotion in the part, so he responded to any special excitement on the night. Twice, a star Iago provoked an extraordinary performance from him. In 1817 Junius Brutus Booth, an actor who had made a study of Kean and had astonished audiences at Covent Garden with a copy of his Richard III, seemed briefly to challenge Kean's supremacy. Kean flatteringly invited him to enter into a contract with his own management at Drury Lane and to play, among other parts, Iago. The critic for *Blackwood's Magazine* (April 1818) remembered that on that night, 20 February 1817,

141 Lewes, *Actors*, p. 269.   142 Vandenhoff, *Notebook*, p. 22.
143 Robinson, *Diary*, I, p. 225; Hunt, *Dramatic Criticism*, p. 201; Lewes, *Actors*, p. 5.
144 Lewes, *Actors*, p. 37.   145 Robson, *Playgoer*, pp. 114, 9.
146 Lewes, *Actors*, pp. 5, 6.

Kean's performance was 'the noblest exhibition of human genius we ever witnessed'. Booth was billed for 25 February, but he never appeared: 'Kean's Othello smothered Desdemona and my Iago too', he admitted later.[147] Later in Kean's career, hoarse from drink and crippled by gout, Kean trounced the Iago of the tragedian who was to be his successor, William Charles Macready: 'how puny he appeared beside Macready', Lewes recalled, 'until the third act when, roused by Iago's taunts and insinuations he moved towards him with a gouty hobble, seized him by the throat, and in a well-known explosion "Villain, be sure thou prove . . ." [3.3.360] he seemed to swell into a stature which made Macready appear small'. Taken 'as a whole' the performance was 'patchy', but, says Lewes, 'it was irradiated with such flashes that I would again risk broken ribs for the chance of a good place in the pit to see anything like it'.

Lewes, like those before him, thought Othello to be 'the most trying [i.e. testing] of all Shakespeare's parts', and it was 'Kean's masterpiece'.[148] It was fitting therefore that he should take his leave of the stage in it. His son Charles was his Iago, and as the performance progressed it became clear that Kean was becoming too ill to be revived, even by hot brandy and water. Finally, at 'Villain, be sure thou prove', he 'trembled – stopped – tottered – reeled; Charles . . . went forward and extended his arms; the father made another effort . . . but it was of no use, and with a whispered moan "I am dying, – speak to them for me," he sank insensible into Charles's arms'.[149]

Three weeks later, on 15 May 1833, he died. It was in a sense the death of Othello himself, at least for a generation. In 1883 Dutton Cook looked back over the period and doubted whether 'since the times of Edmund Kean, a generally accepted Othello has been forthcoming'.[150] The stage history of the play for the following forty years or so is marked by a rising interest in Iago.

Race and sex; slavery and satire

The reason for Othello's decline goes back to an earlier point about his emotional extremes. Actors and critics of the eighteenth century took these in their stride (always excepting the fit and the eavesdropping), neither pointing to Othello's African origins nor arguing them away. Dr Johnson could concede that he yielded 'too readily to suspicion'[151] and could admire and pity him just the same. John Hill in 1750 could cheerfully say that 'tragedy may . . . represent to us cruel, nay barbarous and savage actions in

147 Hackett, *Notes and Comments*, p. 307.   148 Lewes, *Actors*, pp. 4, 5, 11.
149 Quoted from Hawkins, *Life*, II, p. 379, in *Variorum*, p. 404.
150 Cook, *Nights*, II, p. 318.   151 Johnson, *On Shakespeare*, p. 143.

[principal] persons . . . but then these are always the effect of some violent transport of rage, not of a temper in a person naturally brutal'.[152] The black face was, in effect, neither here nor there. There was no pressing reason to abandon it, nor to make it part of a thoroughgoing foreign costume. Boaden, it is true, said that above the general's uniform it 'begets a ludicrous association at first sight',[153] and perhaps it was for that reason that Barry (according to the frontispiece of a 1777 edition of the play) adopted a vaguely oriental costume. But he surely had not always worn it, for when J. P. Kemble assumed 'the Moorish habit'[154] in 1787, he was praised for it as though it were not yet customary.

Now, in the early decades of the nineteenth century, cruel, barbarous and savage actions were no longer so lightly taken. On the one hand, according to the German critic Schlegel, they gave Othello's blackness tremendous significance: 'What a fortunate mistake', he wrote, 'that the Moor, under which a baptized Saracen of the northern coast of Africa was unquestionably meant in the novel [Cinthio's narrative], has been made in every respect a negro!' Othello is 'tamed only in appearance . . . by foreign laws of honour, and by nobler and milder manners. His jealousy . . . is of that sensual kind from which in burning climes has sprung the disgraceful treatment of women . . . The mere physical force of passion puts to flight in one moment all his acquired and accustomed virtues.'[155]

On the other hand, there were critics who preferred to sink this whole aspect of Othello. We have seen Hazlitt distinguishing Othello from the fierceness of the African Zanga. Coleridge goes further and refuses to allow that jealousy is the passion in question at all: 'it was a moral indignation and regret that virtue should so fall . . . There is no ferocity in Othello; his mind is majestic and composed.'[156] In Lamb's view only vulgar people would think anything else: they 'shed tears', he wrote, 'because a blackamoor in a fit of jealousy kills his innocent white wife', but 'of the texture of Othello's mind, the inward construction marvellously laid open . . . of the grounds of passion, its correspondence to a great or heroic nature', they know nothing. It is as though the actual story were irrelevant. As for the blackness itself, it was better not to go to the theatre at all:

I appeal to everyone that has seen Othello played whether he did not sink . . . Othello's mind in his colour; whether he did not find something extremely revolting in the courtship and wedded caresses of Othello and Desdemona; and whether the actual sight of the thing did not over-weigh all that beautiful compromise which we make in reading.[157]

152 Hill, *The Actor*, p. 142.   153 Boaden, *Correspondence*, 1, p. 593 (footnote).
154 *Public Advertiser*, 29 October 1787.   155 Quoted in *Variorum*, p. 431.
156 Coleridge, *On Shakespeare*, p. 195.   157 Lamb, *Works*, 1, pp. 102, 108.

One recalls Steele at the beginning of the century making the opposite point about the reader 'in his closet'.

The problem with jealousy is sex. A. C. Bradley, the early twentieth-century exponent of the 'noble' Moor approach, saw this clearly: 'sexual jealousy brings with it a sense of shame and humiliation . . . [it] converts human nature into chaos, and liberates the beast in man; and it does this in relation to one of the most intense and also the most ideal of human feelings'.[158] The only way the nineteenth-century theatre could get rid of the beast in Othello was first to deny his jealousy and then to de-sex his love. The strategy can be seen in this echo of Coleridge by John Forster in 1836: 'Jealousy is not the grand feature of [Othello's] passion', he wrote, 'his love for Desdemona . . . is presented to us rather as that grand principle of virtue, tenderness, and affectionate admiration of beauty and good into which all the hopes and habits of an active life had at length settled down, and which is to carry him happily and calmly and with a tranquil mind through the "vale of years".'[159]

Othello's 'race', moreover, made de-sexualisation a matter of urgency. Earlier, this black and white marriage had been an absurdity, at worst an impropriety. Now, like Lamb, Coleridge judged that 'as we are constituted . . . it would be something monstrous to conceive this beautiful Venetian girl falling in love with a veritable negro'.[160] The stage did what it could to preserve Desdemona's purity. Her white satin gown became so much a part of her character that when Fanny Kemble, Sarah Siddons's niece, chose to appear in black and gold, like a Venetian noblewoman in a Titian painting, she said, she expected 'to be much exclaimed against'.[161] A debate arose in the *Examiner* in 1814 as to whether or not Iago was right in saying that Desdemona's love for Othello was merely a 'lust of the blood and a permission of the will.' Leigh Hunt, while admiring her amiable and generous qualities, thought her 'as little qualified to go by the side of Una [to whom, with her milk-white lamb, Wordsworth had compared her] as a wanton Italian by the side of one of the most perfect of our countrywomen'.[162] It was a line of thought hotly pursued in America. Joseph Quincy Adams even thought she deserved what she got: 'upon the stage, her fondling with Othello is disgusting; who in real life would have her for a sister, daughter or wife?' he asked.[163]

158 Bradley, *Tragedy*, p. 144.   159 Forster, *Essays*, p. 20.
160 Coleridge, *On Shakespeare*, p. 188.   161 Kemble, *Records*, III, p. 368.
162 Hunt, *Dramatic Criticism*, p. 80.
163 See Hackett, *Notes and Comments*, p. 225. See also Quincy Adams's essay on Desdemona, in ibid., pp. 234–49.

Joyce Green MacDonald[164] has written about the fear and ridicule of black people at this period in America, especially when they performed Shakespeare, as they did in Manhattan in the 1820s. She describes England too, in the early 1830s when the black American tragedian, Ira Aldridge, toured the country in a variety of roles, including Othello. Arriving in London in April 1833, at the height of the campaign to defeat the bill to emancipate British-owned slaves in Jamaica, Aldridge's performances of Shakespeare seemed to challenge one of the very bases of slavery – the contention that black people were intellectually inferior. Some newspapers were complimentary, but the views of the *Athenaeum* give an idea of what was at stake. Aldridge, it said, should never have been allowed to play Othello – 'Othello, forsooth!' – because 'it is impossible that Mr Aldridge should fully comprehend the meaning and force or even the words he utters'. The success of the anti-slavery bill in July 1833 only made matters worse. Theoretically, black attempts on Shakespeare became more possible, and on *Othello* in particular, where Shakespeare concerns himself with the very thing most feared – miscegenation. Aldridge's engagement at Covent Garden was, in fact, cut short, owing, it was said, to the fastidiousness of the friends of Ellen Tree (his Desdemona) 'envious of the Moor's familiarity with her fair face'.[165]

Another kind of answer to black encroachments of this kind was burlesque. Burlesque draws the sting, as MacDonald points out, eroding 'the secret fear at the heart of the play' by making 'satirically explicit the contours of the racial unconscious from which *Othello* draws its power in performance'.[166] In 1834 an operatic burlesque of the play by Maurice G. Dowling opened in Liverpool, moving two years later to the Strand Theatre in London. Here Othello is unashamedly 'a Nigger', strumming on his banjo. His speech to the Senate begins: 'Massa him neber do de ting dat wrong; / Him tell him all about it in him song' and continues, to the tune of 'Yankee Doodle', 'Potent, grave and rev'rend sir / Very noble Massa –'. The whole thing, in rhyming doggerel and songs with choruses like 'Tol de rol' or 'Och hubbaboo', is pitched below stairs with Desdemona a servant girl – no more scandalous a partner for Othello than Rymer's 'little drab or small-coal wench'. She listens to his 'tales bewitching' while curling her hair in the 'kitchen', tales which she found so 'tender' that she fell across the 'fender.' The 'turn . . . / And turn again' speech (4.1.244–5) becomes

---

164 MacDonald, 'Acting Black'.
165 Quoted (without precise dates) by Marshall and Stock, *Ira Aldridge*, pp. 126–7 and 130–1.
166 MacDonald, 'Acting Black', 247.

Sir, if she get her living she must earn him
And if you've got a mangle she can turn him.
Yes she can turn and turn and so go on
For ebber, or till all the work be done.

Othello then appears to offer Lodovico 'a glass of – goats and monkeys' – 'I'd rather not', says Lodovico, and Othello goes out muttering 'Razors and donkeys.' 'It is the cause' from 5.2 is sung to the tune of 'King of the Cannibal Islands.'

William Charles Macready

The whole idea of playing Othello was thus deeply compromised by the time Macready took over from Kean. From now on, any Othello would have to steer a careful course: exotic (it was said that Macready 'wore rich Eastern garments, strongly scented with musk')[167] but not sub-Saharan; wild but not barbarous; dignified but not tame. His own social sensitivities could only have complicated matters. The son of a provincial actor–manager, he had never intended to be an actor. Acting was regarded as a doubtful profession, little better than being a vagabond. But his father's financial difficulties had forced him into it, and throughout his life (like his great friend Charles Dickens) he was sensitive about his respectability. One feels it in the pen-strokes across his prompt copy of *Othello*, for which he used Kemble's revised edition. Kemble had struck out the 'thigh' in Cassio's dream; Macready strikes out the plucking kisses too. 'Happiness to their sheets' (2.3.25) is neatly altered to 'Happiness to them'. All the 'whores' in 4.2, the 'brothel' scene so-called, which Kemble had kept, become 'strumpets' or, for the sake of variety, 'one'. Desdemona cannot even say, as she wakes before the murder, 'Will you come to bed, my lord?' (5.2.24) The whole nexus of sexual and racial fear seems to have tightened round him.

Macready's diaries show him constantly trying for grandeur, fighting off the memory of Kean, and – not surprisingly – nervous: 'sat down to read Othello; the idea of which . . . gave me a sensation of nervousness'; 'Practised part of Othello, to which I do not find I yet give that real pathos and terrible fury that belongs to the character'; and in a withering note to himself – 'elaborate but not abandoned'.[168] He did what he could. He wept, or rather (according to Hazlitt) 'whined and whimpered'; at one point in 1.3, the Senate scene, he 'goes off like a shot', continued Hazlitt, 'and startles our sense of hearing'.[169] In the last scene, one of his Desdemonas, Fanny

167 Kirk, 'Shakespeare's Tragedies'.
168 Macready, *Reminiscences*, I, pp. 364, 468, 471.   169 Hazlitt V, p. 339.

3 Willam Charles Macready 'thrusting . . . his dark despairing face through the curtains of the bed when Emilia calls to him'.

Kemble, said that she dreaded 'his personal violence. I quail at the idea of his laying hold of me in those terrible passionate scenes.'[170] After the murder he hit on a thrilling effect: 'the thrusting of his dark despairing face, through the curtains of the bed when Emilia calls to him'.[171] It is even recorded that a woman hysterically fainted one evening at this moment.[172] Once, on 1 November 1843, he pleased himself: 'Acted Othello in a very grand and impassioned manner, never better', he wrote.[173]

But it was a losing battle. 'In all the touching domesticities of tragedy', wrote Lewes of Macready, 'he is unrivalled. But he fails in the characters which demand impassioned grandeur . . . His Macbeth and Othello have fine touches, but they are essentially unheroic – their passion is fretful and irritable, instead of being broad, vehement, overwhelming.'[174] John Forster Kirk, an admirer of Macready agreed. Taken as a whole, he said, Macready's Othello

170 Kemble, *Records*, III, p. 386.   171 Marston, *Recent Actors*, I, p. 83.
172 Forster, *Essays*, p. 24.   173 Macready, *Reminiscences*, II, p. 219.
174 Forster and Lewes, *Essays*, p. 132.

never satisfied either his audiences or himself. He had not grasped the conception – baffled as it seemed to me by its very simplicity and freedom from intellectual subtleties. He was haughty, irate, vehement, not grandly terrible or deeply pathetic . . . there was no suggestion of Oriental repose, mellifluous flow of words, or lava-like torrents of passion.[175]

On 15 August 1840, the correspondent of the *Theatrical Journal* looked back over the careers of Macready and Kean and declared that there were two ways of doing the Moor: 'on the one hand . . . retaining all the fiery qualities of his native clime with little or no restraint; on the other hand his original nature and warm passions, being in some degree under self-control, in consequence of having been accustomed to the high bearing and polished manners of the Venetian state'. The first, he says, was Kean's manner, the second, Macready's. The distinction measures the distance Othello had travelled from 'Africa'. Kean's 'smothered' performance of 1817 seemed, by contrast with Macready in 1840, to be the very thing it was originally praised for not being.

Middle-class audiences and naturalism

Macready was baffled by Othello, but he made up for it with gorgeous, historically accurate scenery and costumes, and a well-rehearsed cast. Shakespeare, the National Poet, deserved no less. Macready and his successors were both creating and reacting to a new kind of audience, interested as never before by comforts and appearances, and anxious to be 'improved'. Where once they would respond 'with an instantaneous shout of enthusiastic applause' when an actor carried them away, now in the middle of the century they 'sit for the most part in silent admiration . . . the stalls, boxes and even the pit are too genteel to clap their hands; and the Olympian deities are awed into silence by their isolation and the surrounding chill'.[176]

Once more, the contrast between one generation and the next seemed so great that when in 1856 Charles Dillon played an Othello that was 'natural, not at all declamatory, sometimes familiar, always domestic', the *Athenaeum* (6 December 1856) thought that 'a new era in Shakespearean performances' had arrived. For one thing, the actors sat: 'the great scenes between the Moor

---

175 Kirk, 'Shakespeare's Tragedies'. Kirk imagines the Orient here rather as Edward
      Said describes the popular perception of it – as a place of 'sensuality, promise, ter-
      ror, sublimity, idyllic pleasure, intense energy' (*Orientalism*, pp. 118–19). From
      the early nineteenth century, commentators often reach for this 'chameleonlike',
      'free-floating Orient', as Said puts it, as a way of defining what Othello is.
176 J. W. Cole, *Charles Kean*, I, pp. 92–3.

and his tempter were for the most part gone through in a sitting position', it noted with surprise. In 1861, Charles Fechter went even further, lolling and lounging, shaking hands, opening and shutting doors with keys. The *Athenaeum* (26 October 1861) devoted more space to these things than to the acting: 'the furniture was so disposed that . . . the characters could lean upon it and adopt either a sitting or a standing attitude . . . Mr Ryder as Iago availed himself of the council table when left to himself . . . The result was that the performance had an air of naturalness and reality sufficient of itself to command success.' The critic notes that Fechter lacked the 'physical force' for the 'vehement display' of jealousy, but this is a trifling point against the 'natural and conversational tone . . . as satisfactory as it was novel'.

Others were less content. Realism, felt Lewes, worked on *Othello* 'like poison'; it turned the play into a French *drame*.[177] Fechter was indeed half French (his father came from Alsace) and his greatest success had been as Armand Duval in *La dame aux camelias*. But an Armand Duval was no model for Othello, thought Henry Ottley: 'the weak dalliance which M. Fechter makes to pass between [Othello and Desdemona]', the kissing and playing with curls and 'then more kissing usque ad nauseam', all 'this sort of thing consists very well with French notions of sentiment' but it 'shocks us as unworthy of the personages and the poet'.[178]

Fechter's readings and cuts do suggest a literal-minded, rational approach to the play. For example, 'It' in 'It is the cause, it is the cause, my soul' turned out to be the colour of his skin – something he tried to convey by looking at himself in 'a handglass like a hairbrush that he had deliberately gone to fetch from Desdemona's bed'.[179] In the same spirit, he cut Othello's mystical history of the handkerchief (3.4.51–71); but equally, he brought back Bianca so that Othello could see her give it to Cassio. His most significant rationalisation of the play, however, lay in his treatment of Othello's jealousy. On 24 October 1861, the *Morning Herald* wrote that 'a striking change has been introduced; it is not until late in the scene that Othello is made to yield to a suspicion of his wife's falsehood. He appears to disregard or to utterly misunderstand the innuendos of Iago, then to accept them as general reflections not applicable to himself any more than to anyone else.' Only at Iago's 'She did deceive her father' (3.3.208) did he catch on. This, thought Lewes, makes Othello convinced by force of argument, when his feeling is really 'founded on Iago's suggestions and the smallest possible external evidence'.[180]

---

177 Lewes, *Actors*, pp. 147, 146. 178 Ottley, p. 21.
179 Morley, *Journal*, p. 231. 180 Lewes, *Actors*, p. 162.

This is especially interesting in the context of the discussion earlier, about Shakespeare's alterations to Cinthio. Neither Kean nor Macready had provoked Lewes to this sort of objection. He even thought that Othello should have a '*vague* feeling which he dares not shape into a suspicion' during the preceding dialogue with Desdemona, after Iago has dropped his remark about Cassio stealing away 'so guilty-like' (3.3.99).[181] There is evidence that Kean was overcome with real horror as early as Iago's 'O beware my lord of jealousy' (see commentary at 3.3.92ff.), and if, as seems likely, Helena Faucit's attack on Othello is derived from her knowledge of the play in performance, then the supposition is confirmed.

Fechter's Othello was well received, however, by precisely the kind of audience that called it into being. Ottley fumed as he made the connection:

> when critics speak without rebuke of M. Fechter's delivering the speeches of Othello in a 'colloquial style', in a 'free and easy manner', and all as 'familiar discoursing' – what are we to think of their notions of Shakespeare's work? And when we are told that the performance was of a character to be relished by the educated classes in the boxes and stalls, though not perhaps entirely to the taste of that 'many-headed beast', the public, what can be the writer's idea of the purpose with which Shakespeare wrote?[182]

Edwin Forrest and G. V. Brooke

Edwin Forrest, Macready's American contemporary and bitter rival, was the favourite of just that 'many-headed beast' in his own country. He was a man of 'mastodonian muscularity', and his parts were chosen chiefly with a view to his own 'private legs and larynx', wrote Charles T. Congdon.[183] When Forrest visited England in 1845, the *Spectator* (29 March 1845) was scornful: 'his passion is a violent effort of physical vehemence. He bullies Iago and treats Desdemona with brutal ferocity: even his tenderness is affected, and his smile is like the grin of a wolf showing its fangs. The killing of Desdemona was a cold-blooded butchery.' And yet for some, this was a welcome corrective. It was said that apart from Salvini, Forrest was 'the only actor within living memory [who] dared present the true unidealised Othello'.[184]

Here was a clash of cultures – raw versus cooked. Raw was more exciting and one reviewer spoke of applause 'such as we have seldom before witnessed in a London theatre . . . [at 'I had rather be a toad'] the look of ghastly horror

181 Ibid., p. 158.   182 Ottley, pp. 5, 6.
183 Quoted in Barrett, *Edwin Forrest*, p. 136.
184 Lawrence, *Gustavus Vaughan Brooke*, p. 84.

with which the utterance . . . was accompanied electrified the audience, who rising in all parts of the house,' continued to greet the performer with most enthusiastic applause'. And an early biographer reported that once in the handkerchief scene 'the glare of his eye when his wife could not produce the fatal napkin was almost supernatural, and the lady who sat in the same box with me, clutched convulsively at her husband's arm for protection'.[185]

Forrest was entirely simple-minded: 'where a tender word occurred, it was spoken tenderly; where a fierce word fiercely', said John Forster, who, though a partisan of Macready's, is circumstantial enough to deserve attention (see e.g. commentary at 5.2.334ff.). But perhaps his literalness was a form of direct identification. It was said that after a certain evening in 1848, when he found his wife 'standing between the knees of Mr Jamieson who was sitting on the sofa with his hands on her person', he identified with the Moor very directly indeed.[186]

This was not the only way left of making *Othello* thrilling. Gustavus Vaughan Brooke did it in the traditional Romantic vein. When he first played the part at the Olympic Theatre in 1848, he quelled the brawl in the second act with a terrific sweep of his scimitar: 'the picturesque grandeur of the action and the magnificence of the pose so struck a fellow in the gallery that he roared out "Abd'l Kader by G – !" [the Emir of Algeria, about whose gallantry the papers were then full]. This exclamation touched the keynote of sympathy: the house rose at it, the pit sprang to its feet, the boxes swelled the general chorus of applause and from that moment the success of the actor was assured.'[187] Brooke was neither brutal like Forrest – in fact all 'the mournful side of Othello's position he had conceived with great' delicacy', said *The Times* – but neither was he lachrymose like Macready. In fact he reminded the critic of the *Morning Post* of Kean,[188] and the same thought occurred to Westland Marston at his delivery of 'O, fool, fool, fool!' (5.2.319).[189] But although his success was assured in 1848, by 1853 and in the more fashionable Drury Lane, he seemed to the *Athenaeum* (10 September 1853), to neglect 'the more delicate expressions which intimate subtle feeling, and those nice phases of emotion which indicate the highest intellectual art'. Brooke left soon after for Australia, and made a name for himself in Melbourne.

---

185 See Rees, *Edwin Forrest*, p. 132; Harrison, *Edwin Forrest*, p. 64.
186 Forster, *Essays*, p. 21; Alger, *Edwin Forrest*, I, p. 497.
187 Lawrence, *Gustavus Vaughan Brooke*, p. 78.
188 Quotes from *The Times* and *Morning Post* in Lawrence, *Gustavus Vaughan Brooke*, pp. 81, 82.
189 Marston, *Recent Actors*, II, p. 174.

In their opposite ways Brooke and Forrest went against the current of an age that was fast carrying Othello in the direction of Hamlet. Edwin Booth, the great American Hamlet, would play Othello like 'a young Jesuit student, calm, cultivated and subdued'; and Forbes-Robertson, the great English Hamlet, would play him like 'Plato's philosopher–King', as one person remembered him – adding, 'if you like, more Hamlet than Othello'.[190]

Othello on the Continent: France

Meanwhile, the French and the Italians were going in the opposite direction. When the Italian actors Tommaso Salvini and Ernesto Rossi surprised London and New York in the 1870s and 80s with a terrifyingly animal Othello, it was not a bolt from the blue. The American critic J. R. Towse, in raptures over Salvini, pronounced the last scene 'utterly, abominably un-Shakespearian, if you will, but supremely, paralyzingly real'.[191] Outside the English-speaking world Shakespeare had long had a reputation for being abominable but real. Largely on the say-so of Voltaire (the first Frenchman to take an interest in Shakespeare), he had come to be known as a man of the people, full of violence and absurdity, ignorant of the classical unities, and yet capable of sublime moments.

When French translations appeared, Voltaire could not long remain the sole arbiter. In 1745 parts of several of the plays were published, including *Othello*, translated by La Place, to which the translator prefixed a discourse on the English stage. This gave great offence to Voltaire's party for it praised Shakespeare more warmly, and condemned him more faintly than had been usual. Furthermore La Place brings forward 'an eminent Englishman' and allows him space in which to say that although the classical rules may be very correct, they send him to sleep.[192] *Othello*, which had been 'corrected' by Voltaire in his *Zaïre*, went on being translated – four more times between 1773 and 1785 – but it was not performed until 1792.

This was in Ducis's translation, or rather version, altered and watered down. Othello himself is not black but 'jaune et cuivré', a coppery yellow, and Ducis cleans up the sullied imaginations of both Iago and Othello. In fact, Iago (or Pézarre) is a very minor character. Ducis felt him to be too monstrous – 'les Français ne pourraient jamais au moment y souffrir sa

190 *New York Herald*, 25 April 1869; undated clipping from *MG*, Enthoven Collection, Theatre Museum, London.
191 Towse, *Sixty Years*, p. 163.
192 Lounsbury, *Shakespeare and Voltaire*, p. 171.

présence',[193] Instead, he emphasises the relation between Brabantio and Desdemona (or Hédelmône) – thus making *Othello* a play about filial disobedience rather than sexual jealousy. But to the Parisian audience, it was heady enough. Perhaps as much as anything it was the acting of the French tragedian Talma as Othello, which, according to an English correspondent, 'burst out upon the coldness and fastidiousness of the French pit, with a force against which all critical scorn was helpless – he broke down all rules, and carried away his audience with a torrent of emotions new and strange to the French stage'. The death of Desdemona – such things were reported, not enacted, in the classical theatre – caused an uproar: 'Tears, groans, and menaces resounded from all parts of the theatre . . . several of the prettiest women in Paris fainted in the most conspicuous boxes . . . Ducis was alarmed for his tragedy, for his fame, and for his life.' He wrote an alternative ending in which Brabantio or Odalbert rushes on to the stage just as the dagger is raised (Ducis thought the pillow too cruel) and prevents the murder. The play was published with both endings, but Talma disapproved of the alteration. One evening backstage Ducis saw him 'striding away in one of the dark passages' muttering '"Shall I kill her? – No, the audience will not suffer it! Yet, what do I care – I will kill her; they shall learn to suffer it – Yes, I have made up my mind – she must be killed!"' And so she was, and continued to be.[194]

But it was not only the ending that made the play daring. The whole thing was a challenge to the *ancien régime*. A letter by a certain Citoyen Flins written to Citoyen Talma, and published in the *Journal de Paris* (16 November 1792), reassures the anxious actor that times have changed: that classical tragedy has gone out with formal gardens and the monarchy, that whereas five years ago 'les hommes de la cour' would have laughed at the idea of a beautiful young white girl marrying a Moor, now Philanthropy has triumphed, blacks (*mulâtres*) have the rights of citizens, and the aristocracy of colour is dead. Nor will Desdemona's song seem surprising (Ducis included the willow-song scene), or the sight of her bed scandalous, 'because republicans, who have better manners than the subjects of a monarchy, will not be, as they are, slaves to that false delicacy which is the hypocrisy of decency'. In one place, Ducis even refers to his hero as 'le sans-culotte Othello',[195] a reference, perhaps, to the heroic Toussaint l'Ouverture, who had led a black revolution on the French colony of San Domingo only the year before, in 1791.

---

193 Ducis's explanations and apologies can be found in his preface to *Othello* in Ducis, *Œuvres de J. -F. Ducis.*
194 'Talma', *BM*, September 1825.
195 See Gilman, *Othello in French*, pp. 57–8, 69.

There was, however, a long way to go. When some years later, in 1822, an English troupe of players performed Shakespeare's *Othello* in Paris, they were jeered. Ducis's version obeys tragic decorum so far as to cut 2.3, the drunken scene, so that when Cassio became fuddled there were shouts of derisive laughter: 'A drunken man in a tragedy! Shades of Racine and Corneille! . . .' From then on, apart from Othello's entrance in that scene (at which 'the house seemed electrified'), the play continued in dumb show: 'Desdemona was put to bed and smothered amid roars of laughter . . . Othello stabbed himself to prove that suicide was a most mirth-provoking catastrophe.'[196] Some of this hostility was simply anti-English; Waterloo still rankled. But in 1827–8, when Macready and the now decaying Edmund Kean were successfully received in Paris, there was still resistance to their *Othello*.[197]

The story had by now become so well known in its various forms – not only through Voltaire's *Zaïre* and Ducis's translation, but, from 1816, through Rossini's opera *Otello*, and a ballet by Vigano – that when, in 1829, a group of French writers wished to pronounce the death of classicism they seized upon *Othello*, newly translated by Alfred de Vigny, as their instrument. Such was the grip of classical decorum, wrote de Vigny, that the characters in 'correct' plays spent all their time 'preciously preserving that one sentiment which has animated them from start to finish, without allowing their imagination to stray a step, and preoccupied with one business only, that of starting a denouement and delaying it without ceasing to talk about it'. Shakespeare, he wrote, with his crowded plots, peopled by individuals rather than abstractions, would explode all this. Furthermore, for the first time there would be no poetic substitution, no letter or bracelet, for the word 'handkerchief' – 'to the horror of the faint-hearted . . . but to the satisfaction of the public, who, the majority of them, were in the habit of calling a handkerchief, a handkerchief'.[198] On 4 October 1829 'the battle between classicism and romanticism was joined', wrote the Duc de Broglie.[199]

There are, in fact, many evasions in de Vigny's translation. But some of what de Vigny softens was not being said at all on the English stage. The Barbary horse (1.1.111–12) which de Vigny includes was cut by Kemble. The wedding sheets, which become 'robe de mariée', were struck out by Macready. De Vigny even tries to translate 'when the blood is made dull with the act of sport', which had disappeared long before,

196 'English Players in Paris', *New Monthly Magazine and Literary Journal*, 5, 1822.
197 See Haig, 'Vigny and *Othello*'.
198 Vigny, his introductory 'letter' to his translation, in *Œuvres*, II, pp. 80, 88.
199 Broglie, 'Sur *Othello*', p. 271.

in the 1755/60 acting edition. What is remarkable is not the omissions, but the restorations. Bianca is still out, but (as in Ducis's version) the willow-song scene – in which, says de Vigny, Desdemona 'doit peu à peu déshabiller' – is in.

Furthermore, French criticism was much tougher-minded than English criticism. De Broglie readily concedes that Othello becomes

> irrational, deaf to truth, insensible to tenderness, inaccessible to moral evidence . . . at the same time taking pleasure, with a cruel joy, in describing to himself in detail his outrage in most revolting terms, crying "blood! blood! blood!" and ending by falling unconscious with rage and despair . . . he brutally strikes Desdemona in front of everyone. In public and in private he treats her like a slut, emptying bitter sarcasms and humiliating epithets on her . . .

After Lamb, Hazlitt and Coleridge, de Broglie might be talking of a different play. Equally, he makes no attempt to elevate the kind of reaction in the audience:

> from the moment Iago says 'Ha, I like not that', to the moment the curtain falls, the spectator cannot draw breath. You could hear a fly buzz . . . the spectator looks at this scene . . . with something of that anxiety which takes hold of us when in a court of justice we witness the vain efforts of the miserable ones dragged off to execution.[200]

English critics of the same period would never have allowed themselves such a comparison. And when, later, Shaw did make it – he spoke of the play's 'police court morality and commonplace thought'[201] – it was only to denigrate the play.

Ira Aldridge: *Othello* in Russia

It was the fate of *Othello* to be involved in artistic and political change on the Continent, while in England and America it remained stuck in a limbo of Shakespearean veneration. In 1852 the American black actor Ira Aldridge, having found it impossible to get a serious hearing in his own country, or in anything but minor or provincial theatres in England, started a tour in Europe, visiting Brussels, Cologne, Berlin, giving a command performance at the Court Theatre in Potsdam and going on to Prague, Cracow and Vienna. His biographers, Herbert Marshall and Mildred Stock, have written the story of his extraordinary continental success, the medals and orders, the packed houses, the society invitations, the portraits, and the enthusiasm

200 Ibid., p. 330.   201 Shaw, *Our Theatres*, III, p. 315.

4 Ira Aldridge as Othello 'represented by him at the Royal Opera House, Berlin, before their Majesties, the King and Queen and Court of Prussia; at the Court Theatre, Dresden, before the King, Queen and Court of Saxony, and the Imperial Court of Austria' (original caption).

of actors, artists and intellectuals. They point out that he was particularly fortunate in touring Europe so soon after the revolutions of 1848 when the spirit of liberalism was still alive.

Certainly, continental reviews were notably free of insulting personal comment. The *Athenaeum* had felt 'repugnance' at 'the labial peculiarity of which we had been forewarned', and had approved with surprise 'the finger nails expressively apparent' on the 'ungloved hand'. In Germany the press was, if anything, gushing. Here was

> a Shakespearean figure in the fullness of its power and passion and fantasy . . . realized with the most exhaustive expressiveness. After this Othello it would be an anticlimax to have seen an ordinary Othello again. What abandonment, passion, beauty, greatness, sense . . . A Negro from Africa's western coast had to come to show me the real Othello.

It must be admitted that the word 'sense' there comes as something of a relief.[202]

It was in Russia, where Aldridge went in 1858, and in 1862–6, that his blackness and his powers as an actor seem to have made the deepest impression. In 1857 Alexander II's draft for the liberation of the serfs had been published (though the statute was not promulgated until 1861), so that when Aldridge appeared in St Petersburg in November 1858, he and his Othello hit a nerve: 'the liberation of the Negro in the United States', wrote K. Zvantsev,

> . . . becomes something *internal*, not only for the enslaved people, but for all of us. That is why, for us, at this particular time, the role of Othello performed by an artist of genius, with all its subtleties of tribal and climatic character, has a universal mighty significance . . . From Othello is torn the deep cry, 'Oh misery, misery, misery!' and in that misery of the African artist is heard the far-off groans of his own people, oppressed by unbelievable slavery, and more than that – the groans of the whole of suffering mankind.[203]

Not until Paul Robeson would Othello be seen in quite this light again.

But apart from his colour, Aldridge's 'democratic' style of acting was a revelation, just as Talma's had been to the Parisians: 'he does not bother about the majestic stride, but moves about completely naturally, not like a tragedian, but like a human being', wrote one critic. Of course this kind of criticism had a way of making Aldridge's 'naturalness' more 'natural' still – as here where another reviewer noticed 'so many unusual, savage and uncontrolled elements, entirely unknown to us until now' that

> it appears quite strange and often, even, not altogether skilled, but the talent of the artist is so tremendous that it . . . carries us into another world . . . In the role of Othello Mr Aldridge was extraordinary – he is a genuine tiger and one is terrified for the artists who play Desdemona and Iago, for it seems that actually they will come to harm . . .

202 Marshall and Stock, *Ira Aldridge*, pp. 213–14, 181.
203 Quoted in ibid., pp. 221–2.

Russia became Aldridge's most permanent home. He toured provincial Russia, visiting places at which even Russian actors never stopped. According to Sergei Durylin, who published a biography of Aldridge in 1940, his tours represented 'a whole epoch in the cultural life of each town'. And Catherine Tolstoy noted in her *Memoirs* that his influence on the great Russian actors was such that 'the acting of many of them afterwards became simpler, livelier, and more worked out'.[204]

Italy

As in France, so in Italy, classicism and the three unities ruled; and although *Othello* was known and played (Rossini's opera aside) during the first half of the nineteenth century, it was always in 'corrected' versions with happy endings. In 1842 Gustavo Modena tried to stage a relatively faithful version but when Iago shouted up at Brabantio's window 'the public began to murmur "What's this? a tragedy or a farce?"' and when Brabantio appeared in his nightclothes 'the public went from murmurs to laughter and hissing. They had read "tragedia" on the poster; and they thought they were watching a scene by Goldoni. . .'.[205] It ended in a shambles.

But in 1856, two Italian actors, Ernesto Rossi and Tommaso Salvini, began to meet with some success. When Salvini went to Paris he took Voltaire's *Zaïre* with him as well, just in case, but *Zaïre* did not draw, he records, and *Othello* paid the expenses of the season. But it was in 1863, at a performance in Naples, that he received his accolade: 'I cannot describe the cries of enthusiasm which issued from the throats of those thousands of persons in exaltation', he wrote, 'or the delirious demonstrations which accompanied those scenes of love, jealousy and fury; and when the Moor . . . cuts short his days . . . a chill ran though every vein, and, as if the audience had been stricken dumb, ten seconds went by in total silence. Then came a tempest of cries and plaudits . . .'[206]

Ernesto Rossi's Othello was arousing similar enthusiasm. Both actors had their partisans; pamphlets and counter-pamphlets were written in support of each against the other, and since both made long triumphant tours abroad (always performing in Italian), the debate was added to by foreign critics, all comparing them against their own home-grown traditions. Agreement is general in describing Rossi as more 'African' than Salvini: that is, according to their views, more sensuous in love and more bestial in hate. Salvini was thought to show both the European and the African: dignified, courteous

---

204 Quoted in ibid., pp. 225; 224–5; 276; 238.
205 Quoted in Busi, *Otello in Italia*, p. 159.
206 Salvini, *Leaves*, pp. 98–9, 116–17.

5 Salvini's Othello *in extremis.*

and restrained up to a point, and during the fourth and fifth acts, a volcano, a tiger and so on. What is not agreed is the relative rightness of these two interpretations. In Italy it was possible to dispute the point. In England and America, it was impossible. Rossi was simply too crude. It was all that many people could do to watch Salvini without disgust. And yet in Italy an admirer of Rossi could write that Salvini was 'the mannered cipher of classical art'.[207]

Italian and French critics, on the other hand, were fascinated by Rossi's explicitness. When he performed in Paris in 1866, one commentator, Fernand Laffont, wrote of his 'Come Desdemona; I have but an hour/

207 Quoted in Busi, *Otello in Italia*, p. 197.

Of love . . .' (1.3.294–6), that 'it is impossible to imagine the loving savagery that he was able to put into this sentence . . . He enveloped his beloved in one of those immense looks that in themselves are a whole poem. It was all at once both lascivious and ideal.'[208] It depends what you mean by a poem – how ideal it has to be and how much lasciviousness you can allow before it stops being ideal. Not very much according to William Winter, the American critic and admirer of Edwin Booth (Junius Brutus's son). Rossi greeted Desdemona on Cyprus, Winter said disapprovingly 'in a spirit of gloating, uxorious animalism'; 'should the character and experience [of Othello] be interpreted before the public as poetry or as prose?' he asks, and he answers firmly: 'the love of Othello for Desdemona is devotional not sensual'.[209]

Italians versus Anglo-Saxons

If Rossi and Salvini divided the goats from the sheep in Italy, Salvini and Irving or Edwin Booth divided them in England. The whole debate moved up a notch. Not that those who admired Salvini were goatish exactly, but they didn't see Othello in terms of late nineteenth-century Englishness. William Winter could pronounce (rather like the often-quoted lady from Maryland who said that 'Othello *was* a *white* man')[210] that Shakespeare had 'unequivocally drawn [him] as an Englishman'.[211] Likewise, Booth could express complete surprise when a friend told him that Shakespeare had intended Othello for a '"beast" – . . . did you ever?!!! I cannot possibly see the least animalism in him – to my mind he is pure and noble; even in his rage . . . I perceive no bestiality.'[212] But to many people the 'pure and noble' tradition was bearing shrivelled fruit.

Of Edwin Booth's Othello, Dutton Cook said that he 'appeared to be labouring to lay and light a train of gunpowder, which all his efforts could only induce to fizz, never to flame'.[213] Irving (who exchanged the parts of Iago and Othello with Booth at the Lyceum in 1881), though less embarrassing than he had been in 1876 when he first played the part, was similarly impotent: he 'screamed and ranted and raved', wrote Ellen Terry; 'I could not bear to see him in the part. It was painful to me.'[214] Like Macready, he hung himself with rich robes, 'jewels sparkle from his turban and depend from his ears'; there were 'strings of pearls . . . [and] gold and silver ornaments'.[215] He

208 Quoted in ibid., p. 176.   209 Winter, *Shakespeare*, pp. 295–6; 287; 288.
210 Quoted in, *Variorum*, p. 395.   211 Winter, *Shakespeare*, p. 249.
212 Quoted in Carlisle, *Green Room*, p. 206.   213 Cook, *Nights*, II, p. 305.
214 Terry, *Story*, p. 206.   215 Cook, *Nights*, II, p. 326.

made up blacker than was usual. But all to no avail. He was 'European rather than African', with 'nothing whatever, except his swarthy complexion and taste for gorgeous and oriental costumes to indicate his origin'.[216] Martin-Harvey, Irving's devoted fellow-actor, confided in his autobiography that 'to be plain, Irving was grotesque as Othello'.[217] There is, moreover, a sense of resignation in most reviews, as though Othello were out of range for English and American actors. The *Athenaeum* (22 January 1881) said categorically that 'in characters that are at once romantic, imaginative and impassioned, English-speaking actors seem wholly at fault'.

Salvini's appearances in England and America only drove the point home. His performance was in some ways crude, thought Henry James, overlooking 'the gradations and transitions which Shakespeare had marked in a hundred places, the manly melancholy, the note of deep reflection', but it had 'the quality that thrills and excites, and this quality deepens with great strides to the magnificent climax'. It lay in his presence as much as anything else, he thought:

> his powerful, active, manly frame, his noble, serious, vividly expressive face, his splendid smile, his Italian eye, his superb, voluminous voice, his carriage, his tone, his ease, the assurance he instantly gives that he holds the whole part in his hands and can make of it exactly what he chooses, – all this descends upon the spectator's mind with a richness which immediately converts attention into faith, and expectation into sympathy. He is a magnificent creature, and you are already on his side . . . you find yourself looking at him, not so much as an actor, but as a hero.[218]

By contrast one hardly knows what Irving and Booth looked like in the part. We know their costumes, and their interpretations can be pieced together – tenderness, dignity, sorrow – but the physical equivalents of these things are minimal. Irving greeted Desdemona on Cyprus for example with 'no greedy haste, no fierce satisfaction; only the comfort of returning to loved arms and a companion heart'.[219] It is difficult to see that, except in terms of what it is not. And when something more vivid presents itself it is faintly ridiculous: Irving in the Senate scene 'held [Desdemona's] veil . . . with rather an effeminate air of affection, and obsequiousness the while she delivered her first speech to her father'.[220] Even when Salvini was not expressing sensual passion he threw his meaning into a physical gesture which almost made

216 *A*, 14 May 1881.   217 Martin-Harvey, *Autobiography*, p. 42.
218 James, *Art*, p. 172.   219 *Theatre*, 1 June 1881.
220 Cook, *Nights*, II, p. 325.

words redundant. Just before he spoke 'chaos is come again' he made a pause 'followed by a gesture', said Lewes 'which *explained* the words . . . the world vanishing into a chaos at such a monstrous state of feeling'.[221]

Women figure largely among Salvini's commentators – Madge Kendal who had played Desdemona to Ira Aldridge, Fanny Kemble,[222] Ellen Terry, Emma Lazarus. It's not surprising. Salvini woke the whole play up, turned it on, brought Desdemona back into it to be loved and hated, rather than used as a pretext for high-minded sorrow. When on Cyprus he 'fiercely swept into his swarthy arms the pale loveliness of Desdemona', wrote Clara Morris,

> 'twas like a tiger's spring upon a lamb . . . the English Shakespeare's Othello was lost in an Italian Othello. Passion choked, his gloating eyes burned with the mere lust of the 'sooty Moor' for that white creature of Venice. It was revolting, and with a shiver I exclaimed aloud 'Ugh, you splendid brute!'[223]

Like it or not, he 'liberated the beast' in Othello, and Clara Morris liked it.

Ellen Terry wrote that Salvini's Othello was 'the grandest, biggest, most glorious thing', and at the same time it was restrained. 'Men have no need to dam up a little purling brook', she said, 'but Salvini held himself in, and still his groan was like a tempest, his passion huge.'[224] In this respect he was like Kean. But he was unlike Kean in that he was able to sustain the whole of the part, the quiet first acts as well as the later frenzies. Lewes, fortunate in having seen both, preferred Kean at certain moments, but thought that Salvini's 'representation as a whole was of more sustained excellence'.[225] Kean had clearly been uninterested in the oratorical, public side of Othello. He had come alive at the extremes of private emotion. He had a peculiarly intimate feeling for words: 'the sensual life of verse springs warm from the lips of Kean', said Keats.[226] By contrast, Salvini's greatest moments were when he took action. He omitted the eavesdropping scene because he knew Othello would 'spring upon Cassio and rend him in pieces'.[227] His seizing and shaking and flinging down of Iago at 'Be sure thou prove my love a whore', and his circling the stage before pouncing on Desdemona, are the moments which attracted the most comment. And it somehow fits with this that his other most impressive moment was in his public speech to the Senate. His delivery, said Fanny Kemble, was 'admirable in its soldier-like simplicity'.[228] If Kean was the poet, Salvini was the warrior.

221 Lewes, *Actors*, p. 268.
222 See Kendal, *Dame Madge Kendal*, p. 223, and Kemble, in *TB*, July 1884.
223 Morris, *Confidences*, p. 240.   224 Terry, *Story*, p. 204.
225 Lewes, *Actors*, p. 267.   226 *Champion*, 21 December 1817.
227 Salvini, 'Impressions'.   228 Kemble, *TB*, July 1884.

No doubt it helped that Salvini was blithely unaware of possible problems. How could Othello behave differently, given Iago's honest and reluctant suggestions, he asks?[229] His playing of the part struck Emma Lazarus as a simple three-fold sequence, from nobility, to 'a necessary development of everything that is evil and brutal in him', and back again. She had no quarrel with this. Each phase convinced and moved her. At the end, she said, he 'suddenly nerves himself anew, starts up with the old majesty of carriage and commanding trumpet-tones, and by the concluding six lines of the play, connects the Othello of Desdemona's love with the Othello who assassinated her'.[230] One is reminded of Verdi's closing device where Otello dies on a kiss to the melody of their first love-duet. Salvini's power lay not in explaining or reconciling these disparities, but in showing them.

Edwin Booth's notes written for Furness and published beneath the text in his *Variorum* edition of the play (some of which are included in the commentary), show an actor wincing his way through the play, finger on lips. In that context, Salvini's Othello must have been like someone walking loudly into a hushed sick-room. Even Henry James puts his hands up a little. The gradations, he says, the transitions, the 'metaphysical side' of Shakespeare are neglected. And yet, he concedes, 'to be played at all, he must be played, as it were, superficially'. James dances about on the brink, but he does jump in. It is the 'portrait of an African by an Italian', he says, and although there are those 'to whom Italians and Africans have almost equally little to say', he clearly does not count himself one of them.[231]

The Italians provoked much debate about the nature of Othello, a debate that continued into the twentieth century. In it there is one persistent thread – not about African-ness, but about Englishness: about what Englishness means, whether it's Shakespearean, and whether it qualifies or disqualifies the actor of Othello. Henry James says he can imagine that 'a great English Othello would touch us more nearly still' than Salvini. It is natural, he says, for English people to wish for more pathos, for 'a tenderness hushed to horror'. Pathos, tenderness, a 'metaphysical' quality (whatever that means – 'hard to indicate and easy to miss', said James) seemed to him intrinsically English, so that, in a sense, the ambiguity in his phrase 'a great English Othello', seems apposite. Ostensibly he means 'an Othello acted by a great English actor'. But he also seems to mean that such an actor would make Othello English, something he 'really' is – 'an English Othello'.[232]

The Italians kept coming: Salvini and Rossi were followed by other visiting Italians, Ermete Novelli and the Sicilian Giovanni Grasso. But English

---

229 Salvini, 'Impressions'.   230 Lazarus, 'Tommaso Salvini'.
231 James, *Art*, pp. 173–4.   232 Ibid., pp. 189, 174, 173.

actors went on being 'English' (or as good as – Arabian would do, according to Beerbohm Tree, 'a stately Arab of the best caste').[233] In 1902, Johnston Forbes-Robertson fulfilled the Jamesian ideal with a performance filled with 'a tenderness and a pathos that are absolutely irresistible in their poignancy' (*ILN*, 20 December 1902), but which Richard Dickins found a picture 'drawn in the washiest of watercolours'.[234] The play was also being beautifully and picturesquely mounted. In 1911 Oscar Asche had 'supers' sweeping 'across the stage in wide arcs, one arc after another preceding Asche's debarkation in Cyprus, which was thus, as in Verdi's opera, worked up into a tremendous, spectacular climax'.[235] In 1912 Beerbohm Tree, using a much cut and rearranged text (see commentary *passim*), mounted a sumptuous production, his set designers, Percy Macqnoid and Joseph Harker, 'rioting among Carpaccio pictures'. His wife Maud Holt Tree rhapsodised about the 'haunting music by Coleridge Taylor [that] threaded in and out of the play, accentuating the dreamlike loveliness of the scenery, accenting the passion and pathos and majesty of the words'.[236]

But, for all that, Tree's Othello was 'self-consciously noble . . . restless, vague, affected', and his beautiful arrangements could not prevent the greatest praise from going to Iago, Laurence Irving (Henry's son): 'we have seen nothing more absorbing than that deadly gaiety of Mr Irving's' (*O*, 14 April 1912).

Iago's ascendancy: Fechter, Booth and Irving

It was by then a familiar phenomenon. One rarely hears of the Salvini Iagos and then only derogatively (his own was 'a commonplace Mephistophelian villain'),[237] but in the Booth and Irving season it was quite clear that Iago had emerged as the most interesting role. It had long been recognised that some tragedians were better at Iago than Othello – Garrick had been one, J. B. Booth was another, Macready another. But not until Fechter, when Othello as a part had begun to decline, did a good Iago attract such excited praise as Othello had done.

Herman Merivale was convinced that Iago 'is the central figure rightly played'. 'Fechter played it so', he adds; 'they [the rest of the cast] were his puppets.'[238] Westland Marston describes Fechter as 'gay [i.e. merry], agreeable, ingratiating', and 'amused by the sense of superiority to his

233 Tree, 'Herbert and I', p. 148.   234 Dickins, *Forty Years*, p. 106.
235 Graves, '*Othello* Recalled'.   236 Tree, 'Herbert and I', p. 148.
237 Foss, *The Author*, p. 79.   238 Merivale, *Bar, Stage*, p. 149.

puppets, and the ease with which he played on them'.[239] But Fechter was not entirely the cordial, comfortable villain that Hazlitt saw in Kean. There was still, according to the *Athenaeum* (8 March 1862), 'a subtle malignity . . . the furtive smile and the curled lip'. The *Athenaeum* even put its finger on what has become a familiar theme in modern criticism: the audience, it said, were made 'partakers of his secret intentions. We were made . . . in some sort to sympathise with his fatal success.' But then it doubts that the part will be popular for long: 'the attention naturally wearies when fixed on a mere intellectual development devoted to an immoral end'.

The correspondent was wrong. How seriously an audience resists Iago's fascination is a measure of how seriously it takes Othello. It is an irony that the denial of Iago's appeal led to his vulgarisation as a scowling, sneering, pantomime villain, which in turn exposed Othello for a gull and a simpleton – the very thing that would make Iago the fascinating 'central figure'. As a critic for *Macmillan's Magazine* (July 1881) put it: 'we marvel at the genius who could create Othello, but for the man himself we really feel not much more perhaps than a half-familiar, half-contemptuous pity . . . we cannot but feel a touch of scorn for a man so easily gulled . . . But it is Iago himself who interests us, the very man; in his presence we forget Shakespeare for a time.' Critics at this period often imagine that Shakespeare was not responsible for the ignoble things in his plays. When Othello is bestial he is un-Shakespearean. When Iago is entertaining, Shakespeare is forgotten.

In the hands of Booth and Irving, Iago became an elegant Italianate villain: the first an 'incarnation of smooth, eager, supple, and fathomless devilry', the other 'startling, picturesque, irregular, brilliant sometimes, sometimes less brilliant than bizarre'.[240] Booth wore 'a crimson-peaked hat and curling feather' and 'an Italian look [with] . . . an Italian ease and variety'. Irving was something between 'a Spanish bull-fighter and an Italian bandit'.[241] The one was a watchful figure in the shadows; the other a flippant, grape-pip-spitting swaggerer. Irving was more entertaining, but *Macmillan's Magazine* (July 1881) thought Booth more in character. In fact the critic felt that Irving's by-play, though striking, was irritating. He was 'never for an instant still, always playing with his cap, or his dress, or his mustachios, slapping Roderigo on the back, throwing his arm round his neck, now sitting on a table, now leaning against a pillar . . . after a time it wearies'. Irving's Iago bore a strong resemblance to his Richard III, a part in which he revelled – and his tactile familiarities foreshadow several modern Iagos.

239 Marston, *Recent Actors*, II, p. 197.
240 Towse, *Sixty Years*, p. 190; *MM*, July 1881.
241 Cook, *Nights*, II, pp. 302, 319.

Booth was, in fact, older than Irving, and had been playing Iago (with his father J. B. Booth as Othello) since the 1850s all over the United States. His whole method of acting was therefore more deliberate and old-fashioned than Irving's, and his Iago struck Ellen Terry as fatally obvious: 'deadly commonplace . . . always the snake in the grass'.[242] Dutton Cook enlarges: 'there is little gaiety in his manner . . . he laughs and jests, but in a mocking, malignant spirit, with a subcurrent of bitterness and venom . . . even his sprightlier moods are attended by grim shadows or may be said to cast sinister reflections'. He was, said Cook, 'the Evil Principle'.[243] This, no doubt would have pleased Hazlitt, but times had moved on. In Irving's Lyceum production, it was 'as though a splash of crimson had been introduced into a delicate nocturne by Whistler'.[244] The future belonged to Irving with his lighter touch (though everything is relative: see Irving in commentary at the end of Act 1).

A brief detour: Verdi to the rescue

A 'crimson' Iago, however, did belong in opera. In Verdi's *Otello* (premiered in Milan in 1887) Iago is deliberately made into an Evil Principle, with a stunningly sinister 'Credo' in which he avows his faith in Original Sin. In fact, Booth's gesture over Othello's dead body (see commentary at 5.2.352 SD) is repeated in the curtain-dropping attitude of Victor Maurel, Verdi's Iago, over Otello's unconscious body after the fit. Like Booth, Victor Maurel stood with one foot on Otello and triumphantly exclaimed 'Ecco il leone' – and then went one better (according to the stage direction in the score) by holding up the handkerchief and dropping it on to Otello's upturned face.

When Verdi's *Otello* came to London in 1889, it was as though all the magnificence that had gone out of the stage play had found a home. Othello's grandeur had passed out of reach, at least with English-speaking actors. That grandeur transferred to Iago seemed somehow out of date, and out of keeping. The two things had come together briefly when Edwin Booth played Iago to Salvini's Othello, but it was not a lasting partnership. In Verdi's opera the combination is made permanent in the music and the characterisation. All Salvini's public, heroic Othello is there in the triumphant 'Esultate' of Othello's first entrance on Cyprus (Verdi cuts the Venice scenes), and all Booth's diabolism is there in Iago's 'Credo'. It is a simplification of Shakespeare's play, but it is the only place left where Lewes's '*largo* of execution'

242 Terry, *Story*, p. 206.
243 Cook, *Nights*, II, p. 303.   244 Dickins, *Forty Years*, p. 40.

6 'Villian, be sure thou prove my love a whore': the moment from Verdi's *Othello*, premiered at La Scala, Milan, February 1887.

was safe from the refinements of increasingly unconvinced and embarrassed actors.

Bernard Shaw, like Thomas Rymer and others, thought Shakespeare's play 'the most impossible far-fetched nonsense'. Othello's jealousy has no 'natural reason', he said, Iago's trick is 'farcical', and the whole fraud is covered up by 'splendid words . . . such music!' Verdi's opera only proved the point, he thought. It showed that Verdi was less indebted to Shakespeare than Shakespeare was to Verdi: '*Othello* is a play written in the style of Italian opera.'[245] He was thinking of Othello's histrionics, of the vow of vengeance, for example, which he thought belonged intrinsically to opera. But he forgot that Shakespeare leaves room for dissent, for irony. Verdi doesn't. That moment in the opera is meant to be overwhelmingly impressive.

Verdi's freedom from ambiguity saves him from the precariousness of Shakespeare, from the shaky balance between tragedy and comedy which, since the middle of the nineteenth century, has always threatened Othello's position. It is true that Maurel's Iago attracted most comment. The emphasis of the libretto, the novelty of his music, especially the 'Credo', and Maurel's expressive acting made him the acknowledged centre of the piece: 'his delivery . . . of the famous mockery of the Credo is simply horrible in its diabolical cynicism' wrote *The Times* (6 July 1889). Beerbohm Tree was so impressed that he modelled his own (disastrous) Iago on Maurel's.[246] But, unlike the play at that period, Iago's success did not undermine Othello. Verdi's librettist, Arrigo Boito, once remarked: 'Eight bars are enough to restore a sentiment to life; a rhythm can reestablish a character; music . . . has a logic all its own; both freer and more rapid than the logic of spoken thought.'[247] Boito's observations are apposite here. Whatever Iago's effect, Othello's music guarantees him. It renders him unassailably the hero, the warrior, the lover – all the things that seemed so straightforward on the eighteenth- and early nineteenth-century Shakespearean stage. In fact, Verdi's *Otello* could be the nearest we can get to the effect Shakespeare's *Othello* made before doubt set in.

The first decades of the twentieth century: disillusion

Meanwhile, the prospects for the stage play were not good. Even Italian actors began now to fall into some of the traps that had caught the English half a century before. We read of Giovanni Emanuel in 1886 playing Othello with surprisingly familiar naturalism, all declamation scrupulously eschewed.[248] Ermete Novelli, who performed Othello in New York in 1907, went further, saying that he never did on the stage what he had not seen in real life – problematic where Othello is concerned. Othello's suicide, for example, had to wait until he saw someone cutting his throat with a razor: 'And then I

245 Shaw, 'A Dressing-Room Secret', pp. 235–6; *London Music*, p. 394.
246 Tree, 'Herbert and I', p. 23.   247 Quoted in Budden, *Verdi*, III, p. 309.
248 Busi, *Otello in Italia*, pp. 210ff.

say: "*That* is the way. *Now* I know how the Moor died. *At last* I can play the part". And that night I begin rehearsals of *Othello*.'[249] Ermete Zacconi, a pupil of Emanuel, chose to concentrate on the fit, and interpreted Othello, with the help of medical treatises, as a clinical study in epilepsy. In 1920 Amadeo Chiantoni staged a production which was accused of reducing the tragedy to 'the modern proportions of a gloomy bourgeois drama'. In 1933, perhaps in reaction, Scharoff produced a huge *Othello* in the courtyard of the Palazzo Ducale in Venice, where the play had to be filled up with Verdian crowds, dancing and music. It was said that when Othello appeared 'at the top of the "scala dei Giganti" one almost expected the shrill vocal fan-fare of the "Esultate"' which greets Otello's arrival on Cyprus in the opera.[250]

In England and America the play slipped back into the sleep from which Salvini had woken it. Oscar Asche in 1907, 1908 and 1911, and Baliol Holloway in 1922 and 1927 stand out: the first for the massive magnificence associated with Salvini,[251] and the second for realising the barbarity that Asche only suggested: 'there was no pretence that, despite his complexion, his soul was Hamlet's', wrote Agate, 'neither were his transports and his tendernesses for Desdemona quite those which we use on this side of the Mediterranean. He had no northerly consideration for her, and she had neither existence nor identity except in so far as she was his. This Othello was wounded, one felt, not only in his love, but in his *amour-propre* and most of all his sense of property.'[252] Holloway strikes an entirely new note on the English-speaking stage, anticipating F. R. Leavis's 'brutal egoist' view of Othello, and outdoing Leavis's disciple, Olivier.

More typical was Ion Swinley who could meet Desdemona's hand with his own, said Herbert Farjeon, 'calmly – a northern hand to the last knuckle.'[253] Godfrey Tearle, who first played Othello in 1921, and again in 1948 and 49, was hailed as the 'noblest [Othello] of our day',[254] but it was an Othello firmly in the tradition of 'little redeeming touches intended by the actor to alleviate the bestiality and brutality suggested by the lines' (*ST*, 24 April 1921). There was a contest, said the reviewer, 'between gentility and animalism', and the critic was occasionally 'thrilled' by his 'sheer savagery and absence of control.' But Charles Graves in the *Scotsman* (4 April 1959) concluded, at least in the 1948 revival, that 'in almost every other line he stressed Othello's nobility . . . It was almost too controlled.'

249 Winter, *Shakespeare*, pp. 303–4.
250 Busi, *Otello in Italia*, pp. 236ff.; 259; 263.   251 Crosse, *Playgoing*, p. 27.
252 Agate, *Chronicles*, pp. 280–1.   253 Farjeon, *Scene*, p. 164.
254 Trewin, *Theatre*, p. 300.

In fact productions lacked so consistently what Agate called 'that passionate saturation, the negation of which constitutes the English temper',[255] that one critic (Stephen Williams in the *Evening Standard*, 9 May 1935) gave up on the play altogether. Some, he said, think Shakespeare 'the unmitred bishop of everything the English people describe as "nice" ', so that 'our actors . . . are too apt to make a "gentleman" of one who loved – and hated – not wisely but too well'. The only time he had seen an actor realise the 'ugly and terrifying savagery' of Othello was in Verdi's opera with Frank Mullings as Otello. A Verdian actor could, it seems, transform the reluctant medium of music into 'beastlike noises', while his brother Shakespearean was hard put to it even to follow the willing medium of Shakespeare's words. Wilfred Walter, in 1932, was described by Agate as being about 'as temperamental as an usher in a well-behaved public school.' Ernest Milton, also in 1932, was a nervous Hamlet whose frenzies were 'tantrums' and 'bagpipe dronings'.[256] Abraham Sofaer, in 1935, 'let cadenced declamation get the better of emotion', and 'expounded rather than expressed his rapturous devotion' to Desdemona.[257] In 1938 an unheroic, reasonable-sounding Ralph Richardson 'blacked as if by boot polish' and wearing 'a frizzy wig' was allowed by Tyrone Guthrie to be hopelessly upstaged by Olivier's 'madcap' Iago.[258] The play, instead of being about 'a lion killed by a viper' turned into one about a 'torreador playing a bull', said Raymond Mortimer (*NS and N*, 19 February 1938). It dwindled, he felt, into a 'thriller, about a villain who ruins an amiable and well-bred simpleton'. 'As a lover he fails', said Darlington; there were no 'consuming fires of possessive passion without which the story is nonsense'.[259]

What were once guilty un-Shakespearean doubts about the play itself now become commonplace. The Birmingham Repertory Company's modern-dress production in 1929 was a catalyst. Modernity brought the play closer, said the *Birmingham Gazette* (25 February 1929), but by the same token

> we are more driven to ask if the psychology of the piece is sound. Is it likely that
> Othello would give a ready ear to the evil promptings of Iago instead of
> knocking him flat at the first murmur of insinuation, or that any woman of spirit
> would continue to consort with her lord instead of smacking his face and leaving
> him when he had called her a strumpet?

Desdemona's cropped hair only made the question more pressing. As the *Manchester Guardian* (25 February 1929) put it: 'the comparative scantiness

255 Agate, *Chronicles*, p. 291.   256 Ibid., pp. 290, 295.
257 *DT*, 22 January 1935 and *O*, 27 January 1935.
258 Williamson, *Old Vic Drama*, p. 95; *DT*, 9 February 1938.
259 *DT*, 9 February 1938.

of modern dress lays bare in addition to feminine backs and arms, the whole dramatic machinery'.

Thereafter the reviews become more irritated: '*Othello* is the least rewarding of the Shakespearean tragedies for the pains that are lavished on it', said *Punch* (30 January 1935), and the *Daily Telegraph* (9 February 1938) said that it was the 'most difficult of Shakespeare's plays because if it falls short of greatness it fails altogether'. On the other hand certain kinds of failure were welcome. Ivor Brown writing in the *Observer* (27 January 1935) liked Sofaer's remoteness because 'it spared us the brutishness', and the *Daily Telegraph* (9 February 1938), reviewing the Ralph Richardson *Othello*, liked Olivier's Iago simply because it was distracting: 'much of *Othello* is almost intolerable and inexplicable', he said; 'relief therefore is vitally important: we must have some rest from the flood of grossness'.

Paul Robeson: *Othello* and racism

The only remarkable production at this period was the one at the Savoy in 1930 in which Paul Robeson played Othello, and Peggy Ashcroft Desdemona. Even then the interest of the occasion had more to do with the emergence of serious black acting than with the quality of the production. Racial prejudice in America made it as unthinkable for Robeson to perform Shakespeare there as it had been for Ira Aldridge a century before. The American stage historian, Charles Shattuck, argued against white actors of Othello even using black make-up on the grounds that 'no average audience could be assembled nowadays which could take in without distraction the circumstance of white woman and black man. Troublesome feelings will arise, even against better judgement, to muddy the clear current of sympathy for the hero.'[260] In England a black actor was possible at least – though daring. The *Daily Express* (20 May 1930), for example, headlined its review 'Kissing scene' and 'Coloured audience in stalls', while the reviewer reported overhearing people wondering how a black actor could be allowed to kiss a white actress.

These were mutterings, however. The more serious and central objection was that Robeson himself, while having the bulk (not helped by Elizabethan 'padded trunks, square shoes and a ruff')[261] and the voice for Othello, lacked his confidence. It is hardly surprising, and Robeson himself, looking back on that first attempt, is reported to have told Margaret Webster, who directed his New York *Othello* in 1943, that he was 'so overwhelmed by the thought of playing Shakespeare at all, especially in London, with his unmistakable

260 Shattuck, 'Shakespeare's *Othello*'.   261 Gielgud, *An Actor*, p. 88.

7 Paul Robeson in Margaret Webster's production (pre-New York opening in Cambridge, MA, 1942).

American accent, that he never reached the point of looking Othello squarely in the eye'.[262]

But there was also an interpretative reason for his subdued performance. On the Sunday before the opening night there appeared in the *Observer* (18 May 1930) an interview in which he stated his belief that the play was about racial prejudice: 'it is a tragedy of racial conflict; a tragedy of honour rather than of jealousy . . . it is because he is an alien among white people that his mind works so quickly, for he feels dishonour more deeply . . . '. And he added that he found in Shakespeare a 'superb sympathy for the underdog'. In the event, Robeson played Othello precisely *as* an underdog: 'he lacked command', wrote Farjeon; 'he was the under-dog from the start. The cares of "Old Man River" were still upon him. He was a member of a subject race, still dragging the chains of his ancestors.'[263]

262 Webster, *Daughter*, pp. 106–7.   263 Farjeon, *Scene*, p. 166.

But there was praise too – for his 'great simplicity and directness' *(Punch,* 25 May 1930), and for a 'tranquil dignity and a melancholy infinitely sad . . . which grows as the tempest of fury, scorn and hatred draws to its full, possessing our minds and giving a kind of noble plainness to the tragedy' (*T,* 20 May 1930). Dover Wilson thought his acting, on the whole, magnificent, and the fact that he was black 'seemed to floodlight the whole drama . . . new points, fresh nuances were constantly emerging'.[264] *The Times* agreed, but thought that his colour mattered mostly for the light it shed on Desdemona: it 'brings home to us with how much daring the young girl chose a black hero'. As for Desdemona herself, Agate called Peggy Ashcroft 'exquisite', though Farjeon found her 'a little on the vegetarian side'. Everyone agreed with him, though, that the willow-song scene was 'intensely moving'.[265] Maurice Browne as Iago was a failure, the staging unaccountably required the actors to spend most of their time as far away from the audience as possible, and the whole thing was badly lit. The production lost £7,000.[266]

Far more significant was the 1943 production in New York, directed by Margaret Webster, which subsequently toured the United States (north of the Mason–Dixon line; Robeson refused to perform in segregated houses) and Canada. The production was an extraordinary phenomenon, 'a declaration', wrote Webster, 'and its success an event in which the performance itself was of less importance than the public response'. It had been difficult, on racial grounds, to find a Desdemona. Maurice Evans had refused Iago, believing that a black Othello would never succeed.[267] The war, in which black GIs served alongside white, added to the general sense of racial unease. Every night there was an 'audible gasp' from the audience when Robeson first kissed Desdemona (Uta Hagen) on Cyprus.[268] One night in Detroit, where there had recently been race riots, someone happened to sneeze at that moment, and the cast froze in terror until they realised what the sound was.[269] All the same, the show broke all previous records for a Shakespeare play.

Some of this was Webster's doing. Speed and clarity were her objects. She cut about nine hundred lines and all her business was aimed at underlining the story. Like Robeson, she believed that the play was about race: that 'Othello was . . . quiveringly aware of what the judgement of the world would be upon his marriage' and that his sensitivity to this was 'one of the potent factors in his acceptance of the possibility of Desdemona's infidelity'.[270] But

264 Wilson, *Othello*, p. x.   265 Agate, *Chronicles*, p. 288; Farjeon, *Scene*, p. 167.
266 Bishop, *Betters*, p. 47.   267 Webster, *Daughter*, pp. 106, 107.
268 Quoted by Carroll, p. 105.   269 Quoted in ibid., p. 56.
270 Webster, *Without Tears*, p. 238.

although they were in agreement, there were difficulties. Robeson himself was not a natural actor. He moved badly; he could not manage his hands;[271] his voice became 'preachy' in the stormy scenes, 'he never got out of the pulpit';[272] the cast acted round him 'as if he were a Maypole and everyone else the streamers', as one member put it.[273] If anyone acted it was José Ferrer as Iago, 'a nimble Satan, goading and prodding his victim to madness' (*Victoria Daily Times*, 13 January 1945).

Webster wrote of Robeson's Othello that 'there was plenty of power, but no flash'. She tried, naively, to ignite him in rehearsal by asking him to think of some painful memory of racist insult.[274] But although he felt acutely the humiliations of the American black man (while on tour there were hotels that barred him, or refused him the use of the lift), it does not follow – indeed the reverse may be true – that such feelings can be transferred to the stage. It cannot have helped that Webster's understanding of the emotions involved was itself racist – however unwittingly so: 'the gulf [between him and Desdemona]' she wrote later, ' is a gulf between two races, the one old in the soft ways of civilization, the other close to the jungle and burning desert sands. Iago . . . does not reckon with the full primitive power of passion which he unleashes.'[275] How far Robeson fell short of Othello's 'primitive power of passion' because he felt such an exhibition to be demeaning we cannot know.

In the event, it scarcely mattered. Earle Hyman, one of the small band of American black actors who inherited the part from him, wrote that Robeson didn't need to act, he 'simply *was* Othello'.[276] Lois Potter makes the point that this is hardly a compliment, but that it was true in a sense that Robeson himself encouraged. With both Aldridge and Robeson, audiences tended 'to read the actor's situation into the characters he played'. In Russia, Aldridge's Othello was the voice of the suffering: slaves, serfs, humanity at large. In the USA, Robeson's was the voice of black America – and of his own struggle with the House Committee on Un-American Activities.[277] But beyond that, Hyman also meant a certain quality about Robeson himself: 'the majesty- there is no other word for it – of his sheer presence on stage was electric'.[278] He was a figure of international renown and in the words of the stage manager, Francis Letton, 'everywhere we went he was adored': 'every night long lines of people waited . . . to speak to him – black and white . . . and he spoke with every one of them. He was a truly *great* man.'[279]

271 Carroll, pp. 119–20.   272 Webster, *Daughter*, p. 109.   273 Carroll, p. 111.
274 Webster, *Daughter*, pp. 110–12.   275 Webster, *Today*, p. 235.
276 Hyman, 'Ego in Love', p. 23.   277 Potter, *Othello*, pp. 132–3.
278 Hyman, 'Ego in Love', p. 23.   279 Quoted in Carroll, p. 121.

Robeson's Othello attracted a public that broke all social and racial barri-
ers. Soldiers and sailors home on leave from the war came to see his Othello,
as did cab-drivers, trade union officials, and people who said to each other in
the interval 'Now for heaven's sake, *don't* tell me what happens.'[280] Webster's
most prized letter came from a GI who wrote:

> Last Saturday night I saw *Othello*. It took a lot of coaxing to get four soldiers to
> spend a Saturday night of the first weekend leave in a month, in a theatre,
> watching something by Will Shakespeare. You didn't know what was at stake
> when the curtain went up – my life practically. Well, what followed is only
> natural. We all of us, for those brief hours, went into a trance; we were living
> every emotion of the play. (One was a first Sarge, and my dear Miss Webster,
> that which moves a first Sargeant is almost miraculous) . . . Incidentally, going
> back on the troop train (it's a six hour ride) for the first time in my army career,
> I saw five soldiers sprawled over the seats, feet in the air, sleeves rolled up, shirts
> open talking not about the babe they met in the Broadway Brewery, but of all
> things, a thing called *Othello*.[281]

Frederick Valk

The *New York Times* (20 October 1943) acknowledged that Webster's production had rescued the play from tediousness. Meanwhile, England continued to wait. In 1940 and 41 Donald Wolfit had been playing a very black
Othello, 'with a Christy Minstrel appearance', said the *Daily Mail* (13 February 1940), but although he was at moments 'touchingly simple' (*T*, 13 February 1940), he didn't altogether convince – in spite of writhing 'like a contortionist' in the fit, and foaming at the mouth.[282] At last, rescue came in
the form of Frederick Valk, a German Czech – a foreigner again. Valk's
Othello, according to Ken Tynan, represented 'a transfusion of bubbling
hot blood into the invalid frame of our drama'.[283] This was of Valk's 1947
production, with Donald Wolfit as Iago, but it would have done as well for
his 1942 appearance with Bernard Miles. Valk had none of Salvini's heroism
and splendour. He tended to be compared to a buffalo, or a bear, rather than
to a tiger.[284] It was after seeing Valk, that Ivor Brown called *Othello* 'bull-
baiting', and felt 'anew the brutal ugliness which genius somehow flecked
with exquisite and noble things' (*O*, 26 July 1942).

That was the general complaint: he lacked 'poetry'.[285] The very thing
that had sapped the English tradition was now missed. Agate argued for

---

280 Ibid., p. 39.   281 Webster, *Daughter*, p. 115.
282 Graves, '*Othello* Recalled'.   283 Tynan, *A View*, p. 157.
284 Agate, *Chronicles*, p. 306; Williamson, *Old Vic Drama*, p. 155.
285 Williamson, *Old Vic Drama*, p. 156.

Valk by saying that 'no amount of beautiful verse-speaking can save' an actor who is not Othello.[286] The Bradleyan idea that Othello is 'the poet born' seemed to Agate worth compromising for the sake of what he saw as a separate and somehow quintessential Othello. Tynan in 1947, expanding the anti-poetic argument, saw Valk as 'piercing to the core of elemental and therefore wordless things'. Indeed Tynan's highest praise was that Valk's performance was 'not beautiful'. He did not even know whether it was 'a good Othello': 'I cannot believe there is blood in the man's veins: it must be some vile compound of corrosive venoms . . . Why, he was to be touched into mad lambent flame in an instant; he broke every law of our stage-craft this beserk Colossus.'

It was probably the most unnerving performance that English audiences had had to endure. They had never before had to listen to the verse itself being battered to pieces. Salvini had always spoken in Italian, even with an English-speaking cast. But here was a man with often unintelligible English. Tynan's enthusiasm amounts almost to a declaration against the language, as though the only way to recover Othello was to wreck the poetry. The consequence was, curiously, a kind of melodiousness: 'impious lullabies' whose 'strains moved to pity as great verse should'.[287]

Meanwhile, Othello became a part for English actors to avoid. Michael Redgrave, explaining why he never tried it, said that he did not understand 'all that jealousy in Othello. I really don't. I suppose it means I am too rational to play it . . . I'm afraid of Othello . . . I don't think I could do it.'[288] Laurence Olivier resisted all persuasion at this period, knowing it to be 'a terror . . . almost impossible' as he confided later to Tynan.[289] Anthony Quayle performed it in 1950, 52 and 54, but Philip Hope-Wallace thought that 'he seemed no more than a kindly coloured gentleman who was being vilely treated' (*MG*, 17 March 1954). In 1956 neither Richard Burton, 'roaring through his whiskers', nor John Neville 'a tormented sheikh' (they exchanged Othello and Iago at the Old Vic) could entirely dispel Tynan's initial opinion that they were 'two born Cassios'.[290] Gielgud tried it in 1961 but had to admit failure.[291] Everyone who hazarded themselves fell short one way or another. Godfrey Tearle alone received acclaim, in 1948 at Stratford – but for the old noble Othello. He was, wrote Hobson, 'so easily noble of presence that he does not require to tell us he comes from men of royal siege, of such commanding stature of mind . . . of such shattered faith in purity . . .' (*ST*, 8 August 1948). But still, as in 1921, he didn't risk the fit.

---

286 Agate, *Chronicles*, p. 306.   287 See Tynan, *A View*, pp. 59–61.
288 Findlater, *Redgrave*, p. 141.   289 In Cole and Chinoy, *Actors*, p. 413.
290 Tynan, *Curtains*, p. 119.   291 Gielgud, *Directions*, p. 46.

Orson Welles's film

Orson Welles's stage production of *Othello* in 1951 was not a success. His Othello, according to Tynan, was no more than 'a huge shrug . . . his face expressed wryness and strangulation but little else. And his bodily relaxation frequently verged on sloth.'[292] In the jealous scenes he could 'only stand as if stunned, his eyes fixed and glaring', said Eric Keown in *Punch* (31 October 1951). More interesting was his film, released in America in 1952, but in the UK not until 1956. Not that the performances themselves were remarkable. The drama lay in the photography. Welles's camera expressed all the sense of risk and chaos that was absent from the stage: the skewing, disordering dangerousness of Iago, the mythic but somehow toppling grandeur of Othello and (since he saw her that way) the static and helpless beauty of Desdemona.

Twenty-five years after its release, Jack J. Jorgens eloquently praised the film as 'a mannerist montage of broken continuities, wrenched perspectives, clashing images and surreal sound'[293] but it wasn't until its remastered re-release in 1992 that it became more generally known and studied. Critics at the time were bemused: 'the screen is in a perpetual state of incoherent turmoil', wrote Virginia Graham in the *Spectator* (2 March 1956), 'the camera rushing distractedly across Alexander Trauner's remarkable sets on its way to unidentified places, picking up as it goes a leg perhaps, half a face, a dog'. Shakespeare's text was also in turmoil – 'hashed up', says Graham. Still, the result she felt, was a 'spell-binding fantasy', a 'tricksy, splendidly mad drama, the visual effects of which are often staggering and the verbal almost wholly inaudible'. To the largely conformist public taste of the UK and McCarthyite USA, however, Welles's filmic language was an affront. One critic called him 'that big prankish schoolboy', and remarked patronisingly that his film might just help some 'real director' of the future 'to make *Othello* into a worthy film'.[294]

There is, however, one aspect of the film which places Welles himself firmly within the conformist ranks that he otherwise so rudely broke – the treatment of Desdemona. Jorgens identifies two styles: the Othello-style, heroic and lyrical, and the Iago-style, skewed and chaotic. Virginia Vaughan adds to these the Desdemona-style. In contrast to the other two, with their 'disjunctive editing, rapid changes in scale, and manipulations of space', the Desdemona-style is characterised by 'moments of light and stillness'. Desdemona's luminous face, her diaphanous figure, her pale halo-like or symbolically netted hair, all are presented in their '*to-be-looked-at-ness*', as

292 Tynan, *Curtains*, p. 14.
293 Jorgens, *Film*, p. 191.   294 Rothwell, *Screen*, p. 78.

objects of male desire.[295] Barbara Hodgdon notes further, 'the repeated high-angle shots that so intensify her objectification or widen and magnify the distance between [Othello and Desdemona]'.[296] Sometimes she is reduced to a mere dot. Lois Potter quotes the *Observer* critic, C. A. Lejeune, saying: 'I shall always recall her, as a tiny dot at the foot of an immense staircase, gazing adoringly at the monumental bulk of Mr Welles on some upper landing, waiting for the great man to come out of his pose and toss her the cue for a line.'[297]

Both Vaughan and Potter point to the real-life situation behind the making of the film: how Welles hunted, not for a woman who could act the part, but for a collection of physical attributes that he could photograph, even if, in the end, they belonged to different actresses. The first two Desdemonas withdrew from the film almost immediately, and when the third, Suzanne Cloutier, repelled his advances, Welles toyed with the idea of dubbing her voice – in effect silencing her. Welles does in fact silence Desdemona in many places and, as Potter points out, Othello often appears to be talking to himself rather than to her. 'Cloutier's Desdemona', she writes, 'is more in the nineteenth century tradition than any other',[298] and it is in the spirit of that century that Welles omits Desdemona's willow song – except for a barely audible humming at one point, brief and off-camera.

Iago in the early twentieth century

During the 1920s actors of Iago followed Irving in portraying him as a frivolous, sophisticated, intellectual villain. True, Laurence Irving, his son, had given the role a touch of the Artful Dodger: 'no aristocrat of villains', wrote the *Manchester Guardian* (10 April 1912). But he had still been Mephistophelian in spirit. Dashingly, he wore a long red cloak in the first scene, and a black doublet and hose, 'splashed waspish-wise, with yellow' (*DT*, 10 April 1912). One magazine illustrator even showed him sprouting little horns. He used his father's grape-pip business (*Morning Leader*, 10 April 1912), and added something of his own – catching flies and burning them in a candle flame (see notes at 1.3.365ff.). In 1921 Basil Rathbone, Tearle's Iago, even 'suggested that in his leisure hours the Ancient was something of an aesthete' (*ST*, 24 April 1921). Similarly, Neil Porter (with Baliol Holloway) in 1927, was 'obviously an intellectual'.[299] But there must still have lingered

---

295 Vaughan, *A Contextual History*, p. 212.
296 Hodgdon, 'Kiss me Deadly', p. 225.
297 (26 February 1956), quoted in Potter, *Othello*, p. 143.
298 Ibid., p. 143.   299 Agate, *Chronicles*, p. 281.

M? LAURENCE
IRVING
AS 'IAGO'

8 Laurence Irving 'craftily qualifying' Cassio's drink.

the old mask-dropping knowingness, for Rathbone, the 'aesthete', struck Desmond MacCarthy as inclining to 'the catlike, wicked-grinning, demon-detective tradition'.[300] And when in 1932 Ralph Richardson presented 'so singly honest a face that even the audience could read nothing else', he was rebuked by Agate for being 'very good Richardson, but indifferent Shakespeare'.[301]

The idea, however, gained ground. In 1935 Maurice Evans's Iago (Sofaer was Othello) had a 'very honest fairhaired appearance, suggesting a decent simple subaltern . . . young, open of countenance, light and gay [i.e. merry] of speech and step'. Yet still, like Agate, the reviewer wanted more of 'the deep plotting of an evil nature' (*Punch*, 30 January 1935). Olivier's Iago in 1938 swung back the other way with 'the regular Italianate villain', as Raymond

300 MacCarthy, *Theatre*, p. 71.   301 Agate, *Chronicles*, p. 291.

Mortimer put it (*NS and N*, 19 February 1938). In fact Olivier and his director, Tyrone Guthrie, had intended something much more up to date, something that was explored again, but more carefully, by David Suchet in Terry Hands's production, namely a gay (in the modern sense) Iago. But no one in 1938 seems to have noticed it. Olivier described himself in rehearsal once, flinging his arms round Richardson's neck and kissing him. At which, Richardson 'more in sorrow than in anger, sort of patted me and said, "Dear fellow, dear boy", much more pitying me for having lost control of myself, than despising me for being a very bad actor'.[302]

Bernard Miles was original in modern times for making Iago the low scoundrel that he was in the eighteenth and for much of the nineteenth centuries. Audrey Williamson thought this made sense of his envy, but (in a curious piece of social prejudice) she thought it deprived him of 'imagination': 'there is imagination in Iago as well as proletarian coarseness. He is an artist in crime who exults in his creative malevolence.'[303] Hazlitt's old idea – brought to fruition in Booth's satanic and Irving's Macchiavellian interpretations – was still alive, it seems. Nevertheless Quayle continued in Miles's direction: his 'mouthwiping, nose-scratching Iago was not born in Venice', wrote Hobson, 'the polish of the cities is not on him; he wears a rough jerkin, and his manner is not smooth either; he is a stubborn, scheming country lad. . .'. Such imagination as he had was voyeuristic rather than artistic: 'he inflames himself as well as Othello by his lechery of thought'. He gave Hobson the impression of being exhausted by his own evil: 'when he is alone there are moments at which he comes close to fainting'[304] – something that Ian McKellen brilliantly developed in Trevor Nunn's production in 1989. This is the first time (that I have come across) where it is suggested that Iago and Othello become almost equally entangled in the emotions of the play. Not everyone saw it like that. H. K. Fisher thought Quayle's performance vulgar, and that it 'very nearly threw the play off its balance.' He declared categorically that '*Othello* is the tragedy of one man – Othello.'[305]

Laurence Olivier and Leavis

That was the position F. R. Leavis took, though not in the sense intended by Fisher. In Leavis's scheme (Othello is himself the cause of his own disintegration, Iago merely the mechanical device by which the fraud of his nobility is exposed. This was the approach, when it came to it, that Olivier took with

302 Cole and Chinoy, *Actors*, pp. 413–14.
303 Williamson, *Old Vic Drama*, p. 157.
304 Hobson, *Theatre*, p. 69.   305 Fisher, *Life and Letters*.

9 Laurence Olivier as Othello in 1964.

his director, John Dexter, and it had the added advantage of downgrading Iago. Olivier, knowing only too well what an Iago can do to his Othello, made it a condition that he should have, not 'a witty Macchiavellian Iago, [but] . . . a solid honest to God NCO'.[306] Olivier and Dexter believed themselves to be departing from tradition, in that they were showing Othello as 'only a goodish fellow which had merely fixed the ear-mark of nobility on himself'. Self-love and self-delusion were to be the sources of his downfall – 'plus that he is a savage man', said Olivier, and then, in a curiously revealing

306 Tynan, *National Theatre Production*, p. 2.

and embarrassed disclaimer, he added, 'not on account of his colour; I don't mean that. . . '.[307] Tynan reported that, in rehearsal, Dexter told the cast that Othello 'is a pompous, word-spinning arrogant black general'[308] Extracts from Leavis's essay[309] were duly printed in the programmes, and the public primed to expect a brutal egoist.

That is what Dover Wilson saw, and he wrote an anguished letter to *The Times*[310] saying that all the performances that he had ever seen of *Othello* had accepted the Bradleyan principle of the essential dignity of man, but that here, especially in the second half, was a 'Leavis *Othello*' in which 'I could discover no dignity . . . at all, while the end was to me, not terrible, but horrible beyond words.' And yet, bearing in mind the stage history – Salvini's throat-hacking suicide, the 'amour-propre' of Holloway, the inglorious rages of Valk – the absolute originality of Dexter's production is questionable. It was certainly original in actually announcing Othello's ignobility, and this on its own may have gone far towards antagonising people. In fact Dover Wilson admits that 'unhappily I could not follow the expressions on his [Olivier's] face with my imperfect sight except every now and then'. Many critics simply did not concern themselves with the Leavisian advertisement, or, if they considered the matter, came to conclusions that were almost the opposite of what was officially intended.

The whole question of whether Othello is noble or ignoble seems to have been swept away so often by terrific performances, and to have mattered so much in mediocre ones, that one wonders whether it is important. It occupies the central position in *The Masks of Othello* (1961) by Marvin Rosenberg, whose object is to collect evidence from every century to show that actors intended Othello to be noble, that they acted him that way, and that therefore Shakespeare meant him to be so. Certainly it was the background assumption in every performance from Betterton to Robeson, and no doubt before and occasionally after, but it was never the thing that determined a great performance. Salvini thought he was being noble all the time; he even said that his love for Desdemona was entirely unsensual and poetic. If we were to believe his account of himself, we might imagine his performance to have looked like Edwin Booth's.[311] But when he got on the stage other things happened. Chaste, poetical love was flatly contradicted. Audiences were moved to terror and pity in the most unholy ways. If 'black insanity' overcomes Othello, to use Henry James's phrase about Salvini,[312] questions

307 'The Great Sir Laurence', *LI* (18 May 1964).
308 Tynan, *National Theatre Production*, p. 4.
309 Leavis, F. R., 'Diabolic Intellect'.   310 See Gregory, *Cuckoo*, pp. 254–5.
311 Salvini, 'Impressions'.   312 James, *Art*, p. 173.

of nobility or ignobility seem beside the point. As it happened, Salvini's notion of nobility remained undisturbed by Othello's deeds. If an English actor needs to think of Othello as a brutal egoist before he can get to grips with him, the distinction becomes a matter of tactics. The outcome may not be very different.

Of course the 'brutal egoist' approach runs the risk of alienating the audience so much that they cannot feel for the man at all. But Leavis's bark was worse than Olivier's bite. People found themselves moved in spite of everything, or if they were not it was not because he was Leavisian, but rather because Olivier's 'technical mastery' was so evident (*T*, 22 April 1964). In fact John Russell Brown felt that Olivier's interpretation was not 'as remarkable as the artistry which presented it.'[313] A large part of this 'mastery' and 'artistry' was the elaborate transformation that Olivier wrought on his voice, his features, his gait (see commentary at his first entrance, 1.2) and his gestures.

Since 1964 and since the making of the film of Dexter's production, attitudes have changed. As we shall see, blacking up by white actors is now regarded as unacceptable. The very completeness of the job in Olivier's case, and the manner in which he describes it in his autobiography, smacks of white 'possession' of the black body. Barbara Hodgdon quotes Olivier on the blacks and browns he applied, the blueberry for the lips, the tight curled wig and 'that glorious half yard of chiffon with which I polished myself all over until I shone'. 'I am, I . . . I am Othello', he concludes, ' . . . but Olivier is in charge. The actor is in control. The actor breathes into the nostrils of the character and the character comes to life . . . Othello is my character – he's mine. He belongs to no one else; he belongs to me.' Of course it could be said that this is the actor's ritual, his technique for getting into the part. But there is something peculiarly triumphalist and aggressive about Olivier here, and it is no surprise that Hodgdon draws the analogy with the white claim on colonial property.[314]

At the time, reaction was mixed: 'It could have been a caricature', wrote Ronald Bryden, 'an embarrassment. Instead, after the second performance, a well-known Negro actor rose in the stalls bravoeing. For obviously it was done with love' (*NS*, 1 May 1964). Some doubted the wisdom of it, not on racial grounds but because it was a distraction. Robert Speaight questioned whether 'the negroid physiognomy which Olivier was at such pains to create was necessary to establish' his characterisation.[315] In so far as critics took it into account, other than as a phenomenon in its own right, it led them

313 Brown, 'Three Kinds'.
314 Hodgdon, 'Race-ing Othello', p. 26.   315 Speaight, 'Shakespeare', p. 379.

to conclude that Othello's brutality was either of the jungle and essentially his own, or that, as one of Nature's innocents, he had taken the infection from a trivial and mean white society. The second opinion was held, perhaps predictably, by the Russian critic, Alexander Anikst – though, in exchanging the brute for the simpleton, he hardly improves matters: 'A civilization that is false and untrue kills the simple-minded man, it kills Man . . . this is what Laurence Olivier the actor, and John Dexter the producer show us.'[316] Harold Hobson also suggests it, though without resorting to the idea of simple-mindedness: 'before the evil and the cruelty and the unscrupulousness of the white men, the civilization of Othello is stripped off . . . it cannot stand fire' (*ST*, 26 April 1964). Naturally, when liberal-minded white audiences are presented with a black man – real or painted – it is difficult for them to follow the orthodox Leavisian view.

And yet in a vague way, unconnected with interpretative argument, Olivier was felt to be bringing the play into the modern world. Harold Hobson (in the same review) felt that

> there is here a concern with the relations between the black and the white races which give to this production a contemporary urgency lacking in its predecessors. With . . . an uncomfortable mixture of arrogance and inferiority, Sir Laurence makes this *Othello* a world-drama as well as a tale of individual poignancy and betrayal.

How well considered was that concern with relations between the races is open to doubt. Charles Marowitz gave as a reason for his own version of the play, *An Othello*, the fact that he had 'felt a great frustration always seeing Othello from a contemporary standpoint . . . and never having those anticipations satisfied'. He had much sympathy with Olivier's approach, but felt that by imitating the details of black behaviour, he stood out from the play in a way which only emphasised what the play was not about: 'The play had no truck with attitudes towards contemporary negritude and the skills of imitation not only did not strengthen the fable, but positively diverted it from its true centre.'[317]

So, in the end, the old question remains of whether or not this Othello carried his audiences with him. There were those that hated him, but many who were both amazed and moved. Olivier's 'casual pain' at 'Not a jot, not a jot' seemed to Harold Hobson 'extremely moving' (*ST*, 26 April 1964). Bamber Gascoigne (*O*, 26 April 1964), felt that the sense of 'sexual promise' between him and Desdemona was 'electric'; but he was also 'tender and

316 Quoted in Tynan, *National Theatre Production*, p. 109.
317 'Charles Marowitz Directs'.

tormented' with her, said Hobson, and Philip Hope-Wallace felt that at the
end 'cradling his dead wife in his arms [he] struck deeper chords than I have
ever heard from him'(*G*, 22 April 1964). Felix Barker (*EN*, 8 September
1965) has a story of an audience in Moscow – which the production visited
in 1965 – sweeping 'down the central gang-way . . . hurling flowers and
clapping', all except for 'a woman in black sitting while all around her were on
their feet, crying "Bravo" . . . was she anti-Shakespeare, anti-British? . . . then
she turned slightly . . . Tears were running down her cheeks. She was too
overwhelmed to get up.'

Experiments with *Othello*

Olivier's concentration on Othello's race reflected a new alertness to the
subject which was bound to find more conscious and coherent expression in
other kinds of production. In 1969, Murray Carlin published *Not Now, Sweet
Desdemona*, a play first performed the year before at Makerere University
College, Uganda. It is a dialogue between two actors, one Jamaican and
the other white South African, as they rehearse the parts of Othello and
Desdemona. In real life they are lovers, and in the course of the rehearsal
they have a ferocious quarrel in which 'Othello' rejects 'Desdemona's' view
that the play is about love and jealousy, and insists that it is about race and
power. In particular, it is about the white liberal manipulation of the black
man: 'They want power, and they get it, through love – because they're too
sensitive to get it by force . . . That's your Desdemona . . . Othello is her
personal black man.' The play is an eloquent, often humorous, and, in the
end, affecting critique, which anticipates many of the arguments put forward
in the late 1980s and 90s.

In 1972, Charles Marowitz went further and rewrote *Othello* itself. His *An
Othello* tunes the story in to Malcolm X and Eldridge Cleaver. The actors
themselves recede before the ideology of Black Power. Here Iago is as black
as Othello, uttering obscenities in his own hip dialect, a revolutionary Black
Panther to Othello's Uncle Tom – or, as Malcolm X terms it, a Field Nigger
to Othello's House Nigger.[318] Here, Desdemona, referred to throughout as
'white pussy' (John Mortimer's neighbour in the theatre 'nearly fell off the
bench with laughter every time anyone said "white pussy"'),[319] is unfaithful
before our eyes with Cassio, and with half the cast besides. Iago incites
Othello not to jealousy but to revenge – on 'whitey' for 'all the wrongs of
the past'. In this new role he becomes, in a sense, Othello's good angel,
half-goading, half-imploring him to renounce his toadying past, and, when

318 See ibid.   319 *O*, 11 June 1972.

it comes to it, not to do whitey's work by killing himself. At the end, in his last long speech Othello pauses uncertainly before 'and smote him thus', at which point Lodovico and the Duke move in and cut his throat. The last tableau is of Iago cradling Othello in his arms, and then 'with a curious kind of love' dragging his body out.

It is striking how well Marowitz's Shakespeare lends itself to his propaganda. Othello's speeches to the senate at 1.3.76ff. – 'Most potent, grave, and reverend signiors, / My very noble and approved good masters' – sound very much like sucking-up, like (as Iago puts it)

> sweet-talkin' . . . All that shit about 'hair-breadth 'scapes' and
> 'Anthropophagi' . . . and how you was hip enough to leave all those
> cotton-pickin' coons behind you, 'cause you knew where all that gravy
> lay . . . And it weren't with those Stephen Fetchit water-melon-munchin'
> darkies. No, you bet your sweet little ass, it weren't. It was in Mr Charlie's army,
> ey black boy?

Marowitz utterly demystifies Othello, removes all sense of strangeness and romance. He takes away his love for Desdemona and hers for him, and replaces it with a delight in stolen goods. By the same token, there is no real anguish at her loss. What he adds is a keen sense for the modern analogy. When the Venetian senate makes use of Othello and disposes of him as it suits its purposes, Vietnam springs to mind so pat that there is almost a sense of double-take. Could this be what Shakespeare was driving at? The critics were sometimes shocked, but always intrigued. John Mortimer in the *Observer* (11 June 1972) was scornful, and yet admitted that he had 'been discussing it and arguing about it ever since I saw it'.

The same sense that the play's overriding interest lies in the general corruption of Othello's environment, rather than in his particular sorrow and collapse, resulted in another but quite different directorial experiment, this time in Italy. In 1970 Virginio Puecher took the basic comic structure of the play, and the conventional *commedia dell'arte* types with which he felt it to be peopled – ridiculous old father, villain, gull – and used them to show that *Othello* is really a hideous game played by the agents of a degenerate society upon an outsider who does not know the rules. In order to emphasise the unwilled, totally artificial and conventional quality of the game, and at the same time to bring home its heartlessness, he set the production in a circus ring, with Shakespeare's insignificant clown elevated to the position of narrator, commentator and shadowy mocker, scraping at an out-of-tune violin, mingling among the characters, imitating them, sometimes reading them their parts and stage directions in advance. (The Georgian director Sturua used this device in his version of *Richard III* which visited Edinburgh and London in 1980.) Rather than play down the comedy, or attempt to lose it in Othello's tragedy, Puecher did everything to emphasise it, leaving the tragedy to take care of itself. The Senators were doddering old fools who gathered with voyeuristic curiosity around Othello as he told them his love story, but got bored half way through, dozed off, muttering and mumbling in disappointment. Othello, in blackface that resembled a clown's whiteface, was shoved unceremoniously under a table for the eavesdropping scene. It was an ambitious experiment, and not entirely successful, but it is interesting for being the first, as far as I know, to try to harness the very farce that has for so long, at least since Rymer, been held against the play.[320]

In 1976, Peter Zadek in Hamburg took the same idea of using blackface as a form of deliberate caricature, but went further in an outrageous interpretation of Othello as a King Kong figure, scratching himself for lice. Desdemona wore a bikini and Othello's black make-up came off on her, as was intended. Iago was a stud beach-boy who kept the strawberry handkerchief as a bulge in his crotch. Finally, Othello hung the brutally murdered body of Desdemona over a curtain line, her bottom exposed to the audience, before cutting his throat and smearing himself with the blood. As with his 1972 production of *The Merchant of Venice*, this *Othello* was meant to be understood as 'racist' rather than racist – in other words, a display of racism intended as an exposé of it.[321]

A less nihilistic though equally anarchic experiment was Jack Good's rock opera *Catch My Soul*, based on *Othello*, performed at the Roundhouse in 1970–1. Here, with 'ferocious' music and 'frenetic' dancing, 'the satanic furies raging at the heart of the tragedy' were released, said John Barber. Shakespeare's text, he said, was 'chopped into messes', but 'the result . . . has an Elizabethan power and energy' (*DT*, 22 December 1970). It was set in America's deep south, a half-Christian, half-voodoo world, in which Lance LeGault's Iago, 'his artistic roots deep in the blues and the rhetoric of Southern Baptist revivalism', wrote Nicholas Garnham, acted as master of ceremonies (*L*, 31 December 1970). Garnham felt that the power of the piece lay in its 'magic and ritual' and his only complaint was that it did not go far enough in jettisoning language: 'Rock proclaims the death of language and therefore of thought', he wrote, echoing Tynan on Valk. But an impressed Benedict Nightingale (*NS*, 25 December 1970), far from feeling encouraged to think, confessed that he could scarcely give 'a detached balanced response . . . bunched and stunned' as he was in the second row of the Roundhouse.

320 See Busi, *Otello in Italia*, pp. 291–302.
321 See Engle, 'Audience, Style and Language', pp. 100–2.

Some 'straight' productions

During the early seventies the play seems to have changed course, with
the director's hand becoming more evident – as it was in Shakespearean
performance generally. And yet no one was to be 'bunched and stunned' by
any of these directorial treatments. Perhaps Bernard Miles at the Mermaid
in 1971 (playing Iago again) hoped a naked Desdemona in the last act would
send shock waves, but it passed without outrage. It seemed reasonable enough
that she might try to win her lord again by going to bed without her nightie.
The whole much-publicised exercise did not save a production of which
Punch (29 September 1971) could ask with asperity: 'where's the colour, the
life, conviction, surprise, excitement, and basic believable vitality, the fury
and evil in the words?'

The production directed by John Barton which ran simultaneously at
Stratford in 1971 was far more successful in its failure to overwhelm. For
that was its deliberate choice. Just as Puecher allowed the comedy its head, so
Barton allowed Iago, Emrys James, his. This Iago was played as the 'obsessively disgruntled NCO' that Olivier imagined after his experiences in the
army (*S*, 25 September 1971). The colonial, mid-nineteenth-century military setting, carefully sustained in every detail, the cigars, the uniforms,
the heel-clicking, the saluting; the barrack-room atmosphere; the soldiers
picking up whores, and tangling occasionally with the 'natives' – all this
favoured Iago's story, sharpened the audience's sense of rank, and gave an
edge to Iago's envy at Cassio's promotion. Michael Billington in the *Guardian*
(10 September 1971) felt that it also seemed 'to isolate and make Desdemona
more vulnerable, and the innate brutality of the play more obviously naturalistic'. It was just as well, for Othello (Brewster Mason) hardly assisted.
'Some vital fire was missing', said Derek Mahon in the *Listener* (16 September 1971), 'some edge of arrogance born of old unease, perhaps, to prepare
us for his too swift conviction of Desdemona's guilt'.

Admittedly Barton cut some of Othello's more extravagant utterances,
such as 'I'll tear her all to pieces' (more was excised for the Aldwych 1972
season than for the Stratford 1971 season), but the omissions could not convincingly trim Shakespeare's Othello to Mason's reduction. Irving Wardle
in *The Times* (10 September 1971) took his genial relaxation to mean that
he was intended to represent 'a supremely confident egoist, too sure of his
own powers to take anyone else seriously'; Benedict Nightingale in the *New
Statesman* (17 September 1971) felt that he existed simply 'in order that Iago
may exploit and expose his superficiality'. Perhaps Leavis was in the background again, but if so it was with a difference. Where once Leavis was used
to support a central Othello and a secondary Iago, now, by contrast, a more
faithfully Leavisian speciousness in Othello made him theatrically secondary.

Iago, the mere 'mechanics' in Leavis's criticism, becomes, in the theatre, the only person interesting to watch. And yet somehow, perhaps because the circumstantial life of the play was so carefully observed, or because Iago was so brilliantly played – 'a pasty-faced under-dog in crumpled battledress', according to Wardle (same review) 'turning to confide in the audience with blubbery lips stretched into a gloatingly intimate smile' – the lack of a vital Othello did not sink the production. Hurren in the *Spectator* (25 September 1971) was alive to the singularity of this: it is, he said, 'the miracle of John Barton's production that this much of *Othello* can be missing, and yet not be fatally missed'.

Emrys James's Iago marks an interesting development in the life of that character – one which was prepared for by Quayle, even by Frank Finlay, Olivier's Iago. It is the idea of extraordinary evil arising out of nothing very special. Only a post-Hitlerian world that knew about the vileness of apparent non-descripts could imagine such a thing. Such wickedness had previously required a terrific sneer, or a dark and troubled spirit, or a dashing dangerousness to be credible. A satanic connection even. Much more frightening to us now, because much more real, is the little man, the bureaucrat. Irving Wardle compared Emrys James's Iago to 'as harmless a nonentity as Eichmann; an eternal dogsbody hovering on the margin of the group to be sent on little errands' (*T*, 10 September 1971). Bob Peck, in Ronald Eyre's RSC production (1979), continued in the same spirit with a deliberately 'flat and expressionless' Iago: a 'dogged North Country NCO . . . never more dangerous than in understatement . . . a hate machine created by the slow dehumanising process of professional warfare' (*S Tel*, 12 August 1979; *O*, 2 August 1979).

Michael Bryant in Peter Hall's 1980 production gave the idea of the insignificant little chap a twist by making him 'positively cosy', according to Irving Wardle in *The Times* (21 March 1980). He was a 'cherubic smiler, radiating benevolence', he said. In the same way Bob Hoskins in Jonathan Miller's 1981 BBC television production stroked and comforted Desdemona at the end of 4.2 with truly motherly tenderness. Bryant's envy was not of rank, but of Cassio's and Othello's sexuality. Emilia was plainly an object of desire, and his suspicion of Othello with her, said Peter Jenkins (*S*, 29 March 1980), was a species of 'voyeurism': he is a man 'small in stature and morally deformed, a grey dumpy little man, kinky and repressed, someone seriously disturbed.' Jonathan Miller also saw Iago as disturbed, an almost text-book psychopath.[322] But he did not pin down his envy as Hall had done – and as David Suchet's homosexual Iago was to do. It was congenital, an itch

322 See Fenwick, 'The Production', p. 26.

against everything happy or beautiful. It would seem that, having brought Iago out into the everyday world, the obvious next step was to take a closer look – something the camera is ideally suited to. What the layman calls a 'nasty bastard' (Hoskins's description),[323] and the psychologist a 'criminal psychopath', seemed to merge as Miller's camera lingered on that sweaty, giggling face.

The solidity of Iago in these productions of the seventies and early eighties was part of a new care for the play in all its much-neglected aspects. Until then it had been an opportunity for one or other of the main parts, rarely for both together; but beginning with Barton one observes a more general distribution of intelligence and roundedness. Cushman, describing Barton's *Othello* in *Plays and Players* (October 1971) speaks of 'spacious three-dimensional Shakespeare, the kind you can take a walk around and explore'. Billington in the *Guardian* (10 September 1971) writes of its being conceived with 'great thought and emotional precision'. In Ronald Eyre's production there was 'overall a high level of intelligent verse-speaking' (*L*, 16 August 1979): 'everyone was working in needle-point and letting the feelings generally grow on us by implication, rather than stating them directly'. It was possible to single out Suzanne Bertish's Desdemona as particularly fine, or James Laurenson's Cassio, or Willoughby Grant's Duke. It was altogether a 'thoughtful, absorbing piece of theatre', wrote Steve Grant in the *Observer* (2 August 1979). Or again, in Peter Hall's production (1980) all the secondary characters were precisely and richly characterised: the 'honourable stupidity' of Michael Gambon's Roderigo (*TLS*, 28 March 1980), Stephen Moore's Cassio, 'deeply moving' in his loss of 'reputation' (*ST*, 23 March 1980), the 'unexpected jewel' of Penelope Wilton's Bianca (*TLS*, 28 March 1980). And on television, Jonathan Miller's Desdemona (Penelope Wilton again) was unexpectedly important, partly because of her own skill, but also because the whole production, with its cool interiors and almost obsessively quiet acting, keyed itself into her orderly wifely world.

But where in all this did Othello stand? He was as elusive as ever. He did not flourish in this new world. At the worst he became something of an embarrassment, an eccentric guest stumbling in on an intelligent conversation, out of another period, another play. He could be kept quiet by drugging, as in Barton's production, where Brewster Mason's Othello was played 'almost ritualistically. His movements are voluptuous, his eyes dreamy, he seems stunned rather than roused by Iago' (*G*, 10 September 1971). Donald Sinden in Ronald Eyre's production seemed to have 'strayed into this working world from a stained glass window' (*FT*, 8 August 1979); 'he gave us great

---

323 Ibid., pp. 27–8.

wodges of emotion, very well done', said the *Listener* (16 August 1979) but out of keeping with the 'needlepoint' performances around him. Scofield, in 1980, was even more elaborately unconnected, giving a performance which seemed to have been 'worked up in front of a mirror, brought along to the stage door and then inserted into the production' (*ST*, 23 March 1980). It was 'so different from the rest of the interpretations on the stage that are much more naturalistic', said Alexander Walker on *Critics' Forum*,[324] 'that one listens to it almost as . . . a throwback to an earlier tradition in theatrical history'.

Both Sinden and Scofield actually raised laughs at some of Othello's extravagant moments. Sinden, according to some critics, never quite convinced, though wanting to; Scofield with his extraordinarily affected voice and movements did not seem even to want to. Of course Leavis – particularly in Scofield's case – was the great defence: the man is hollow anyway, so the argument runs. That at least is what John Carey on *Critics' Forum* thought Peter Hall meant. The difficulty with it was that the results were not only chilling (as chilling as 'noble' Moors had been) but embarrassing, as when Scofield in Carey's words, 'rather carefully lies on the floor and knocks his head against it . . . or . . . lowers himself onto the deathbed and moos three times like a cow'.

In America, where Robeson had left Othello in the hands principally of black actors – notably Earle Hyman in the 1950s and James Earl Jones in the 1960s and 70s – the Leavis approach was, for obvious reasons, less prevalent. The Moor had been played with some power by both actors, but Jones's 1982 production, with Christopher Plummer as Iago, seems to have been the most stirring. It was not especially distinguished as a whole. Some of the cast 'wouldn't be missed if they slept through their cues', said the *New York Post*[325] of the 1981 showing at Stratford, Connecticut. And although improvements were made for the Broadway run, not much interest was directed beyond Iago and Othello.

But, granting those limitations, the production gives a sense of constraints being lifted, of the actor seizing the space to make Othello large without embarrassment: 'this Othello is a Big man', said the *New York Post*, 'with a Big voice, given to Big theatrical gestures, and capable of playing Big emotions without flinching.' At the same time, James Earl Jones was also intensely human, as, for example, his interpretation of 'away, away, away' shows (see commentary at 4.2.40). In the same way, Christopher Plummer's

---

324 BBC Radio 3, 29 March 1980.
325 Undated clipping from the Schomberg Collection, New York Public Library. The next two references are to this clipping.

Iago touched on the demonic without being less human. He used 'despair' as his source of energy, said Walter Kerr in the *New York Times* (14 February 1982), the knowledge that nothing will ever help him to preferment: 'the energy itself is demonic in its thrust, incapable of stillness, yet eternally clear in its ferocious busyness . . . when . . . repose is impossible, one must race forward to ruin.' Thus the two protagonists interlocked. The *New York Post* talks of a 'chemistry between these two giants' and about their being absorbed in their 'titanic games'. There is something old-fashioned-sounding about these performances, and yet there was a note of excitement in the reviews which had not been heard for a long time.

Reappraisal: history

Perhaps 'old-fashioned' was the operative word. After the above was written, James Earl Jones published his autobiography (with Penelope Niven) in which he stated his belief that Othello has 'no sense of inferiority as the Western black man sometimes has'.[326] Lois Potter perceptively calls his interpretation 'the utopian Othello'. Utopias are typically defined by a mixture of idealism and nostalgia, and it is significant that, of his seven productions of *Othello* between 1956 and 1982, James Earl Jones preferred the one in 1964 – the height of America's civil rights movement, a time of pride and defiance.

But history was not to be so easily set aside. Othello was not to be disconnected from 'the Western black man' – nor for that matter was Desdemona, from the modern woman (of which more later). During the late eighties and nineties, the play was to become a focus for post-colonial and feminist studies. The story of a black man up against a white society, and of a woman murdered within a male society, has such obvious contemporary resonances, that parallels between *Othello* and the O. J. Simpson trial have been almost routinely drawn – at least in the USA. In the theatre, however, the play has not always been able to reflect those preoccupations with the same certainty.

It will be remembered that, in 1987, Ben Okri saw *Othello* for the first time – Terry Hands's RSC production – and felt urgently the need for an Othello more firmly rooted in his historical context. The pain it gave him to witness a black man so deracinated overshadowed the pain of the story itself. As far as the story went, more pain would have been welcome. Ben Kingsley, half-English and half-Indian, played Othello in his own barely non-white skin, as a Coleridgian Arab Moor. This, thought Okri, removed the play's racial and sexual tensions at a stroke: 'If you take away Othello's

326 Quoted in Potter, *Othello*, p. 161

colour then you don't really have the depths of the tragedy . . . To reduce the colour is to diminish the force of the sex. Working together they can be quite unbearable.'

Okri's frustration with the play and his ambivalence over its casting is characteristic of *Othello* commentary across the last two decades. On the one hand he acknowledges 'the chromatic tension of the play'. On the other, he feels that really Othello is 'a white man's myth', that 'in the castle of Othello's skin Shakespeare poured whiteness'. The question then arises: if Othello really is, as Okri says, 'a blackened white man', then why not black up a white man?[327] Jonathan Miller did in 1981, using a lightly tanned Anthony Hopkins in his BBC television film, but was fiercely criticised for it. Miller's defence was that the play was not about race, but about jealousy. A black actor would only reinforce racist assumptions. Potter comments, fairly, that 'Miller was, and still is, accused of racism precisely because he did not make race an issue.'[328]

But it is not in order to deny race as an issue that critics such as Okri – or more recently, S. E. Ogude and Sheila Rose Bland – have rediscovered Othello as a blackfaced white man. On the contrary, it is in order to magnify the element of racial caricature, as they see it, in Shakespeare's Othello. Ogude even proposes a production in which, under the heat of the lights, the blackface begins to melt and 'Othello becomes a monstrosity of colours: the wine-red lips and snow-white eyes against a background of messy blackness.'[329]

An alternative to caricature,[330] and an answer to frustration, is outright adaptation – as a way of directly interrogating the play. After all, as Jyotsna Singh points out, 'the end of Shakespeare's play *cannot foresee* the violence and conflict of colonial history'.[331] Murray Carlin's modern South Africa and Marowitz's American deep south are ways of forcing the issue. Again, in 1999, Caleen Sinnette Jennings set her play, *Casting Othello*, in a modern, socially mobile, black and white, urban USA – a place ripe with all the inter-race/gender/class fears and resentments that Shakespeare's play is almost 'about' – but never quite satisfyingly enough.

Modern Britain is equally ripe. In 2001, the sceenwriter Andrew Davies's adaptation of *Othello* was shown on British television (ITV). Davies sacrificed the language and changed certain elements of the plot, but he gained a specific political setting that made explicit the teasing racial topicality of

327 Okri, 'Meditations', *West Africa*, 23 and 30 March 1987.
328 Potter, *Othello*, p. 154.   329 Ogude, 'Literature and Racism', p. 163.
330 See also Bland, 'How I Would Direct *Othello*'.
331 Singh,' Othello's Identity', p. 291.

the original. The context was London's Metropolitan Police, a body that had been found 'institutionally racist' by the official enquiry set up after the racist murder in 1993 of Stephen Lawrence, a black teenage Londoner. No one had been successfully prosecuted (nor has anyone at the time of writing) and despite their efforts, the police force had been shown to have deeply racist elements within it. Davies deftly transforms Othello's Generalship into his appointment by the Prime Minister as the first black Commissioner of the Met. Round this man (Eamonn Walker), Davies weaves two tales. The first is more or less Shakespeare's story, of love and betrayal involving Othello, his upper-class wife Dessie (Keeley Hawes), and his friend Ben Jago (Christopher Ecclestone). Jago, in a shift from Shakespeare, has been Othello's mentor, and is thus provided with one unequivocal motive – poisonous jealousy of his protégé's promotion over his head. The other tale is the investigation into a racist killing by the police (an echo, perhaps, of the Rodney King case in Los Angeles in 1992), on which the idealistic Othello stakes his reputation. It is a powerful piece, which communicates just that sense of black isolation that Okri felt for Shakespeare's Othello, while at the same time giving it immediate social and political weight.

Because his context is live and current, so much simply slots into place. Davies has only to pan the camera round a roomful of white police officers; to overhear a casually racist chat in the gents'; or show us politicians eager to play their black appointment in the media – and immediately we feel the full weight of the white Establishment. History presses closely too, as Othello tells his friends about his Caribbean birthplace, St Lucia, with its one-time slave plantations, where his grandmother still lives. It was from there that he first came to England, wishing, he confesses, that he was white. As the contemporary scene with its social gradations and historical underpinnings assemble themselves, all Jago's hints at what upper-class white women ('super-subtle Venetians', 1.3.343–4) get up to, hit home. We know these women, their accents, their schools, their money (Davies paints them in too), so we know precisely how far they are outside Othello's experience. Everything joins up – Othello's personal breakdown and the larger picture.

It is evident that the play is richly susceptible to modern adaptation. At the same time, circumstances can combine to make adaptation unnecessary. That, at least, is what Janet Suzman felt from the vantage point of South Africa in 1987, and more particularly from the Market Theatre, Johannesburg – 'loomed over by the terrible concrete of the Lubianka's terrible twin, John Vorster Square'.[332]

---

332 Suzman, 'Parables', p. 257.

Othello in South Africa

With apartheid still in place, and with the law against mixed marriages not long repealed (in 1985), the production was loaded with political context. So much so that when Suzman was invited in 1995, after the dismantlement of apartheid, to give the Tanner Lectures on Human Values, it took a paper on its own to explain to her Oxford audience what the system had meant for a production of *Othello*. Only then could she give, in the second lecture, her account of the production itself. Othello was played by John Kani, a South African actor whose first language is not English and who therefore not only looked but – more than black British and American Othellos – sounded different. Kani's family had suffered cruelly under apartheid; his brother had been shot dead by the police. He himself had wanted to be a freedom fighter before he became an actor. Now, living in Soweto, he had to 'run the gamut of police roadblocks every day' just to get into rehearsal.[333]

In effect, apartheid turned *Othello* into a form of protest theatre. That is how Suzman and Kani argued it with the exiled African National Congress, whose boycott against foreign cultural and sporting events might have prevented Suzman, as an expatriate, from going ahead. She describes a conversation with Wally Serote, the cultural attaché of the ANC in London, in which she answered his concern that there was only one 'representative of the people' in the play, by saying that 'the people' were to be represented by Othello 'as a victim of white oppression, and that the oppressor, represented by Iago, got his comeuppance'.

No doubt she was simplifying, but her view of the play as a whole confirms that outline: 'a microcosm of not only South Africa, but any society in the West', complete with the 'bigots (Iago and Roderigo . . .), the armchair liberals (Brabantio, Gratiano), the pragmatists . . . (Emilia, Lodovico), and those who simply don't see colour at all (Desdemona, Cassio)'. It was her picture of Iago especially that rooted the concept: 'the spitting image of extreme Afrikanerdom's very own icon, Eugene Terreblanche'. They were both military men with the gift of the gab: brutal, vulgar, racist and, supposedly, trustworthy. Her choice for Iago was Richard Haines, tall and burley, a Boer General to the life, she said.[334]

In performance, as we have seen, Iago can create an unholy intimacy with an audience in spite of itself, and he often becomes more fascinating to watch than Othello. Suzman and Haines avoided this danger by keeping Iago public. He was the sick face of Afrikanerdom, of state-sponsored prejudice, rather than a psychotic individual: finger in nostril at 'baboon' (1.3.310),

333 Ibid., p. 285.   334 Ibid, pp. 257, 279, 280–1.

10 John Kani as Othello and Joanna Weinberg as Desdemona at the Market Theatre,
Johannesburg, 1987.

thumb up between two fingers at 'Virtue? A Fig!' (313), spitting viciously at every opportunity, hee-hawing and miming a monstrous donkey's penis at 'led by the nose / As asses are' (383–4) – he was a cartoon figure pointing out beyond the theatre, rather than in towards his psyche (see commentary generally).

By contrast, it was Kani's Othello who became fascinating to watch: fairly small (like Kean, but unlike the common expectation), lithe, gentle-seeming, soft-spoken, and with a rare radiant smile. His attraction for Desdemona was immediately credible and the two of them had a chemistry which went far towards explaining why Haines's Iago, for all its power, could not unbalance the production. Joanna Weinberg played Desdemona with dignity and candour – and with a directness of passion that made sense of her words about 'downright violence and storm of fortunes' (1.3.245). The video[335] of the production brings this out very clearly, the camera, as Barbara Hodgdon points out, making Desdemona's 'trajectory of desire', 'her look', the key to our sense of 'Kani's exoticism and the sexual bond between them'.[336]

This heightened feeling between them also helped, paradoxically, to explain Othello's credulousness. In the video, the ability of the camera to isolate heads in close shot, to pan down bodies, to shut out the rest of the cast and, with the help of music, to create moments of intense privacy – all this works to remove the couple from the ordinary world (see commentary, particularly at 2.1.173 SD; also at e.g. 1.3.294–6, and 2.3.1–11). By the time Iago sets to work on Othello in the third act, we have a powerful sense of Kani's emotional delicacy. It is as though he already has a skin too few. Without the traditional paper-signing business to distract Othello's attention and delay his understanding (see commentary at 3.3.92ff.), Kani is alert from the outset, rising to suspicion and despair as quickly as Othellos did in the eighteenth and early nineteenth centuries. By the time he makes his farewell to arms (348b ff.), he is already on the edge, his agony vividly expressed both in his acting and in Suzman's use of sound – a nightmare mix with a drumbeat, like an insistant head pulse (see also commentary at 4.1).

---

335 According to Suzman, the play could have run for much longer than its six-week limit. So, 'not having the funds to tour the production . . . I decided we must film it for television . . . we taped this giant play in six days flat' (Suzman, 'Parables', p. 294). Given the closeness between this video and the stage production, I have used it not only for its filmic values, but also, particularly in the commentary, to indicate actors' business.

336 Hodgdon, 'Race-ing *Othello*', p. 28.

The parallel with the periods of Spranger Barry and Edmund Kean is illuminating. These were times when the blackness of Othello seemed to matter least, when his 'barbaric' extremes were described (on the whole and always excepting Schlegel) with little reference to race. In a modern context however, as Hodgdon concedes, Othello's extremes are bound to play into 'some spectators' desire to experience Othello's "wildness" . . . to find their expectations of a primitive blackness fulfilled'. Thus a modern Othello seems to be stuck in an impossible trap. Hodgdon argues a way out by saying that Suzman avoids using these 'wild' elements 'as denigrating narratives of cultural othering', and that 'by trivializing and problematizing their racist content, [she] turns them into positive modes of self-definition'.[337]

It is a conundrum for any production of *Othello*. Ultimately, neither director nor actors can completely control an audience. If a performance confirms prejudices, the 'right' way of looking is wishful thinking. Suzman reports that at the first kiss between Othello and Desdemona, some members of the audience would walk out.[338] For them the racist content had not been at all trivialised. As for the ones who stayed, did they understand, for example, that the last scene 'articulates the demand for "the negro" which Suzman's representation of the negro disrupts', as Hodgdon argues? That Kani's huge demonic shadow cast on the white screen, followed by his actual appearance, naked to the waist, padding animal-like on bare feet – that this was not Kani performing 'the other', but Othello *performing* 'the other', parodying the white man's dream of the black man?[339]

Suzman herself must have had worries about this scene. In explaining why she rejected the idea of modern dress for the production (they used Renaissance costume), she gives several reasons. One of them was Desdemona's unmodern submissiveness, and another was Othello at 5.2: 'How', she asks, 'without being risible in the eyes of an urban black audience, could Othello discard, in the final act, his borrowed finery [i.e. his modern clothes] to revert to his unprotected African self?'[340] In the event, her urban black audiences decided for themselves that this *Othello* spoke for them. The theatre's 'normal 10 to 15 percent black audience for a European play', Suzman reported, 'jumped to an unprecedented 40, 50, and then 60 percent'. They came, she guessed, because 'the black guy gets to be in charge of his own death at the end, and because the white guy gets found out'. And looking back, post-apartheid, she suspected 'that it will not happen again; it was a play that had found its time and place'.[341]

---

337 Hodgdon, 'Race-ing *Othello*', p. 29.   338 Suzman, 'Parables', p. 293.
339 Hodgdon, 'Race-ing *Othello*', p. 30.   340 Suzman, 'Parables', p. 284.
341 Ibid., p. 294.

The white flight

Back in England, time and place were elusive. No black actor had performed Othello on a major English stage since Robeson in 1959. No white actor had either, since Anthony Hopkins in 1981. Blacking up had become a kind of scandal. Ian McKellen declared that it was 'as disgusting these days as a "nigger minstrel show"'.[342] Olivier's film, looked at in more sensitive times, had not helped, as we have seen.

Ben Kingsley filled the gap in 1985–7, but the programme notes had to work hard advertising his African–Indian background and his role as Ghandi in the Oscar-winning film. By way of conceptual alibi, it was said that Kingsley's pale Othello and Suchet's Iago were not meant to be sharply distinguishable anyway, because they were spiritually twinned: 'two faces of the same disturbed spirit', as Kingsley says in an essay on his role.[343] David Suchet elaborates the point, proposing a bisexual tendency in Iago, and a confused love / hate for Othello.[344] The production as a whole supported the idea of a solipsistic relationship. Ralph Koltai's set was 'a gladiatorial arena' in which, says Kingsley, 'we could grapple only with our passions and each other'.[345] But the homoerotic theme was curiously reductive, deflecting attention, as Potter points out, both from Desdemona and from any 'political appraisal of the play'.[346]

Trevor Nunn: wives . . . and husbands

In 1989, Trevor Nunn took the necessary step and cast a black Othello: Willard White, the Jamaican-born bass baritone opera singer, who had sung Porgy in Nunn's production of *Porgy and Bess* the year before at Glyndebourne.

Nunn's casting was not, however, an overt political statement. The period was vaguely mid-to -late nineteenth century: 'Chekhov crossed with the American Civil War' (*TLS*, 8 September 1989), or the Franco-Prussian war (*T*, 26 August 1989) with a dash of *Death in Venice* in Cassio's and Roderigo's civvies. As it had been with John Barton, the point of the setting was military rather than racial, 'an almost loving recreation of a military camp' thought Potter.[347] People noted the shrilling cicadas, the sun-drenched light, the bugles calling, and the sound of hymn tunes being played on an old organ. 'Spiritually', however, according to the *Spectator*, the audience was located 'inside the four walls of bourgeois naturalist drama' (2 September 1989).

---

342 Quoted in Potter, *Othello*, p. 153.   343 Kingsley, 'Othello', p. 171.
344 See Suchet, 'Iago', pp. 179–99.   345 Kingsley, 'Othello', pp. 170, 171.
346 Potter, *Othello*, p. 165.   347 Ibid., pp. 188–9.

These particular four walls were very close together. The play, with a full text lasting almost four hours, was staged at the old Other Place in Stratford-upon-Avon, a cramped tin shack that has since been demolished. This was where Ian McKellen and Judi Dench had performed Nunn's famous *Macbeth* in 1976 – another play suited to claustrophobic conditions. Now McKellen, carrying those associations, was Nunn's Iago, and with Willard White, Imogen Stubbs as Desdemona and Zoë Wanamaker as Emilia, he was part of a tight, tense marital foursome.

As with John Barton's production, Nunn's *Othello* was noted for its attention to all the subordinate parts and for its 'lovingly dwelt-on almost novelistic detail' (*I*, 2 October 1989). To some the novelism was excessive – literal-minded and over-explanatory. Cassio, for example, in his drunken sleep actually threw a leg over Iago, which undermined 'the perverted originality of Iago's ruse' (*I*, 2 October 1989. See commentary at 2.3.303–29; also at 3.3.39ff.). Nevertheless, the closeness and the detail gave the audience an almost physical sense of involvment: 'This business between Iago and the Moor is an intensely personal matter', wrote the *Spectator*, 'we see it, indeed we feel it, in close-up' (2 September 1989). It also favoured Iago. His was 'the virtuoso performance of the evening' (*TLS*, 8 Septembr 1989), 'precisely thought out in every detail . . . a trim, vicious and compulsively tidy mother-hen, whose manhood is sublimated in professional resentment and in keeping order in the army' (*ST*, 27 August 1989).

Surprisingly though, this production did not exile Othello, as earlier productions had done. Some reviewers grumbled about White's verse-speaking and acting and he himself admitted, as Robeson had done, that he was 'totally intimidated by the whole cast because they were actors and I was a singer' (*Wall Street Journal*, 6 October 1989). But Robert Smallwood felt that though his 'careful' approach to the verse 'distanced him a little from it . . . In a curious almost disturbing way, this seemed to fit the role . . . the alien among the Venetians, the black opera singer among the white Shakespeareans.'[348] His voice – 'a basso as profundo as the sea' (*T*, 26 August 1989) – reminded people of Robeson, as did his massive presence (and unlike Robeson, he moved well). But, beyond that, the *Times* critic was also impressed by his 'actorly imagination and eye for detail': in the 'temptation scene', so-called, 'the way in which White's eyes, narrowing and turning inwards, mirror the clouding of his mind is riveting to watch'. Given the special difficulty of carrying off a credible Othello, this same critic's remark that White 'can never be asinine', was less patronising than it might sound. But, as so often when black actors are involved, praise is apt to hit the wrong note, as here,

---

348 Smallwood, 'Shakespeare', p. 113.

unwittingly, in the *Spectator* (2 September 1989): 'When furrowing his massive brow in pained confusion or roaring some of the briefer lines of verse when he is on the rack, the effect is riveting. The monumental simplicity of the man is perfectly captured.'

What is new about the critical reaction this time is the amount of space given to the women. Since Shakespeare leaves them relatively lightly sketched, they are particularly open to novelistic development. Desdemona's frivolity as she awaited Othello's arrival on Cyprus was suddenly interrupted by a violent burst of tears; she announced the dinner that Othello is late for with a pocket watch plonked flirtatiously down on the table in front of him; Cassio gave her a box of chocolates which she locked away and, later, she and Emilia had a secret binge together. Emilia whistled desolately and smoked a pipe like Masha in the *The Three Sisters*; she watched Iago watching Othello and Desdemona kissing, and averted her head in misery; when she wasn't doing much she glared critically in silent desperation. These are only some of the moments that reviewers picked up and interpreted with an analytical care that has rarely been given to the characters before.

Thus the impact on the women of that all-absorbing duo – Othello-and-Iago – came into clearer focus than ever before. The *Observer* (27 August, 1989) even noted that the play became 'among many things, a lesson for women in the destructiveness of men'. Zoë Wanamaker's Emilia in particular brought this out: 'what has her existence with Iago been like, one wondered; why does she still yearn for attention and affection from him?' This was the effect on Robert Smallwood, for whom the part of Emilia had never seemed so significant.[349] And it has been the effect on many since, for whom the video of the TV production has only served to keep the question alive and more insistent.[350] As a consequence, Iago's moments with her took on new life and definition: 'everything between Iago and Emilia' wrote the *Wall Street Journal* (6 October 1989) 'seems sweaty and covert'. The *Listener* clearly saw in Emilia's face a history of 'brutal treatment at the hands of Iago' (7 September 1989; see commentary at 2.1.191b–3a; 3.3.87 and 302–21). Equally, it was in relation to Desdemona that Willard White often drew

---

349 Ibid., p. 112.
350 See, for example, Carol Chillington Rutter, 'Looking at Shakespeare's Women'. As Rutter notes, this film was 'shot in a studio . . . a much more actorly film than Parker's: there are no exteriors, no location settings . . . the camera concentrates on actors' bodies in their domestic settings' (p. 257). With this in mind, I have used it in the commentary to supplement contemporaneous accounts of the stage performance.

comment: 'he's at his best with Imogen Stubbs as Desdemona', wrote the *Sunday Times* (27 August 1989), and for Smallwood, as with several others, the two moments that stood out were his lifting and whirling her joyfully up on to the luggage at 2.1 and jeeringly on to the stool in 4.2[351] (see commentary).

All the same, White and Stubbs did not come across as lovers in the saturated, passionate manner of Kani and Weinberg. The lifting and whirling is a world away from the embraces of Suzman's pair. Stubbs was noted, not always approvingly, for a certain childishness. The *Sunday Times* (27 August 1989) praised her for catching 'that fugitive moment between girlhood and womanhood', but the *Listener* (13 October 1989) thought her too 'sickly sweet', and *Punch* 'too frail and chirpy, with a babyish voice and manner that make it hard to credit her with having boldly flirted with Othello' (13 October 1989). Where once it took modern dress to make critics wish for a more modern Desdemona, now they wanted one even in nineteenth-century costume. Barbara Hodgdon even argues (from the video) that the production's sexual reticence leaves a vacuum which is filled for the spectator by Iago's racist mythology of black sexuality and fear of miscegenation.[352]

The relationship between the women was more generally agreed to have been rightly emphasised: 'very moving', wrote Smallwood, 'the compassionate affection of the disillusioned Emilia supporting the bewildered naivety of the grief-stricken girl'.[353] Indeed, the *Stage* thought that 'the quality of their friendship evolves as the one really valid relationship in the play' (7 September 1989). The word 'evolves' is significant. In their extended scene together, the willow-song scene, it took time. At one point, Desdemona hugged Emilia, but the hug was not returned (see commentary, 4.3.55). The turning point came when 'the women share contraband – a box of chocolates locked in the one drawer Othello couldn't open when he ransacked the room – and gossip – more contraband'.[354] As Emilia finished her speech about husbands, she leant down and embraced Desdemona.

Trevor Nunn's legacy: Sam Mendes . . .

A gap of eight years followed Nunn's production before *Othello* was again seen on a major stage in England. When Sam Mendes brought it to the National Theatre in London (with David Harewood as Othello, Simon

351 Smallwood, 'Shakespeare', p. 113.
352 Hodgdon, 'Race-ing *Othello*', pp. 32–3.
353 Smallwood, 'Shakespeare', p. 112.
354 Rutter, 'Looking at Shakespeare's women', p. 257.

11 Zoë Wanamaker as Emilia and Imogen Stubbs as Desdemona in 4.3 (Trevor Nunn, 1989).

Russell Beale as Iago and Claire Skinner as Desdemona), there was much debate about the reasons for this unheard-of neglect, about the fortuitous freshness that it gave the play, about casting difficulties, and the desirableness, or otherwise, of restricting the part of Othello to black actors. While the production itself was noted, like Nunn's, for its attention to domestic detail, this other discussion created a kind of racial meta-politics around it: 'A ridiculous situation', complained the *Financial Times* (18 September 1997) about the taboo on white actors in the part: 'I should like to see Adrian Lester [who had been Mendes's first choice for Othello] play Iago to Michael Gambon's Othello, but will I?' That call for two-way colour-blind casting was echoed by Charles Spencer in the *Daily Telegraph* (same day): 'it is surely absurd that the traffic is all one way'.

It seems that the Robeson-effect (that only 'the real thing' would do) was losing its edge. Robeson had had the advantage of surprise not just in *Othello*, but in Shakespeare at all. Now in the late nineties, that kind of statement no longer needed to be made. David Harewood himself drew attention to the 'black British heritage of actors who've been classically trained in British theatre, in cinema, in television', and to the amount of reverse traffic: 'white comedians delivering comedy in a black way, white kids on the street talking in a black way' (*I*, 16 September 1997). There is almost a post-racial feeling in a few of the reviews, a sense that in a multicultural society we should have outgrown the literalism of racial division. Christopher Cannon, writing in the *TLS* (3 October 1997), made no comment on Mendes's casting, but he thought the whole production racially simple-minded. It was all so obvious: in the design (black and white chequered floor), in the lighting (black shadows and white shafts of light), in the fetishising of David Harewood's body ('the production seems to think there is something scandalous about the decision simply to show black skin') and lastly in staging 'a lingering kiss' between him and Desdemona 'as if its interracial circumstance might still have the power to shock'. Shakespeare asks us to look beyond colour, Cannon argued, whereas 'in its assumption that darkness and light convey deep meaning, this production's understanding of "race" remains at the level of those in the play who believe Iago'.

Other reviewers did not notice that they were meant to be shocked – thus, in their way, proving Cannon's point that colour no longer has that power. It wasn't so much the black and white skins that they noticed, but Harewood's muscles and Claire Skinner's fragility, as well as the fact that there was a 'chemistry between them in the first two acts [that] ensures we feel the full impact of their tragedy' (*What's On In London*, 24 September 1997). Again, as with Imogen Stubbs, critics were quick to commend the forcefulness of Skinner ('no milksop', *T*, 18 September 1997) or to regret signs of weakness ('slightly too fragile . . . to suggest the character's "downright violence"', *G*, 18 September 1997). The other complaint was that Othello was too young (though his youth did help the 'chemistry') – Mendes had had to cut Othello's line about having declined into the vale of years. In fact, in a sign of the apolitical atmosphere of the production, the age gap between Othello and Desdemona seemed to matter as much as any other difference:

'like the differences of colour and culture, [it] is vital, both to our sense of the bravery and beauty of their love and to the deep insecurities in the hero' (*I*, 18 September 1997).

Otherwise, appreciation ran along conventional lines. Reviewers loved the production for its speed and tension ('the plot seems to hurtle') and for the Trevor Nunn-like attention to detail, 'precise and rich' (*T*, 18 September 1997). Just as with Nunn, the setting was military and colonial, louvred and shuttered against the sun, though this time the period itself, sometime in the 1930s or 40s, was less nostalgic – indeed it brought 'the play uncomfortably close to home' thought Charles Spencer (*DT*, 18 September 1997). But then there was a studied stylishness about the production, which kept it at a distance too. With stark lighting effects, and blackouts between scenes instead of entrances and exits, the production reminded people of film noir: 'This is the "Othello" that Orson Welles tried to make and never quite succeeded; heavily filmic, dark as any French thriller' wrote Sheridan Morley (*IHT*, 24 September 1997).

Above all they loved it for Simon Russell Beale's Iago, a charismatic actor who, like McKellen, had a 'rare grasp of detail: every gesture and inflection has its effect' (*Glasgow Herald*, 20 September 1997). Like McKellen he was a buttoned-up NCO, but unlike McKellen he was physically repulsive: 'a frog-like creature with a shaved head (and sinister crease of flesh at the base of his neck)', said Robert Butler (*IoS*, 21 September 1997). All the hatred and sexual disgust that McKellen expressed in his ramrod-straight back, his clipped flat northern voice, and in 'the mysterious folds and lines of his face', Beale expressed in bulgy clamminess: 'the only surprise is that he doesn't leave a trail of slime' (*DT*, 18 September 1997).

But although Beale was said by many to steal the show, there were others who insisted that David Harewood held his own. Or rather that Mendes had interlocked them as a contrasting pair. 'In an age which finds it hard to believe in the very idea of nobility – at any rate in its masculine, heroic form', said John Gross (*STel*, 21 September 1997), Harewood rose to the challenge: his 'grandeur, humour, ardour, anguish and his nobility of voice and physique form an ideal contrast to Beale's gnarled ugliness' (*FT*, 18 September 1997). The only serious complaint was that he broke the verse into 'three-word parcels with long pauses in improbable places' (*TLS*, 3 October 1997).

. . . and Michael Attenborough

Michael Attenborough's production of *Othello* was the first in the main house at Stratford to be cast with a black Othello (Ray Fearon) since Robeson in 1959. Again Nunn's influence can be felt, in the setting and period:

Cyprus as a military outpost, Edwardian this time, with uniforms for the men (red jackets, red trouser-stripes and ceremonial swords) and long summery dresses for the women. Once more, here was a devilishly virtuouso Iago (Richard McCabe), and, as in Mendes's production, a young Othello with 'rippling pecs and six-pack stomach' (*TO*, 28 April, 1999). He too had his line about being declined into the vale of years, cut.

This time, however, it seemed to matter more. As with Harewood's, Fearon's youth removed one of the causes, felt to be equal with all the others, for Othello's insecurity. But it also deprived the character of 'weight' (*G*, 22 April 1999). Harewood had a noble baritone voice and could convey grandeur despite his youth. The lighter-voiced Fearon had to avoid 'the vocal beef and trumpetry' of the part, as Alistair Macaulay put it, aiming instead at 'sincerity . . . inwardness; and clarity' (*FT*, 23 April 1999). There was agreement that he was moving, but also that more 'volume and depth' were needed: 'emotionally and musically, this is the Diet Coke version' (*IoS*, 25 April 1999).

Beside him was Richard McCabe's 'pudgy-faced, Essex-toned' and more than usually comic Iago (*TO*, 28 April 1999). Beale had veered close to camp and farce on occasion (see *What's On*, 24 September 1997), but McCabe approached the comedy in the role as Iago's deliberately adopted persona (see *IoS*, 25 April 1999). Matey with the audience and everyone onstage, underneath there seethed 'sexual jealousy, professional resentment and above all, a deep-seated complex rooted in class and sexual inferiority' (*MS*, 27 May 1999). This new element of class envy was also picked up by the *Spectator* (1 May 1999), who saw McCabe's 'wise-cracking' Iago not as 'dedicated to evil in the abstract but simply to the destruction of Othello and the entire officer class'. In fact, by a curious reversal, it was McCabe's Iago who was the outsider in the officers' mess, rather than Othello 'who never quite conveys the sense of coming from an alien culture' (*MS*, 27 May 1999).

If, as the *Independent on Sunday* thought, 'a heavier Othello and a graver Iago would engulf us more swiftly and deeply in the tragedy', the women made up for it. Michael Billington thought that 'McCabe aside, the production's strongest suit lies in its feminist emphasis' (*G*, 22 April 1999). Zoë Waites's Desdemona was 'a strong woman capable of "downright violence"', with a 'grave beauty' in her voice that is 'rare in this role' (*FT*, 23 April 1999); and Rachel Joyce's Emilia was 'a tough woman burning with resentment at her sex's maltreatment' (*G*, 22 April 1999).

Taking these three productions together – Nunn's, Mendes's and Attenborough's – it is noticeable that the question of Othello's nobility has moved from the moral to the aesthetic field. Critics are no longer especially interested in deciding whether Othello is or isn't noble, should or shouldn't be forgiven. What counts is the process of his undoing, not how to judge it. Nobility as style, though, is still important – in his presence, his voice, and his way with the verse. Those 'three-word parcels' of Harewood's, and Fearon's 'habit of breaking up Othello's sentences Into Individual (*pause*) Words' *(FT,* 23 April 1999) were regretted not only for the lost emotion, but for the lost grandeur as well.

But perhaps the most interesting development during this decade is the reduced level of racial comment. Instead we have lengthy arguments about Othello's age, almost as though 'the real thing' had turned out not to make enough of a difference after all. Ray Fearon had recently played a success-ful Romeo with Zoë Waites as Juliet, and it is tempting to speculate on the (presumably intended) confusion sown by colour-blind casting in gen-eral – where coloured casting becomes as blinding as colour-blind casting. In Fearon's case, if a critic made a point about difference, it was likely to be either about age, or about something else that wasn't colour. *Time Out,* for example, pointed to Fearon's 'muscular self-assurance' in contrast to the 'uptight' Venetians (28 April 1999). If Fearon's isolating 'coffee-coloured skin' was mentioned (as in the *MoS,* 25 April 1999), it was only by way of contrast to the greater isolation of Iago.

By the same token, there was much less comment about Othello's 'instinc-tive emotions', or his 'monumental simplicity' – phrases that were used about Willard White's Othello (see *O,* 27 August 1989; *S,* 2 September 1989; see also *LR,* November 1989). In fact the gullibility question seemed alto-gether less prominent: 'it would take a man of iron to hold his own against such cunning' said the *MoS* (same issue). Whether this has to do with lib-eralism, political correctness or genuine colour blindness, it is difficult to determine.

Oliver Parker's film, 1995

Despite the respect accorded to the Othellos in the above productions, many of the reviews maintained that, on each occasion, the play belonged to its Iago – McKellen, Beale or McCabe. Alistair Macaulay's summary of the difference between the Othello and Iago of Harewood and Beale suggests the reason: 'Othello is large of soul, poetic in manner, mighty in utterance; he belongs to tradition. The Iago of Simon Russell Beale is fleet of thought, small in scale, mean of spirit, prosaic in style; and startlingly modern' *(FT,* 18 September 1997).

Iago's modernity is irresistible, and never more so than when in front of the camera. It is no surprise then, that Parker's film also seems to be dominated by its Iago – Kenneth Branagh, with his famously throw-away modern inflections. As Samuel Crowl puts it: 'Parker allows Kenneth Branagh's Iago to appropriate the camera, to make it his intimate . . . We get Iago's knowingly conspiratorial soliloquies in tight closeup, often begun in profile so that Branagh can then draw us in to Iago's cunning gutter imagination with just the slightest turn of his head to confide in us directly'.[355] But it isn't just Branagh. Compounding his effect is Parker's treatment of Laurence Fishburne's Othello.

If you take away most of what belongs on Othello's side of the balance – the 'utterance' that Alistair Macaulay speaks of – the scale is bound to tip towards Iago. Cuts are to be expected in film, of course, but, as Samuel Crowl puts it, 'Parker's camera replaces Othello's text with his texture'.[356] What we get is Fishburne looking wonderful, dignified (even *in extremis*), young (again), sexy and exotic – ear-rings, scars and tatoos. Barbara Hodgdon writes that Laurence Fishburne 'plays Othello precisely against . . . stereotypes of black masculinity and on his own terms'.[357] But, paradoxically, his 'own terms' are at least partly defined by the stereotype itself – if only in order to avoid it. Fishburne is a powerful actor in any event, but the film is preoccupied with what he looks like – just as it is with the women. His face and body are never allowed seriously to disarrange themselves. Furthermore, the colour palette for Parker's film is rich and warm so that the difference between him and the others is not very marked – dark gold and gold, rather than black and white. In fact, in the context of so many nationalities and voices – Italian for Brabantio and the Duke (André Oumansky and Gabrielle Ferzetti), French–Swiss for Desdemona (Irene Jacob), English for Iago (Kenneth Branagh) – Fishburne's colour and his indeterminate English seem just another aspect of the film's internationalism, and another example of that nineties tendency towards de-race-ing *Othello*.

Naturally in the circumstances, Fishburne never says 'Haply for I am black', nor finds Desdemona's visage as 'black / As mine own face' (3.3.265, 388–9). But that is the least of it. It's not just that the 'arias' are truncated (for example, his farewell to war) or excised (e.g. the Pontic Sea speech), or that the camera often pans away from him when he does speak (for example, for the flashback that illustrates his speech to the Senate about wooing Desdemona). But much that might sound extreme or eccentric is gone too: for example, his odd moment of excess when he greets Desdemona on Cyprus – about death and fate and being choked with 'too much of joy'. Othello's text is alive with erotic detail: the 'young and sweating devil' in Desdemona's hand; Heaven stopping its nose at her deed; the lewd or ugly

355 Crowl, 'Othello', p. 41.
356 Ibid.   357 Hodgdon, 'Race-ing *Othello* ii', p. 90.

creatures that he shares with Iago, goats and monkeys and 'summer flies . . . in the shambles', all of which disappear for Fishburne.

Instead, the film expresses (or rather, literalises) Othello's abused imagination by way of a series of flashed-up sequences of Cassio and Desdemona flirting and making love – the internal film, we are to suppose, that Othello is playing to himself. This not only diminishes Othello, deflecting our attention from him as victim of his own and Iago's (male) fantasies, but it diminishes Desdemona too. As Carol Rutter points out, it works 'perversely and reductively to instantiate and validate the misogynistic stereotypes . . . that Shakespeare's play circulates'. The play's distinction between male erotic delusion and the 'real' Desdemona is blurred, and Shakespeare's 'interrogation of masculinity' is derailed by 'making women somehow at fault for male fantasy'.[358] Not entirely derailed, though. Irene Jacob acts the 'real' Desdemona with openness and candour, avoiding all hint of coyness; and Anna Patrick as Emilia, her part having been drastically cut throughout, triumphantly turns the tables at the end (see commentary at 5.2).

Turning white black

If mainstream productions in England have not gone out of their way to make race into the central theme, experiments and variations on the idea have been made elsewhere. A film directed by Liz White, made and financed entirely by African–Americans in 1960 (but not shown until 1980, at Howard University) used the play to explore the idea of difference among black people. Othello was cast as a 'young, passionate, emotionally sensitive African' and the rest of the cast as lighter-skinned African–Americans, characterised by 'a tone of urban American sophistication'. The cultural difference was evident, while the racial difference in Shakespeare's play was softened, making the last act 'viable as tragedy', says Peter S. Donaldson. The film used a Freudian model of the relations between Africa and black America, so that the Americans, in rejecting Othello, 'reject a part of themselves', while he 'denies the claims of consanguinity and disavows shared history'.[359]

A common thread in these experiments is the blacking of part or all of the play's white cast, making Othello himself less of an extraordinary and inexplicable exception. Hugh Quarshie himself directed an *Othello* at the Greenwich Theatre in 1989 in which Iago was played by a light-skinned black actor, the idea being 'to suggest a natural affinity' between him and Othello, and 'to lessen the force of the argument that Othello behaves as he

358 Rutter, 'Looking at Shakespeare's Women', p. 256.
359 Donaldson, *Shakespearean Films*, pp. 129, 136.

does because he is black'. But beyond these reasons lay a real fascination with Iago himself – a part that is otherwise denied black actors – as a man who leaps all boundaries: 'a man subject to infinite aspiration, not regulated by moral codes, cultural tradition or racial solidarity, but impelled by his imagination and intellectual curiosity'.[360]

The following year in Washington DC, Hal Scott directed another *Othello* with a black Iago (André Braugher) – and with a black Emilia too (Franchelle Stewart-Dorn). The point here seemed to be a solidarity of sorts, as in Marowitz's *An Othello*. At 'Now art thou my lieutenant' and 'I am your own forever' (3.3.479–80), both Othello (Avery Brooks) and Iago raised their arms in a Black Power salute; and during the fit at 4.1, Iago (like other Iagos – see commentary) held Othello in his arms. As with the Quarshie production, reviewers were sometimes baffled by the mismatch between text and casting, but Potter reports that Brooks's message was clear enough to the pupils of a largely black school visited by the production: 'It was one black man undercutting another', said one of them.[361]

The production that took racial experiment in an unexpected direction was Jude Kelly's 'photo-negative' *Othello* in 1997, again in Washington DC, at the Shakespeare Theatre, with Patrick Stewart (of *Star Trek* fame) as Othello. Here it was not just Iago (Ron Canada) and Emila (Franchelle Stewart-Dorn again), but the entire cast that was black, except for Othello, Bianca (who is often cast black), Montano, Cypriot walk-ons and Brabantio's servants. Kelly's idea, of course, was to put the boot on the other foot: 'What's fascinating for me', she said,

> is that you have 22 African–American actors onstage who know what racism is about and one white British actor who . . . has never experienced it the way they have. So the images flip back and forth. What it all means, I think, will depend very much on the color of the person who's watching (*WP*, 12 November 1997).

For most of the run, the colour of the people watching was predominantly white. In an interview with Stewart, Miranda Johnson-Haddad asked him about the reactions of audiences and he recalled a change in the atmosphere late in the run, an increasing volatility, when non-subscribers began to come.[362] He does not specify whether African–Americans were among them in any large numbers, but in any case, for the photo-negative experiment to work fully – transmitting the same unease to whites as Ben Okri felt in 1987, for example – the whites in the audience would have needed to be in a minority.

360 Quarshie, 'Second Thoughts', p. 21.   361 Potter, *Othello*, pp. 173–4.
362 Johnson-Haddad, 'Patrick Stewart', 12.

12 Jude Kelly's 'photo-negative' production, Washington DC, 1997.

Nevertheless, as Michael Kahn, the artistic director of the theatre, pointed out, Washington DC, which has a majority black population, was 'a fruitful place for this project': 'the issue of race and racial difference is actively part of this city's dialogue, all the time, every single day . . . it concerns people deeply, not just intellectually' (*WP*, 12 November 1997). The contribution that this Othello made to that dialogue is not clearcut, especially since Kelly and Stewart chose not to reverse the language along with the casting. Thus, for example, a black Iago still uttered his racially offensive lines about 'an old black ram' to a black Brabantio, and a white Othello still admired 'that whiter skin of hers than snow' of a black Desdemona.

The immediate reaction was sometimes one of disappointment:

For a white audience to see a white actor and character scorned in vicious racist terms could have been a scathing theater experience, but the whole issue just seems confused. What is the audience supposed to think when Stewart, an actor whose mouth is like a slit in his face, is derided with the remark 'thick lips'? [several further examples follow] Racial derogations end up seeming meaningless, even harmless – surely not what Kelly intended.'

(*WP*, 18 November 1997)

In a seminar paper for the Shakespeare Association of America the following year, James Loehlin described some of his own moments of bafflement or double-take in an effort to discover what exactly the experiment did accomplish. Specific instances appear in the commentary, but along the way Loehlin makes the interesting point that Kelly's race reversals seemed at times analogous to the gender reversals in Shakespeare's comedies, and that in forcing the audience to 'monitor their own responses throughout' they achieved a similar questioning of constructed identity. In the same way Miranda Johnson-Haddad saw at work in the casting the theme that animates the play itself – 'of how we interpret what we see'.[363]

But what is striking about both Loehlin's and Johnson-Haddad's accounts is the extent to which gender politics seems to have equalled, if not to have overshadowed, racial politics, as the really explosive element in the production. Franchelle Stewart-Dorn played Emilia as 'a cowed and brutalised woman', who clearly expected to be beaten by Iago – even flinching from Cassio's greeting for fear of her husband's reaction. It was, according to Loehlin, a 'remarkable performance' which 'gave Emilia a stature as important as Othello's in the dynamics of the production'.[364] The abuse Desdemona suffers was also pointed up, particularly at 4.2, when 'Othello, increasingly enraged, flung Desdemona up against a wall of the armory (where this scene was set) . . . and seemed to rape her on stage.'[365]

In the end, the flaws in this production mattered less than the fact that it made people examine assumptions and expectations. One moment from Johnson-Haddad's account stands out. She has been explaining that Ron Canada's Iago was as eaten up with jealousy as Othello, with the result that when they were together at 3.3, 'visually, the effect was most interesting': 'this *looked* like *Othello* (a jealous black man and a white man on stage together), but the roles were reversed'.[366] The double-take, presumably, is that the white man is jealous too – so why does it look as though there is only one jealous man onstage, and he the black man?

Summings-up and trend-spotting are dangerous. Given the disquiet over *Othello* expressed by black actors and writers, the way is open for a more radical assault than Jude Kelly's on that analogy between theatrical role-playing and racially constructed identity. In their way, Puecher and Zadek have explored the issue, but perhaps someone will pick up on the idea, only half a joke, in Murray Carlin's *Not Now Sweet Desdemona*, of a black Othello in whiteface.[367] After all, part of the colonial experience is 'the divided

---

363 Johnson-Haddad, 'Shakespeare Theatre *Othello*', p. 11.
364 Loehlin, '*Othello*', np.
365 Johnson-Haddad, 'Shakespeare Theatre *Othello*', p. 10.   366 Ibid.
367 'I've got a brilliant idea!', says Carlin's Othello, 'Suppose I play Othello in *white make-up*! . . . White actors have always played Othello in blackface. Why shouldn't a black actor play him in whiteface?'

subjectivity of the black man, aptly defined by Frantz Fanon as the "Black Skin, White masks" syndrome'.[368] Othello himself, in his last speech makes that very division when he takes the malignant and turbaned Turk and smites him – that is himself – thus.

The mainstream (or rather the RSC) is now shortening the gaps between productions of *Othello*. The ten-year interval between Willard White and Ray Fearon became five years as another *Othello*, directed by Gregory Doran, opened at Stratford-upon-Avon in February 2004. Sello Maake ka Ncube was Othello, and Anthony Sher, Iago. Both are South African and both have worked together at the Market Theatre in Johannesburg. It is tempting to draw a line from Suzman and Doran into the future, and to expect that the old colonial settings used by Barton, Nunn, Mendes and Attenborough will begin to feel the draught of more recent history.

368 Singh, 'Othello's Identity', p. 291.

OTHELLO

LIST OF CHARACTERS

OTHELLO, *'the Moor', a general in the service of Venice*
BRABANTIO, *'father to Desdemona', a Venetian Senator*
CASSIO, *'an honourable lieutenant' to Othello*
IAGO, *'a villain', ensign to Othello*
RODERIGO, *'a gulled gentleman'*
DUKE OF VENICE
SENATORS *of Venice*
MONTANO, *'Governor of Cyprus'*
GENTLEMEN *'of Cyprus'*
LODOVICO, *a noble Venetian, kinsman of Brabantio*
GRATIANO, *a noble Venetian, brother of Brabantio*
SAILORS
CLOWN, *servant of Othello*
DESDEMONA, *'wife to Othello' and daughter of Brabantio*
EMILIA, *'wife to Iago'*
BIANCA, *'a courtesan', mistress of Cassio*
MESSENGER
HERALD
OFFICERS
GENTLEMEN
MUSICIANS
ATTENDANTS

OTHELLO, THE MOOR OF VENICE

There is little comment on the sets for *Othello* during the eighteenth century. A 1766 Drury Lane promptbook indicates 'the balcony promptside' [i.e. stage left] and the 'Rialto opposite prompt' [i.e. stage right]. Macready's promptbook has 'Brabantio's palace occupying part of the scene and the wings LH'. If Brabantio's window was in 'flat L', his house was part of the scenery proper, whereas the 'balcony' of 1766 was probably the box over a proscenium door.

In modern times an adaptable permanent set is usual: e.g. for Barton in 1971, Julia Trevelyan Oman designed 'a semi-circular colonnade of timber that can be screened or curtained to provide anything from the defences of Cyprus to Desdemona's bedroom' (*FT*, 13 September 1971); for Ronald Eyre, Pamela Howard gave the play 'a tang of the sea' (*S*, 29 March 1980) by having a 'granite floor backed by what looked like an Assyrian squash court which itself opens out and down to a giant wharf structure of six wooden beams' (*O*, 2 August 1979). Peter Hall's set, designed by John Bury, was minimalist: 'a rectangular acting area backed with a high square wall with a central door behind a handsome porch on top of it'. Bury 'elaborates by shining projections on to the backscreen that help locate the scenes' (*FT*, 22 March 1980). Janet Suzman's set at the Market Theatre, Johannesburg, was 'an empty space, with a simple central podium, which could become a chair or a bed . . . to afford the actors maximum prominence' (Suzman, 'Parables', p. 284). Trevor Nunn's stage was bare for Act 1, except for some rugs (*T*, 26 August 1989). Sam Mendes (1997) had a permanent set of 'heavy wooden blinds, beyond and above a deep verandah', which seemed 'to trap the characters as if in a cul de sac' (*T*, 18 September 1997), while a 'rug and some cushions and the tiled floor provide the only colour' (*The Lady*, 7 October 1997). For Jude Kelly, Robert Innes Hopkins had 'a huge round dais . . . paved with real stone, . . . oddly raked . . . somehow tilting in two directions simultaneously . . . Upstage centre stood a huge wooden door, set beneath a massive pediment' – part of a structure that included two windows (Johnson-Haddad, 'Shakespeare Theatre *Othello*', p. 9) each with its own pediment.

ACT I, SCENE I

Enter RODERIGO *and* IAGO.

Some productions have omitted this scene – possibly because, as Harold Hobson thought, Othello's entry at 1.2 is 'too late' for him to catch up with Iago in the audience's interest (Hobson, *Theatre*, p. 72). According to E. T. Mason, who wrote a minute account of Salvini's New York performances, that actor opened the play at 1.2 (Mason, p. 1). The Italian acting version, though, has 1.1 intact. Frank Benson also cut the first scene (Trewin, *Benson*, p. 137), while Oscar Asche in 1908 opened with the Duke and Senators in conference (promptbook). Other productions, so far from omitting, have enlarged Shakespeare's opening scenes. In an earlier revival, 1907, Asche opened 'with Roderigo and Iago witnessing the flight of Desdemona from her father's house'. Richard Dickins thought it 'ridiculous to suppose that even so foolish a gentleman as Roderigo . . . would stand quietly by, not even attempting to rouse Brabantio's household, sleeping within a few feet of him, while the woman he loved walked away . . .' (Dickins, *Forty Years*, pp. 143–4). In 1987, Janet Suzman also shows Iago watching Desdemona's flight (video). Oliver Parker's film (1995) develops her whole adventure: first with a night-time shot of an approaching gondola carrying her and a black man (mysteriously not Othello) who raises a white mask to his face as he passes the camera; then with shots of her hurrying through the streets, briefly glimpsed by Iago and Roderigo; and lastly with the secret marriage itself, spied on by Roderigo and Iago who simultaneously conduct their opening dialogue. In 1990, Hal Scott dispensed with everything except the bed itself, crimson-draped and centre stage. Othello and Desdemona approached it, disrobed, and to the sound of an African 'talking drum', 'they embraced and lay down across the bed, which was then drawn back into the shadows and off-stage . . .' (Johnson-Haddad, 'Shakespeare Theatre at the Folger', 477)

   Orson Welles, in his film, emphasises the fateful nature of the play by opening with a funeral procession of Desdemona and Othello, their corpses carried in a dead march against the sky-line before disappearing into blackness. Iago is then led through the crowd by his neck and hoisted up in a cage above the walls of Famagusta castle. The bars of this cage establish a visual motif which the film pursues in various ways – criss-crossing shadows, barred and leaded windows, lattices, Desdemona's netted hair, a tesselated courtyard – all of which signify 'the net that shall enmesh them all' (see Rothwell, *Screen*,

RODERIGO Tush, never tell me, I take it much unkindly
　　　　　That thou, Iago, who hast had my purse
　　　　　As if the strings were thine shouldst know of this.
IAGO 'Sblood, but you will not hear me.
　　　　　If ever I did dream of such a matter,　　　　　　　　5
　　　　　Abhor me.
RODERIGO Thou told'st me thou didst hold him in thy hate.
IAGO Despise me if I do not: three great ones of the city,
　　　　　In personal suit to make me his lieutenant,
　　　　　Off-capped to him; and by the faith of man,　　　　10
　　　　　I know my price, I am worth no worse a place.
　　　　　But he, as loving his own pride and purposes,
　　　　　Evades them with a bombast circumstance,
　　　　　Horribly stuffed with epithets of war,
　　　　　And in conclusion,　　　　　　　　　　　　　　　15
　　　　　Non-suits my mediators. For 'Certes', says he,
　　　　　'I have already chosen my officer.'

p. 81). Welles's opening dialogue, when it comes, is conducted during the actual marriage ceremony of Desdemona and Othello.

0 SD　Macready had Roderigo 'entering . . . repelling the expostulations of Iago and, as avoiding him, crosses over to L and back to R' (promptbook).

　　　　Francis Gentleman gives the eighteenth-century view of Roderigo: 'in performance he requires nothing but smartness of figure, airiness of deportment and pertness of expression. The addition of a vacant cast of features must be of advantage' (*Bell*, p. 153). In the nineteenth century, 'the low comedian was traditionally cast for Roderigo; and Roderigo consequently was presented, not as a foolish Venetian gentleman about town, but as a clown' (St John, *Correspondence*, p. xix). Arthur Pinero, in the Irving–Booth production in 1881, broke the custom by being 'quite as earnest in his way as Iago himself' (*MM*, July 1881). But the approach remained unusual, for in 1938 Stephen Murray was noted for infusing 'a touch of real pathos into this mindless ass. For the first time that I remember, I felt myself sorry for him falling into Iago's hands' (*DT*, 9 January 1938). A serio-comic Roderigo is not uncommon in modern times. Michael Gambon expressed 'an implacable, almost honourable stupidity, which helps to make the point that anything in the way of silliness, rashness, even wanton absurdity goes with true love' (*TLS*, 28 March 1980). Oliver Parker's Roderigo took the point to the verge of caricature, making him a swivel-eyed obsessive, scarcely comic at all.

17　　Richard Haines's Iago sticks a finger up his nostril in a gesture that becomes part of a repertoire of obscenities (Suzman video). Ian McKellen's Iago sarcastically imitates Willard White's deep bass voice and accent as Othello (video). Kelly's 'photo-negative' Iago, Ron Canada, 'parodied Patrick Stewart's mellifluous patrician voice' here so that he was

And what was he?
Forsooth, a great arithmetician,
One Michael Cassio, a Florentine, .   20
A fellow almost damned in a fair wife,
That never set a squadron in the field,
Nor the devision of a battle knows
More than a spinster, unless the bookish theoric,
Wherein the togèd consuls can propose   25
As masterly as he. Mere prattle without practice
Is all his soldiership. But he, sir, had the election,
And I, of whom his eyes had seen the proof
At Rhodes, at Cyprus, and on other grounds
Christian and heathen, must be lee'd and calmed   30
By debitor and creditor; this counter-caster,
He, in good time, must his lieutenant be,
And I, God bless the mark, his Moorship's ancient.
RODERIGO By heaven, I rather would have been his hangman.
IAGO Why, there's no remedy. 'Tis the curse of service;   35
Preferment goes by letter and affection,
Not by the old gradation, where each second
Stood heir to the first. Now sir, be judge yourself
Whether I in any just term am affined
To love the Moor.
RODERIGO   I would not follow him then.   40
IAGO O sir, content you.
I follow him to serve my turn upon him.

'simultaneously a black American mocking the elevated diction of a white Englishman, and white soldier resentfully mimicing a black officer who dares to take on such high-flown airs and graces' (Loehlin, *'Othello'*).

19   In Michael Attenborough's 1999 production, Richard McCabe, whose Iago spoke with biting pedantry, gave 'arithmetician' six syllables (RSC archive film).

20–1 Margaret Webster made Roderigo interrupt with 'Cassio?' thus breaking the long speech and underlining an important step in the story. She cut 21, keeping Iago's envy uncomplicatedly military (Carroll).

24b–31 These lines and most of Iago's next two speeches are cut in Bell's edition and in Kemble's – the latter edition was used by Kean and Macready. Iago's second speech was still largely cut (lines 43–59) at the end of the century: in Ellen Terry's promptbook these lines are struck through.

33   Modern Iagos often mock the words 'Moorship' and 'Moor' by pronouncing them as 'Moo-ership' and 'Moo-er' (e.g. Richard Haines, Ian McKellen and Richard McCabe).

41–66 Parker's film allows Kenneth Branagh only enough of this speech to make the narrative clear. Parker cuts everything except 41–4a, 59–61 and 66b.

Truth, identity

We cannot all be masters, nor all masters
Cannot be truly followed. You shall mark
Many a duteous and knee-crooking knave,   45
That doting on his own obsequious bondage,
Wears out his time much like his master's ass
For nought but provender, and when he's old, cashiered.
Whip me such honest knaves. Others there are
Who, trimmed in forms and visages of duty,   50
Keep yet their hearts attending on themselves,
And throwing but shows of service on their lords,
Do well thrive by them; and when they have lined their
        coats,
Do themselves homage. These fellows have some soul,
And such a one do I profess myself.   55
For, sir,
It is as sure as you are Roderigo,
Were I the Moor, I would not be Iago;
In following him, I follow but myself.
Heaven is my judge, not I for love and duty,   60
But seeming so for my peculiar end.
For when my outward action doth demonstrate
The native act and figure of my heart
In complement extern, 'tis not long after
But I will wear my heart upon my sleeve   65
For daws to peck at. I am not what I am.
RODERIGO What a full fortune does the thick-lips owe,
        If he can carry it thus!
IAGO   Call up her father:
        Rouse him, make after him, poison his delight,

---

43   'The sardonic grace with which he [Christopher Plummer] pretends resignation' here, made
     on Walter Kerr an 'indelible' impression 'to be stored away in a permanent Shakespeare
     prompt book – if only there were one' (*NYT*, 14 February 1982).

54   In Kelly's production, Canada's stress on 'soul' gave the word a twentieth-century twist,
     forcing the spectator 'into a flurry of questions – who's speaking? When do we hear the
     black actor and when the racist white soldier?' (Loehlin, '*Othello*').

60–1 Richard Haines gives the two-fingers sign with both hands and then oilily mimes washing
     them (Suzman video).

66   Bell's edition rationalises 'I am not what I am' to give: 'I am not what I seem'. Kemble was
     singular in preferring the quarto's 'doves' to 'daws', and Macready in his promptbook
     deletes it, substituting the Folio's 'daws'.

69   J. B. Booth, on 'Rouse him: make after him', emphasised '*him*' so as to indicate Othello
     (Gould, *Tragedian*, p. 83).

Proclaim him in the street, incense her kinsmen,   70
And though he in a fertile climate dwell,
Plague him with flies: though that his joy be joy,
Yet throw such chances of vexation on't
As it may lose some colour.
RODERIGO Here is her father's house; I'll call aloud.   75
IAGO Do, with like timorous accent and dire yell,
    As when, by night and negligence, the fire
    Is spied in populous cities.
RODERIGO What ho, Brabantio! Signior Brabantio, ho!
IAGO Awake! What ho, Brabantio! Thieves, thieves!   80
    Look to your house, your daughter, and your bags!
    Thieves, thieves!

BRABANTIO [*appears*] *above at a window.*

BRABANTIO What is the reason of this terrible summons?
    What is the matter there?

75ff.   Webster made Iago say 'Aye' after 'her father's house', and Roderigo said the rest of the line
        as a question. Then Iago pushed Roderigo towards Brabantio's house, and ran off
        downstage, leaving Roderigo to face the window (Carroll).

76ff.   J. B. Booth 'uttered these words without heat, with a devilish unconcern, as if pleased with
        the fancy of terror and dismay; and playing meanwhile with his sword-hilt or pulling at his
        gauntlets. He then strikes on the door of Brabantio's house and speaking through the
        key-hole, sounds the resonant alarm "What ho, Brabantio!" Yet in saying this, we felt his
        mind was "playing with some inward bait". The duplicity, the double nature, the devil in
        him, was subtly manifest' (Gould, *Tragedian*, p. 83).

80   Here Webster's Iago ran centre, jumped on a bench below the window and stamping his
        foot on each cry of 'thieves!' he then jumped off and ran into an archway, stage right, to
        hide (Carroll).

82 SD Edwin Booth remarks: 'Brabantio should be seen through the open window at his book or
        papers; this would account for his appearance instead of his servants" (*Variorum*).
            On Brabantio, Francis Gentleman comments: 'in representation he should be sustained
        by a venerable appearance and a medium degree of the pathetic' (Bell, p. 156). Edwin Booth
        felt that 'the pathetic' played so large a part in Brabantio that the role, though small, was
        rightly given to the 'First Old Man' in the company (*Variorum*). But the part often goes for
        little. Audrey Williamson noted that Alexander Knox in Guthrie's production, 'refreshingly
        stimulated that elderly bore Brabantio by unexpectedly playing for tragedy' (Williamson,
        Old Vic Drama, p. 98). Nunn's Brabantio, Clive Swift, drew much praise for uncovering a
        'tragedy-within-a-tragedy' in the old man's plight (*G*, 26 August 1989).

RODERIGO Signior, is all your family within? 85
IAGO Are your doors locked?
BRABANTIO   Why, wherefore ask you this?
IAGO Zounds, sir, you're robbed; for shame, put on your gown;
        Your heart is burst; you have lost half your soul;
        Even now, now, very now, an old black ram
        Is tupping your white ewe. Arise, arise; 90
        Awake the snorting citizens with the bell,
        Or else the devil will make a grandsire of you.
        Arise, I say!
BRABANTIO   What, have you lost your wits?
RODERIGO Most reverend signior, do you know my voice?
BRABANTIO Not I; what are you? 95
RODERIGO My name is Roderigo.
BRABANTIO   The worser welcome;
        I have charged thee not to haunt about my doors;
        In honest plainness thou hast heard me say
        My daughter is not for thee. And now in madness,
        Being full of supper and distempering draughts, 100
        Upon malicious bravery dost thou come
        To start my quiet.
RODERIGO Sir, sir, sir –
BRABANTIO   But thou must needs be sure
        My spirit and my place have in them power
        To make this bitter to thee.
RODERIGO   Patience, good sir. 105
BRABANTIO What tell'st thou me of robbing? This is Venice;
        My house is not a grange.

89–90a   In Bell's edition Gentleman italicises these lines because, 'for sake of decency', they 'should
         be omitted though usually spoken'. Kemble made the cut, and that remained the practice
         throughout the nineteenth century. De Vigny (*Le More*) translates Shakespeare's specifically
         sexual 'ram and ewe' image into the merely predatory one of a black vulture preying on a
         dove. Likewise Salvini's translation had a black wolf taking a white lamb.

90b–3a   Hazlitt described Edmund Kean's delivery of these lines as having 'the tightness of a
         drumhead, and was muffled (perhaps purposely so) into the bargain' (Hazlitt, v, p. 217).

103a   T. R. Gould, writing in 1868, asked 'why cannot some actor who represents "the silly
         gentleman" make him interrupt the old man at intervals in order to get a hearing, instead of
         repeating "Sir, sir, sir," all at once, as is invariably done upon the stage' (*Tragedian*, 84).
         Edwin Booth thought it should be spoken impatiently but without interrupting Brabantio
         (*Variorum*). Margaret Webster interspersed the 'sirs' among the preceding lines (Carroll).

RODERIGO   Most grave Brabantio,
      In simple and pure soul I come to you.
IAGO Zounds, sir; you are one of those that will not serve God if the
      devil bid you. Because we come to do you service and you think   110
      we are ruffians, you'll have your daughter covered with a Barbary
      horse, you'll have your nephews neigh to you, you'll have
      coursers for cousins, and jennets for germans.
BRABANTIO What profane wretch art thou?
IAGO I am one, sir, that comes to tell you your daughter and the Moor   115
      are now making the beast with two backs.
BRABANTIO Thou art a villain.
IAGO   You are a senator.
BRABANTIO This thou shalt answer; I know thee, Roderigo.
RODERIGO Sir, I will answer anything. But I beseech you
      If't be your pleasure and most wise consent   120
      (As partly I find it is) that your fair daughter,
      At this odd-even and dull watch o'the night,
      Transported with no worse nor better guard,
      But with a knave of common hire, a gondolier,
      To the gross clasps of a lascivious Moor: 125
      If this be known to you, and your allowance,
      We then have done you bold and saucy wrongs.

109–10   'Actors usually commit the ludicrous mistake of bringing down the emphasis plump on
          "devil" as if the highest motive for serving God were the devil's bidding! J. B. Booth said:
          "that will not serve *God*, if the devil *bid* you", giving the plain meaning that the devil's
          bidding was no argument *against* serving God' (Gould, *Tragedian*, p. 84).

111–16   Francis Gentleman puts everything after 'ruffians' down to 116 into italics to indicate his
          disapproval of what was said on the stage. Kemble's edition cuts 110 ('Because we
          come . . .') to l. 113, keeping, however, 115–16. Macready cut these last two lines as well.
          Alfred de Vigny in his translation notes that he has omitted some of Iago's expressions,
          especially those beginning 'I am one, sir, that comes to tell you . . .' adding that 'tous les
          acteurs célèbres de l'Angleterre, Kean, Kemble [Charles], Young et Macready, retranchent
          habituellement les paroles trop libres' (de Vigny, *Le More*, footnote pp. 106–7). Fechter,
          Edwin Booth and Ellen Terry all cut the lines about the Barbary horse and the beast with two
          backs. Samuel Phelps's promptbook alters 116 to 'your daughter and the Moor are e'en now
          together'. Salvini's translation has '. . . che la figlia vostra / Al Moro e in braccio' (. . . that
          your daughter is in the Moor's arms).

117b   Richard Haines blows a raspberry here and makes an obscene gesture (Suzman video).

120–36a Bell's edition shows this cut, and the cut remained throughout the nineteenth century.
          Webster also cut here, but only down to 131 (Carroll).

125   Here Ron Canada's 'photo-negative' Iago 'hooted and gambolled in imitation of a gorilla'
          (Loehlin, '*Othello*').

But if you know not this, my manners tell me,
We have your wrong rebuke. Do not believe
That from the sense of all civility   130
I thus would play and trifle with your reverence.
Your daughter, if you have not given her leave,
I say again, hath made a gross revolt,
Tying her duty, beauty, wit, and fortunes
In an extravagant and wheeling stranger   135
Of here and everywhere. Straight satisfy yourself.
If she be in her chamber or your house,
Let loose on me the justice of the state
For thus deluding you.

BRABANTIO   Strike on the tinder, ho!
Give me a taper; call up all my people.   140
This accident is not unlike my dream;   ·
Belief of it oppresses me already.
Light, I say, light!   *Exit*

IAGO   Farewell, for I must leave you.
It seems not meet nor wholesome to my place
To be produced, as if I stay I shall,   145
Against the Moor. For I do know the state,
However this may gall him with some check,
Cannot with safety cast him; for he's embarked
With such loud reason to the Cyprus wars,
Which even now stands in act, that, for their souls,   150
Another of his fathom they have none
To lead their business; in which regard,
Though I do hate him as I do hell's pains,
Yet, for necessity of present life,
I must show out a flag and sign of love,   155
Which is indeed but sign. That you shall surely find him,
Lead to the Sagittary the raisèd search,
And there will I be with him. So farewell.   *Exit*

146a–52a This cut is recorded in Bell, as it is in Webster's promptbook. Fechter cuts right down to and including 156a. Parker cuts the whole speech.

151   At 'fathom' Edwin Booth advised touching 'your head to indicate *judgement* not your breast to imply courage' (*Variorum*).

156b–8   Here Ian McKellen's Iago wrote down the address of the Sagittary in a little notebook and tore it out for Roderigo (promptbook and video).

158   In Beerbohm Tree's production Iago made his exit by gondola (promptbook).

158 SD.2   In Kelly's production, Brabantio's servants were white, cringing and servile 'in white waiter's coats' like black servants in Hollywood films, while his armed retainers were black, generally macho, 'with black leather jackets and knit caps'. These stereotypes, colour-reversed or not,

Enter Brabantio in his nightgown, and SERVANTS *with torches.*

BRABANTIO It is too true an evil. Gone she is,
        And what's to come of my despisèd time   160
        Is nought but bitterness. Now Roderigo,
        Where didst thou see her? O unhappy girl!
        With the Moor, say'st thou? Who would be a father?
        How didst thou know 'twas she? O she deceives me
        Past thought! What said she to you? Get more tapers,   165
        Raise all my kindred. Are they married, think you?
RODERIGO Truly I think they are.
BRABANTIO O heaven! How got she out? O treason of the blood!
        Fathers, from hence trust not your daughters' minds
        By what you see them act. Is there not charms   170
        By which the property of youth and maidhood
        May be abused? Have you not read, Roderigo,
        Of some such thing?
RODERIGO   Yes, sir, I have indeed.
BRABANTIO Call up my brother. O that you had had her!
        Some one way, some another. Do you know   175
        Where we may apprehend her and the Moor?
RODERIGO I think I can discover him, if you please
        To get good guard and go along with me.
BRABANTIO Pray you lead on. At every house I'll call;
        I may command at most. Get weapons, ho!   180
        And raise some special officers of night:
        On, good Roderigo; I'll deserve your pains.

                                                    Exeunt

---

        forced 'each audience member . . . back on his or her own uncomfortable library of racial
        associations . . . to try to unpack the meaning of the scene' (Loehlin, *'Othello'*).
168   Bell records 'my blood' for 'the blood', making Brabantio's outrage purely parental, and
        losing Shakespeare's suggestion of animal passion. Edwin Booth similarly took the word to
        mean only kinship, for he says that the line should echo Shylock's 'my own flesh and blood
        to rebel!' (*Variorum*).
176ff Beerbohm Tree brought on a gondola here, with a 'super' in it to paddle Brabantio and
        Roderigo off (promptbook).

ACT I, SCENE 2

Enter OTHELLO, IAGO *and* ATTENDANTS *with torches.*

The 1766 promptbook indicates that the 'French Town' scene should be 'slipped into the first groove' for the Sagittary. But there is usually no change of set here. Macready merely indicated 'the lamps' should be a little darkened (promptbook). Webster had the lights change from a greenish to a reddish glow (promptbook).

0 SD   Othello has little to say during his first moments onstage, but some actors have made this as eloquent as any other moment in the play. Winter said that 'at the beginning', J. E. McCullough 'did not, even remotely, suggest a man predestined to a tragic fate, and in that particular his Othello was practically unique . . . He was . . . absolutely happy . . . The calm glance of surprise at Iago as that miscreant uttered his lie . . . the composure of "'Tis better as it is", the modesty of "Let him do his spite" . . . were perfectly accordant with the equanimity and sweet gravity of the character, and finely effective' (Winter, *Shakespeare*, pp. 283–4). Of Salvini, Emma Lazarus wrote: 'From the moment of his entrance upon the scene, with the effect of his bronzed and turbaned face and towering figure, heightened by the long white burnous which falls in ample folds to his feet, in their curving Moorish shoes, the superb picturesqueness of his appearance, and the dignity of his gestures and movements fully bear out the magniloquence which Shakespeare places in his mouth' (*C*, November 1881).

Fechter's entrance was calculatedly unheroic. His stage direction reads 'Enter Othello leaning on Iago', and Lewes commented: 'When he appears leaning on the shoulder of Iago (the great general and his ensign!) . . . he is certainly *natural* – but according to whose nature?' (Lewes, *Actors*, p. 148). Ira Aldridge impressed Theophile Gautier: 'his eyes half closed as though dazzled by an Afric sun, his manner orientally carefree with that Negroid grace of movement which no European can imitate' (quoted by Marshall and Stock, *Ira Aldridge*, p. 229). Olivier did attempt to imitate it: 'He came on smelling a rose, laughing softly with a private delight, barefooted, ankleted, black . . . He sauntered downstage, with a loose, bare-heeled roll of the buttocks; came to rest feet splayed apart, hip lounging outward' (Ronald Bryden, *NS*, 1 May 1964). Ben Kingsley was almost Ghandi-like: 'On to a stage of midnight black, with everyone on it wearing black, steps a strange aloof figure in a dazzling white robe. A grey-bearded ancient, mysteriously smiling, he might be some grave Indian mystic on a visit to an unknown planet' (*DT*, 26 September 1985). Television perhaps demands the naturalism that Lewes so detested in Fechter. Anthony Hopkins in Jonathan

IAGO   Though in the trade of war I have slain men,
      Yet do I hold it very stuff o'the conscience
      To do no contrived murder. I lack iniquity
      Sometimes to do me service. Nine or ten times
      I had thought to have yerked him here, under the ribs.   5
OTHELLO   'Tis better as it is.
IAGO   Nay, but he prated,
      And spoke such scurvy and provoking terms
      Against your honour,
      That, with the little godliness I have,
      I did full hard forbear him. But I pray, sir,   10
      Are you fast married? For be sure of this,
      That the magnifico is much beloved,
      And hath in his effect a voice potential
      As double as the duke's. He will divorce you,
      Or put upon you what restraint and grievance   15
      The law, with all his might to enforce it on,
      Will give him cable.
OTHELLO   Let him do his spite;
      My services which I have done the signiory
      Shall out-tongue his complaints. 'Tis yet to know –

Miller's BBC production comes on chummily doing up Iago's collar. In Suzman's video, John Kani enters smelling a red rose in a deliberate evocation of Olivier. Perhaps it was here in Kelly's production that a 'smiling Desdemona [Patrice Johnson] leaned out of the window . . . and scattered rose petals on the head of Othello, who stood below laughing delightedly and lifting up his hands as he twirled slowly and luxuriously in the falling petals' (Johnson-Haddad, 'Shakespeare Theatre *Othello*', p. 9).

2–3   Bell's edition records 'base and infamous' for 'stuff o' the conscience', and 'a contrived' for 'no contrived'.

6   Fechter's stage direction is: 'Goes to the house and opens the door with a golden key.' Olivier playfully brushes Iago's face with his rose (film). Perhaps it was here that David Harewood, Mendes's Othello, slapped Iago playfully on the chest – at which Simon Russell Beale's Iago gave 'a second's pause before he [could] overcome his private distaste and allow a ghastly fake smile to break over his features' (*I*, 18 September 1997).

11   At 'Are you fast married?' Salvini 'smiles, showing well-assured confidence in the strength and safety of his position' (Mason, p. 2). Olivier too gives a lazy laugh here (film); and Suzman's camera closes in on John Kani's blissful smile (video).

12–14a   Webster made Othello show anger at the suggestion of Brabantio's influence, and she cut the strictly unnecessary 13–14a (Carroll).

17b   Fechter spoke this 'on the threshold of the open door' (his stage direction). Robeson crossed downstage especially for it, making it a public declaration (Carroll).

Which, when I know that boasting is an honour, 20
I shall provulgate – I fetch my life and being
From men of royal siege, and my demerits
May speak unbonneted to as proud a fortune
As this that I have reached. For know, Iago,
But that I love the gentle Desdemona, 25
I would not my unhousèd free condition
Put into circumscription and confine
For the sea's worth. But look what lights come yond!
IAGO Those are the raisèd father and his friends;
You were best go in.
OTHELLO   Not I; I must be found. 30
My parts, my title, and my perfect soul
Shall manifest me rightly. Is it they?
IAGO By Janus, I think no.

Enter CASSIO, *with* OFFICERS *and torches.*

30b Here, by way of emphasising his desire to be 'found', Fechter shut the door and took out the
key (his stage direction). G. H. Lewes commented: 'When Fechter takes out his door-key to
let himself into his house, and on coming back relocks the door and pockets the key, the
intention is, doubtless, to give an air of reality; the *effect* is to make us forget the "noble
Moor", and to think of a sepoy' (Lewes, *Actors*, pp. 147–8).

33 Webster altered 'no' to 'so' – simpler, and the Janus allusion might not have been picked up
anyway (Carroll).

33SD Cassio is described by Gentleman as 'a very amiable, but except his drunken scene which
we esteem disgraceful to tragedy, a very uninteresting personage' (Gentleman, *Censor*,
p. 153). Cassio is rarely mentioned in the eighteenth and nineteenth centuries. Charles
Kemble at the beginning of the nineteenth century and William Terris at the end of it both
distinguished themselves by not caricaturing drunkenness and – at least in Kemble's case –
conveying real grief afterwards. Modern Cassios sometimes touch tragedy at that moment
(see notes at 2.3). In general, Cassio's difficulty is to be convincing both as Othello's
second-in-command and as a lady's man. William Terris, Irving's Cassio in 1881, was said to
excel because he was 'equally at home in camp or court' (*MM*, July 1881). Leo Genn in
Sofaer's production was merely 'dashing', and 'absurdly young and irresponsible to be in so
much authority' (*Punch*, 30 January 1935). David Calder in Barton's production went too far
the other way: a 'shouting bully', fitter for the command of a 'down-county regiment than
adorning the Staff' (*FT*, 13 September 1971). Janet Suzman's Cassio was a handsome blond
wonderboy in green velvet (video). Kelly's production, which emphasised the insensitivity
to women of men in a military environment, included Cassio in this: 'he was caddish with
Bianca' and 'demanding and tactless with Desdemona' (Loehlin, 'Othello').

OTHELLO The servants of the duke and my lieutenant!
          The goodness of the night upon you, friends.   35
          What is the news?
CASSIO   The duke does greet you, general,
          And he requires your haste-post-haste appearance
          Even on the instant.
OTHELLO   What is the matter, think you?
CASSIO   Something from Cyprus, as I may divine.
          It is a business of some heat. The galleys   40
          Have sent a dozen sequent messengers
          This very night at one another's heels;
          And many of the consuls, raised and met,
          Are at the duke's already. You have been hotly called for,
          When, being not at your lodging to be found,   45
          The senate hath sent about three several quests
          To search you out.
OTHELLO   'Tis well I am found by you.
          I will but spend a word here in the house,
          And go with you.   *[Exit]*
CASSIO   Ancient, what makes he here?
IAGO Faith, he tonight hath boarded a land carrack;   50
          If it prove lawful prize, he's made for ever.
CASSIO I do not understand.
IAGO   He's married.
CASSIO   To who?

          [Enter Othello.]

IAGO Marry, to – Come, captain, will you go?
OTHELLO   Have with you.
CASSIO Here comes another troop to seek for you.

    Enter BRABANTIO, RODERIGO *and* OFFICERS *with lights and*
                     weapons.

IAGO It is Brabantio; general, be advised,   55
          He comes to bad intent.
OTHELLO   Holla, stand there!
RODERIGO Signior, it is the Moor.
BRABANTIO   Down with him, thief!

44 Here Olivier laughs delightedly and makes his departure humming (film).
56b–61 Janet Suzman cut this episode.

IAGO You, Roderigo? Come, sir, I am for you.

OTHELLO Keep up your bright swords, for the dew will rust them.

        Good signior, you shall more command with years   60

        Than with your weapons.

BRABANTIO O thou foul thief! Where hast thou stowed my daughter?

        Damned as thou art, thou hast enchanted her,

        For I'll refer me to all things of sense,

        If she in chains of magic were not bound,   65

        Whether a maid so tender, fair, and happy,

        So opposite to marriage that she shunned

        The wealthy curlèd darlings of our nation,

        Would ever have, t'incur a general mock,

        Run from her guardage to the sooty bosom   70

        Of such a thing as thou – to fear, not to delight.

        Judge me the world, if 'tis not gross in sense

58   Edwin Booth comments that Iago singles out Roderigo so as to protect him, or rather his purse: 'make the audience understand this by your manner of singling him out – a look will do it' (*Variorum*).

59   When Kean spoke this line, wrote Keats, 'we feel that his throat had commanded where swords were as thick as reeds. From eternal risk, he speaks as though his body were unassailable' (*Champion*, 21 December 1817). Salvini said the first part of the sentence 'in a loud tone of command . . . then . . . after a slight pause, and with a smile, "for the dew will rust them"' (Mason, p. 3). Robeson, in 1930, 'said the line with a casualness which amounted almost to meaninglessness' (Agate, *Chronicles*, p. 286). Olivier delivered it 'almost affably with a trace of sarcastic condescension in the second half of the line' (Tynan, *National Theatre Production*, p. 6). In Barton's production Othello prevailed by firing a gun – a mistake, thought Robert Cushman (*P and P*, October 1971). Nunn's Willard White spoke the line in a 'low boom', and 'the sense is that . . . this Othello has the power to put out a battle before it begins' (*Literary Review*, November 1989).

60–1   Edwin Booth: 'Be very respectful to Brabantio; resent his abuse merely with a look of momentary anger' (*Variorum*).

64–76   Cut by Fechter, and in Ellen Terry's promptbook. Bell's edition records 72–6 as cut, and Kemble follows suit.

68   Here Clive Swift in Nunn's production pointed up Othello's strangeness by stressing the pronoun 'our' (video).

70ff.   John Kani's Othello suffers the insult quietly, merely closing his eyes momentarily. The rest of Brabantio's speech from 71b is cut (video). Jude Kelly's Brabantio, Darrell Carey, held up his hand next to Othello's 'highlighting the visual/verbal disjunction' (Loehlin, '*Othello*').

That thou hast practised on her with foul charms,
Abused her delicate youth with drugs or minerals
That weakens motion. I'll have't disputed on;   75
'Tis probable and palpable to thinking.
I therefore apprehend and do attach thee
For an abuser of the world, a practiser
Of arts inhibited and out of warrant.
Lay hold upon him. If he do resist,   80
Subdue him at his peril.
OTHELLO   Hold your hands,
Both you of my inclining and the rest.
Were it my cue to fight, I should have known it
Without a prompter. Where will you that I go
To answer this your charge?
BRABANTIO   To prison, till fit time   85
Of law and course of direct session
Call thee to answer.
OTHELLO   What if I do obey?
How may the duke be therewith satisfied,
Whose messengers are here about my side
Upon some present business of the state   90
To bring me to him?
OFFICER   'Tis true, most worthy signior;
The duke's in council, and your noble self

73   Here Salvini 'smiles disdainfully and turns towards Iago whose hand he clasps' (Mason, p. 4).

77   Webster turned the old-fashioned 'attach' into 'attack' (Carroll).

78–9 Edwin Booth: 'Othello and Cassio exchange smiles of pity for the old man's credulity' (*Variorum*).

81b Edwin Booth: 'Now Othello's friends draw. Othello stands between the two parties with sheathed scimitar held up; its crescent shape lends a little Oriental atmosphere to the picture. 'Tis harmless' (*Variorum*). Salvini, centre stage, 'restrains the opposing parties by an imperious gesture, extending his arms and looking at first one, then the other' (Mason, p. 5). Anthony Hopkins's television Othello (Jonathan Miller, BBC) puts the sword blades down with the touch of a finger.

83–4 On these lines Kean 'always brought down the house from the natural, yet pointed expression, conversational, yet full of meaning, with which he gave it; it conveyed a wonderful mixture of sarcasm and courtesy' (Vandenhoff, *Notebook*, p. 22). 'Mr Forrest, after indulging in a fencer's attitude, turned round with a pointed sneer to Cassio and Iago – "Were it my cue – to *fight*! – I *should* have *known* it – without – a prompter!"' (Forster, *Essays*, p. 18).

85   'To prison': here Olivier smiles and shakes his head as if to say 'you'd be lucky' (film).

I am sure is sent for.
BRABANTIO   How? The duke in council?
In this time of the night? Bring him away;
Mine's not an idle cause. The duke himself,   95
Or any of my brothers of the state,
Cannot but feel this wrong as 'twere their own;
For if such actions may have passage free,
Bondslaves and pagans shall our statesmen be.

Exeunt

93b–9   In Salvini's production, Iago 'starts forward' as Brabantio's party exits 'as if to attack them,
but is restrained by Othello, who lays his hand upon Iago's arm, and then motions him and
the rest to follow him to the council chamber' (Mason, p. 5). In Webster's promptbook the
stage directions indicate a bustle of departure. Brabantio arrives downstage for the last line,
makes a false exit, comes back for Roderigo who has been motioned by Iago to follow
Brabantio. After the general departure there is a blackout and quick curtain.

ACT I, SCENE 3

Enter DUKE *and* SENATORS, *set at a table with lights, and*
ATTENDANTS.

DUKE There is no composition in these news
　　　　That gives them credit.
I SENATOR　　　　　　　　　　Indeed they are disproportioned.
　　　　My letters say a hundred and seven galleys.

This is the first opportunity in the play for light and colour and splendour. The 1766
promptbook shows that the 'French Town' shutters were drawn back to reveal the Senate
House. Pollock's toy theatre sets and figures, based on early nineteenth-century stage
tradition, show the Duke on a raised 'throne' at the back with the Senators flanking him – all
wearing doublet and hose, with plumes in their hats. In 1837 Macready set them in the Hall
of the Doges surrounded by paintings by Titian and Tintoretto – added to which there was
'that most picturesque little touch in the centre, where sits the secretary . . . with his
blue-gowned back to the audience, and his face intent on the enormous book before him'
(*Examiner*, 22 October 1837). However, Macready's promptbook has a diagram showing
this arrangement crossed out, and another arrangement with the Council of Ten along the
side substituted. Samuel Phelps's promptbook has the same change. This, according to
Edwin Booth, was done so that 'the characters need not turn their backs on the audience
when addresssing the Duke' (*Variorum*). Rossi and Novelli used the old arrangement, and
were criticised for being either unnatural or inaudible. Beerbohm Tree's 'court house blazes
with the pomp and circumstance of the richest state in the world' (*DT*, 10 April 1912). Robert
Edmund Jones, Webster's designer, had officers in black and gold and red-robed Senators
wearing fur-trimmed hats (Carroll).

　　　Productions set in more modern times are less gaudy. Trevor Nunn's Senators were a
high-collared, buttoned-up war cabinet, their table littered with maps and documents,
brandy and cigars (promptbook and video); Michael Attenborough also had everyone in
dark suits and ties. A large globe was placed downstage centre (RSC archive film); Sam
Mendes's production, set in the 1930s or 40s, had pinstriped officials who (like Nunn's)
'cradle brandy glasses, puff on cigars and pore over maps. The late-night atmosphere is one
of disciplined urgency' (*IoS*, 21 September 1997).

1–47　If the quarto reflects theatre practice, this opening section of 1.3 has always offered an
opportunity for cutting. But the quarto's dropping of the unexplained Signior Angelo, at 16,

DUKE And mine, a hundred and forty.
2 SENATOR   And mine, two hundred;
　　　But though they jump not on a just accompt –   5
　　　As in these cases where the aim reports
　　　'Tis oft with difference – yet do they all confirm
　　　A Turkish fleet, and bearing up to Cyprus.
DUKE Nay, it is possible enough to judgement:
　　　I do not so secure me in the error,   10
　　　But the main article I do approve
　　　In fearful sense.
SAILOR (*Within*)   What ho! What ho! What ho!
OFFICER A messenger from the galleys.

                    Enter a SAILOR.

DUKE   Now, what's the business?
SAILOR The Turkish preparation makes for Rhodes;
　　　So was I bid report here to the state   15
　　　By Signior Angelo.
DUKE How say you by this change?
1 SENATOR   This cannot be,
　　　By no assay of reason. 'Tis a pageant
　　　To keep us in false gaze. When we consider
　　　The importancy of Cyprus to the Turk,   20
　　　And let ourselves again but understand
　　　That as it more concerns the Turk than Rhodes,
　　　So may he with more facile question bear it,
　　　For that it stands not in such warlike brace,
　　　But altogether lacks the abilities   25
　　　That Rhodes is dressed in. If we make thought of this,
　　　We must not think the Turk is so unskilful
　　　To leave that latest which concerns him first,
　　　Neglecting an attempt of ease and gain
　　　To wake and wage a danger profitless.   30

and the unnecessary 24–30, is modest compared with later cuts. Bell's edition, followed by
Kemble, cuts 19–31, but Fechter omitted 9–12, 14–32 and 44–6. Irving cut everything except
the Duke's first line and the Messenger's news starting at 33. In Edwin Booth's edition ('as
produced by Edwin Booth', 1869) the dialogue is distributed among the Senators, the Duke
not being present. Then presumably the front scene opened to 'discover' the Duke and
other Senators in the council chamber. This arrangement was used by Webster, the first part
of the scene being played in front of a 'traveller' curtain, which opened to reveal the Senate
chamber (Carroll).

DUKE Nay, in all confidence he's not for Rhodes.
OFFICER Here is more news.

Enter a MESSENGER.

MESSENGER The Ottomites, reverend and gracious,
  Steering with due course toward the isle of Rhodes
  Have there injointed with an after fleet.   35
1 SENATOR Ay, so I thought. How many, as you guess?
MESSENGER Of thirty sail, and now they do restem
  Their backward course, bearing with frank appearance
  Their purposes toward Cyprus. Signior Montano,
  Your trusty and most valiant servitor,   40
  With his free duty recommends you thus,
  And prays you to believe him.
DUKE 'Tis certain then for Cyprus.
  Marcus Luccicos, is not he in town?
1 SENATOR He's now in Florence.
DUKE   Write from us to him   45
  Post-post-haste dispatch.
1 SENATOR Here comes Brabantio and the valiant Moor.

Enter BRABANTIO, OTHELLO, CASSIO, IAGO, RODERIGO *and*
      OFFICERS.

DUKE Valiant Othello we must straight employ you
  Against the general enemy Ottoman.
  [*To Brabantio*] I did not see you: welcome, gentle
   signior;   50
  We lacked your counsel and your help tonight.
BRABANTIO So did I yours. Good your grace, pardon me:
  Neither my place nor aught I heard of business

33–9 In Mendes's production 'a desk officer puts down the phone and relays the news that the
  Turkish fleet is heading from Rhodes to Cyprus' (*IoS*, 21 September 1997).
47 Janet Suzman's First Senator used Iago's sarcastic pronunciation of 'Moo-er' for 'Moor'
  (video).
47 SD Edwin Booth's entrance here resembled his first entrance as Hamlet: 'no smile mars his
  solemnity, and walking slowly down the stage the well-known *pose* is taken, one arm across
  the breast, and the hand of the other gracefully supporting the resting chin (Hamlet in
  Othello) absorbing all the gloom into himself ' (*New York Evening Mail*, 24 April 1869).
  Oscar Asche was oriental, Charles Graves remembered, 'salaaming gravely almost to the
  ground' (*Scotsman*, 4 April 1959). David Harewood, in Mendes's production, 'enters
  wearing a dinner jacket, his black tie hanging loose. He might be a sporting hero, dropping
  in after an awards dinner' (*IoS*, 21 September 1997).

Hath raised me from my bed, nor doth the general care
Take hold on me; for my particular grief   55
Is of so flood-gate and o'erbearing nature
That it engluts and swallows other sorrows
And yet is still itself.
DUKE   Why, what's the matter?
BRABANTIO My daughter! O, my daughter!
SENATORS   Dead?
BRABANTIO   Ay, to me.
She is abused, stol'n from me, and corrupted   60
By spells and medicines bought of mountebanks;
For nature so preposterously to err,
Being not deficient, blind, or lame of sense,
Sans witchcraft could not.
DUKE Whoe'er he be that in this foul proceeding   65
Hath thus beguiled your daughter of herself,
And you of her, the bloody book of law
You shall yourself read in the bitter letter
After your own sense, yea, though our proper son
Stood in your action.
BRABANTIO   Humbly I thank your grace.   70
Here is the man: this Moor, whom now it seems

60ff.   At Brabantio's accusations of witchcraft Edwin Booth's Othello exchanged smiles with
        Cassio, as he had at 1.2.78. Salvini 'sighs and turns slightly . . . wearied and disgusted. The
        action is very slight, not emphasised' (Mason, p. 7). In Webster's production the Senators
        began 'to ad lib murmurs' during Brabantio's speech, beginning slowly and rising to a
        crescendo (Carroll). 'When being accused by Brabantio [Olivier] strikes a pose of heroic
        nonchalance, his left hand flamboyantly languishing on the hilt of his sword. Occasionally
        he crosses himself, chiefly it would seem, because he does the movement so beautifully'
        (*O*, 26 April 1964).

71ff.   Fechter built up the lead-in to Othello's first long address to the Senate: 'While Brabantio
        complains to the Duke, he looks like a man conscious of a good reply in store . . . He begins
        so instantly upon the Duke's question, "What in your own part can you say to this?" that
        Brabantio's interpolation, "Nothing, but this is so", comes as an interruption . . . he utters
        the "no more" [line 81] as one violently repelling a foul imputation . . . with fierce gesture of
        advance towards the table. Upon this, senators rise, as if they almost expected an attack,
        and Othello gives the next eight or nine lines, "Rude am I in my speech" etc., as a special
        apology called for by that show of violence . . . The device is new and ingenious, it gives a
        lively break to the speech and carries it to the end in true colloquial fashion' (Morley,
        Journal, pp. 227–8). Fechter's innovation shocked those who had always expected a formal
        address here. Also it made an 'unseemly scene . . . which reflects scandal equally upon
        Brabantio and Othello' (Ottley, p. 16). Salvini also treated Brabantio's 'Nothing, but this is

Your special mandate for the state affairs
Hath hither brought.
ALL   We are very sorry for't.
DUKE [*To Othello*] What in your own part can you say to this?
BRABANTIO Nothing, but this is so.   75
OTHELLO Most potent, grave, and reverend signiors,
My very noble and approved good masters,
That I have tane away this old man's daughter,
It is most true; true I have married her;
The very head and front of my offending   80
Hath this extent, no more. Rude am I in my speech
And little blessed with the soft phrase of peace,
For since these arms of mine had seven years' pith
Till now some nine moons wasted, they have used
Their dearest action in the tented field;   85
And little of this great world can I speak
More than pertains to feats of broil and battle;
And therefore little shall I grace my cause

so' as an interruption, but he 'restrains himself courteously, without glancing towards
Brabantio, and awaits his opportunity to speak' (Mason, p. 8). Olivier, during these
passages, 'hooded his eyes in a pouting ebony mask: an old chief listening watchfully in
tribal conclave' (*NS*, 1 May 1964). When Mendes's Duke discovered that it's Othello that
Brabantio is complaining about, the audience gave 'a quick appreciative laugh. The sort that
says: nice twist' (*IoS*, 21 September 1997).

76–94   According to Ottley, Kean was 'calm, impressive, dignified, modest all at once – his voice
flowing in musical cadence from end to end' (p. 16). Salvini spoke 'Rude am I in my speech'
'with a slight smile . . . using the finest and most musical tones of his voice . . . a slight pause
between the several phrases, "What things [sic], what charms, what conjuration"; smiling
good-naturedly; expressing lofty indifference and amused contempt in regard to Brabantio's
accusations' (Mason, p. 9). When Olivier named the Senators 'my masters', 'it was proudly
edged: he had been a slave, their inquisition recalled his slavery, he reminded them in turn
of his service and generalship' (*NS*, 1 May 1964). Where Othello is acted by a black actor,
the aggression offered earlier by some Othellos (described above) is sometimes reversed.
In Webster's production, a Senator made a movement towards Robeson during this speech,
and had to be restrained. Angry murmuring became so loud that Lodovico had to cry 'Let
him speak' (Carroll). Similarly, in Suzman's production, there is a scandalised tut-tutting at
'true I have married her', and one Senator angrily cried out 'Against all rules of nature'
(video). Michael Attenborough had one of the Senators stand up suddenly, as though in
protest (RSC archive film).

83–7   Omitted from the Smock Alley text.

In speaking for myself. Yet, by your gracious patience,
I will a round unvarnished tale deliver   90
Of my whole course of love: what drugs, what charms,
What conjuration and what mighty magic –
For such proceedings I am charged withal –
I won his daughter.
BRABANTIO   A maiden never bold;
Of spirit so still and quiet that her motion   95
Blushed at herself; and she, in spite of nature,
Of years, of country, credit, everything,
To fall in love with what she feared to look on?
It is a judgement maimed and most imperfect
That will confess perfection so could err   100
Against all rules of nature, and must be driven
To find out practices of cunning hell
Why this should be. I therefore vouch again
That with some mixtures powerful o'er the blood
Or with some dram conjured to this effect   105
He wrought upon her.
DUKE   To vouch this is no proof
Without more wider and more overt test
Than these thin habits and poor likelihoods
Of modern seeming do prefer against him.
I SENATOR But, Othello, speak: 110
Did you by indirect and forcèd courses
Subdue and poison this young maid's affections?
Or came it by request and such fair question
As soul to soul affordeth?
OTHELLO   I do beseech you
Send for the lady to the Sagittary   115
And let her speak of me before her father.
If you do find me foul in her report,
The trust, the office I do hold of you,
Not only take away, but let your sentence
Even fall upon my life.
DUKE   Fetch Desdemona hither.   120
OTHELLO Ancient, conduct them: you best know the place.
                    [*Exit Iago with two or three Attendants*]
And till she come, as truly as to heaven
I do confess the vices of my blood,

99–103a The '1755' edition cuts, and the cut remains in Bell's edition.
121 SD   In Phelps's promptbook Iago beckons to Roderigo 'who follows him out on tiptoe'.

So justly to your grave ears I'll present
How I did thrive in this fair lady's love,   125
And she in mine.
DUKE   Say it, Othello.
OTHELLO Her father loved me, oft invited me,

127-69   Of the two speeches to the Senate this one is often regarded as Othello's first great test, and
actors have been narrowly observed in it. Garrick was urged by Henry Aston, or 'a friend', to
be more modest, to defer more to his judges: Othello 'was certainly the hero of the drama,
[but] that part of his character was for a while to be suspended . . . [Garrick's] deportment
would very well have become Othello had he been under trial as a captive at some foreign
tribunal' (Boaden, *Correspondence*, 1, p. 30). Samuel Foote compared old Quin to young
Spranger Barry: Quin's 'tale, from want of variety, is not quite so entertaining to us as it was
to Desdemona; and the young one's . . . from diffidence, [was] rather too flat and insipid'
(Foote, *Treatise*, pp. 25–6). But John Bernard reported that on one occasion 'when Barry
had finished his address . . . three rounds of applause spoke the feelings of the house; and
when the Duke . . . observed "I think this tale would win my daughter too", the audience
sympathized so truly . . . that their hands by spontaneous effect, came again together'
(Bernard, *Retrospections*, 1, p. 18). Kemble 'though most critically correct in his address to
the Senate . . . was more anxious to do justice to the text of his author than the feelings of
Othello' (*Public Advertiser*, 29 October 1787).

Lewes thought Kean 'very bad' here. 'This long simple narrative was the kind of speech
he could not manage at all. He gabbled over it, impatient to arrive at the phrase "And this is
all the witchcraft I have used [sic]. Here comes the lady; let her witness it." His delivery of
this "point" always startled the audience into applause by its incisive tone and abrupt
transition' (Lewes, *Actors*, pp. 5–6).

Like the earlier speech, something oratorical was expected here. When Fechter made it
'simply an honest apology for a natural action colloquially delivered' (*Daily News*, 24
October 1861), Ottley noted that it 'failed to bring down a hand'. And yet, at 'Her father
loved me' he gave 'an amount of emotion and emphasis on the word "loved" which
savoured of rhodomontade, and which very properly called for a motion of dissent from
Brabantio' (Ottley, pp. 14, 17). Edwin Booth treated the speech 'like a well-delivered appeal
of an elderly schoolboy begging off a flogging' (*New York Herald*, 25 April 1869).

Mason describes Salvini in New York gesturing at 'cannibals' 'as if repelling maneaters',
and at the men with misplaced heads, he touched his head and then his breast. He even
imitated Desdemona's voice at ''twas strange, 'twas passing strange' (Mason, pp. 12–13). But
an account in the *Gazette de France* sets Salvini's stillness against Rossi's pantomime:
'Salvini advances quietly, nobly . . . He pleads [his case] without moving a step . . . M.
Rossi . . . played this scene in exactly the opposite manner; . . . his gestures added the force
of pantomime to his words; . . . he walked to and fro; . . . his Othello deemed it

> Still questioned me the story of my life
> From year to year – the battles, sieges, fortunes
> That I have passed.   130
> I ran it through, even from my boyish days

necessary at moments to summon . . . a smile, irony, familiarity, affected simplicity. Othello as enacted by Rossi conquered as much by his cleverness as by his heart. Othello as enacted by Salvini disdains these subtleties; he does not even think of such fears' (quoted by Emma Lazarus, *C*, November 1881).

This was Robeson's best moment, thought many critics: 'Here the intelligent actor came to the aid of the cultured musician' (*Christian Science Monitor*, 11 August 1943). The story of the Anthropophagi was obviously treated as a joke, for Webster's promptbook directs all the Senators except Brabantio to laugh outright after 'shoulders'.

Olivier was, like Salvini, 'still and central', but he combined self-confident pride with some of Rossi's pointedness: his first line was directed at Brabantio 'in tones of wondering rebuke'. He uttered 'Anthropophagi' 'by way of kindly parenthetical explanation, as if to say: "that, in case you didn't know, is the scholarly term for these creatures". He also manages to convey his sardonic awareness that that is just the kind of story that Europeans would expect Africans to tell.' At 'Upon this hint I spake' he gave 'a smiling shrug . . . dwelling on "hint" as a jocular understatement and forcing the senators to share his pleasure'. The word 'witchcraft' was isolated as though it had inverted commas. He spoke it 'deliberately making the second vowel harsh and African, and pointedly eyeing Brabantio . . . he is at once the Duke's servant and the white man's master' (Tynan, *National Theatre Production*, p. 6). Ronald Bryden described him here as 'easy with sexual confidence', which gave an extra dimension to Iago's envy: 'a small white man's sexual jealousy of the black, a jealousy sliding into ambiguous fascination' (*NS*, 1 May 1964).

James Earl Jones, in a New York production of the same year, was generally much less elaborate, but 'there is a touching openness in his explanation . . . It is easy to understand, in his smiling, guileless adoration, how complete is his contentment, and how vulnerable it can become' (*NYT*, 15 July 1964). In Jonathan Miller's BBC television production Hopkins speaks the speech modestly, and engagingly, *piano pianissimo*. All the figures are very still, heads only moving, with the odd hand gesture. Oliver Parker illustrates Othello's speech in a flashback here. We see him walking with Brabantio in his garden, while Desdemona tries to catch their conversation. We see her caressing the battle scars on Othello's shaved head, and Othello wiping her tears away with the strawberry-embroidered handkerchief. Patrick Stewart gave the line about being sold to slavery 'with pained restraint' as though not wishing to dwell on it. 'Gratiano, however, threw up his hands in exasperation and turned away, as if to say, "Oh, . . . he's playing the race card."' At the cannibals, Stewart 'sidled up very close to the Duke, who leaned rigidly away from him . . . in a stiff-upper-lip parody of colonial horror at savage ways' (Loehlin, '*Othello*').

To the very moment that he bade me tell it;
Wherein I spake of most disastrous chances,
Of moving accidents by flood and field,
Of hair-breadth scapes i'th'imminent deadly breach,   135
Of being taken by the insolent foe
And sold to slavery; of my redemption thence,
And with it all my travels' history:
Wherein of antres vast and deserts idle,
Rough quarries, rocks, and hills whose heads touch
        heaven,   140
It was my hint to speak – such was the process:
And of the cannibals that each other eat,
The Anthropophagi, and men whose heads
Do grow beneath their shoulders. This to hear
Would Desdemona seriously incline;   145

138–44 In spite of its fame this speech described above has often been shortened and even altered. An acting edition of 1770 records six new lines in place of 138–44: 'Of battles bravely, hardly fought; of victories / For which the conqueror mourned, so many fall: / Sometimes I told the story of a siege / Wherein I had to combat plagues and famine; / Soldiers unpaid; fearful to fight, / Yet bold in dangerous mutiny.' George Winchester Stone thinks that David Ross, an Othello at Covent Garden, was responsible for these lines ('Garrick and *Othello*', PQ, 45, January 1966, pp. 304–20). Bell's 1773 edition includes them, so they were obviously in use at both houses. Kemble restored the original lines, but the Shakespearean passage was obviously disliked, for 'D-G', the editor of Cumberland's 1829 acting edition, puts it in inverted commas with a note to say that Edmund Kean generally omitted it. William Oxberry's note in his acting edition of 1819 explains why: the passage, he says, is 'sometimes omitted, and we think discreetly . . . [it] justifies Iago's subsequent sneers at the Moor, who here, in his courtship of Desdemona was "bragging and telling her fantastical lies"'. However, the eighteenth-century substitution was never restored. William B. Wood, a Philadelphian who saw Edmund Kean, showed him the lines, which, he says, he 'distinctly' remembered finding 'in an old Covent Garden promptbook of our early library, not in the printed text, but interwritten upon a blank leaf. Kean had never seen them before.' The only puzzle is that Wood speaks of them as ocurring just 'after' 'men whose heads / Do grow beneath their shoulders' not instead of that passage (Wood, *Recollections*, p. 265). Fechter cut the whole passage from 'antres vast' to the Anthropophagi, and also the line about 'hair-breadth scapes'. The latter is an awkward mouthful, and perhaps he couldn't trust his French accent with it. Irving cut the cannibals and the men with heads below their shoulders, and it was still a doubtful passage at the end of the century, for Ellen Terry crosses it out in her promptbook and then writes 'in' in the margin.

But still the house affairs would draw her thence,
Which ever as she could with haste dispatch
She'd come again, and with a greedy ear
Devour up my discourse; which I observing
Took once a pliant hour and found good means   150
To draw from her a prayer of earnest heart
That I would all my pilgrimage dilate
Whereof by parcels she had something heard,
But not intentively. I did consent,
And often did beguile her of her tears   155
When I did speak of some distressful stroke
That my youth suffered. My story being done,
She gave me for my pains a world of sighs:
She swore, in faith, 'twas strange, 'twas passing strange,
'Twas pitiful, 'twas wondrous pitiful;   160
She wished she had not heard it, yet she wished
That heaven had made her such a man. She thanked me,
And bade me, if I had a friend that loved her,
I should but teach him how to tell my story,
And that would woo her. Upon this hint I spake: 165
She loved me for the dangers I had passed,
And I loved her that she did pity them.
This only is the witchcraft I have used.
Here comes the lady: let her witness it.

Enter DESDEMONA, *Iago and Attendants.*

162   In her promptbook Ellen Terry underlines 'her' (heavily), and 'man' suggesting that
Desdemona wished that she herself had been such a man. As M. R. Ridley points out in his
Arden edition, the alternative reading i.e. 'she wished Heaven had made such a man *for* her'
is more 'forward'. Ellen Terry's emphasis takes pains to avoid that implication.

166–8   John Kani kneels to Brabantio on 'She loved me', and to illustrate his non-existent witchcraft
he shakes imaginary dice, and 'scatters' them on the floor (video).

169 SD   In Bell's and Kemble's editions Desdemona does not enter until 176, just before Brabantio
says 'Come hither, gentle mistress.' At Desdemona's entrance all eyes in the audience seem
to have turned towards Othello. An innovation of Fechter's illuminates tradition: 'when
Desdemona . . . makes her appearance as a witness, good sense . . . would prompt Othello
to hold aloof from her, nor offer the slightest . . . attention which might be supposed to
exercise an influence over her . . . And so it has always been acted'. But Fechter 'with the
impetuosity of a boy and the gallantry of a Frenchman . . . springs forward "to lead in
Desdemona" [Fechter's stage direction]; and upon Brabantio calling to her . . . still keeps
hold of her' (Ottley, p. 17). Irving followed Fechter, 'as though she were a dangerous witness

DUKE I think this tale would win my daughter too.   170
     Good Brabantio, take up this mangled matter at the best:
     Men do their broken weapons rather use
     Than their bare hands.
BRABANTIO   I pray you hear her speak.
     If she confess that she was half the wooer,
     Destruction on my head if my bad blame   175
     Light on the man! Come hither, gentle mistress;
     Do you perceive in all this noble company
     Where most you owe obedience?
DESDEMONA   My noble father,
     I do perceive here a divided duty:

against him, and he desired to school her . . . – and afterwards held her veil for her with rather an effeminate air of affection and obsequiousness, the while she delivered her first speech to her father' (Cook, *Nights*, II, p. 325). Salvini did not rush to greet her, but from where he stood 'he covers [her] with a glance of indescribable tenderness' (Knight, *Theatrical Notes*, p. 21). Edwin Booth thought Othello should turn his back on her (*Variorum*), and the Sicilian actor Grasso parodied this by shutting his eyes tight and keeping them so 'in the manner of a child at hide-and-seek' (Beerbohm, *Theatres*, p. 575). When Robeson helped to take off her blue velvet cloak it was, said a correspondent, as though he were touching glass (*Denver Post*, 6 April 1945). Ben Kingsley seemed 'to spot' Desdemona when she entered 'through eyes in the back of his head' (*L*, 3 October 1985). When Imogen Stubbs entered in Trevor Nunn's production 'the shy conspiratorial look [she] shoots at Othello . . . instantly tells us they have been bracing themselves for this moment of public exposure' (*G*. 26 August 1989).

178b–87a   Praise for a contemporary of Sarah Siddons, Mrs Pope, also tells us how this speech was usually given at the time: 'It was not a word she spoke . . . but it was her polite and tender manner of saluting her husband from the opposite side of the stage . . . The grace and delicacy of her action . . . has not only not been equalled, but it has never been attempted by any other. Othello generally stands as much unnoted by his fair bride, except perhaps by a glance of the eye, whilst she recites this speech, as any other individual present' (*Bell's Weekly Messenger*, 2 April 1797). Of Sarah Siddons's delivery, Boaden wrote: 'I question whether equal discrimination was ever before given to these lines: "My noble father, I do perceive HERE, a *divided* duty; To YOU I am bound etc. But *here's* my husband"' (*Siddons*, I, p. 258). Ellen Terry's promptbook is also full of such distinctions, with 'you' and 'lord of duty', and 'I' and 'daughter' and 'here's my husband' all strongly underlined. In 1926, Lena Ashwell complained that actresses normally give the lines 'as though it were an impersonal essay on the duties of the daughter, as contrasted with those of the wife' (Ashwell, *Reflections*, p. 113).

To you I am bound for life and education;   180
My life and education both do learn me
How to respect you. You are lord of all my duty;
I am hitherto your daughter. But here's my husband;
And so much duty as my mother showed
To you, preferring you before her father,   185
So much I challenge that I may profess
Due to the Moor my lord.

BARBANTIO   God bu'y! I have done.
Please it your grace, on to the state affairs.
I had rather to adopt a child than get it.
Come hither, Moor: 190
I here do give thee that with all my heart
Which, but thou hast already, with all my heart
I would keep from thee. For your sake, jewel,
I am glad at soul I have no other child,
For thy escape would teach me tyranny   195
To hang clogs on them. I have done, my lord.

DUKE Let me speak like yourself and lay a sentence
Which as a grise or step may help these lovers
Into your favour.

189–96   Though lines 192–6 of this passage were cut, together with the following rhyming passages, from Bell's, Kemble's and Fechter's editions – Ellen Terry too persisting in the omission – the speech offers Brabantio a fine opportunity, as Edwin Booth remarks: 'Let the actor speak these lines with anguish, and he'll find out why the "first Old Man" is generally cast for so small a part; the audience will tell him' (*Variorum*). Sprague speaks of 'a number of promptbooks' directing Brabantio to join the lovers' hands, commenting that this could 'only be carried out with the bitterest irony' (Sprague, p. 188). Margaret Webster directed Brabantio to push Desdemona into Othello's arms (Carroll). Guthrie's Brabantio, Alexander Knox, was so moving here that when later it was said that his heart had broken, you believed it: 'it had cracked before one's eyes' (Williamson, *Old Vic Drama*, p. 98). Desdemona too can make an effect here, as in a production in 1924 at the Old Vic when 'in her controlled agitation' she stretched out a hand to Othello behind her. But Ion Swinley as Othello instead of making his hand 'leap to the encounter', moved it 'slowly towards Desdemona's and took it calmly – a northern hand to the last knuckle' (Farjeon, *Scene*, p. 164). At the end of this speech Webster's Cassio comes forward and 'smiles and kisses her hand' (Carroll).

197–218   Bell's edition records that this rhyming exchange was cut in the theatre, and ever since then it has been usual to omit it. In Nunn's production, however, Clive Swift's Brabantio spoke lines 208–9, and 'with a savage fury and impeccable logic . . . that suddenly make the war preparations seem irrelevant' (*G*, 26 August 1989).

When remedies are past the griefs are ended   200
By seeing the worst which late on hopes depended.
To mourn a mischief that is past and gone
Is the next way to draw new mischief on.
What cannot be preserved when fortune takes,
Patience her injury a mockery makes.   205
The robbed that smiles steals something from the thief;
He robs himself that spends a bootless grief.

BRABANTIO So let the Turk of Cyprus us beguile,
We lose it not so long as we can smile;
He bears the sentence well that nothing bears   210
But the free comfort which from thence he hears;
But he bears both the sentence and the sorrow
That to pay grief must of poor patience borrow.
These sentences, to sugar or to gall,
Being strong on both sides, are equivocal.   215
But words are words; I never yet did hear
That the bruised heart was piercèd through the ear.
Beseech you now, to the affairs of the state.

DUKE The Turk with a most mighty preparation makes for Cyprus.
Othello, the fortitude of the place is best known to you; and 220
though we have there a substitute of most allowed sufficiency,
yet opinion, a more sovereign mistress of effects, throws a
more safer voice on you. You must therefore be content to
slubber the gloss of your new fortunes with this more stubborn
and boisterous expedition.   225

OTHELLO The tyrant custom, most grave Senators,
Hath made the flinty and steel couch of war
My thrice-driven bed of down. I do agnise
A natural and prompt alacrity

220ff. Here Edwin Booth describes a piece of unobtrusive acting for Iago: 'Othello leaves
Desdemona with Cassio, who regards her with tender, yet respectful admiration. Iago, at the
back, watches them curiously, but let him not be obtrusive; he must keep in the background
and assume this expression, and feel the curiousness even if only one person in the whole
audience sees or understands it; the "censure", as Hamlet calls it, of that one is worth all the
rest' (*Variorum*).

228ff. Hazlitt complained that Macready 'goes off like a shot and startles our sense of hearing . . .
as if he was impatient to exculpate himself from some charge, or wanted to take them at
their word lest they should retract' (Hazlitt, V, p. 339).

I find in hardness, and do undertake   230
These present wars against the Ottomites.
Most humbly, therefore, bending to your state,
I crave fit disposition for my wife,
Due reference of place and exhibition
With such accommodation and besort   235
As levels with her breeding.

DUKE   If you please,
Be't at her father's.

BRABANTIO   I'll not have it so.

OTHELLO Nor I.

DESDEMONA   Nor I; I would not there reside
To put my father in impatient thoughts
By being in his eye. Most gracious duke,   240
To my unfolding lend your prosperous ear
And let me find a charter in your voice
T'assist my simpleness.

DUKE   What would you, Desdemona?

DESDEMONA That I did love the Moor to live with him,
My downright violence and storm of fortunes   245
May trumpet to the world. My heart's subdued
Even to the very quality of my lord.
I saw Othello's visage in his mind

230–1   When Robeson (1943) gave his undertaking to fight, the 'entire group cheers', and Lodovico
says 'Bravo, Othello, that is it, we can use your arm.' He then shook Othello's hand, and
kissed Desdemona's (Carroll).

238a   Othello's 'Nor I': 'Not harshly', warns Edwin Booth, 'but firmly' (*Variorum*).

240ff.   Macready's promptbook directs that Desdemona should kneel here, and in the following
lines 'Othello raises her.' An interesting alternative manuscript direction – 'Cassio raises
her' – is crossed out.

246ff.   Of Sarah Siddons, Boaden writes: 'I was greatly delighted with the generous warmth that
animated the supplication of Desdemona to go with Othello to the wars' (*Siddons*, II,
p. 155). A similar animation informs Ellen Terry's marginal notes 'quick' and 'q' opposite the
half-lines at 236–7 and Desdemona's following speeches. Salvini's gaze here at Desdemona
became 'burning', and 'forgetful of all restraints he approaches and almost folds her in his
arms; but awaking in time to recollection of the august presence in which he stands, he
turns from her with a gesture of apology' (Knight, *Theatrical Notes*, p. 21).

247   The quarto has 'pleasure' for 'quality', which Olivier chose by way of emphasising the
eroticism of their love (film). Orson Welles went further and made it 'pleasures' which
Desdemona uttered with 'a coy glance' (*S*, 26 October 1951).

And to his honours and his valiant parts
Did I my soul and fortunes consecrate.   250
So that, dear lords, if I be left behind
A moth of peace, and he go to the war,
The rites for which I love him are bereft me,
And I a heavy interim shall support
By his dear absence. Let me go with him.   255
OTHELLO Let her have your voice.
Vouch with me, heaven, I therefore beg it not
To please the palate of my appetite,
Nor to comply with heat the young affects
In my distinct and proper satisfaction,   260
But to be free and bounteous to her mind.
And heaven defend your good souls that you think
I will your serious and great business scant
For she is with me. No, when light-winged toys
Of feathered Cupid seel with wanton dullness   265
My speculative and officed instruments,
That my disports corrupt and taint my business,
Let housewives make a skillet of my helm,
And all indign and base adversities
Make head against my estimation!   270
DUKE Be it as you shall privately determine,
Either for her stay or going. Th'affair cries haste,
And speed must answer it. You must hence tonight.
DESDEMONA Tonight, my lord?
DUKE   This night.

252   Fechter excises the one poetic phrase – 'a moth of peace' – from these lines. Salvini at least
       had the excuse of translation to render the sense thus flatly: 'se in pace io resto . . .' (if I stay
       here, in peace).
255   At the end of Desdemona's speech Webster's Senators muttered things like 'We send no
       maidens into battle' and 'What have we here?' (Carroll).
256–70 The Smock Alley text omits lines 268–72a. Bell's edition uses the quarto's: 'Your voices
       lords: beseech you, let her will / Have a free way.' The only omissions to the rest of the
       speech are the slightly risky (but also difficult to understand) lines 259–60 and 268 – the
       'skillet of my helm' line. Kemble goes further, cutting everything after the opening lines,
       achieving compression but at the same time avoiding Othello's unseemly defence against
       wantonness. The same cut is made in Fechter's edition, and in Ellen Terry's and Oscar
       Asche's promptbooks. Webster's promptbook cuts only 264b–70. On the word 'skillet',
       there is general laughter in Nunn's production (video).
273   Edwin Booth remembered Roderigo here, who 'shows alarm at this, but Iago quiets him.
       This must not interfere with the action of the scene, but merely be suggested' (*Variorum*).

OTHELLO   With all my heart.
DUKE At nine i'the morning, here we'll meet again.   275
          Othello, leave some officer behind
          And he shall our commission bring to you
          With such things else of quality and respect
          As doth import you.
OTHELLO   So please your grace, my ancient:
          A man he is of honesty and trust.   280
          To his conveyance I assign my wife,
          With what else needful your good grace shall think
          To be sent after me.
DUKE   Let it be so.
          Good night to everyone. [*To Brabantio*] And noble
              signior,
          If virtue no delighted beauty lack,   285
          Your son-in-law is far more fair than black.
1 SENATOR Adieu, brave Moor; use Desdemona well.
BRABANTIO Look to her, Moor, if thou hast eyes to see:
          She has deceived her father and may thee.
OTHELLO My life upon her faith!
              Exeunt [Duke, Brabantio, Cassio, Senators and Attendants]

274 Nunn's Imogen Stubbs 'emits a squeal of excitement' on 'Tonight', 'as if it's her first trip
     abroad' (*G*, 26 August 1989). During the following dialogue before Brabantio's exit she tried
     'to reach him round the council table, first one way then the other . . . to settle their quarrel
     with an embrace' (Smallwood, 'Shakespeare', p. 112). Salvini forestalled any reproach at his
     prompt 'With all my heart', by looking 'painfully surprised at the Duke's command; he turns
     toward Desdemona, and restrains himself from protesting against the abruptness of his
     departure' (Mason, p. 18).
286 In Kelly's production, the Duke said this 'as a forced, embarrassed attempt to defuse the
     racial tension with, as it were, a slightly off-colour joke' (Loehlin, '*Othello*'). In Mendes's
     production, 'the chuckle from the officers that accompanies this remark suggests that they
     all know Othello isn't one of them, but they need him badly – and right now they don't
     intend to dwell on it' (*IoS*, 21 September 1997).
288–9 Kemble chose the more dramatic quarto reading here: 'have a quick eye to see', and this
     reading became traditional, as one gathers from Ottley's fury at Fechter's use of the Folio
     reading: 'upon what authority he changes the well-known lines . . . to . . . "if thou hast eyes
     to see"' (p. 18). William Winter thought Salvini 'introduced a denotement of coarseness and
     jealousy, giving a violent start, and looking from father to daughter with a quick flickering,
     tigerish glare' (Winter, *Shakespeare*, p. 289). John Kani, in Suzman's production, lays his
     fist across his heart, in a 'Roman' salute (video).

> Honest Iago   290
> My Desdemona must I leave to thee;
> I prithee, let thy wife attend on her,
> And bring her after in the best advantage.
> Come, Desdemona, I have but an hour
> Of love, of worldly matters and direction   295
> To spend with thee. We must obey the time.
>
> *Exeunt Othello and Desdemona*

290 SD   Macready's promptbook reads 'Desdemona crosses and kneels to Brabantio, who throws her from him.' This is followed by Phelps, who has Othello raise her. Fechter made Desdemona try to kiss the hand of Brabantio who, less spectacularly, merely 'disengages' himself (his stage direction). Oscar Asche has Desdemona kneel and take Brabantio's hand, adding that as Othello passes Iago, 'the latter salutes him and curses him behind his back' (promptbook). Orson Welles's film makes a tragic figure of Brabantio as he exits here, reminiscent of Shylock at the end of the trial scene. Nunn's Brabantio, Clive Swift, showed 'that the play gives us one small tragedy before the end of Act I' (Smallwood, 'Shakespeare', p. 111).

290   Salvini uttered 'My life upon her faith!' as a parting shot at Brabantio, 'rapidly [following] him up the stage'. Then he paused, 'utters an indignant exclamation, and makes a threatening gesture toward Brabantio' (Mason, p. 20). Of his London performances, Fanny Kemble speaks only of his 'sudden folding Desdemona in his arms as Brabantio goes out' (*TB*, July 1884). Olivier speaks the line with complete confidence, dismissing Brabantio's warning with raised hand and a sort of whooshing sound (film).

294–6   Rossi made it clear what that hour was for: 'His eyes shone, his face trembled as though in the power of some feverish hope. He enveloped his beloved in one of those immense looks that in themselves are a whole poem. It was all at once both lascivious and ideal' (Fernand Laffont, *Le Panthéon de l'Industrie et des Arts*, 9 June 1866, quoted in Busi, *Otello*, p. 176). In his film, Orson Welles had Othello speak the lines over Desdemona as she lies, illumined and hair-haloed, in her gauzy-curtained bed. Janet Suzman's video seizes this moment to emphasise the physical love between John Kani's Othello and Joanna Weinberg's Desdemona, with a long kiss in close shot (video). At the Market Theatre in Johannesburg where the production was first staged, 'black lips on white ones' proved too much for some white members of the audience, who walked out (*T*, 26 October 1987). But a kiss is not the invariable modern practice. Neither Oliver Parker's film nor Michael Attenborough's production made much of this opportunity.

296 SD   The 1766 promptbook shows a change of scene here to the 'N Chamber', but with Macready and thereafter it became usual to leave Iago and Roderigo in the council chamber. In Macready's promptbook Iago is about to exit as well, but is called back by Roderigo who has lingered behind and is leaning against the proscenium.

RODERIGO Iago.

IAGO What say'st thou, noble heart?

RODERIGO What will I do, think'st thou?

IAGO Why, go to bed and sleep.   300

RODERIGO I will incontinently drown myself.

IAGO If thou dost, I shall never love thee after. Why, thou silly
gentleman?

RODERIGO It is silliness to live, when to live is torment: and then
we have a prescription to die, when death is our physician.   305

IAGO O villainous! I have looked upon the world for four times seven
years, and since I could distinguish betwixt a benefit and an
injury, I never found a man that knew how to love himself. Ere
I would say I would drown myself for the love of a guinea-hen,
I would change my humanity with a baboon.   310

RODERIGO What should I do? I confess it is my shame to be so fond,
but it is not in my virtue to amend it.

IAGO Virtue? A fig! 'Tis in ourselves that we are thus or thus. Our
bodies are our gardens, to the which our wills are gardeners. So

297ff.   Fechter's Iago surprised London audiences with 'the inelegant act of sitting upon a table,
one leg swinging in the air (à la Captain Macheath)' (Ottley, p. 10). But naturalism was to be
characteristic of Iago from then on. In Beerbohm Tree's production, Laurence Irving sat
down in Brabantio's chair, putting his hat and the standard he had been carrying on the
table, and examining the papers there from time to time during the scene (promptbook).
José Ferrer, in Webster's production, pulled a stool round at 308, 'with his left foot and sits.
He picks his teeth', according to the promptbook. In Ronald Eyre's production, there was
instead a sense of bustle with Iago checking luggage for Cyprus, soldier by soldier, during
the scene (promptbook), but Peter Hall (and more recent producers) have returned to the
idle insolence of Iago and Roderigo making free with the senatorial chairs (promptbook).
    At some point in the eighteenth century, and during the nineteenth, this scene was, in
Gentleman's words 'very much and very properly [as he thought] reduced from the original
prolixity' (Bell, footnote). The cuts are noted below.

301ff.   Michael Grandage, Trevor Nunn's Roderigo, threw a tantrum here, kicking and banging his
fists on the floor (promptbook and video).

310   On 'baboon', Richard Haines in Suzman's production sticks a finger in his nostril again
(video).

311–24   Bell's edition records this cut. Kemble, followed by Fechter, also cut. Salvini keeps more, but
feebly translates 'our raging motions, our carnal stings, our unbitted lusts' as 'instinti, e
sensi, e brame' ('instincts, and senses, and desires').

313ff.   On 'Virtue? A fig!', Richard Haines pokes his thumb up between two fingers (video). Ian
McKellen's Iago took Roderigo by the chin and in illustration of 'wills' and 'reason' pressed

that if we will plant nettles or sow lettuce, set hyssop and weed   315
up thyme, supply it with one gender of herbs or distract it
with many, either to have it sterile with idleness or manured with
industry, why the power and corrigible authority of this lies in
our wills. If the balance of our lives had not one scale of reason
to poise another of sensuality, the blood and baseness of our   320
natures would conduct us to most preposterous conclusions. But
we have reason to cool our raging motions, our carnal stings,
our unbitted lusts; whereof I take this, that you call love, to be
a sect or scion.
RODERIGO It cannot be.   325
IAGO It is merely a lust of the blood and a permission of the will. Come,
be a man. Drown thyself? Drown cats and blind puppies. I
have professed me thy friend, and I confess me knit to thy
deserving with cables of perdurable toughness. I could never
better stead thee than now. Put money in thy purse. Follow   330
thou these wars; defeat thy favour with an usurped beard. I say,
put money in thy purse. It cannot be that Desdemona should
long continue her love to the Moor – put money in thy

Roderigo's temples or tapped his head; on 'carnal stings' he hugged and stroked him
(promptbook and video). Richard McCabe, in Michael Attenborough's production, also
massaged Roderigo's head on 'we have reason', but was otherwise much less tactile than
McKellen (RSC archive film).

326–47   Boaden praises Henderson particularly for his skill in this scene which was remarkable for
making the 'eleven times repeated phrase' ['put money in thy purse'] 'untiring to the ear'
(Boaden, *Siddons*, II, pp. 29–30). As Iago, Olivier 'clowned the "put money" speech to such
an extent that many of the audience decided that he was a comic character, and
thenceforward were prepared to laugh at anything he said' (Crosse, *Playgoing*, p. 122). In
Parker's film, the first 'Put money in thy purse' (330) comes across as a new and
spontaneous idea. The last time it occurs, Branagh says 'Put' and Roderigo wearily finishes
the sentence.

331   Iago's idea of a beard for Roderigo was dropped in Bell's edition and Kemble's.

333–47   Recorded as cut in Bell's edition, but perhaps, on occasion, it was restored (see Boaden's
praise of Henderson, above). At any rate Kemble restored the sentence about their love
having 'a violent commencement', and the eloquently cynical line 'if sanctimony and a frail
vow . . .'. Fechter had no ear for this and cut it again, but Edwin Booth and Irving restored it
anxious only to remove the spicy lines about food and Desdemona's sated appetite. Oscar
Asche even included the 'food' lines omitting only 'when she is sated with his body . . .'
(promptbook). Webster reversed this cut, judging 'luscious as locusts' and 'coloquintida' to
be unintelligible (promptbook). Webster's teeth-picking José Ferrer showed a casualness
during this speech which the *Boston Globe* (11 August 1942) found excessive. The

purse – nor he his to her. It was a violent commencement, and
thou shalt see an answerable sequestration – put but money in thy   335
purse. These Moors are changeable in their wills – fill thy purse
with money. The food that to him now is as luscious as locusts
shall be to him shortly as acerb as the coloquintida. She
must change for youth; when she is sated with his body she
will find the error of her choice. Therefore put money in thy   340
purse. If thou wilt needs damn thyself, do it a more delicate way
than drowning. Make all the money thou canst. If sanctimony
and a frail vow betwixt an erring barbarian and a super-subtle
Venetian be not too hard for my wits and all the tribe of hell, thou
shalt enjoy her – therefore make money. A pox of drowning   345
thyself! It is clean out of the way. Seek thou rather to be hanged
in compassing thy joy than to be drowned and go without her.
RODERIGO Wilt thou be fast to my hopes, if I depend on the issue?
IAGO Thou art sure of me. Go make money. I have told thee often, and
I retell thee again and again, I hate the Moor. My cause is   350
hearted: thine hath no less reason. Let us be conjunctive in
our revenge against him. If thou canst cuckold him, thou dost
thyself a pleasure, me a sport. There are many events in the womb
of time which will be delivered. Traverse! Go, provide thy money.
We will have more of this tomorrow. Adieu.   355
RODERIGO Where shall we meet i'the morning?
IAGO At my lodging.
RODERIGO I'll be with thee betimes.
IAGO Go to; farewell. Do you hear, Roderigo?
RODERIGO What say you?   360
IAGO No more of drowning, do you hear?
RODERIGO I am changed.
IAGO Go to; farewell. Put money enough in your purse.
RODERIGO I'll sell all my land.   *Exit*
IAGO Thus do I ever make my fool my purse;   365

promptbook shows that he rubbed his fingers together at the word 'money', slapped
Roderigo on the shoulder, and gave him a push here and there. This was very much
Laurence Irving's manner – more surprising in 1912 – who 'pats and prods and punches
Roderigo' (*Bradford Telegraph*, 10 April 1912). Richard Haines spits on the floor at 'as acid
[for Q1's 'acerb'] as coloquintida' (Suzman's video).

350–2 Fechter changed 'cuckold', which even Macready kept, to 'deceive'. In Michael
Attenborough's production, they both giggled on 'I hate the Moor' (pronounced 'Moo-er')
and shook hands on 'Let us be conjunctive . . .' (RSC archive film).

365ff. In Bell's edition, Gentleman sprinkles this speech with dashes, e.g. after 'true' and 'well' and
'now' and at 'How? How? – – Let's see – – ' and so on. These frequent pauses

For I mine own gained knowledge should profane
If I would time expend with such a snipe
But for my sport and profit. I hate the Moor,
And it is thought abroad that 'twixt my sheets
He's done my office. I know not if't be true   370
Yet I, for mere suspicion in that kind,
Will do as if for surety. He holds me well:
The better shall my purpose work on him.
Cassio's a proper man: let me see now;
To get his place and to plume up my will   375
In double knavery. How? How? Let's see.
After some time, to abuse Othello's ear
That he is too familiar with his wife;
He hath a person and a smooth dispose
To be suspected, framed to make women false.   380

support the eighteenth-century version of Iago as a heavy villain. It was here, according to Kirkman, that Macklin made such an impression: 'full of subtlety, irascibility and villainy . . . mean, hypocritical and vindictive . . .' (Kirkman, *Memoirs*, 1, pp. 300–1). Macready was coolly meditative: ' it is a lesson . . . to see Mr Macready's change of countenance at . . . "I have't – it is engendered" ' (*TJ*, 10 October 1840). He changed 369–70 to 'that with my wife / He has wrought me shame' (promptbook). Phelps has '. . . that with my wife / He hath supplied my place' (promptbook).

Fechter watched Roderigo make his exit, then broke 'into a loud laugh' (his stage direction). He leant 'his forehead on his hands . . . muttering between his teeth' at 'How, how?' ', then slowly raised his face which 'brightens with a diabolical smile'. At 'I have't' he 'walks forward triumphantly' and, as Merivale remembered, 'broke into one clear laugh of triumphant enjoyment . . . sharply turned and put his finger to his lips, and went' (Merivale, *Bar, Stage*, p. 149). Irving similarly covered 'his brooding brow with his long lean hand, then as the fiendish solution occurred to him, he suddenly withdrew his hand and discovered a face expressing triumphant malignity with the words "I have't" ' (Martin-Harvey, *Autobiography*, pp. 42–3). Laurence Irving was cooler, 'lazily catching flies and burning them in the candle' (Foss, *The Author*, p. 81). Then, he 'picks up standard, spits on it, puts it over shoulder' and goes out (promptbook).

Ronald Eyre 'has the other four principals concerned (Emilia, Desdemona, Cassio and the Moor himself) line up silently on the stage behind him, so that Iago may view them almost as if they were waxworks, before arranging them into his evil patterns. It is a simple, stunningly good stage effect . . .' (*Punch*, 22 August 1979). Walter Kerr spoke of the 'terrible ashen agony on Mr Plummer's face whenever he is left alone to do his plotting. His nimble driven mind keeps turning over, inventing, inventing' (*NYT*, 14 February 1982). In the video, Ian McKellen almost retches up the word 'hate' at 368. He seemed 'like a man used to

The Moor is of a free and open nature,
That thinks men honest that but seem to be so,
And will as tenderly be led by the nose
As asses are.
I have't. It is engendered. Hell and night   385
Must bring this monstrous birth to the world's light. *Exit*

talking to himself; lonely, slightly drunk, sexually hung up'. He 'has a fascinating mannerism
that serves almost as a signature . . . a rotating finger, pointed at his head as if to wind up his
wits' (*Literary Review*, November 1989). At 382 he pocketed some of the Duke's cigars
(promptbook), and on the concluding lines there was a 'thrilling moment' when 'as though
[Iago] had engendered them, the thunder and lightening which usher in the next act . . .
melodramatically erupt' (*I*, 2 October 1989). Oliver Parker suggests Iago's hellish intellect
here by having Branagh peer at the camera through pieces of chess on a board, flames
flickering behind him and music rising to a crescendo. In Mendes's production, at 369–70,
Simon Russell Beale's 'chubby hand knocks an in-tray flying across the room. He squeezes
into a chair and thinks how best to get his revenge. "How? How?" he asks, as if searching
for a clue in a crossword. He gets an idea ("It is engendered"), picks up a paper and
switches on the radio. It's bravura stuff' (*IoS*, 21 September 1997). In contrast, Suzman's
Richard Haines delivers this speech with triumphant vulgarity, standing on the arms of the
Doge's throne. At 383–4 he puts a finger in both nostrils, and gives a grotesque imitation of
a donkey, hee-hawing and miming a monstrous penis; and on the last two lines, he
indicates a huge womb (video).

ACT 2, SCENE 1

Enter MONTANO *and two* GENTLEMEN.

The 1766 Drury Lane prompt copy indicates the 'Port Tunis' flats at the second groove – flats which represented a 'Castle Scene'. Fechter had a painted backdrop showing 'the harbour at Cyprus, with storm raging and tempest-tossed wrecks', but Ottley ridiculed the idea of a 'storm-driven wreck remaining prominent in the centre of the picture, for a full half-hour or so, with nobody going to its rescue' (Ottley, p. 13). In New York, Edwin Booth was more happily grandiose: 'It is indeed a novelty to see a turreted building rising forty-five feet high, with bastions and towers standing out against a lighted void of atmosphere, with a great sweep of sky we know not how far behind it in which white clouds seem from their very distance to hang suspended' (*New York World*, 16 April 1869). Beerbohm Tree did the storm with sound, rather than paint: 'when we go to Cyprus . . . the night is loud with storm. A wonderful sea comes rolling against the quay with surge and thunder. As the light breaks through the clouds you find a picture of the gorgeous East . . .' (*DT*, 10 April 1912). The props list for this scene specifies vines with bunches of grapes. Also flags were made to blow on the castle walls (Bristol Theatre Collection). Modern productions are in striking contrast: for Peter Hall, John Bury achieved 'the move to Cyprus . . . with minimum fuss by projecting clouds on the wall, using the upper level as a look-out tower, and rearranging the furniture to form a guardroom' (Roger Warren, 'Shakespeare in Performance, 1980', *Sh.S*, 34, p. 154). Jonathan Miller suggested the storm through the words alone, the whole thing being observed from within his still and airy interior. For Nunn's production, Bob Crowley designed a 'white verandah with latticed Venetian blinds above . . . a late nineteenth-century military outpost, forever blazing in the sweltering heat of day' (*G*, 3 October 1989). Here 'Cyprus is revealed as a dusty parade-ground, where the sound of bugles and the muezzin's cry suggest not confinement but a threatening sense of space' (*L*, 7 September 1989). Mendes created a similar atmosphere with his 'sunbleached, garrissoned outpost, all louvred windows and parquet floors where the military have too much leisure' (*G*, 18 September 1997). Kelly's designer, Robert Innes Hopkins, had 'a ruined structure suggestive of battlements, above which flew the golden Cypriot flag against a backdrop sky of rich cerulean blue' (Johnson-Haddad, 'Shakespeare Theatre *Othello*', p. 9).

MONTANO What from the cape can you discern at sea?
1 GENTLEMAN Nothing at all; it is a high-wrought flood.
    I cannot 'twixt the heaven and the main
    Descry a sail.
MONTANO Methinks the wind does speak aloud at land,   5
    A fuller blast ne'er shook our battlements.
    If it hath ruffianed so upon the sea,
    What ribs of oak, when mountains melt on them,
    Can hold the mortise? What shall we hear of this?
2 GENTLEMAN A segregation of the Turkish fleet: 10
    For do but stand upon the banning shore,
    The chidden billow seems to pelt the clouds;
    The wind-shaked surge, with high and monstrous mane,
    Seems to cast water on the burning Bear
    And quench the guards of th'ever-fixèd Pole.   15
    I never did like molestation view
    On the enchafèd flood.
MONTANO   If that the Turkish fleet
    Be not ensheltered and embayed, they are drowned:
    It is impossible they bear it out.

            Enter a third GENTLEMAN.

3 GENTLEMAN News, lads! Our wars are done: 20
    The desperate tempest hath so banged the Turks
    That their designment halts. A noble ship of Venice
    Hath seen a grievous wrack and sufferance
    On most part of their fleet.
MONTANO How? Is this true?
3 GENTLEMAN   The ship is here put in,   25
    A Veronesa; Michael Cassio,
    Lieutenant to the warlike Moor Othello,
    Is come on shore; the Moor himself at sea,
    And is in full commission here for Cyprus.
MONTANO I am glad on't; 'tis a worthy governor.   30
3 GENTLEMAN But this same Cassio, though he speak of comfort
    Touching the Turkish loss, yet he looks sadly
    And prays the Moor be safe; for they were parted
    With foul and violent tempest.
MONTANO   Pray heaven he be;
    For I have served him, and the man commands   35

1–42   The '1755' edition cuts the opening dialogue, starting the scene at Cassio's entrance. Most eighteenth- and nineteenth-century acting editions made the same cut.

Like a full soldier. Let's to the seaside, ho!
As well to see the vessel that's come in
As to throw out our eyes for brave Othello,
Even till we make the main and th'aerial blue
An indistinct regard.
3 GENTLEMAN   Come, let's do so;   40
For every minute is expectancy
Of more arrivance.

Enter CASSIO.

CASSIO Thanks, you the valiant of this warlike isle
That so approve the Moor. O, let the heavens
Give him defence against the elements,   45
For I have lost him on a dangerous sea.
MONTANO Is he well shipped?
CASSIO His bark is stoutly timbered, and his pilot
Of very expert and approved allowance;
Therefore my hopes, not surfeited to death,   50
Stand in bold cure.
      [*A shout*] *within, 'A sail, a sail, a sail!'*

Enter a MESSENGER.

CASSIO What noise?
MESSENGER The town is empty; on the brow o'the sea
Stand ranks of people and they cry, 'A sail!'
CASSIO My hopes do shape him for the governor.   55
      A shot [*is heard within*].
2 GENTLEMAN They do discharge their shot of courtesy;
Our friends at least.
CASSIO   I pray you, sir, go forth,
And give us truth who 'tis that is arrived.
2 GENTLEMAN I shall.   *Exit*
MONTANO But, good lieutenant, is your general wived?   60
CASSIO Most fortunately: he hath achieved a maid
That paragons description and wild fame;
One that excels the quirks of blazoning pens
And in th'essential vesture of creation
Does tire the ingener.

Enter Second Gentleman.

                  How now? Who's put in?   65
2 GENTLEMAN 'Tis one Iago, ancient to the general.
CASSIO He's had most favourable and happy speed:

Tempests themselves, high seas, and howling winds,
The guttered rocks and congregated sands,
Traitors enscarped to clog the guiltless keel,   70
As having sense of beauty do omit
Their mortal natures, letting go safely by
The divine Desdemona.
MONTANO   What is she?
CASSIO She that I spake of, our great captain's captain,
        Left in the conduct of the bold Iago,   75
        Whose footing here anticipates our thoughts
        A se'nnight's speed. Great Jove Othello guard
        And swell his sail with thine own powerful breath,
        That he may bless this bay with his tall ship,
        Make love's quick pants in Desdemona's arms,   80
        Give renewed fire to our extinct spirits,
        And bring all Cyprus comfort.

        Enter DESDEMONA, IAGO, EMILIA *and* RODERIGO.

                                O, behold,
        The riches of the ship is come on shore!

0, 74–82, Bell's edition and Kemble's cut most of Cassio's effusions. Macready restored line 84 and
84   directed that 'all kneel' and 'all uncover and bow to Desdemona' (promptbook). Webster
         had Bianca enter during Cassio's second speech and chuck him under the chin, at which a
         citizen pulled her away (Carroll).

82b–173 Boaden said that in general during this scene, before Othello's entrance, he was especially
         struck by Sarah Siddons's 'elegant deportment, cordial manners and smothered anxiety . . .
         which would have enchanted Shakespeare himself . . .' (Boaden, *Siddons*, II, p. 156).

83 SD In Fechter's edition 'Desdemona appears at the back and passes along the arcades,
         surrounded by people to whom she distributes alms.' The idea prefigures Verdi's opera
         where, a little later, after Iago first plants suspicion in Otello's mind, Desdemona appears at
         the back of the stage surrounded by women and children and sailors distributing and
         receiving gifts. In Peter Hall's production Desdemona entered under Iago's protection, he
         'shielding her with his cloak' (promptbook). In the video of Nunn's production they make
         their entrance soaked to the skin, coughing and sneezing, towelling their hair, Emilia (Zoë
         Wanamaker) and Desdemona settling down on boxes and packing cases and Iago offering
         brandy tots all round.

         Of eighteenth-century Emilias, Boaden wrote: 'Kept unwillingly in the background,
         longing to break forth . . . she contrives by outdressing her lady, and the aid of a rich plume
         of *feathers*, to do almost nothing through *four* tedious acts, but waves her *promise* to the

You men of Cyprus, let her have your knees.
Hail to thee, lady! And the grace of heaven,   85
Before, behind thee, and on every hand,
Enwheel thee round.
DESDEMONA   I thank you, valiant Cassio.
What tidings can you tell me of my lord?
CASSIO He is not yet arrived; nor know I aught
But that he's well, and will be shortly here.   90
DESDEMONA O, but I fear – how lost you company?
CASSIO The great contention of the sea and skies
Parted our fellowship.
       [*A shout*] *within, 'A sail, a sail!'* [*A shot is heard.*]
But hark, a sail!
2 GENTLEMAN They give their greeting to the citadel:
This likewise is a friend.
CASSIO   See for the news.   95
       [*Exit Second Gentleman*]
Good ancient, you are welcome. [*To Emilia*] Welcome,
mistress.

spectators that at last their patience shall be repaid' (*Siddons*, I, pp. 72–3). Boaden goes on
to complain of their 'heroic' size, and how, 'like another Glumdalclitch', they tower over
their Desdemonas (footnote on p. 74). At the end of the nineteenth century the complaint
was that Emilias were too old: 'old enough to be Desdemona's mother, nor scarcely likely to
awaken jealousy in the most suspicious breast' (*MM*, July 1881). Emilia's feminism has
attracted special interest in modern times, but already in 1902 Merivale saw that 'the lucky
actress of that little part' could command the sympathy 'denied to all the rest' (Merivale,
Bar, Stage, p. 149). When Sybil Thorndyke played it in 1930, she dominated the play (Foss,
The Author, p. 81) and Edith Evans in 1932 'gave us the only real emotion of the afternoon'
(Agate, *Chronicles*, p. 290). Recently productions have been especially alert to the sexual
relations between Emilia and Iago. Both Zoë Wanamaker (dir. Nunn), and Franchelle
Stewart-Dorn (dir. Kelly) forcefully suggested marriages of mental and/or physical abuse,
thus giving Emilia an even greater weight and significance in the play as a whole.

85–7   In the video, Janet Suzman's Cassio here lifts Desdemona up and swings her round. Michael
           Attenborough's Cassio did the same (RSC archive film).

6–9SD and ff.   Edwin Booth wrote: 'Kiss her face; not as is frequently done, her hand. Iago winces slightly
           for he "suspects Cassio with his nightcap"' (*Variorum*). In Suzman's video, Richard Haines,
           Suzman's Iago, reacts with private fury, as Cassio lifts Emilia up. Nunn's Cassio, Sean Baker,
           kissed Emilia's hand and cheek, and Iago, who had been towelling her hair, hit her lightly
           with it (promptbook). Kelly's Emilia (Stewart-Dorn) 'flinched' at Cassio's kiss, 'in terror of
           Iago's reaction' (Loehlin, 'Othello').

Let it not gall your patience, good Iago,
That I extend my manners. 'Tis my breeding
That gives me this bold show of courtesy.
[*He kisses Emilia.*]
IAGO Sir, would she give you so much of her lips   100
As of her tongue she oft bestows on me
You would have enough.
DESDEMONA Alas, she has no speech.
IAGO   In faith, too much:
I find it still when I have list to sleep.
Marry, before your ladyship, I grant   105
She puts her tongue a little in her heart
And chides with thinking.
EMILIA   You've little cause to say so.
IAGO Come on, come on; you are pictures out of doors, bells in
your parlours, wild-cats in your kitchens, saints in your injuries,
devils being offended, players in your housewifery, and   110
housewives in your beds.
DESDEMONA O fie upon thee, slanderer!
IAGO Nay, it is true, or else I am a Turk:
You rise to play and go to bed to work.

During the following dialogue (which from the '1755' edition onwards, throughout the nineteenth century, was reduced by the omission of 123–41), actresses have tried to show Desdemona's abstraction from Iago's lewd merriment. Boaden speaks of Sarah Siddons's '*endurance* of Iago's ribaldry' (Boaden, *Kemble*, I, p. 259). Webster had Desdemona going upstage to scan the harbour at 108 just as Iago was getting going. And a little later at 128 and 135 she made Bianca react to the lines, flirting and bridling, thus relieving Desdemona of having to listen actively (Carroll). Peter Hall arranged much bustle during this dialogue: organising food and drink, hot soup, taking off cloaks, laying table etc. Desdemona alone neither eats nor drinks (promptbook). Yvonne Bryceland's Emilia 'was particularly convincing in her greed . . . in contrast to Desdemona's abstinence' (*Cahiers Elizabéthains*, October 1980). In the video of Nunn's production, McKellen's Iago is the bustler, hugging, shoulder-massaging, shadow-boxing with Cassio, and giving Roderigo's forehead a reminding tap as he passes. Some critics noted a Chekhovian atmosphere at moments in Nunn's production. This was one of them. 'The forced merriment comes across as the willed time-killing in *Three Sisters,* less the whiling away of a few specific minutes, than the attempt to shake off a pervasive ennui' (*I*, 2 October 1989).

113 Richard Haines, always the racist, pulls chinese eyes here (Suzman's video).

114 Gentleman protests here: 'Iago expresses himself most indecently to his wife and barefacedly to Desdemona' (Bell). However, Kemble kept the line, and it stayed until Macready cut it (promptbook).

EMILIA You shall not write my praise.

IAGO   No, let me not.   115

DESDEMONA What wouldst thou write of me, if thou shouldst
          praise me?

IAGO O, gentle lady, do not put me to't,
          For I am nothing if not critical.

DESDEMONA Come on, assay. There's one gone to the harbour?

IAGO Ay, madam.   120

DESDEMONA [*Aside*] I am not merry, but I do beguile
          The thing I am by seeming otherwise –
          Come, how wouldst thou praise me?

IAGO I am about it, but indeed my invention
          Comes from my pate as birdlime does from frieze –   125
          It plucks out brains and all. But my muse labours,
          And thus she is delivered:
          'If she be fair and wise, fairness and wit,
          The one's for use, the other useth it.'

DESDEMONA Well praised! How if she be black and witty?   130

IAGO 'If she be black, and thereto have a wit,
          She'll find a white that shall her blackness fit.'

DESDEMONA Worse and worse.

EMILIA   How if fair and foolish?

IAGO 'She never yet was foolish that was fair,
          For even her folly helped her to an heir.'   135

DESDEMONA These are old fond paradoxes to make fools laugh
          i'th'alehouse. What miserable praise hast thou for her that's foul
          and foolish?

IAGO 'There's none so foul and foolish thereunto,
          But does foul pranks which fair and wise ones do.'   140

DESDEMONA O heavy ignorance! Thou praisest the worst best. But
          what praise couldst thou bestow on a deserving woman indeed?
          One that in the authority of her merit did justly put on the vouch
          of very malice itself?

IAGO 'She that was ever fair, and never proud,   145

117–18   Walter Kerr wished again for a 'permanent Shakespeare promptbook' in which to record
          the 'earnest humility with which [Christopher Plummer] begs off being asked to praise
          Desdemona for fear of *seeming* a hypocrite' (*NYT*, 14 February 1982).

145–55   J. B. Booth as Iago was 'the poet caught in the very act of invention: with just those pauses,
          abstractions, flashes, and occasional career of speech, when a line or two came out entire –
          which befit the passage' (Gould, *Tragedian*, p. 85). Likewise, Macready 'hesitates in the
          delivery, as if he was making the lines as he proceeded . . .' (*TJ*, 10 October 1840). Ottley
          was scandalised by Fechter's Iago who 'leans cross-armed on the top of a capstan, and with

Had tongue at will, and yet was never loud;
Never lacked gold, and yet went never gay;
Fled from her wish, and yet said "Now I may";
She that being angered, her revenge being nigh,
Bade her wrong stay, and her displeasure fly;   150
She that in wisdom never was so frail
To change the cod's head for the salmon's tail;
She that could think and ne'er disclose her mind,
See suitors following and not look behind;
She was a wight, if ever such wight were –'   155
DESDEMONA To do what?
IAGO 'To suckle fools and chronicle small beer.'
DESDEMONA O, most lame and impotent conclusion! Do not learn of
  him, Emilia, though he be thy husband. How say you, Cassio, is
  he not a most profane and liberal counsellor?   160
CASSIO He speaks home, madam; you may relish him more in the
  soldier than in the scholar.
IAGO [*Aside*] He takes her by the palm. Ay, well said; whisper.
  With as little a web as this will I ensnare as great a fly as Cassio.
  Ay, smile upon her, do. I will gyve thee in thine own courtship.   165
  You say true, 'tis so indeed. If such tricks as these strip you out
  of your lieutenantry, it had been better you had not kissed your
  three fingers so oft, which now again you are most apt to play the

familiar smirk, stares first at the wife of his general, and then at her attendant, his own wife.
The proprieties are certainly ignored by the cautious ancient in this . . .' (Ottley, p. 11).
Nunn's Chekhovian manner was particularly evident here. Towards the end of Iago's
sexually suggestive rhymes, a general silence fell, leaving only the sound of Emilia forlornly
whistling (promptbook and video).

154–5   Edwin Booth: 'a glance at Roderigo would imply that Desdemona is the "wight" particularly
referred to. Roderigo has long been an unnoticed follower' (*Variorum*). Ronald Eyre made
this idea much more explicit and significant by having Desdemona herself look round and
see not Roderigo, but Cassio (promptbook).

163–71   Directors have been at pains to give Cassio and Desdemona something plausible to do here.
Kemble's stage direction has Cassio taking 'Desdemona by the hand to introduce her to the
gentlemen of Cyprus; he talks with her during Iago's speech'. Macready directed that she be
taken 'up the stage as high as the first wing' where she was introduced to Montano as well
(promptbook). Edwin Booth insisted that 'the hands of both should be ungloved. They
seldom are so', but that Cassio should kiss his three fingers 'as though describing some
pleasing act or scene, not as though complimenting Desdemona' (*Variorum*). Irving as Iago
drew the audience's attention to himself by eating grapes as he watched them: 'slowly . . .
spitting out the seeds, as if each one represented a worthy virtue to be put out of his mouth'

sir in. Very good, well kissed, an excellent courtesy! 'Tis so
indeed. Yet again your fingers to your lips? Would they were　170
clyster-pipes for your sake!
                    Trumpets within.
            The Moor! I know his trumpet.
CASSIO   'Tis truly so.
DESDEMONA Let's meet him and receive him.
CASSIO   Lo, where he comes!

            Enter OTHELLO *and* ATTENDANTS.

OTHELLO O, my fair warrior!

(Terry, *Story*, p. 206). But one critic preferred 'Mr Booth's still, respectful attitude, leaning against the sun-dial, . . . seeming careless . . . yet ever watching his prey with sly, sleepless vigilance' (*MM*, July 1881). Ronald Eyre had a brazier to which Cassio took Desdemona to warm her hands (promptbook). In Nunn's production, Desdemona burst into tears here, and Cassio naturally put his arm round her (promptbook and video). In Parker's film, Branagh watches the pair behind him reflected in his fruit-knife.

173 SD and 174–91　Most comment concentrates on Othello, but Sarah Siddons was said to have been 'full of passion' in her reception of Othello (*London Magazine*, March 1785), and, a century later, Ellen Terry suggests something similar with her marginal note 'all happy – joyous – *young*' (promptbook). Othello's arrival here has been treated either as a triumphal entry, or as a lovers' reunion, or as both. In the eighteenth and early nineteenth centuries it was a lovers' reunion. An imitator of Barton Booth, one Stephens, was advised by Aaron Hill not to run 'so eagerly to the arms of Desdemona', but to preserve 'a certain stately, yet tender advance, not tripping lightly to her embrace; but a little quickening the step, more strongly extending the arms, gently inclining the breast, not the head, and sending your look, as it were, before you, with a kind of amorous delight, in approaching her' (Aaron Hill, *Works*, I, p. 218).

Spranger Barry, wrote Foote, 'from the sweetness and compass of [his] voice . . . is much superior to Mr Q[uin]. There is indeed a mixture of distress in his joy, which . . . I would be glad he would part with' (Foote, *Treatise*, p. 27). But Barry here, according to 'J.T.', was only 'a judicious copy of Mr Garrick, who first showed in how much the grumbling of . . . Mr Quin, was ill-suited for the delicate tenderness which the poet has interwoven with the soul of the black warrior' (*J.T., Letter*, p. 16).

Lewes contrasted Kean and Fechter: 'Kean's tones, "O my fair warrior!" are still ringing in my ears, though a quarter of a century must have elapsed since I heard them; but I cannot recall Fechter's tones, heard only the other night. I only recall a vision of him holding his wife at most "proper" distance, kissing her hand, his tone free from all tremulous emotion . . . and from Desdemona he turns to the gentlemen of Cyprus as affable and calm

DESDEMONA   My dear Othello!
OTHELLO It gives me wonder great as my content   175
            To see you here before me. O, my soul's joy,
            If after every tempest come such calms,
            May the winds blow till they have wakened death,
            And let the labouring bark climb hills of seas,
            Olympus-high, and duck again as low   180
            As hell's from heaven. If it were now to die,

as if he had but just come home from a morning stroll' (Lewes, *Actors*, pp. 150–1). Fechter's stage direction suggests grand opera. Othello appeared at the back 'surrounded by his followers and attended by people who shout! Behind him come . . . the squire carrying Othello's armour, the banner bearer, the flag embroidered with the Lion of St Mark; the page, the helmet, the gauntlets and the truncheon on a velvet cushion.'

Edwin Booth was careful to avoid physicality: 'they embrace, with delicacy. There is nothing of the animal in this "noble savage" '. Lines 181–2 were to be 'uttered in low foreboding terms' thus treating them as a portent, rather than as the expression of present contentment. And at the kiss, he notes 'I think their *heartthrobs* are better than kisses' (*Variorum*). Irving, likewise, showed 'no greedy haste, no fierce satisfaction; only the comfort of returning to loved arms and a companion heart' (*Theatre*, 1 June 1881).

The nineteenth-century Italians were less inhibited: Rossi greeted Desdemona, said Winter, 'in a spirit of gloating uxorious animalism' (*Shakespeare*, pp. 295–6). Salvini had a triumphal entrance with crowds and trumpets (Mason, p. 21), but then he 'threw down his sword, raised his face to hers with tears of joy in his eyes, and as he held her in his embrace spoke that marvellous line "If it were now to die . . ." ' (Kendal, *Dame Madge Kendal*, p. 223). Fanny Kemble noted that at 'O my soul's joy!' there was 'a sudden choking of his utterance which brought a similar sensation into the throats of those that hear him' (*TB*, July 1884).

Verdi's opera opens with the storm, and the frenetically delayed climax of Otello's arrival is announced with cries of 'Evviva!' and a triumphant 'Esultate!' from Otello. Desdemona is not present, so nothing else is called for here. Verdi probably influenced Salvini's New York production, and also Oscar Asche's, in which 'supers swept across the stage in wide arcs, one arc after another, preceding Asche's debarkation in Cyprus which was thus worked up into a tremendous spectacular climax' (*Scotsman*, 4 April 1959).

Robeson entered to a cheering crowd and the strains of Warlock's Capriol Suite (Carroll). In America, the kiss caused 'an audible gasp' every night (tape supplied to Carroll from member of cast). English actors were cool: Jack Hawkins missed 'the underlying hysteria which alone can account for the exuberance of the fear which is the very cause of his relief' (H. K. Fisher, *Life and Letters*, vol. 54, July 1947). But Olivier was 'beside himself with deep internal joy, wreathed in smiles and barely able to speak' (Tynan, *National Theatre Production*, p. 7).

'Twere now to be most happy; for I fear
My soul hath her content so absolute
That not another comfort like to this
Succeeds in unknown fate.
DESDEMONA   The heavens forbid   185
But that our loves and comforts should increase,
Even as our days do grow.
OTHELLO   Amen to that, sweet powers!
I cannot speak enough of this content;
It stops me here; it is too much of joy.
                    They kiss.
And this, and this, the greatest discords be   190
That e'er our hearts shall make.
IAGO [*Aside*]   O, you are well tuned now!
But I'll set down the pegs that make this music,
As honest as I am.
OTHELLO   Come, let us to the castle.
News, friends; our wars are done; the Turks are drowned.

In the video of Suzman's production, Othello appears at the top of some stairs and Desdemona runs up towards him, Cassio's sword in her hand, cueing Othello's 'O my fair warrior'. A slow-motion sequence follows, during which, to the sound of lutes and violins, they approach each other and embrace, the camera alternating the point of view between them and thus containing them in a bubble of intense privacy: 'Both music and slow motion not only function to romanticise their meeting . . . but to separate their seemingly ideal relationship from its perception by others' (Hodgdon, 'Race-ing Othello', p. 28). This is in contrast to Oliver Parker's treatment, where the lovers' embrace (with Othello in armour on horseback and everything cut except 175–6) is seen from the point of view of an onlooking crowd whose reaction becomes one of faintly comic embarrassment. In Nunn's production, Othello dashed on and at line 179 'sweeps her up off the ground as if over the hill of sea' (*Literary Review*, November 1989). He then plumped her on to a piece of luggage, like a child, and walked round her until, on 'Amen to that', she jumped into his arms and he spun her round (promptbook and video). During their kiss, the video version cuts to McKellen's watching and smiling face. Attenborough's Cassio (Henry Ian Cusick) was embarrassed 'at [Othello's] hungry fondlings of Desdemona' here. And Othello's obliviousness to this 'makes it more than usually credible that he should be so blind to Iago' (*S*, 1 May 1999).

191b–3a In the video, Suzman has lute music here, which makes sense of Iago's 'well tuned' and 'pegs'. In Nunn's production, Emilia watched Desdemona and Othello and was 'surprised to find her attention to their embrace interrupted by a rough affectionless kiss from her husband' (Smallwood, 'Shakespeare', p. 112). In Parker's film, the camera pans to Branagh's smiling face in the crowd, and we hear his unsmiling words in voice-over.

194–5 Olivier 'greets the Cypriots as old friends; they are closer to him in blood than the Venetians' (Tynan, *National Theatre Production*, p. 7) This is the cue for general celebrations in

How does my old acquaitance of this isle? 195
Honey, you shall be well desired in Cyprus;
I have found great love amongst them. O my sweet,
I prattle out of fashion and I dote
In mine own comforts. I prithee, good Iago,
Go to the bay and disembark my coffers; 200
Bring thou the master to the citadel;
He is a good one, and his worthiness
Does challenge much respect. Come, Desdemona,
Once more well met at Cyprus!
Exeunt [all except Iago and Roderigo]
IAGO [*To a departing Attendant*] Do thou meet me presently at the 205
harbour. [*To Roderigo*] Come hither. If thou be'st valiant – as
they say base men being in love have then a nobility in their
natures more than is native to them – list me. The lieutenant
tonight watches on the court of guard. First, I must tell thee this:
Desdemona is directly in love with him. 210
RODERIGO With him? Why, 'tis not possible!
IAGO Lay thy finger thus, and let thy soul be instructed. Mark me
with what violence she first loved the Moor but for bragging and
telling her fantastical lies. And will she love him still for prating?
Let not thy discreet heart think it. Her eye must be fed. And 215
what delight shall she have to look on the devil? When the blood

Parker's film, with the burning of a Turk in effigy, and a feast at which Desdemona dances before Othello and their guests. Jude Kelly's colour reversals (black Venetians versus light-skinned Cypriots) made a point of the racial difference between the two sets of soldiery. Stewart thus greeted Montano 'with a warm embrace' (Johnson-Haddad, 'Shakespeare Theatre *Othello*', p. 10).

204 Beerbohm Tree had all the cast stage a tableau on the steps up to the castle door, just before the curtain fell (promptbook). John Barton's Iago actually took a group photograph at this point (promptbook). In Suzman's video, the moment is full of erotic promise. In Michael Attenborough's production, Iago swiped Emilia's bottom with a towel as she exited (RSC archive film).

216b–35 Like the earlier dialogue between Roderigo and Iago at the end of 1.3, this one was, from the '1755' edition onwards, throughout the nineteenth century, drastically cut. The editions of Bell, Kemble, Fechter, Edwin Booth and Irving, as well as Ellen Terry's and Oscar Asche's promptbooks, all show this cut. Webster introduced a comic misunderstanding for Roderigo here. When Iago comes to 'who stands so eminently in the degree of this fortune as . . .' he slaps Roderigo's shoulder, at which Roderigo looks forward, expecting his own name. Disappointed, he says 'eh?' and repeats 'Cassio' (Carroll). Suzman makes the same joke (video). In Nunn's video, Ian McKellen utters this speech smoking savagely as the thoughts come fast, hugging Roderigo, fixing his cross straps, mothering him.

is made dull with the act of sport, there should be, again to
inflame it and to give satiety a fresh appetite, loveliness in
favour, sympathy in years, manners and beauties: all which the
Moor is defective in. Now for want of these required conveniences, 220
her delicate tenderness will find itself abused, begin to heave the
gorge, disrelish and abhor the Moor. Very nature will instruct
her in it, and compel her to some second choice. Now, sir, this
granted – as it is a most pregnant and unforced position – who
stands so eminent in the degree of this fortune as Cassio does? – a 225
knave very voluble; no further conscionable than in putting on
the mere form of civil and humane seeming for the better
compassing of his salt and most hidden loose affection.
Why none; why none – a slipper and subtle knave, a finder
out of occasions, that has an eye can stamp and counterfeit 230
advantages, though true advantage never present itself; a
devilish knave! Besides, the knave is handsome, young, and hath
all those requisites in him that folly and green minds look after.
A pestilent complete knave; and the woman hath found him
already. 235

RODERIGO I cannot believe that in her; she's full of most blest
condition.

IAGO Blest fig's end! The wine she drinks is made of grapes. If she
had been blest she would never have loved the Moor. Blest
pudding! Didst thou not see her paddle with the palm of his 240
hand? Didst not mark that?

RODERIGO Yes, that I did; but that was but courtesy.

IAGO Lechery, by this hand: an index and obscure prologue to the
history of lust and foul thoughts. They met so near with their lips
that their breaths embraced together – villainous thoughts, 245

---

238   In Suzman's video, at 'Blest fig's end!', Richard Haines again thrusts a thumb up between
two fingers.

244b–8   (' . . . Pish!') cut from Bell onwards, in most nineteenth-century acting editions. The '1755'
edition cuts only from 'villainous thoughts' to 'the incorporate conclusion', but at the other
end of the period, Oscar Asche takes the cut back to 238 – 'If she had been blest . . .'
Interestingly, Webster makes the same cut as the '1755' edition – perhaps Iago went too far,
given the riskiness of the whole enterprise in America at that time (Carroll).

Modern productions have relished these speeches. At 'their breaths met so near', Nunn's
video has McKellen thrusting his face into Roderigo's; at 'incorporate', Ronald Eyre's Iago,
Bob Peck, touched the top of Roderigo's thigh (promptbook). Branagh does the same in
Parker's film, and, though heavily cut, his lewd images are delivered under a cart on which a
lusty couple are heard illustrating their meaning.

Roderigo! When these mutualities so marshal the way, hard
at hand comes the master and main exercise, the incorporate
conclusion. Pish! But, sir, be you ruled by me. I have brought
you from Venice; watch you tonight; for the command, I'll lay't
upon you. Cassio knows you not; I'll not be far from you. Do you   250
find some occasion to anger Cassio, either by speaking too loud or
tainting his discipline, or from what other course you please,
which the time shall more favourably minister.
RODERIGO Well.
IAGO Sir, he's rash and very sudden on choler, and haply with his   255
truncheon may strike at you: provoke him that he may; for even
out of that will I cause these of Cyprus to mutiny, whose
qualification shall come into no true taste again but by the
displanting of Cassio. So shall you have a shorter journey to your
desires by the means I shall then have to prefer them, and the   260
impediment most profitably removed without the which there
were no expectation of our prosperity.
RODERIGO I will do this, if you can bring it to any opportunity.
IAGO I warrant thee. Meet me by and by at the citadel. I must fetch
his necessaries ashore. Farewell.   265
RODERIGO Adieu.   *Exit*
IAGO That Cassio loves her, I do well believe't;
       That she loves him, 'tis apt and of great credit.
       The Moor, howbeit that I endure him not,
       Is of a constant, loving, noble nature;   270
       And I dare think he'll prove to Desdemona
       A most dear husband. Now, I do love her too,
       Not out of absolute lust – though peradventure
       I stand accountant for as great a sin –
       But partly led to diet my revenge,   275
       For that I do suspect the lusty Moor
       Hath leaped into my seat, the thought whereof
       Doth like a poisonous mineral gnaw my inwards;

256   Here Ronald Eyre's Roderigo went weak at the knees and had to be supported to prevent
      him from fainting (promptbook).
273b–4   J. B. Booth spoke the parenthesis with 'gratuitous fiendishness . . . looking to heaven with
      defiant forehead and gesture, and with a cold and mocking smile' (Gould, *Tragedian*,
      pp. 86–7).
276–7   Macready amends to: 'the adulterous Moor / Hath fixed a shame on me . . .' (promptbook).
276–8   Of Simon Russell Beale, one critic wrote: 'How lightly, quickly, to us he drops his suspicion
      that he himself has been cuckolded by Othello . . . he hardly inflects the words at all, and yet
      we know his very soul is bilious' (*FT*, 18 September 1997).

And nothing can or shall content my soul
Till I am evened with him, wife for wife;   280
Or failing so, yet that I put the Moor
At least into a jealousy so strong
That judgement cannot cure. Which thing to do,
If this poor trash of Venice, whom I trace
For his quick hunting, stand the putting on,   285
I'll have our Michael Cassio on the hip,
Abuse him to the Moor in the rank garb –
For I fear Cassio with my night-cap too –
Make the Moor thank me, love me, and reward me,
For making him egregiously an ass,   290
And practising upon his peace and quiet
Even to madness. 'Tis here, but yet confused;
Knavery's plain face is never seen till used.   *Exit*

280   On 'wife for wife' Ian McKellen slipped his mask enough to show his own jealousy,
       'pounding his fists on his knees' (*T*, 26 August 1989). In Suzman's video, Richard Haines
       thrusts an obscene fist up for each wife.

288   Even 'night-cap' was too much for Macready, who altered the line to: 'For I have fears of
       Cassio's foulplay too' (promptbook). Webster cut it, probably for the sake of simplicity
       (Carroll).

289–93 Here Webster's Iago, José Ferrer, sneered after 'love me', tapped his head at 'madness', and
       snapped his fingers at the conclusion. His soliloquies 'never failed to bring a roar of
       delighted applause from the audience' (personal letter to Carroll, 25 June 1976). David
       Suchet put 'more than a touch of longing in his voice' at 289 (*S*, 18 January 1986), and in the
       video, Ian McKellen speaks it with desperation. Richard Haines, as usual, sticks his fingers in
       his nose at 'ass', and on 'madness' he prolongs each syllable, ending the word with a hiss
       (video). Richard McCabe lifted his voice on the word, giving it a kind of soft madness in
       itself (RSC archive film). Oliver Parker's film cuts the whole soliloquy, and shows instead
       Othello and Desdemona, in a shower of red petals, consummating their marriage – a point
       Shakespeare leaves unsettled.

ACT 2, SCENE 2

Enter Othello's HERALD *with a proclamation.*

HERALD It is Othello's pleasure, our noble and valiant general, that upon certain tidings now arrived importing the mere perdition of the Turkish fleet, every man put himself into triumph: some to dance, some to make bonfires, each man to what sport and revels his addiction leads him; for besides these beneficial news, it is   5 the celebration of his nuptial. So much was his pleasure should be proclaimed. All offices are open, and there is full liberty of feasting from this present hour of five till the bell have told eleven. Heaven bless the isle of Cyprus and our noble general Othello!   *Exit*   10

Bell records this little scene as having been cut by then, and most nineteenth-century productions omitted it. Beerbohm Tree took the opportunity to mark the celebrations with dancers. Barton at the Aldwych had drums and trumpets and a sword dance (1972 promptbook); Attenborough had marching to the regimental band and fireworks for the General in full dress uniform and his wife in a big Edwardian hat (video). Jude Kelly ran this scene into the next one, setting both in the Venetian barracks, where a potentially ugly racial scrap between the Venetians and the Cypriots began to develop: 'A Cypriot soldier entered up centre to deliver Othello's proclamation, but faltered and was shouted down by the Venetians.' More Cypriots joined in, but were outnumbered, and the Venetians mocked them with a parody of a Cypriot dance (Loehlin, '*Othello*').

ACT 2, SCENE 3

Enter OTHELLO, DESDEMONA, CASSIO *and* ATTENDANTS.

OTHELLO Good Michael, look you to the guard tonight.
        Let's teach ourselves that honourable stop,
        Not to out-sport discretion.
CASSIO Iago hath direction what to do;
        But notwithstanding with my personal eye   5
        Will I look to't.
OTHELLO   Iago is most honest.
        Michael, good night; tomorrow with your earliest
        Let me have speech with you – Come, my dear love,
        The purchase made, the fruits are to ensue;
        That profit's yet to come 'tween me and you.   10

Kemble set this scene in 'the Guard house before the castle'. Macready's promptbook indicates 'Gates or Arch' and 'Gates open. Small portals R and L. 4 torches R and L. Officers precede Othello to the Gate and on his entrance to the castle follow him in.' Nunn set the stage as a barrack-room dormitory, with regulation camp beds, grey blankets, washstands, kitbags, billycans, towels, razors, first-aid box, etc. (promptbook).

1–11   In Suzman's video, Othello and Desdemona are unable to resist each other here. She draws his shirt aside and kisses his shoulder; the camera pans down their bodies, offers a glimpse of the strawberry handkerchief, and shows us Desdemona's fingers dropping the bunch of daffodils that Cassio has earlier presented to her. As the lovers exit, Othello, with a laugh, gives Cassio a parting salute. Now alone, Cassio picks up the flowers 'as though to relish Desdemona's lingering touch' (video and Hodgdon, 'Race-ing *Othello*', p. 29). At line 10 Nunn's Othello and Desdemona kissed 'long and hard' (promptbook), and the video shows Iago looking on with haggard face. Patrick Stewart's entry here brought the Cypriot–Venetian brawl (see scene 2 above) to an end: 'after a tense moment, he walked over to the nervous Cypriots, clapped his hands, and began to dance fluently in the style the Venetians had been mocking. Smiling eagerly with relief and pride, the Cypriots began to dance with him in a circle, until Othello broke off with a friendly laugh, patting a Cypriot soldier on the shoulder. His instructions to Cassio "Not to outsport discretion" were clearly intended for his troops at large, and were delivered with [a] combination of good humour and steely authority' (Loehlin, '*Othello*').

Good night.
> *Exeunt Othello, Desdemona [and Attendants]*
> *Enter* IAGO.

CASSIO Welcome, Iago; we must to the watch.
IAGO Not this hour, lieutenant; 'tis not yet ten o'th'clock. Our
general cast us thus early for the love of his Desdemona; who let
us not therefore blame: he hath not yet made wanton the night   15
with her, and she is sport for Jove.
CASSIO She's a most exquisite lady.
IAGO And I'll warrant her full of game.
CASSIO Indeed she is a most fresh and delicate creature.
IAGO What an eye she has! Methinks it sounds a parley to   20
provocation.
CASSIO An inviting eye, and yet methinks right modest.
IAGO And when she speaks, is it not an alarum to love?
CASSIO She is indeed perfection.
IAGO Well, happiness to their sheets! Come, lieutenant, I have a stoup   25
of wine, and here without are a brace of Cyprus gallants, that
would fain have a measure to the health of the black Othello.
CASSIO Not tonight, good Iago; I have very poor and unhappy brains
for drinking. I could well wish courtesy would invent some other
custom of entertainment.   30

12–25   Macready replaced 'he hath not yet made wanton . . .' with 'Is she not a delicate creature?'
(promptbook). But at line 20, he showed that he could act a sexual insinuation, even if he
couldn't utter one. His 'manner of giving this line . . . is of itself quite enough by the
sensuality of its delivery to inflame the lieutenant' (*TJ*, 10 October 1840). Kemble cut 18–19,
and most nineteenth-century editions and promptbooks follow him. Oscar Asche made a
clean sweep, cutting 15–23 (promptbook). At 25, Macready crossed out 'sheets' and altered
'their' to 'them'. Ellen Terry and Oscar Asche dropped the line (promptbooks), but Edwin
Booth and Irving kept it.
　　In Nunn's production both men were lying on their camp beds as they talked, Cassio
with a book (promptbook). As Iago invited Cassio to join the drinking party, he began
uncorking wine bottles, wiping out a washbasin, pouring wine into it (promptbook and
video) In Mendes's production Iago 'discovers the beakily plaintive Cassio [Colin Tierney]
sitting alone with a Penguin classic and half a glass of wine. Over the next few minutes Iago
manages to get him rip-roaringly drunk, as he swings his arm out with ferocious glee
towards Cassio and forces him to down vodka after vodka' (*IoS*, 21 September 1997).
Attenborough's Cassio, Henry Ian Cusick, started even more abstemiously with a glass of
orange juice before Iago seduced him into drinking wine (*SQ*, Summer 2000, 51, p. 220).

IAGO O, they are our friends – but one cup; I'll drink for you.
CASSIO I have drunk but one cup tonight, and that was craftily
qualified too; and behold what innovation it makes here. I am
unfortunate in the infirmity and dare not task my weakness with   35
any more.
IAGO What, man! 'Tis a night of revels; the gallants desire it.
CASSIO Where are they?
IAGO Here at the door; I pray you call them in.
CASSIO I'll do't, but it dislikes me.   *Exit*   40
IAGO If I can fasten but one cup upon him,
    With that which he hath drunk tonight already,
    He'll be as full of quarrel and offence
    As my young mistress' dog. Now my sick fool Roderigo,
    Whom love hath turned almost the wrong side out,   45
    To Desdemona hath tonight caroused
    Potations pottle-deep, and he's to watch.
    Three lads of Cyprus, noble swelling spirits,
    That hold their honours in a wary distance,
    The very elements of this warlike isle,   50
    Have I tonight flustered with flowing cups;
    And they watch too. Now, 'mongst this flock of
        drunkards,
    Am I to put our Cassio in some action
    That may offend the isle. But here they come.   55

Enter Cassio, MONTANO *and* GENTLEMEN.

    If consequence do but approve my dream,
    My boat sails freely, both with wind and stream.   55
CASSIO 'Fore God, they have given me a rouse already.

41ff.   John Hill praised Macklin and Garrick for 'delivering, plainly and without ornament, a
        speech in which we have been used to see a world of unnatural contortion of face' and
        'absurd by-play' (John Hill, *The Actor*, p. 282). Both Tree and Asche indicate in their
        promptbooks that Iago should drug Cassio's wine here. In Suzman's video, Iago takes one
        of Cassio's flowers and smashes it – and everything it signifies – against the wall at 40. In
        Nunn's, Ian McKellen stoops and peers confidentially into the camera for the soliloquy.
44a   On the strength of this, Orson Welles introduces a small dog which trots around throughout
        his film.
44b–53a Webster cut this piece of explanation, perhaps assuming that the event would explain itself
        (Carroll).
56ff.   Macready here was the 'gay reckless soldier', while 'making visible to the spectator his *real*
        character . . . it is absolutely necessary . . . that the performer conveys this idea to the

MONTANO Good faith, a little one; not past a pint, as I am a soldier.

IAGO Some wine, ho!

> [*Sings*]
>
> And let me the cannikin clink, clink,
>
> And let me the cannikin clink;   60
>
> > A soldier's a man,
> >
> > O, man's life's but a span,
>
> Why then, let a soldier drink.
>
> Some wine, boys!

CASSIO 'Fore God, an excellent song.   65

IAGO I learned it in England, where indeed they are most potent in potting. Your Dane, your German, and your swag-bellied Hollander – drink, ho! – are nothing to your English.

CASSIO Is your Englishman so exquisite in his drinking?

IAGO Why, he drinks you with facility your Dane dead drunk; he   70
sweats not to overthrow your Almain; he gives your Hollander a vomit ere the next pottle can be filled.

CASSIO To the health of our general!

MONTANO I am for it, lieutenant, and I'll do you justice.

IAGO O sweet England!   75

> [*Sings*]
>
> King Stephen was and aworthy peer,
>
> > His breeches cost him but a crown;

audience'. At the same time he made the audience feel 'that had we been in Cassio's place, we should most likely have done as he did' (*TJ*, 10 October 1840). In modern productions, this is the cue for barrack-room horseplay. In Nunn's production, Iago pulled down a soldier's trousers at 82 (promptbook) and in a new touch, Cassio's 'No, for I hold him to be unworthy' was provoked by 'his own imminent debagging' (*Punch*, 13 October 1989). Attenborough's production went further with 'a very English regimental drinking contest at which Cassio takes violent objection when the snobby loutish male high jinx turns to mimed fellatio' (*I*, 22 April 1999). Kelly's production, in sharp contrast, took this as an opportunity for racial hostilities. On Othello's earlier exit, the Venetians again began taunting the Cypriots, circling and stamping, and Cassio's line [87–8] was 'a final shouted attempt to maintain order' (Loehlin, '*Othello*').

73   Edwin Booth's Iago 'empties his own glass on the ground' which, as Sprague has pointed out, makes good sense of the following line (Sprague, pp. 190–1).

76–83   John Dexter made the song into 'a homesick soldier's lament, instead of the usual rousing chorus' (Tynan, *National Theatre Production*, p. 7). The last verse was dropped in Bell and Kemble. Kelly's Venetians sang the song at the Cypriots 'with an insulting emphasis on the word "wight" that allowed for the possibility of hearing it as "white"' (Johnson-Haddad, 'Shakespeare Theatre *Othello*', p. 10).

> He held them sixpence all too dear,
>> With that he called the tailor lown.
> He was a wight of high renown,   80
>> And thou art but of low degree;
> 'Tis pride that pulls the country down;
>> Then take thine auld cloak about thee.
>   Some wine, ho!

CASSIO 'Fore God, this is a more exquisite song than the other.   85

IAGO Will you hear't again?

CASSIO No, for I hold him to be unworthy of his place that does those things. Well, God's above all, and there be souls must be saved, and there be souls must not be saved.

IAGO It's true, good lieutenant.   90

CASSIO For mine own part – no offence to the general, nor any man of quality – I hope to be saved.

IAGO And so do I too, lieutenant.

CASSIO Ay, but by your leave, not before me; the lieutenant is to be saved before the ancient. Let's have no more of this; let's to our   95 affairs. God forgive us our sins! Gentlemen, let's look to our business. Do not think, gentlemen, I am drunk; this is my ancient, this is my right hand, and this is my left hand. I am not drunk now, I can stand well enough, and I speak well enough.

85–102   Charles Kemble, brother of John, was famed for his Cassio: 'the insidious creeping up of the "devil" upon his senses, the hilarity of intoxication, the tongue cleaving to the roof of the mouth, and the lips glued together' (Robson, *Playgoer*, pp. 47–8). But Cassios were usually less successful. Irving's William Terris was said to be alone among his contemporaries in remaining 'a gentleman in his cups' (*MM*, July 1881). Charles Kemble's business (Edwin Booth surmised) on 94–9 became tradition: 'Cassio drops his handkerchief and in his effort to recover it, falls on his knees; to account for this position to his companions, he attempts to pray. His clothes being awry, his sword has slipped to his right side, and this confuses him for a moment as to which is his right or his left hand' (*Variorum*). Webster's business was more menacing. 'And thou art but of low degree' was sung by Iago at Cassio and again by a gentleman at line 88. Cassio then made a point of bowing to Montano at 'man of quality' and roughly pushed Iago away at 'not before me' – at which the general talk and laughter stopped. Then at 97 ('drunk') he picked up his sword, pointed it at Iago and threatened another gentleman. He attempted twice to execute a military turn, and faced Iago, who saluted him scornfully, at which he sneered and exited (Carroll). Attenborough's Cassio tried to put his jacket on, but got it back to front, muddling his left and right hands (video). His Iago reacted to Cassio's putdown (94) with 'a look of pure hate, quickly masked' (*G*, 22 April 1999).

ALL Excellent well.   100

CASSIO Why, very well then; you must not think then that I am
    drunk.   *Exit*

MONTANO To the platform, masters. Come, let's set the watch.

IAGO You see this fellow that is gone before,
        He is a soldier fit to stand by Caesar   105
        And give direction. And do but see his vice –
        'Tis to his virtue a just equinox,
        The one as long as th'other. 'Tis pity of him.
        I fear the trust Othello puts him in,
        On some odd time of his infirmity,   110
        Will shake this island.

MONTANO   But is he often thus?

IAGO 'Tis evermore the prologue to his sleep:
        He'll watch the horologe a double set,
        If drink rock not his cradle.

MONTANO   It were well
        The general were put in mind of it.   115
        Perhaps he sees it not, or his good nature
        Prizes the virtue that appears in Cassio
        And looks not on his evils: is not this true?

                    Enter RODERIGO.

IAGO [*Aside to Roderigo*] How now, Roderigo?
        I pray you after the lieutenant, go.   120

                                    Exit Roderigo

MONTANO And 'tis great pity that the noble Moor
        Should hazard such a place as his own second
        With one of an ingraft infirmity;
        It were an honest action to say so
        To the Moor.

IAGO   Not I, for this fair island: 125
        I do love Cassio well, and would do much
        To cure him of this evil.

                    [*A cry of*] '*Help, help!*' *within.*

                        But hark! what noise?

118 SD   Sprague points out that Roderigo's entrance here must be 'covered' onstage, and quotes
          from the promptbook of James Murdoch, an American actor, which indicates a laugh
          offstage, causing Montano to look round just as Roderigo enters (Sprague, p. 191). Peter Hall
          had less compunction. As Roderigo entered, 'reeling', from the right vomitorium, Iago
          turned Montano to face upstage, then picked Roderigo up and pushed him off down the left
          vomitorium (promptbook). Webster avoided the problem by cutting the lines.

Enter Cassio, pursuing Roderigo.

CASSIO Zounds, you rogue, you rascal!

MONTANO What's the matter, lieutenant?

CASSIO A knave teach me my duty!   I'll beat the knave into a   130
twiggen bottle.

RODERIGO Beat me?

CASSIO Dost thou prate, rogue?

> [*He strikes Roderigo.*]

MONTANO Nay, good lieutenant, I pray you, sir, hold your hand.

CASSIO Let me go, sir; or I'll knock you o'er the mazzard.   135

MONTANO Come, come, you're drunk.

CASSIO Drunk?

> *They fight.*

IAGO [*Aside to Roderigo*] Away I say, go out and cry a mutiny.

> [*Exit Roderigo*]

Nay, good lieutenant; God's will, gentlemen!

Help ho! Lieutenant, sir! Montano, sir!   140

Help, masters, here's a goodly watch indeed!

> *A bell rings.*

Who's that which rings the bell? Diabolo, ho!

The town will rise. God's will, lieutenant, hold!

You will be shamed forever.

Enter Othello, and GENTLEMEN *with weapons.*

OTHELLO What is the matter here?

MONTANO   Zounds, I bleed still.   145

134ff.   Irving wrote that 'during the brawl between Cassio and Montano, I used to enjoy a
mischievous sense of mastery by flicking at them with a red cloak, as though they were bulls
in the arena' (*EIM*, September 1893). In John Dexter's production the fight developed into 'a
popular riot, with the mutinous Cypriots rising against their Venetian overlords. Thus
Othello has something more to quell than a private quarrel' (Tynan, *National Theatre
Production*, p. 7). Jude Kelly's Roderigo was dressed as a Cypriot, so that when the fighting
between him and Cassio began, it developed into a race riot, 'in which theatre Venetians
attempted to rape a female Cypriot soldier, who defended herself ferociously with a knife
until she was overpowered' (Johnson-Haddad, 'Shakespeare Theatre *Othello*', p. 10).

144 SD   This is a much-discussed moment. Bell's edition cuts from the entrance straight to 'Hold for
your lives!', and jumps straight to 'Why, how now, ho!' Kemble kept this. Kean was
described as 'rushing with scimitar in hand through the centre gates, shouting "Hold for
your lives"' (quoted by Sprague, p. 192). Gustavus Vaughan Brooke also came 'rushing
down between the combatants . . . [and] as his scimitar swept through the air it collided with
their swords, making a fiery circle in its flight'. At this point someone roared out the name of

         I am hurt to th'death.
OTHELLO   Hold for your lives!
IAGO Hold ho, lieutenant, sir; Montano, gentlemen,
         Have you forgot all place of sense and duty?
         Hold! the general speaks to you; hold, for shame!
OTHELLO Why, how now, ho! From whence ariseth this?   150
         Are we turned Turks, and to ourselves do that
         Which heaven hath forbid the Ottomites?
         For Christian shame, put by this barbarous brawl.
         He that stirs next to carve for his own rage
         Holds his soul light: he dies upon his motion.   155
         Silence that dreadful bell: it frights the isle
         From her propriety. What is the matter, masters?
         Honest Iago, that looks dead with grieving,
         Speak. Who began this? On thy love, I charge thee.
IAGO I do not know. Friends all but now, even now,   160
         In quarter and in terms like bride and groom,
         Divesting them for bed; and then but now –

the Algerian Emir, whose gallantry in rescuing women and children from burning tents was filling the newspapers, and 'the house rose at it, the pit sprang to its feet . . .' (Lawrence, *Gustavus Vaughan Brooke*, p. 78). The *Athenaeum* wished that Edwin Booth had been 'more of a soldier' here, 'and less of a schoolmaster' (7 May 1881). Salvini 'caused a startling effect', said Winter, 'by rushing in and beating down with his naked hands the drawn swords of the combatants' (Winter, *Shakespeare*, p. 289). Forbes-Robertson was not remembered for rushing, but for 'traversing the air on a raised way, a boldly silhouetted figure of austere handsomeness, stalking nobly in profile' (Montague, *Values*, p. 59). In the first part of the twentieth century the moment lost its fascination, and even Olivier took it quietly 'nursing a scimitar; Iago lines the Venetian soldiers up before him, as if on parade' (Tynan, *National Theatre Production*, p. 7). Scofield spoke as though reprimanding 'two children [who] had been sharing a bag of crisps during a sermon' (Ronald Hayman, *P and P*, April 1980). More recently the significance has lain in the unseen bed that Othello has come from. In Nunn's video, Willard White enters bare-chested, putting on his shirt, which gives point to Iago's line 'like bride and groom / Divesting them for bed'. Laurence Fishburne, in Parker's film, comes on draped in a sheet. Ray Fearon was shirtless (video).

156–7a 'The late Mr Barry always gave this direction with distinguished vehemence' (Oxberry, V, p. 29). 'Kean gave it calmly and authoritatively, as a thing of course, and "more in sorrow than in anger" ' (Ottley, p. 19). Fechter said it irritably 'as if he were angry at the bell's preventing his hearing what was to be said' (Lewes, *Actors*, p. 151). Parker's film cuts the bell: 'When Othello appears to restore order . . . no chaos rages, no bell shatters the evening's peace, no riot violates the General's honeymoon' (Samuel Crowl, *SB*, Winter 1996, p. 41).

As if some planet had unwitted men –
Swords out and tilting one at other's breasts
In opposition bloody. I cannot speak   165
Any beginning to this peevish odds:
And would in action glorious I had lost
Those legs that brought me to a part of it.

OTHELLO How comes it, Michael, you are thus forgot?

CASSIO I pray you pardon me, I cannot speak.   170

OTHELLO Worthy Montano, you were wont be civil:
The gravity and stillness of your youth
The world hath noted; and your name is great
In mouths of wisest censure. What's the matter
That you unlace your reputation thus,   175
And spend your rich opinion for the name
Of a night-brawler? Give me answer to it.

MONTANO Worthy Othello, I am hurt to danger;
Your officer Iago can inform you –
While I spare speech, which something now offends me –   180
Of all that I do know; nor know I aught
By me that's said or done amiss this night,
Unless self-charity be sometimes a vice,
And to defend ourselves it be a sin
When violence assails us.

OTHELLO   Now by heaven   185
My blood begins my safer guides to rule,
And passion having my best judgement collied,
Assays to lead the way. Zounds, if I stir,
Or do but lift this arm, the best of you
Shall sink in my rebuke. Give me to know   190
How this foul rout began, who set it on,
And he that is approved in this offence,
Though he had twinned with me, both at a birth,
Shall lose me. What, in a town of war,
Yet wild, the people's hearts brimful of fear,   195
To manage private and domestic quarrel,
In night, and on the court and guard of safety?

---

170   Fechter made his Cassio say this as if he were too drunk, rather than too distressed to
speak: 'what . . . could be more unseemly?' asked Ottley (p. 12).

187–8   Cut in Bell's edition. Gentleman supplies them in a footnote with the opinion that they
'ought to be retained, as beautiful and significant'.

194ff.   Quin here was 'as stoical as at "Fathers we once again are met in Council" ' – entirely
wrong, thought Foote (*Treatise*, p. 27).

'Tis monstrous. Iago, who began't?

MONTANO If partially affined or leagued in office,
Thou dost deliver more or less than truth,   200
Thou art no soldier.

IAGO   Touch me not so near.
I had rather have this tongue cut from my mouth
Than it should do offence to Michael Cassio.
Yet, I persuade myself, to speak the truth
Shall nothing wrong him. This it is, general: 205
Montano and myself being in speech,
There comes a fellow crying out for help,
And Cassio following him with determined sword
To execute upon him. Sir, this gentleman
Steps in to Cassio and entreats his pause;   210
Myself the crying fellow did pursue,
Lest by his clamour – as it so fell out –
The town might fall in fright. He, swift of foot,
Outran my purpose and I returned the rather
For that I heard the clink and fall of swords   215
And Cassio high in oath, which till tonight
I ne'er might say before. When I came back –
For this was brief – I found them close together
At blow and thrust, even as again they were
When you yourself did part them.   220
More of this matter can I not report;
But men are men; the best sometimes forget.
Though Cassio did some little wrong to him,
As men in rage strike those that wish them best,
Yet surely Cassio, I believe, received   225
From him that fled some strange indignity
Which patience could not pass.

OTHELLO   I know, Iago,
Thy honesty and love doth mince this matter,
Making it light to Cassio. Cassio, I love thee,
But never more be officer of mine.   230

Enter Desdemona attended.

205ff.   In the video, Ian McKellen pronounces this like a policeman describing an incident.
229–30   Charles Kemble was particularly impressive here: 'the confusion, the state of *loss of self* . . .
         when he received the rebuke of Othello; and the wonderful truthfulness of his getting sober,
         were beyond description fine – very real' (Robson, *Playgoer*, p. 48).
SD and   According to Foote, Spranger Barry's 'tenderness for Desdemona is happily expressed, and
231–8   the desire of the lover succeeds the fury of the warrior with great propriety'. But the 'fury'

        Look if my gentle love be not raised up!
        I'll make thee an example.
DESDEMONA   What's the matter, dear?
OTHELLO All's well now, sweeting; come away to bed.

itself was disappointing, like 'a gentleman stripping a valet de chambre, and not a General cashiering an officer' (Foote, *Treatise*, p. 28). J. P. Kemble cut Desdemona's entrance (and all the lines referring to her: see Introduction, p. 32) and the cut remained in most nineteenth-century productions thereafter, Phelps's, Irving's and Salvini's being the exceptions. This omission left Othello open to the accusation of excess in his dealings with Cassio. Kean avoided this by speaking the words 'solemnly and sadly as if justifying and explaining a painful act of duty. And then his walk up the stage! so stately and grand, his cloak swaying gracefully with each well-measured step – who that saw it shall forget it!' (Ottley, pp. 19–20). Macready's severity, however, seemed 'unwarranted' (Forster, *Essays*, p. 19), as did Fechter's, who turned it into a vindictive exit line (Ottley, p. 19).

Salvini's restoration of Desdemona explained his severity to Cassio, Joseph Knight observed (Knight, *Notes*, p. 21). Salvini was memorable for wrapping her in his cloak with 'vehement tenderness', like a mother 'folding her child from dangerous exposure' (Fanny Kemble, *TB*, July 1884). Winter thought Salvini's shaking his fist at his friend 'disclosed an innate plebeian quality'. Novelli did worse: he 'twiddled a forefinger . . . under the nose of his "loved" friend' (Winter, *Shakespeare*, pp. 289, 299).

In the twentieth century actors have sometimes been too tame: Ion Swinley spoke the words 'in a low tone, as you or I, or any Englishman in plus-fours might utter them' (Farjeon, *Scene*, p. 164). Agate complained similarly of Wilfred Walter (Agate, *Chronicles*, p. 290). But James Earl Jones's 'blend of personal affection and official bleakness' was 'brilliant – the smile that slowly fades, first from the eyes, leaving them cold as stone . . . the line sounded fresh minted to me' (*New Yorker*, 24 October 1964). Kelly's Desdemona rushed to the near-rape victim, cowering on the ground, whom Othello ignored – shifting 'the scene's emphasis from divisions of race to divisions of gender' (Loehlin, '*Othello*').

Some mark of Cassio's demotion is usual. Macready's Cassio let his sword drop (promptbook). In Barton's production, Othello stripped off Cassio's sash and in Peter Hall's, 'Othello seizes Cassio's baton and gives it to Iago' (promptbooks). In Suzman's video, Iago rips off Cassio's badge, and Cassio gives the same 'Roman' salute that Othello gave at 'My life upon her faith' (1.3.290). Hogdgon writes that this demonstrates not only Cassio's 'frank admiration and loyalty to his commander' but draws an analogy between the cashiered officer and the to-be-rejected Desdemona (Hodgdon, 'Race-ing *Othello*', p. 29). Oliver Parker uses the film medium to suggest Cassio's inner disorientation here. As Iago begins his explanation at line 205, Branagh's voice and image fade while Cassio, now in close-up, seems to lose himself in a droning, tapping, eastern sound that appears to echo from inside his head.

Sir, for your hurts myself will be your surgeon.

[Montano is led off]

Iago, look with care about the town,   235
And silence those whom this vile brawl distracted.
Come, Desdemona, 'tis the soldier's life
To have their balmy slumbers waked with strife.

Exeunt [all but Iago and Cassio]

IAGO What, are you hurt, lieutenant?
CASSIO Ay, past all surgery.   240
IAGO Marry, God forbid!
CASSIO Reputation, reputation, reputation! O, I have lost my
reputation! I have lost the immortal part of myself, and what
remains is bestial. My reputation, Iago, my reputation!
IAGO As I am an honest man, I thought you had received some bodily   245
wound: there is more of sense in that than in reputation.
Reputation is an idle and most false imposition, oft got without
merit and lost without deserving. You have lost no reputation at
all, unless you repute yourself such a loser. What, man! There
are ways to recover the general again. You are but now cast   250
in his mood, a punishment more in policy than in malice, even
so as one would beat his offenceless dog to affright an imperious
lion. Sue to him again, and he's yours.
CASSIO I will rather sue to be despised than to deceive so good a
commander with so light, so drunken, and so indiscreet an   255
officer. Drunk! And speak parrot! And squabble! Swagger!

237-8   Patrick Stewart called for Desdemona 'sharply and a bit imperiously, as if to say that he had
done all that was necessary and she ought not to concern herself further with what was,
after all, a military affair. She obediently followed, and the Cypriots were left to make their
way off amid the baleful glares of the Venetian soldiers' (Loehlin, '*Othello*').

242ff.   Until the last few decades, few Cassios have merited much attention here. Peter Hall's
Stephen Moore, however, made this scene 'one of the most moving moments' of the
evening. When, at 271, he 'grovels on the floor, the action seems fully motivated and
therefore effective', wrote Alan Drury, adding that when Scofield's Othello did the same
thing later 'it is merely an effect' (*L*, 27 March 1980). In the video, Suzman's Cassio speaks
the 'reputation' lines quietly and movingly. Ian McKellen was 'Nurse Iago' here, as the critic
for the *Literary Review* called him (November 1989): solicitously examining Cassio, holding
him while he vomits into a bowl, and tucking him up in bed (promptbook and video). In
contrast, Richard McCabe was distant, upright, patting Cassio awkwardly as they part
(video).

256-7   'Drunk! . . . shadow?' was cut from Bell's, Kemble's and most nineteenth-century texts, and
Webster's. Here Webster's Cassio ripped his insignia off his shoulder and threw it at Iago's
feet (Carroll).

Swear! And discourse fustian with one's own shadow! O thou
invisible spirit of wine, if thou hast no name to be known by, let
us call thee devil!

IAGO What was he that you followed with your sword? What had he   260
done to you?

CASSIO I know not.

IAGO Is't possible?

CASSIO I remember a mass of things, but nothing distinctly: a quarrel,
but nothing wherefore. O God, that men should put an enemy   265
in their mouths to steal away their brains! That we should with joy,
pleasance, revel and applause transform ourselves into beasts!

IAGO Why, but you are now well enough. How came you thus
recovered?

CASSIO It hath pleased the devil drunkenness to give place to the devil   270
wrath; one unperfectness shows me another, to make me frankly
despise myself.

IAGO Come, you are too severe a moraler. As the time, the place, and
the condition of this country stands, I could heartily wish this had
not befallen; but since it is as it is, mend it for your own good.   275

CASSIO I will ask him for my place again; he shall tell me I am a
drunkard. Had I as many mouths as Hydra, such an answer would
stop them all. To be now a sensible man, by and by a fool, and
presently a beast! O strange! Every inordinate cup is unblessed,
and the ingredience is a devil.   280

IAGO Come, come, good wine is a good familiar creature, if it be well
used; exclaim no more against it. And, good lieutenant, I think
you think I love you.

CASSIO I have well approved it, sir. I drunk!

IAGO You or any man living may be drunk at a time, man. I'll   285
tell you what you shall do. Our general's wife is now the general.
I may say so in this respect, for that he hath devoted and given
up himself to the contemplation, mark, and denotement of her
parts and graces. Confess yourself freely to her, importune her
help to put you in your place again. She is of so free, so kind,   290
so apt, so blest a disposition, that she holds it a vice in her
goodness not to do more than she is requested. This broken
joint between you and her husband entreat her to splinter; and

260, 264–5   Fechter remembered here that Iago would be anxious to know whether Cassio had
recognised Roderigo. His direction has Iago scrutinising Cassio, and then relaxing into
laughter when he is sure that Cassio is ignorant.

266–7   Cut from Bell's, Kemble's and most nineteenth-century texts.

286–8   Cut from 'Our general's wife' in Bell's edition, Kemble's and thereafter during the
nineteenth century.

my fortunes against any lay worth naming, this crack of your love
shall grow stronger than it was before.   295
CASSIO You advise me well.
IAGO I protest, in the sincerity of love and honest kindness.
CASSIO I think it freely; and betimes in the morning I will beseech
    the virtuous Desdemona to undertake for me. I am desperate of
    my fortunes if they check me here.   300
IAGO You are in the right. Good night, lieutenant, I must to the watch.
CASSIO Good night, honest Iago.   *Exit*
IAGO And what's he then that says I play the villain,

297   In Parker's film, they embrace, and Branagh gives the camera a straight look over Cassio's
       shoulder.
301   In Barton's production Cassio gave his sword to Iago, and said the line (which comes at
       3.1.38), 'I never knew a Florentine more kind and honest' (promptbook). In Peter Hall's,
       Cassio 'goes to pick up baton, then Iago takes it from him' (promptbook).
303–29 As usual with Iago's speeches, this was subject to heavy cutting. In the '1755' edition,
       308b–20a were cut. Nineteenth-century acting editions thereafter make the same cut (give
       or take a line or so). All the others include, for example, 'Divinity of hell!' (317), and Fechter's
       Iago gave a 'short diabolical laugh' just before it (his stage direction). In general Macready's
       Iago impressed with his 'demoniacal nature and fiendish uncontrolled joy' (*TJ*, 10 October
       1840). Incidentally, he altered 'her body's lust' at 324 to 'her sinful love' (promptbook). It is
       not said where Henry Irving's Iago picked 'his teeth with a dagger and afterwards wipes it
       on his sleeve', but perhaps it was here after the drinking (and perhaps eating) episode (*MM*,
       July 1881). In Peter Hall's production, Michael Bryant was so casual that he almost left the
       stage, returning 'as if as an afterthought' (*Cahiers Elizabéthains*, October 1980). In
       Suzman's video, at 'make, unmake' (313) Richard Haines flops his hands this way and that
       like puppets, and at 'Divinity of hell!' hugs himself, overcome with laughter. Ian McKellen's
       Iago gave the soliloquy sitting on Cassio's bed, and at 315 the sleeping Cassio shifted and
       threw a leg across him (promptbook) – the seed for Iago's later idea and an example of this
       production's 'passion for substantiating things' (*I*, 2 October 1989). On the last line, he
       yawned hugely and fell asleep, exhausted by his night's work (promptbook and video). In
       Parker's film, 'Divinity of hell!' cues in music to heighten the atmosphere and at 327,
       Branagh grabs a blackened brand from the fire, holds it a painful moment, and in a
       meta-filmic gesture, covers the lens with his 'pitchy' hand – as though what he has in mind
       is too dreadful for our sight. In Mendes's production, Simon Russell Beale laid out his
       'diabolical plan with the help of playing cards' (*G*, 18 September 1997), a card each for 'this
       honest fool', the Moor and Desdemona (Potter, *Othello*, p. 198). Richard McCabe stood
       ramrod straight, and maintained his clipped, pedantic delivery: 'no friend to sleep, he needs
       only a basin of water and a quick glance in a polished tray to set his features for another
       day' (*S*, 1 May 1999).

When this advice is free I give, and honest,
Probal to thinking, and indeed the course   305
To win the Moor again? For 'tis most easy
Th'inclining Desdemona to subdue
In any honest suit. She's framed as fruitful
As the free elements; and then for her
To win the Moor, were't to renounce his baptism,   310
All seals and symbols of redeemèd sin,
His soul is so enfettered to her love,
That she may make, unmake, do what she list,
Even as her appetite shall play the god
With his weak function. How am I then a villain   315
To counsel Cassio to this parallel course
Directly to his good? Divinity of hell!
When devils will the blackest sins put on,
They do suggest at first with heavenly shows
As I do now. For whiles this honest fool   320
Plies Desdemona to repair his fortunes,
And she for him pleads strongly to the Moor,
I'll pour this pestilence into his ear:
That she repeals him for her body's lust;
And by how much she strives to do him good,   325
She shall undo her credit with the Moor.
So will I turn her virtue into pitch,
And out of her own goodness make the net
That shall enmesh them all.

Enter Roderigo.

How now, Roderigo?

RODERIGO I do follow here in the chase, not like a hound that hunts,   330
but one that fills up the cry. My money is almost spent; I have
been tonight exceedingly well cudgelled; and I think the issue will
be, I shall have so much experience for my pains; and so, with
no money at all, and a little more wit, return again to Venice.

329 SD   Some productions have omitted this last section of the act – Salvini's, for example, and
Beerbohm Tree's. When Roderigo does enter, he usually does so either 'rubbing his back'
(Fechter's stage direction) or 'torn, bleeding, and with a black eye' (Webster's promptbook),
or, as in Dexter's production, with a bleeding nose, which Iago wiped for him, giving him a
kiss goodbye on the top of his head (film). McKellen nursed him more thoroughly, pouring
water, dabbing eau de cologne, cuddling, bandaging his head, and arranging his hair nicely
over the top (video and promptbook)

IAGO How poor are they that have no patience!   335
       What wound did ever heal but by degrees?
       Thou know'st we work by wit and not by witchcraft,
       And wit depends on dilatory time.
       Does't not go well? Cassio hath beaten thee,
       And thou by that small hurt hath cashiered Cassio.   340
       Though other things grow fair against the sun,
       Yet fruits that blossom first will first be ripe.
       Content thyself awhile. By th'mass, 'tis morning:
       Pleasure and action make the hours seem short.
       Retire thee, go where you are billeted.   345
       Away, I say, thou shalt know more hereafter –
       Nay, get thee gone.

Exit Roderigo

               Two things are to be done.
       My wife must move for Cassio to her mistress –
       I'll set her on.
       Myself the while to draw the Moor apart,   350
       And bring him jump when he may Cassio find
       Soliciting his wife. Ay, that's the way:
       Dull not device by coldness and delay.   *Exit*

ACT 3, SCENE 1

Enter CASSIO, MUSICIANS *and* CLOWN.

CASSIO Masters, play here; I will content your pains.
　　　　Something that's brief, and bid 'Good morrow, general.'
　　　　　　　　　　　　　　[*They play.*]
CLOWN Why, masters, have your instruments been in Naples, that
　　　they speak i'th'nose thus?
1 MUSICIAN How, sir, how? 5
CLOWN Are these, I pray you, wind instruments?
1 MUSICIAN Ay, marry are they, sir.
CLOWN O, thereby hangs a tail.
1 MUSICIAN Whereby hangs a tale, sir?
CLOWN Marry, sir, by many a wind instrument that I know. But, 10
　　　masters, here's money for you; and the general so likes your music
　　　that he desires you, for love's sake, to make no more noise with
　　　it.
1 MUSICIAN Well sir, we will not.
CLOWN If you have any music that may not be heard, to't again; but, 15
　　　as they say, to hear music the general does not greatly care.
1 MUSICIAN We have none such, sir.
CLOWN Then put up your pipes in your bag, for I'll away. Go,
　　　vanish into air, away!
　　　　　　　　　　　　　　　　　　Exeunt Musicians
CASSIO Dost thou hear, mine honest friend? 20
CLOWN No, I hear not your honest friend; I hear you.
CASSIO Prithee keep up thy quillets – there's a poor piece of gold for
　　　thee. If the gentlewoman that attends the general's wife be
　　　stirring, tell her there's one Cassio entreats her a little favour of
　　　speech. Wilt thou do this? 25

This scene was cut from at least as early as the '1755' edition, and it is very rarely played
now, though Peter Hall included it in 1980. Barton in 1971–2 had Arabs singing here, not
under Cassio's direction, but he included some of Emilia's dialogue with Cassio later on in
the scene (promptbooks). Barton's military production gave him the opportunity here to
point up Cassio's humiliation: 'the shock of Cassio's downfall is intensified by his crestfallen
approach to Desdemona in a civilian suit' (*T*, 10 September 1971).

CLOWN She is stirring, sir; if she will stir hither, I shall seem to notify
    unto her.
CASSIO Do, good my friend.

Exit Clown

Enter IAGO.

              In happy time, Iago.
IAGO You have not been abed then?
CASSIO Why, no; the day had broke before we parted.   30
        I have made bold, Iago,
        To send in to your wife. My suit to her
        Is that she will to virtuous Desdemona
        Procure me some access.
IAGO   I'll send her to you presently;
        And I'll devise a mean to draw the Moor   35
        Out of the way, that your converse and business
        May be more free.
CASSIO   I humbly thank you for't.

Exit [Iago]

        I never knew a Florentine more kind and honest.

Enter EMILIA.

EMILIA Good morrow, good lieutenant; I am sorry
        For your displeasure; but all will sure be well.   40
        The general and his wife are talking of it,
        And she speaks for you stoutly. The Moor replies
        That he you hurt is of great fame in Cyprus
        And great affinity, and that in wholesome wisdom
        He might not but refuse you; but he protests he loves you,   45
        And needs no other suitor but his likings
        To take the safest occasion by the front
        To bring you in again.
CASSIO   Yet I beseech you,
        If you think fit, or that it may be done,
        Give me advantage of some brief discourse   50
        With Desdemon alone.
EMILIA   Pray you, come in;
        I will bestow you where you shall have time
        To speak your bosom freely.
CASSIO   I am much bound to you.

Exeunt

ACT 3, SCENE 2

Enter OTHELLO, IAGO *and* GENTLEMEN.

OTHELLO These letters give, Iago, to the pilot,
        And by him do my duties to the senate.
        That done, I will be walking on the works;
        Repair there to me.
IAGO   Well, my good lord, I'll do't.   *[Exit]*
OTHELLO This fortification, gentlemen, shall we see't?   5
GENTLEMEN We'll wait upon your lordship.
                                         Exeunt

This little scene is also usually cut, though Hall and Barton included it.

ACT 3, SCENE 3

Enter DESDEMONA, CASSIO *and* EMILIA.

DESDEMONA Be thou assured, good Cassio, I will do
    All my abilities in thy behalf.
EMILIA Good madam, do; I warrant it grieves my husband
    As if the case were his.
DESDEMONA O, that's an honest fellow. Do not doubt, Cassio,   5
    But I will have my lord and you again
    As friendly as you were.
CASSIO   Bounteous madam,
    Whatever shall become of Michael Cassio,
    He's never anything but your true servant.
DESDEMONA I know't; I thank you. You do love my lord,   10

The 1766 Drury Lane promptbook indicates the 'Wainsc[ote] Chamber' scene, at the second groove, and acting editions of the early nineteenth century continue to place the scene within the castle. When Fechter made it into a cross between Desdemona's boudoir and Othello's operations room, Ottley found it absurd that Othello should share his wife's sitting-room, and 'indelicate' to show Cassio 'dangling at the elbow of Desdemona in her boudoir'. He thought the scene should be set outside, so that Desdemona comes across Cassio 'in her walks'. Most productions since have done just that (Ottley, pp. 24–5).

In Peter Hall's production the lighting followed the progress of Othello's jealousy: 'a translucent canopy was lowered . . . and as the green-eyed monster of jealousy was aroused . . . so the canopy was lit with greens and reds' (*Cahiers Elizabéthians*, October 1980). Nunn had a table upstage, and slatted chairs and a table downstage, with a drinks tray (promptbook). In her video, Suzman has Arab singing, and Nunn the rasp of cicadas (promptbook).

1ff. Fechter had Desdemona winding off silk 'which Emilia (sitting on the stool) holds to her; Cassio stands respectfully before Desdemona who continues her work as she speaks' (Fechter's stage direction). Ottley found Desdemona's 'smiling sympathy' excessive, 'altogether *à la Française*' (Ottley, p. 12). Ellen Terry remarks in the margin of her promptbook 'very bright, merry – young'. Sean Baker, in Nunn's production, entered in white civvies, knelt and presented a box of chocolates to Desdemona who opened it with a little cry and immediately took one (promptbook and video).

> You have known him long, and be you well assured
> He shall in strangeness stand no farther off
> Than in a politic distance.
> CASSIO   Ay, but, lady,
> That policy may either last so long
> Or feed upon such nice and waterish diet,   15
> Or breed itself so out of circumstance,
> That I being absent and my place supplied,
> My general will forget my love and service.
> DESDEMONA Do not doubt that. Before Emilia here,
> I give thee warrant of thy place. Assure thee   20
> If I do vow a friendship, I'll perform it
> To the last article. My lord shall never rest,
> I'll watch him tame and talk him out of patience;
> His bed shall seem a school, his board a shrift;
> I'll intermingle every thing he does   25
> With Cassio's suit. Therefore be merry, Cassio;
> Thy solicitor shall rather die
> Than give thy cause away.

> *Enter* OTHELLO *and* IAGO.

> EMILIA Madam, here comes my lord.
> CASSIO Madam, I'll take my leave.   30
> DESDEMONA Why, stay and hear me speak.
> CASSIO Madam, not now: I am very ill at ease,
>   Unfit for mine own purposes.
> DESDEMONA Well, do your discretion.
>   *Exit Cassio*
> IAGO Ha! I like not that.
> OTHELLO   What dost thou say?   35
> IAGO Nothing, my lord; or if — I know not what.
> OTHELLO Was not that Cassio parted from my wife?

---

24   This was cut in the Smock Alley text and then later by Kemble; it remained so during the
nineteenth century.

34 SD, 35–8   Cumberland's acting edition (1829) directs that Othello should enter 'reading a paper'. From
Morley's descrition of him, Fechter was unusual in suggesting suspiciousness as early as
this: 'I do not understand why . . . Othello sees their parting with a spasm of emotion
preceding "Ha! I like not that". Moreover, nothing . . . immediately after this colloquy
sustained the idea' (Morley, *Journal*, p. 229). Salvini, by contrast, showed 'no anxiety; only
simple, natural curiosity' (Mason, p. 30). Donald Sinden attempted, like Fechter, to convey a
hint of jealousy before Iago's words were uttered (conversation with this editor).

IAGO Cassio, my lord? No, sure I cannot think it
That he would steal away so guilty-like,
Seeing you coming.
OTHELLO   I do believe 'twas he.   40
DESDEMONA How now, my lord?
I have been talking with a suitor here,
A man that languishes in your displeasure.
OTHELLO Who is't you mean?
DESDEMONA Why, your lieutenant, Cassio. Good my lord,   45
If I have any grace or power to move you,
His present reconciliation take.
For if he be not one that truly loves you,
That errs in ignorance, and not in cunning,
I have no judgement in an honest face.   50
I prithee call him back.
OTHELLO   Went he hence now?
DESDEMONA Ay, sooth; so humbled
That he hath left part of his grief with me

39ff.   Edwin Forrest 'for an instant . . . looked at Iago as if much impressed by his emphasis on the
last part of the sentence. Forrest's mind from this moment was particularly drawn to all that
Iago said about Cassio' (Harrison, *Edwin Forrest*, p. 75). Perhaps this was customary, for
when Fechter's Othello showed himself 'free from all misgiving', treating Desdemona 'as a
father might treat a child', Lewes objected – as he never had with Kean or Macready (Lewes,
Actors, pp. 158–9). Fechter's father–child approach, where Desdemona kissed Othello's
beard and he played with her curls (Ottley, pp. 12–13), was elaborated by Salvini, who
seemed sometimes the lover, sometimes 'an old man tenderly caressing the hair of his
grand-daughter', and sometimes 'the good humoured husband created for the purpose of
being forever deceived by women' (Stanislavski, *My Life*, p. 269). Like Fechter, he busied
himself with papers while Desdemona teased him, at one moment (just before 58,
'Tomorrow dinner, then?') actually taking the pen from his hand (Mason, p. 32). Olivier was
in the Fechter–Salvini tradition here, reacting to her 'with paternal chuckles, a man besotted
by the coy white trophy he has conquered' (Tynan, *National Theatre Production*, p. 7).
Anthony Hopkins reacts with a repeated 'sh, sh' to her, as though she were an importunate
child (Jonathan Miller, BBC video). In Suzman's video, the two of them tease each other and
canoodle, Weinberg pretending to cry at one moment, Kani delightedly laughing. In Nunn's
production, Imogen Stubbs brought Othello a glass of lemon which she had forgotten to
sugar. Othello winced, but drank it: 'he will swallow any draught, no matter how bitter, if it
comes from her hand, and that is the point of the scene that follows, but whether it gains
from being anticipated in such physical terms – the audience can see the swirl of pips . . .
and even catch the strong whiff of citrus – is another matter' (*I*, 26 August 1989).

To suffer with him. Good love, call him back.
OTHELLO Not now, sweet Desdemon; some other time.   55
DESDEMONA But shall't be shortly?
OTHELLO   The sonner, sweet, for you.
DESDEMONA Shall't be tonight at supper?
OTHELLO   No, not tonight.
DESDEMONA Tomorrow dinner then?
OTHELLO   I shall not dine at home.
   I meet the captains at the citadel.
DESDEMONA Why, then, tomorrow night, or Tuesday morn,   60
   On Tuesday noon, or night; on Wednesday morn.
   I prithee name the time, but let it not
   Exceed three days. In faith, he's penitent;
   And yet his trespass, in our common reason –
   Save that, they say, the wars must make example   65
   Out of their best – is not almost a fault
   T'incur a private check. When shall he come?
   Tell me, Othello. I wonder in my soul
   What you would ask me that I should deny,
   Or stand so mammering on. What! Michael Cassio,   70
   That came a-wooing with you, and so many a time
   When I have spoke of you dispraisingly
   Hath tane your part, to have so much to do
   To bring him in? By'r Lady, I could do much –
OTHELLO Prithee no more. Let him come when he will;   75
   I will deny thee nothing.
DESDEMONA   Why, this is not a boon;
   'Tis as I should entreat you wear your gloves,
   Or feed on nourishing dishes, or keep you warm,
   Or sue to you to do a peculiar profit

64–7a   Bell's edition omits this, as do nineteenth-century acting editions thereafter. Perhaps
        Desdemona was thought to be straying from her province.

70a   Bell's edition cuts – too colloquial perhaps. Sarah Siddons here was said to be 'beyond
        measure winning' (Boaden, *Kemble*, I, p. 259).

76–83   Desdemona's speech here has been very precarious in earlier centuries. The Smock Alley
        text omits it, and Bell records that it was cut for the stage in the latter part of the eighteenth
        century. Kemble restores it and Macready cut it (promptbook) – but a promptbook owned
        by Fanny Kemble, now at the Stratford-on-Avon Shakespeare Library, has 'in' marked next
        to the scored-out passage, so perhaps she persuaded him to include it – for her, at least.
        Phelps also cut it (promptbook) as did Irving, but Forbes-Robertson kept it. Ellen Terry's
        promptbook, however, omits it.

79–80   Olivier takes special delight in Desdemona just here, and mimes a sort of smiling love-snap
        with his teeth (film).

To your own person. Nay, when I have a suit   80
Wherein I mean to touch your love indeed,
It shall be full of poise and difficult weight,
And fearful to be granted.
OTHELLO   I will deny thee nothing.
Whereon, I do beseech thee, grant me this,
To leave me but a little to myself.   85
DESDEMONA Shall I deny you? No; farewell, my lord.
OTHELLO Farewell, my Desdemona, I'll come to thee straight.
DESDEMONA Emilia, come. Be as your fancies teach you;
Whate'er you be, I am obedient.
                              Exeunt Desdemona and Emilia
OTHELLO Excellent wretch! Perdition catch my soul   90
But I do love thee; and when I love thee not,
Chaos is come again.
IAGO   My noble lord –

87   In Nunn's production, Othello and Desdemona embraced long and lovingly here, while Iago
     and Emilia stood by: 'Everything between Iago and Emilia seems sweaty and covert, and Ms
     Wanamaker . . . brings [this] to bear in one gesture: she watches Iago peering intently at
     Othello and Desdemona's embrace and then, overcome, hurriedly looks away' (*Wall Street
     Journal* (Brussels), 6 October 1989). ' . . . we see his embrace of Desdemona poignantly
     reflected in Emilia's face, as she stands, stage front, thinking of her own brutal treatment at
     the hands of Iago' (*L*, 7 August 1989). After a long kiss, Attenborough's Desdemona, Zoë
     Waites, teased him by emphasising the 'you' and the 'I' (RSC archive film).

D, 90–2 Fechter conducted Desdemona to the same exit that Cassio had just taken, a tapestried
     opening (his stage direction). Ottley thought this full of 'irreconcilable suggestions which it
     is impossible to resist' (Ottley, p. 26). Edwin Booth advised 'joyousness' here, touched by
     'an undertone of sadness – as at their first embrace in Cyprus'. Iago, upstage, sneers
     (*Variorum*). 'How long were their farewells', wrote Stanislavski of Salvini, 'and how their
     eyes talked for them and they made mysterious cabalistic signs to each other . . . And then,
     when Desdemona left him, Othello still followed her with his gaze . . .' (Stanislavski, *My Life*,
     p. 269). Lewes noted that just before the word 'Chaos' there was 'a momentary pause . . .
     followed by a gesture which *explained* the words . . . the world vanishing into chaos at such
     a monstrous state of feeling' (Lewes, *Actors*, p. 268). Godfrey Tearle spoke these words 'as
     though he were saying "When I cease to love you the end of the world will have come"',
     instead of speaking them as 'the expression of the agonized confusion of his spirit when he
     hates her. The line should be broken by a desperate gesture' (MacCarthy, *Theatre*, p. 73).
     Ben Kingsley altered 'wretch' to 'wench', and made a pause before the word 'that is full of
     the impending chaos he predicts' (*FT*, 25 September 1985).

92bff. 'My noble lord . . .' This is the opening of Iago's attack, and the whole rhythm of what
     follows, how eager or reluctant Othello is to catch Iago's drift, has always been watched

OTHELLO What dost thou say, Iago?
IAGO   Did Michael Cassio,
When you wooed my lady, know of your love?

with intense interest. So much comment takes this section of 3.3 at one sweep that it seems best to give these general pictures first. According to Rymer it was known at the Restoration as 'the top scene, the scene that raises *Othello* above all other tragedies in our theatres'. The reason for this, he thought, was its exaggerated 'action'; 'the mops and the mows, the grimace, the grins, and gesticulation' (Rymer, *Short View*, p. 149). Samuel Foote too called it the 'great scene of business'. In going on to complain that actors usually make the mistake here of 'being jealous before they have reason' (Foote, *Treatise*, p. 28), he touches on one of the greatest problems of the play. Foote thinks that 'Ha!' (see note at 166ff.) is too soon, though he may not mean that the actors should show nothing before that moment. We do not know precisely when in the scene the greatest actors before Fechter represented Othello as jealous, possibly because there was nothing precise about it. All we know is that when Fechter left it as late as 210 ('And so she did') it was thought of as 'a striking change' (*Morning Herald*, 24 October 1861, see Introduction, p. 47). That paper continued: 'he appears first to disregard or to utterly misunderstand the innuendos of Iago, then to accept them as general reflections not applicable to himself . . . Next . . . he becomes in the simple honesty of his nature genuinely puzzled.' The result, thought Lewes, was that Fechter disregarded 'the *growth* of jealousy' and made it 'sudden and preposterous' (Lewes, *Actors*, p. 156).

It was said of Spranger Barry that 'his first tendencies to jealousy are beautifully expressed and finely smothered' (*London Chronicle*, 7 March 1757). Perhaps these were evident early on, but identifiable only, as Lewes put it, as 'a *vague* feeling which he dares not shape into a suspicion' (Lewes, *Actors*, p. 158). The *Theatrical Inquisitor* (May 1814) describes Kean's doubt as being already well advanced by 173 ('O misery!'). Leigh Hunt even suggests that Kean expressed doubt almost from the outset. One of his best things, Hunt says, was 'the low and agitated affection of quiet discourse in which he first canvasses the subject with Iago' (Hunt, *Dramatic Criticism*, p. 201). But there was nothing fixed in this. The *Theatrical Inquisitor* speaks of 'the alterations of excruciating suspicion and tender recollection [which] were depicted with a force, a pathos, and a power of expression that were perfectly electrical' (May 1814).

The first attempt at naturalistic business was perhaps also an attempt to ward off the moment. Charles Dillon had Othello 'quietly seated, perusing some state document' when Iago begins, then 'startled by his exclamation "Indeed!"' He then returns to his reading, 'but the thought recurs and he carelessly asks "Discern'st thou aught in that?"' At length Othello is brought to his feet, and 'the paper drops from his hand' (*A*, December 1856). Fechter pressed this same idea to show Othello totally preoccupied. Lewes found the business natural in itself, but 'not natural – that is, not true to the nature of Othello and the

OTHELLO He did from first to last. Why dost thou ask?   95
IAGO But for a satisfaction of my thought;

situation – for him to be dead to the dreadful import of Iago's artful suggestions' (Lewes, *Actors*, p. 157). Salvini used the same desk business, but there went with it, said Lewes, 'the expression of emotion which renders such business significant' (*Actors*, footnote on p. 157).

Salvini was an actor who, according to Robert Louis Stevenson, 'night after night does the same thing differently, but always well' (Stevenson, *Works*, XXIV, p. 63). Thus Mason, who watched Salvini in New York in the 1880s, says that he was 'bothered, bored, teased, anxious to get on with his own work, and impatient of interruption' during the opening speeches of this scene, and that he first showed 'grave anxiety' at Iago's 'Think, my lord!' throwing down his pen and rising at 'Thou dost mean something' (Mason, pp. 35–6). Knight confirms this, but notes too that 'at the first word, [he] suspends his work' (Knight, *Notes*, p. 22). Stanislavski, on the other hand, describes him as still preoccupied with his love for Desdemona, 'looking sideways at his papers of business, idly playing with a goose-feather pen, . . . Iago's first hints about Desdemona only amused Salvini . . .' (Stanislavski, *My Life*, p. 269). Yet even in this idle, contented mood, Salvini could seem momentarily to lose hold of himself: 'but he regained control at once . . . The impossibility of Iago's supposition brings him into even better spirits because he feels such a thing can never happen to him – if for no other reason – Desdemona is so pure' (Ibid., pp. 269–70).

Mason pinpoints his speech at 178b–94 as being the moment when 'he first recognizes the fact that Iago's harping upon jealousy may have some reference to himself' (Mason, p. 40). But whatever the exact timing, Salvini confirmed Lewes in his conviction that Othello is not 'dead' to Iago's insinuations. 'The subtle and varied expression of uneasiness growing into haggard grief – desiring to learn all that was in Iago's mind, yet dreading to know it, – trying to conceal from him the effect of his hints, and more and more losing all control – could not have been more artistically truthful' (Lewes, *Actors*, p. 268).

Irving, in his second production (1881), 'finely exhibited Othello's reluctance to doubt, his struggles with his own misgivings and alarms' (Cook, *Nights*, II, pp. 325–6). Edwin Booth had an identifiable 'moment' – line 179 (ibid., p. 300). Beerbohm Tree gave way almost immediately in spite of being a 'thoughtful' Othello: 'But he never seemed swept away by it, never really its slave' (*Morning Leader*, 10 April 1912).

Robeson's performance in 1930 triggered racial (and racist) explanations for the problem of how soon and how much. Comparing him with the English Godfrey Tearle, one critic opined that Tearle's jealousy seemed irrational and incredible because Englishmen hold 'self-control to be almost the greatest of virtues'. Robeson, by contrast, 'comes of a race whose characteristic is to keep control of its passions only to a point and [then] to throw control to the winds' (*DT*, 20 May 1930). Valk – being a foreigner – could be 'touched into mad, lambent flame in an instant', according to Tynan, and get away with it (Tynan, *A View*, p. 59).

          No further harm.

OTHELLO   Why of thy thought, Iago?

IAGO I did not think he had been acquainted with her.

OTHELLO O yes, and went between us very oft.

IAGO Indeed?   100

OTHELLO Indeed? Ay, indeed. Discern'st thou aught in that?
          Is he not honest?

IAGO Honest, my lord?

OTHELLO Honest? Ay, honest.

IAGO My lord, for aught I know.

OTHELLO   What dost thou think?   105

IAGO Think, my lord?

OTHELLO Think, my lord! By heaven, he echoes me,
          As if there were some monster in his thought
          Too hideous to be shown. Thou dost mean something.
          I heard thee say even now thou lik'st not that,   110
          When Cassio left my wife. What didst not like?
          And when I told thee he was of my counsel
          In my whole course of wooing, thou cried'st 'Indeed?'
          And didst contract and purse thy brow together,
          As if thou then hadst shut up in thy brain   115
          Some horrible conceit. If thou dost love me,
          Show me thy thought.

IAGO My lord, you know I love you.

OTHELLO   I think thou dost;
          And for I know thou'rt full of love and honesty,
          And weigh'st thy words before thou giv'st them breath,   120
          Therefore these stops of thine fright me the more;
          For such things in a false disloyal knave
          Are tricks of custom; but in a man that's just,

Dexter and Olivier departed from the tradition of paperwork: 'both actors must find reasons deeper than accidents of duty to keep them together'. Othello took the initiative 'like a headmaster ordering one prefect to tell tales on another' (Tynan, *National Theatre Production*, p. 7). Later productions – Barton's, Eyre's, Hall's and Nunn's – all used the paper-signing business. In Hall's production, Othello's table had on it a bowl of primroses which Felicity Kendall (Desdemona) had put there before her exit – the symbol of her innocence thus present throughout the scene. Suzman, Oliver Parker and Attenborough avoided paperwork, though the latter two substituted other business – gun-loading and sword-cleaning. Only Suzman left Iago and Othello with nothing but each other, and the result recalls descriptions of Kean: attentive from the outset. Kani was serious at 'What dost think?' (105) rising to suspicion at 'Thou dost mean something' (109) and again at 'fright me the more' (121) (video). Parker uses music to underline the emotional stages of the scene.

They're close dilations, working from the heart,
That passion cannot rule.
IAGO   For Michael Cassio,   125
I dare be sworn I think that he is honest.
OTHELLO I think so too.
IAGO   Men should be what they seem;
Or those that be not, would they might seem none!
OTHELLO Certain, men should be what they seem.
IAGO Why then, I think Cassio's an honest man.   130
OTHELLO Nay, yet there's more in this.
I prithee speak to me as to thy thinkings,
As thou dost ruminate, and give thy worst of thoughts
The worst of words.
IAGO   Good my lord, pardon me;
Though I am bound to every act of duty,   135
I am not bound to that all slaves are free to.
Utter my thoughts! Why, say they are vile and false?
As where's that palace, whereinto foul things
Sometimes intrude not? Who has a breast so pure,
But some uncleanly apprehensions   140
Keep leets and law-days, and in session sit
With meditations lawful?
OTHELLO Thou dost conspire against thy friend, Iago,
If thou but think'st him wronged, and mak'st his ear
A stranger to thy thoughts.
IAGO   I do beseech you,   145
Though I perchance am vicious in my guess –
As I confess it is my nature's plague

127b–8   David Suchet's homosexual Iago stopped short after this utterance as though, terrified at his own iniquity, he had 'peered into the abyss' (*G*, 26 September 1985).
129–30   Fechter spoke 129 'smiling as if in raillery' (his stage direction). Salvini said it as if he felt ' "This is the veriest truism – everyone admits it – why do you inflict it upon me?" ' After Iago spoke the next line 'there is a long pause. Othello regards Iago with searching scrutiny . . . After a moment, Othello smiles, shakes his head and waves his hand slightly, deprecating Iago's lack of frankness . . .' (Mason, p. 37).
131   Olivier speaks this so as to call Iago back from a false exit (film).
139b–42   These lines were cut from Bell's edition and thereafter during the nineteenth century.
145bff.   Hazlitt objected to Kean's Iago in the early stages of this section where there can be no 'superficial gaiety or heedlessness'. These lines especially, he said 'should correspond with the moody dissatisfaction and suspicious, creeping, catlike watchfulness of his general appearance' (Hazlitt, v, pp. 219–20).
147   In Oliver Parker's film, a high, mosquito, violin sound starts at 'my nature's plague'.

>To spy into abuses, and oft my jealousy
>Shapes faults that are not – that your wisdom then,
>From one that so imperfectly conceits,   150
>Would take no notice, nor build yourself a trouble
>Out of his scattering and unsure observance.
>It were not for your quiet, nor your good,
>Nor for my manhood, honesty, and wisdom,
>To let you know my thoughts.
>OTHELLO   What dost thou mean?   155
>IAGO Good name in man and woman, dear my lord,
>Is the immediate jewel of their souls.
>Who steals my purse, steals trash; 'tis something,
>   nothing,
>'Twas mine, 'tis his, and has been slave to thousands:
>But he that filches from me my good name   160
>Robs me of that which not enriches him
>And makes me poor indeed.
>OTHELLO By heaven, I'll know thy thoughts.
>IAGO You cannot, if my heart were in your hand,
>Nor shall not, while 'tis in my custody.   165
>OTHELLO Ha!

148   Here Suchet introduced 'a pregnant pause between the words "my" and "jealousy" . . . sufficient to make you consider that he too might be experiencing some kind of sexual jealousy . . . directed *against Desdemona*' (S, 18 January 1986).

153–5   In Attenborough's production, Richard McCabe sat down and started polishing his sword. Othello walked over, took his sword away and seriously demanded what he meant (RSC archive film).

155b   Olivier here slaps Iago good-humouredly on the shoulder and sits him down with a firm arm round him (film). Reflecting their different interpretations, Suzman has the quarto's 'Zouns' here (video), while Nunn went the other way, crossing out his promptbook's 'Zouns' and substituting the Folio reading (promptbook).

156–63   Colley Cibber here 'shrugs up his shoulders, shakes his noddle, and with a fawning motion in his hands, drawls out these words . . . Othello must be supposed a fool . . . if he does not see through him' (*Grub-Street Journal*, 31 October 1734).

163ff.   In Suzman's video, John Kani is seriously rattled by 163, and Iago's 'cuckold' (169) drives him deeper into despair. Among Parker's many cuts are this cuckold passage and Othello's 'O misery', i.e. 169b–178a. He also cuts 182b ('Exchange me for a goat') to 188. At 163 Fishburne's Othello holds his gun, half playfully, at Iago's chest.

166ff.   Foote wrote that the mistake of showing jealousy too soon was usually made at 'Ha!' Quin, he says, utters it 'as a mark of reflection, B[arry] of Rage' – rage at Iago's obstinacy. This makes sense, thinks Foote, of Iago's next move. Seeing Othello's agitation, and 'with no

IAGO O beware, my lord, of jealousy:
    ⇥ It is the green-eyed monster which doth mock
      The meat it feeds on. That cuckold lives in bliss
      Who certain of his fate loves not his wronger;   170
      But O, what damnèd minutes tells he o'er
      Who dotes, yet doubts, suspects, yet fondly loves?
OTHELLO O misery!
IAGO Poor and content is rich, and rich enough;
      But riches fineless is as poor as winter   175
      To him that ever fears he shall be poor.
      Good God, the souls of all my tribe defend
      From jealousy.

other preparation than the raising a storm . . . he comes plump at once with "O my lord, beware of jealousy"' (Foote, *Treatise*, p. 29). Kean's Othello here gave a 'sudden contraction of his body, as if he had been abruptly stabbed; his hands were tightly clenched, his features horribly contracted, his eyes rolled, his shoulders were drawn up, and his frame writhed' (*TJ*, 19 February 1868). Frank Finlay, Olivier's Iago, came out with 'beware my lord of jealousy' as a piece of 'pure improvisation, a shot in the dark. The notion has never before crossed Othello's mind, and his immediate response is angry incomprehension' (Tynan, *National Theatre Production*, p. 8). Anthony Hopkins walks away, whistling, on 'Ha!', taking Iago's no for an answer, so that Iago's next line is a desperate throw (Jonathan Miller BBC video). David Suchet's Iago seemed almost to be warning himself here (*NS*, 4 October 1985). In Parker's film, the soundtrack reaches a crescendo on 'O beware, my lord, of jealousy', continuing in a low drone.

168   Bell's, Kemble's and Fechter's editions avoid the difficulty of 'mock' and adopt Theobald's conjectured 'make'.

171–2   Fechter's direction here is 'stares in astonishment'.

173   In the first part of the nineteenth century there was a tradition of repeating 'misery' three times. Edwin Booth claims the credit of 'curing' this excess (*Variorum*). The reiteration suggests more distress than was conveyed by later actors, and it fits the description in the *Theatrical Inquisitor* of Kean's 'heartrending expression' here (May 1814). This was where he first made that gesture 'raising his hands and then bringing them down upon his head with clasped fingers' (see Sprague, p. 195). Aldridge kept the old repetition, according to the Russian critic Zvantsev: 'From Othello is torn the deep cry "O misery, misery, misery!" and in that misery of the African artist is heard the far-off groans of his own people . . .' (quoted by Marshall and Stock, *Ira Aldridge*, pp. 221–2). Salvini said it 'merely as an expression of sympathy with any poor wretch in such a plight as Iago had described. The words have no reference to himself' (Mason, p. 39), which is how Olivier (Tynan, *National Theatre Production*, p. 8), Willard White and Ray Fearon said it (videos). By contrast, John Kani in the video growls the words in agony – in the tradition of Kean and Aldridge.

OTHELLO   Why, why is this?
          Think'st thou I'd make a life of jealousy,
          To follow still the changes of the moon   180
          With fresh suspicions? No, to be once in doubt
          Is once to be resolved. Exchange me for a goat
          When I shall turn the business of my soul
          To such exsufflicate and blown surmises
          Matching thy inference. 'Tis not to make me jealous   185
          To say my wife is fair, feeds well, loves company,
          Is free of speech, sings, plays, and dances well:
          Where virtue is, these are more virtuous.
          Nor from mine own weak merits will I draw
          The smallest fear or doubt for her revolt,   190
          For she had eyes and chose me. No, Iago,
          I'll see before I doubt; when I doubt, prove;
          And on the proof, there is no more but this:
          Away at once with love or jealousy!
IAGO I am glad of this; for now I shall have reason   195
          To show the love and duty that I bear you
          With franker spirit. Therefore, as I am bound,
          Receive it from me. I speak not yet of proof.
          Look to your wife, observe her well with Cassio;

179–94   In December 1822 the *New Monthly Magazine* complained of an alteration in Kean's
         delivery here. Instead of 'struggling to reason against [Iago's insinuations] as inapplicable',
         he spoke as though scarcely conscious of what he said, his hands moving 'without impulse
         from the will'. In Nunn's video, Willard White asks the question half laughing. In
         Attenborough's production, Ray Fearon laid the stress on 'I' – as though it were
         inconceivable that he, of all people, would make a life of jealousy (video).
182b–5a This was traditionally cut, from the Smock Alley promptbook, the '1755' edition and onwards
         through the nineteenth century.
189–91a Cut from the Smock Alley text.
    190 J. B. Booth said 'revolt' as if 'he felt, for an instant, how dreadful a thing her revolt might be,
         then dismisses the thought at once' (Gould, *Tragedian*, p. 103).
    194 Edwin Booth advised: 'Touch your breast to signify that *love* is hearted, and your head at
         jealousy to denote that it is a brain disease . . .' (*Variorum*). Here Beerbohm Tree's
         promptbook marks 'breathing hard, laughs, . . . picks up rose [which Desdemona had given
         him at her exit], kisses it. Then takes pen and resumes writing, nothing heard but scratching
         of pen.' Willard White also laughed (promptbook).
    199 In Suzman's video, John Kani is already far gone here (video). In Nunn's, Willard White
         can't believe his ears. He chuckles and starts to write. In Parker's film, the music stops
         abruptly, as though Iago were bringing Othello down to earth hard.

Wear your eyes thus: not jealous, nor secure.   200
I would not have your free and noble nature,
Out of self-bounty, be abused. Look to't.
I know our country disposition well:
In Venice they do let God see the pranks
They dare not show their husbands. Their best
      conscience   205
Is not to leave't undone, but keep't unknown.
OTHELLO Dost thou say so?
IAGO She did deceive her father, marrying you;
   And when she seemed to shake and fear your looks
   She loved them most.
OTHELLO   And so she did.
IAGO   Why, go to then!   210
   She that so young could give out such a seeming
   To seel her father's eyes up close as oak
   He thought 'twas witchcraft – but I am much to blame,
   I humbly do beseech you of your pardon
   For too much loving you.

200   Forrest, as Iago to Kean's Othello, apparently spoke the earlier part of the speech with easy
       frankness until he got to 'nor secure'. Then, 'suddenly, as if the intensity of his
       under-knowledge of evil had automatically broken through . . . he spoke the words "nor
       secure" in a husky tone, sliding down from a high pitch and ending in a whispered horror.
       This fearful suggestiveness produced from Kean a reaction so truly artistic and tremendous
       that the whole house was electrified' (Alger, *Edwin Forrest*, I, p. 145, quoted in *Variorum*).
       Beerbohm Tree's promptbook shows that, between the phrases 'jealous' and 'nor secure',
       Iago 'nearly touches rose, Othello moves it'.
204–5 In Parker's film, Iago's insinuations begin to hit home – Fishburne's breathing comes hard
       here.
208ff. In Suzman's video, Kani weeps here, groaning at the mention of Cassio (225), tears
       dropping fast at 229. Richard Haines's Iago spits just before 'Foh' (234). Finally at 240
       Othello can bear no more and sends Iago off.
210   'And so she did'. Fechter here 'stands aside with his eye fixed on vacancy, as one reasoning
       out in contemplation the path shown him to the hell whither it leads' (Morley, *Journal*,
       p. 229). Lewes thought this mere '*theatrical* effect', for he had until then been 'careless,
       confident, unsuspicious, . . . and then *at once* credulous and overcome' (Lewes, *Actors*,
       pp. 157, 163).
213   Macready 'sighs and sinks his head on his breast' after the word 'witchcraft' (promptbook).
       Salvini, on the other hand, 'turns his eyes threateningly towards Iago, without turning his
       head' and only just restrained himself from drawing his sword (Mason, p. 42).

OTHELLO   I am bound to thee for ever.   215
IAGO I see this hath a little dashed your spirits.
OTHELLO   Not a jot, not a jot.
IAGO   I'faith, I fear it has.
          I hope you will consider what is spoke
          Comes from my love. But I do see you're moved.
          I am to pray you not to strain my speech   220
          To grosser issues nor to larger reach
          Than to suspicion.
OTHELLO I will not.
IAGO   Should you do so, my lord,
          My speech should fall into such vile success
          As my thoughts aimed not at. Cassio's my worthy
                    friend –   225
          My lord, I see you're moved.

215b   Salvini spoke this 'in a very low tone, tremulous with suppressed emotion' and trying 'to
        assume a tone of commonplace courtesy . . . as if he said "I'm greatly obliged to you" '
        (Mason, p. 42).

217   Quin impressed Foote at 'Not a jot, not a jot', trying 'to conceal from Iago, the grief and
        anguish that the doubts of his wife gave him' (Foote, *Treatise*, p. 30). Kean gave 'a plaintive
        choking cry which went to the heart' (Ottley, p. 22), and Mary Cowden Clarke remembered
        him clinging 'to the side-scene . . . as if trying to steady himself against the heart-blow he
        was receiving' (see Sprague, p. 195). The *Morning Post* (21 October 1861) noted 'a sigh like a
        spasm' here in Fechter which was 'perfectly heartbreaking'. It 'drew forth one of the loudest
        bursts of applause of the evening' (*Morning Herald*, 24 October 1861). Salvini amended
        Mason's text here, insisting that he gave the words 'in an indifferent tone'. Mason, however,
        stood by his opinion ('having again seen the performance several times') that Salvini 'first
        essays to speak, but cannot find his voice; then . . . with a ghastly smile, and a tremulous
        waving of his hands, he delivers "Not a jot, not a jot!" in a tone scarcely audible, husky with
        hardly repressed passion' (Mason, footnote on p. 42). Salvini had clearly reached the point
        where he was scarcely separable from Othello, and believed himself to be concealing (as
        Othello) what, as Othello, he could not help disclosing. Olivier spoke this 'with a casual
        pain which is extremely moving' (*ST*, 26 April 1964). Ray Fearon gave it with 'a snort of
        laughter – almost the last we would hear from him' (*SQ*, Summer 2000, 51, p. 221).

226b–28 Cut from the Smock Alley text.

226   Macready here affected a 'pitiful sensibility' at 'No, not much moved' and spoke the line 'in a
        childish treble' (Hazlitt, v, p. 339). Irving, in 1876, spoke with 'delicate plaintiveness' (Cook,
        Nights, II, p. 107). Ellen Terry's promptbook departs interestingly from this with a marginal
        note: '*Blast* him – sudden move' (promptbook). From Godfrey Tearle's delivery, the line
        'could be taken at its face value. It had nothing of the quality given it by most Othellos

OTHELLO   No, not much moved.
      I do not think but Desdemona's honest.
IAGO Long live she so, and long live you to think so!
OTHELLO And yet how nature erring from itself –
IAGO Ay, there's the point: as, to be bold with you,   230
      Not to affect many proposèd matches
      Of her own clime, complexion, and degree,
      Whereto we see in all things nature tends –
      Foh! one may smell, in such, a will most rank,
      Foul disproportion, thoughts unnatural.   235
      But pardon me: I do not in position
      Distinctly speak of her; though I may fear
      Her will, recoiling to her better judgement,
      May fall to match you with her country forms,
      And happily repent.
OTHELLO   Farewell, farewell.   240
      If more thou dost perceive, let me know more;
      Set on thy wife to observe. Leave me, Iago.

        intending to hide an emotion they only thus accentuate' (*Scotsman*, 4 April 1959). Scofield
        gave a 'hint of the instability of the fit scene in "not m-m-much moved"' (*Sh.S*, 34, p. 155).

227–8   Kean spoke 227 as though it were 'a thought flashing conviction on his mind, and irradiating
        his countenance with joy, like sudden sunshine' (Hazlitt, XVIII, p. 263). Richard McCabe in
        Attenborough's production gave the second part of line 228 with 'murderous pauses in it:
        "And long live you to think – so -."' (*SQ*, Summer 2000, 51, p. 221).

229   According to Edwin Booth, his father glanced at his hand here (*Variorum*) and the idea was
        given a literal-mindedly racist twist by Beerbohm Tree who said this 'trying to wipe black off'
        his hands (promptbook). In Parker's film, music starts again at 229, as Othello falls prey to
        Iago's insinuations.

230–40 Edwin Booth described 'the white-lipped icy smile' of his father, J. B. Booth, his 'piercing
        glance at Othello's half-averted face, and the eager utterance, with which [he] spoke the lines
        "Aye, there's the point . . ."' (Grossman, *Edwin Booth*, p. 258). According to F. A. Marshall,
        co-editor of *The Irving Shakespeare*, Edwin Booth said 'to be bold with you' as though it
        referred to Desdemona's boldness with Othello. This he thought ingenious but strained
        (vol VI, p. 93). James Hackett said he was the first to give that reading in 1828 (Hackett,
        Notes and Comments, p. 304). As Branagh's Iago whispers these lines, Parker uses flashback
        here to suggest Othello inwardly picturing Desdemona and Cassio dancing and laughing
        together. The sequence then cuts to Iago helping Othello with his collar in front of a mirror
        so that he is appropriately looking at his reflection at 238–9. See note on Fechter at 242.

234   Kemble turns 'Foh!' into 'Fie!' – a disapproving rather than a nose-holding exclamation.

242   The Smock Alley text, alone among historical acting texts, omitted this line. Fechter, during
        the lead up to it, 'continually glances in the direction of the mirror, till he is worked up to

IAGO [*Going.*] My lord, I take my leave.
OTHELLO Why did I marry? This honest creature doubtless
        Sees and knows more, much more, than he unfolds.   245
IAGO [*Returning.*] My lord, I would I might entreat your honour
        To scan this thing no farther. Leave it to time.
        Although 'tis fit that Cassio have his place –
        For sure he fills it up with great ability –
        Yet if you please to hold him off awhile,   250
        You shall by that perceive him and his means.
        Note if your lady strain his entertainment
        With any strong or vehement importunity –
        Much will be seen in that. In the mean time,
        Let me be thought too busy in my fears –   255
        As worthy cause I have to fear I am –
        And hold her free, I do beseech your honour.
OTHELLO Fear not my government.
IAGO I once more take my leave.   *Exit*
OTHELLO This fellow's of exceeding honesty   260

request Iago to set Emilia "to observe" ', and this he followed with 'an expression of the deepest shame' (*Morning Herald,* 24 October 1861). Dutton Cook noted Irving's 'acute and distressing air of shame' here (Cook, *Nights,* II, p. 107) and Edwin Booth buried his face in his hands, while his Iago smiled in fiendish triumph with 'a rapid clutch of the fingers' (*Variorum*). Godfrey Tearle spoke as by accident, 'followed by a quick checking movement of the hand to the mouth which implied "Did I say that? It was unwise" ' (*Scotsman,* 4 April 1959). Olivier showed such 'shame that he cannot face Iago while delivering the treacherous order' (Tynan, *National Theatre Production,* p. 8). Oliver Parker cuts the line.

242–6   By this time in Nunn's production, Willard White was desperate. After having abruptly dismissed Iago, there was a moment's silence, apart from the drilling cicadas; then he savagely crumpled up a piece of paper which he uncrumpled as Iago entered again (promptbook and video).

244   Olivier emphasised 'I', 'as if to say "I – of all people" ' (Tynan, *National Theatre Production,* p. 8).

246ff.   In Suzman's video, there is a flashback here of Cassio and Desdemona kissing their fingers in farewell.

260–81a   Benjamin Victor gives a rare glimpse of Barton Booth in this speech. At Iago's exit, Othello looks after him and 'after a long pause' began quietly and paused again. 'If I do prove her haggard' was spoken angrily, but then, after 'prey at fortune' he paused 'as to ruminate'. Before 'She's gone' he gave another pause, followed by a 'start of violent passion' for the next section, ending at 'their appetites' (272). 'What follows [was said] in a quicker contemptuous tone' until, seeing Desdemona coming, he was transformed by 'a look of amazement'. After 'Look where she comes!' he paused briefly and spoke the last line and a half with 'the countenance and voice softened' (Victor, *History,* II, pp. 11–13). According to

And knows all qualities, with a learnèd spirit,
Of human dealings. If I do prove her haggard,
Though that her jesses were my dear heart-strings,
I'd whistle her off and let her down the wind
To prey at fortune. Haply for I am black,   265
And have not those soft parts of conversation
That chamberers have, or for I am declined
Into the vale of years – yet that's not much –
She's gone, I am abused, and my relief
Must be to loathe her. O curse of marriage,   270
That we can call these delicate creatures ours
And not their appetites! I had rather be a toad
And live upon the vapour of a dungeon
Than keep a corner in the thing I love
For others' uses. Yet 'tis the plague of great ones,   275
Prerogatived are they less than the base;

Foote the speech is 'a mixture of deliberate reasoning and wild starts of rage'. Quin regarded it in the 'first light only', but Spranger Barry (like Barton Booth), 'gives fire to the one part and sedateness to the other'. Like Barton Booth, his fury begins at 'If I do prove her Haggard'. At 'Haply for I am black', he subsides, but 'the thoughts of her being gone, and that his only relief was to loathe her, hurries him into a fresh tempest of impatience and despair'. Then 'his immediate drop from a whirlwind to a calm, and the tenderness that accompanies the declaration of a belief that it was impossible so divine a form could delight in pollution, this . . . is masterly and affecting' (Foote, *Treatise*, pp. 30–1).

Fechter's rationalism is evident just before 'Haply for I am black', when he catches a glimpse of himself in a mirror and starts (his stage direction). He omitted lines 267b–8. Edwin Booth advised anguish throughout, rather than anger, and suggested neutralising the word 'appetites' by touching 'your *heart*, to signify *likings* or *longings*' (*Variorum*). Beerbohm Tree mimed the hawk with his hand and, at 'Haply for I am black' used a version of Fechter's mirror business (promptbook). This mirror idea was used again by Orson Welles in his film. Scofield gave a premonition of the fit in the way he said 'I-I-loathe her' and in 'a sudden outburst at . . . "haggard"' (*Sh.S*, 34, p. 155). Oliver Parker cuts greatly here – in particular, Othello's hawk image and his consciousness of colour, social inexperience and age as possible reasons for Desdemona's rejection. Instead he concentrates on Othello's inner disintegration with strange music, flashbacks and slightly convulsive movements. David Harewood and Ray Fearon were young Othellos, so 267b–8 were omitted (see Introduction, pp. 102, 104).

69–70a The Smock Alley text omits.

275b–9a The Smock Alley text cuts this, and so does Kemble. Bell's edition cuts only the last two lines. Olivier and John Kani speak the lines proudly (film and video). Nunn cut this passage, as did Oliver Parker.

'Tis destiny unshunnable, like death:
Even then this forkèd plague is fated to us
When we do quicken. Look where she comes.

Enter Desdemona and Emilia.

If she be false, O then heaven mocks itself;   280
    I'll not believe it.
DESDEMONA   How now, my dear Othello?
    Your dinner and the generous islanders,
    By you invited, do attend your presence.
OTHELLO I am to blame.
DESDEMONA   Why do you speak so faintly?
    Are you not well?   285
OTHELLO I have a pain upon my forehead here.
DESDEMONA Faith, that's with watching; 'twill away again.
    Let me but bind it hard, within this hour
    It will be well.
OTHELLO   Your napkin is too little.

---

279 SD   In Nunn's production, Desdemona 'enters carrying a watch to remind him of his lateness for
          supper, and does a stiff-armed parody of a military walk that beautifully points up her
          absolute defencelessness' (*I*, 26 August 1989).

286   Olivier placed 'two fingers above eyebrows, indicating to us (though not to her) the
          cuckold's horns' (Tynan, *National Theatre Production*, p. 8).

288–90   In this episode Salvini seemed to Stanislavski to be saying inwardly 'I want to kiss you and
          am afraid to soil myself. I want to love you and am forced to hate you', alternately
          'spring[ing] away' from her and stretching out his arms to her (Stanislavski, *My Life*,
          pp. 270–1).

289 and SD Forrest 'thrust the handkerchief from her hand – pointed at it emphatically – "Your napkin"
          (with the rigid Kean accent) – passed the forefinger with which he had been pointing at it
          over his brow – "is – too *little*" ' (Forster, *Essays*, p. 22). Fechter risked good sense for
          theatricality and made Othello 'throw down the handkerchief in a rage' (his stage
          direction) – a gesture that Othello might have been expected to recall when Iago mentions
          Desdemona's handkerchief later. Edwin Booth here advised gentle gestures, and forced
          indifference followed by a soulful look and tender embrace (*Variorum*). Olivier 'leads her
          off in a close enfolding embrace that will end in bed' (Tynan, *National Theatre Production*,
          p. 8). In the video, John Kani grabs Desdemona roughly, kisses her and makes as if to rape
          her. Parker cuts 'your napkin is too little' and the dismissive gesture that accompanies it.
          Samuel Crowl regrets that the cut loses the 'pity and irony' inherent in the fact that it isn't
          Desdemona but Othello who causes the handkerchief to go astray (*SB*, Winter 1996, p. 42).
          In Nunn's production, Desdemona felt her pocket for the watch and retrieved it from the

[*He puts the handkerchief from him, and she drops it.*]
Let it alone. Come, I'll go in with you.   290
DESDEMONA I am very sorry that you are not well.
                                    Exeunt Othello and Desdemona
EMILIA I am glad I have found this napkin:
         This was her first remembrance from the Moor.
         My wayward husband hath a hundred times
         Wooed me to steal it; but she so loves the token,   295
         For he conjured her she should ever keep it,
         That she reserves it evermore about her
         To kiss and talk to. I'll have the work tane out
         And give't Iago.
         What he will do with it, heaven knows, not I: 300
         I nothing but to please his fantasy.

                            Enter Iago.

IAGO How now? What do you here alone?

table just as they exited – presumably, to explain why the handkerchief gets forgotten (promptbook). Barton in 1972, Eyre and Mendes all put their interval here after the handkerchief has been dropped, thus making it the play's pivotal moment. Of Eyre's production, Steve Grant remarked that this serves to 'break up a scene which often resembles a sprint from a standing start, so that after the intermission we have a greater impression of jealousy gnawing at the innards' (*O*, 2 August 1979). For Robert Butler reviewing Mendes's production, the handkerchief seemed to be 'challenging one of us to pick it up and prevent a tragedy' (*IoS*, 21 September 1997).

292ff.   Fechter's Emilia 'comes forward with caution, and seizes the handkerchief, which she has watched narrowly since Othello threw it down' (his stage direction). Edwin Booth's, on the other hand, 'by chance sees the handkerchief and picks it up' (*Variorum*). In Nunn's production, Zoë Wanamaker lighted her pipe, sat for a moment and then caught sight of the handkerchief (promptbook). In the video, she speaks line 300 with weary resignation (video). Parker cuts this moment.

302–21   Emilia's 'thing' (303) is cut in Phelps's promptbook, and almost cut in Oscar Asche's which shows the deletion, with a 'stet' [let it stand] in the margin. Webster's production turned this into an amorous struggle between Iago and Emilia, as did Peter Hall's (promptbooks). In generally bringing out the relationship between the couple, Hall made Emilia's 'behaviour in stealing the handkerchief to please [Iago] seem less reprehensible' (*Cahiers Elizabéthains*, October 1980). In recent years, the encounter is used to reveal the sexless, loveless, abusive nature of the relationship. In Suzman's video Richard Haines touches Emilia's neck with his sword on 302 and hits her when she tries to snatch the handkerchief back. In Nunn's

EMILIA Do not you chide; I have a thing for you.
IAGO You have a thing for me? It is a common thing –
EMILIA Ha!   305
IAGO To have a foolish wife.
EMILIA O, is that all? What will you give me now
        For that same handkerchief?
IAGO   What handkerchief?
EMILIA What handkerchief!
        Why, that the Moor first gave to Desdemona,   310
        That which so often you did bid me steal.
IAGO Hast stolen it from her?
EMILIA No, faith; she let it drop by negligence,
        And to th'advantage I being here took't up.
        Look, here it is.
IAGO   A good wench! Give it me.   315
EMILIA What will you do with't, that you have been so earnest
        To have me filch it?
IAGO [*Snatching it.*]   Why, what's that to you?
EMILIA If it be not for some purpose of import, ˊ
        Give't me again. Poor lady, she'll run mad
        When she shall lack it.
IAGO   Be not acknown on't: 320
        I have use for it. Go, leave me.
                                                    Exit Emilia
        I will in Cassio's lodging lose this napkin
        And let him find it. Trifles light as air

production, Ian McKellen gave Emilia 'a psychotically repulsive gesture of affection', a
'barbaric embrace . . . [Emilia] is now reduced to appeasing his lunatic political fantasies'
(*FT*, 26 August 1989). Oliver Parker has Emilia approach Iago in their bedroom as he sleeps,
and attempt to seduce him. Initially indifferent, he is roused by her news at 308–9. He then
brutally begins to indulge her and as brutally breaks off with the cool statement to camera
at 323b–5. The rest of the speech, before and after, is cut. Kelly's Emilia 'made a painful,
pathetic attempt to seduce [Iago], laying the handkerchief across her breasts. When Iago
kissed her, she clung to him desperately, only to have him grab the handkerchief and choke
her with it' (Loehlin, '*Othello*'). Attenborough's Emilia gave the handkerchief to her Iago 'in
the starving hope of a recompensing snog, which he briskly terminates' (*I*, 23 April 1999).

323ff.   In the video, Suzman's Iago, Richard Haines, drops the handkerchief on to his face and
        blows it up into the air. Parker's film pictures Othello's erotic imaginings of Cassio and
        Desdemona, and a flashback to Brabantio's warning at 1.3.289 of which Iago has just
        reminded him (3.3.208).

　　　　Are to the jealous confirmations strong
　　　　As proofs of holy writ. This may do something.　　　　　325
　　　　The Moor already changes with my poison:
　　　　Dangerous conceits are in their natures poisons,
　　　　Which at the first are scarce found to distaste
　　　　But, with a little act upon the blood,
　　　　Burn like the mines of sulphur. I did say so.　　　　　330

　　　　　　　　　Enter Othello.

　　　　Look where he comes! Not poppy nor mandragora,
　　　　Nor all the drowsy syrups of the world,
　　　　Shall ever medicine thee to that sweet sleep
　　　　Which thou owed'st yesterday.
OTHELLO　　　　　　　　　　　Ha, ha, false to me!
IAGO Why, how now, general! No more of that.　　　　　335
OTHELLO Avaunt, be gone! Thou hast set me on the rack.
　　　　I swear 'tis better to be much abused
　　　　Than but to know't a little.
IAGO　　　　　　　　　How now, my lord!
OTHELLO What sense had I of her stolen hours of lust?
　　　　I saw't not, thought it not, it harmed not me.　　　　　340

330 SD　Kean 'entered with the abrupt and wandering step of one to whom the grace or dignity of
　　　　motion were new things, and swallowed up in the fearful bewilderings of a heavy heart'
　　　　(*T*, 14 May 1814). Salvini 'seems to enter as if his inner soul is red-hot . . . he suffers not only
　　　　mentally but physically also' (Stanislavski, *My Life*, p. 271). Olivier returned sniffing his
　　　　fingers 'as if they were tainted by contact with [Desdemona's] body' (Tynan, *National
　　　　Theatre Production*, p. 8). John Kani sobs and groans in the Suzman video.

336　　Kean here 'suddenly raised his eye and pronounced the words . . . with the haughty and
　　　　resentful glance of a man accustomed to authority, and seeing in Iago only the immediate
　　　　instrument of his torture' (*T*, 14 May 1814).

339–44　Foote, who felt that 'anger is rather the passion than sorrow' here, preferred Quin to the
　　　　tearful Barry whom he warned against 'hackneying the passion' (Foote, *Treatise*, p. 31). In
　　　　his early performances Kean 'dropped his arms' in a gesture of 'utter exhaustion'; for the
　　　　first few lines he 'dwelt upon the words as if he was parting with images that he loved. The
　　　　sound of Cassio's name gliding accidentally even from himself broke the spell. The whole
　　　　fierceness of his nature was roused; he sprung from the ground and cried the passage
　　　　aloud with wild and grinning desperation' (*T*, 14 May 1814). Later, in 1817, he modified this,
　　　　and Hazlitt, who felt that '"I found not Cassio's kisses on her lips"' (342) was a speech of
　　　　'pure pathos, of thought and feeling and not of passion' (Hazlitt, v, p. 272), was able to
　　　　report that 'almost every scene or sentence' in Kean's Othello was perfect (ibid., xvIII,
　　　　p. 263). Beerbohm Tree spat at 'Cassio's kisses on her lips' (promptbook).

> I slept the next night well, fed well, was free and merry;
> I found not Cassio's kisses on her lips.
> He that is robbed, not wanting what is stolen,
> Let him not know't and he's not robbed at all.
> IAGO I am sorry to hear this.   345
> OTHELLO I had been happy if the general camp,
> Pioners and all, had tasted her sweet body
> So I had nothing known. O, now for ever
> Farewell the tranquil mind! Farewell content!
> Farewell the plumèd troops, and the big wars   350
> That makes ambition virtue – O farewell!
> Farewell the neighing steed and the shrill trump,
> The spirit-stirring drum, th'ear-piercing fife,
> The royal banner, and all quality,

346–8a   The Smock Alley text cuts this, but no one else does except Fechter. Oscar Asche has 'robbed me of her love' for 'tasted her sweet body' (promptbook).

348b–58   This speech seems not to have become one of the great arias until Kean, whose manner of saying it – like 'the swelling notes of some divine music, like the sound of years of departed happiness' – gave Hazlitt a touchstone for most of Othello's other speeches from this point in the play onwards (Hazlitt, v, p. 272). Again Kean used the gesture described at 3.3.173: 'he raised both hands, clasped them, and so brought them down upon his head, with a most effective gesture of despair' (Gould, *Tragedian*, p. 106). Macready, according to Hazlitt, caught only the weaker side of Kean. He spoke 'Othello's occupation's gone' in a 'childish treble', in the whining, whimpering way he used for 'No, not much moved' (226) (Hazlitt, v, p. 339). Gustavus Vaughan Brooke was especially admired for 'the break of the voice into weeping' at 'Othello's occupation's gone' (Lawrence, *Gustavus Vaughan Brooke*, p. 82). Salvini's tearfulness disappointed Lewes: it was 'not comparable to the deep, manly and *impersonal* pathos of Kean . . . and it seemed to me *over* acted' (Lewes, *Actors*, p. 269).

    Olivier bellowed 'the words as pure, wounded outcry, he hurled back his head until the ululating tongue showed pink against the roof of his mouth like a trumpeting elephant's. As he grew into a great beast, Finlay shrunk beside him, clinging to his shoulder like an ape, hugging his heels like a jackal' (Ronald Bryden, *NS*, 1 May 1964). In Barton's production Brewster Mason's 'deep resonant tones vary little between "She loved me for the dangers I had passed" (1.3.166) and "Farewell the plumèd troops and the big wars". They all come out slow, silky, self-contented, and void of any genuine emotion' (*FT*, 13 September 1971). In the Suzman video, John Kani gives the speech quietly to a soundtrack of nightmarish music. Nunn gave Willard White business: Othello threw all the papers on to the floor and pummelled the table (promptbook) – something which one critic thought was to help White mask 'his true lack of spiritual disintegration' (*Country Life*, 7 September 1989). Parker's film cuts 352–7.

Pride, pomp, and circumstance of glorious war!   355
And, O you mortal engines, whose rude throats
Th'immortal Jove's dread clamours counterfeit,
Farewell! Othello's occupation's gone.

IAGO Is't possible, my lord?

OTHELLO Villain, be sure thou prove my love a whore;   360

---

359   Clearing up Othello's papers, McKellen gave another instance of his characterisation of Iago as a 'trim, vicious and compulsively tidy male mother-hen' (*ST*, 27 August 1989).

360   In Melbourne, G. V. Brooke said 'wanton' instead of 'whore' (*Argus*, 28 February 1855). Edwin Booth has 'drab'.

360–74a A man watching Macready once shouted out 'Choke the devil! choke him!' (see Sprague, p. 199) and most Othellos have done their best here to relieve the audience's feelings. This was one of Barry's best moments: his 'finely smothered' jealousy 'burst out with an amazing wildness of rage . . . when he collars Iago it is actually astonishing how his powers carry him through such a long continued climax of terror . . .' (*London Chronicle*, 7 March 1757). In Bell's edition 'a dog' at line 363 is reinforced by the addition – 'a dog, Iago'. This enables us to place Foote's parody of Macklin, who apparently advised Barry 'that when a man's soul is lost, tossed and crossed, and his entrails *broiling on a gridiron*, bring up the *dog* with a tremendous grind, a Do-o-o-g Iago!' (Cumberland, p. 5).

    Lewes remembered Kean on one outstanding occasion at the end of his career when Macready played Iago: 'how puny he appeared beside Macready until in the third act, . . . he moved towards him with a gouty hobble, seized him by the throat and in a well-known explosion . . . seemed to swell into a stature which made Macready appear small' (Lewes, *Actors*, p. 4). Forrest leapt 'with one electrifying bound . . . his eyeballs rolling and flashing, and his muscles strung, seized the cowering Iago by the throat, and with a startling transition of voice from the mellow mournfully lingering notes to crackling thunderbolts, shrieked [369–70]'. After which he 'rushed to a column and leaned against it . . . to applause' (Alger, *Edwin Forrest*, II, p. 775).

    This was Salvini's greatest moment: 'seizing fiercely Iago by the throat, he crushes the cowering miscreant to the ground, and in the whirlwind of his passion, lifts his foot to stamp the heel upon his head, it might even be to stamp out his brains. Recalled however, to reason, he turns away, and with averted head he stretches out his hand, and penitently, yet with a species of loathing raises the prostrate wretch from the ground' (Knight, *Notes*, pp. 22–3). In 1873 Henry James saw Rossi as Othello in Italy and observed how 'crude' the 'Italian conception' was: 'the great point was his seizing Iago's head and whacking it half-a-dozen times on the floor and then flinging him twenty yards away' (James, *Hours*, p. 211). The tradition was still strong in 1910 when Giovanni Grasso visited London (Beerbohm, *Theatres*, p. 575).

        Be sure of it. Give me the ocular proof,
        Or by the worth of mine eternal soul,
        Thou hadst been better have been born a dog
        Than answer my waked wrath!
IAGO   Is't come to this?
OTHELLO Make me to see't; or, at the least, so prove it   365
        That the probation bear no hinge nor loop
        To hang a doubt on – or woe upon thy life!
IAGO My noble lord –
OTHELLO If thou dost slander her and torture me,
        Never pray more; abandon all remorse;   370
        On horror's head horrors accumulate;
        Do deeds to make heaven weep, all earth amazed:
        For nothing canst thou to damnation add
        Greater than that.
IAGO   O grace! O heaven forgive me!
        Are you a man? Have you a soul? Or sense?   375
        God bu'y you; take mine office. O wretched fool,
        That lov'st to make thine honesty a vice!
        O monstrous world! Take note, take note, O world!
        To be direct and honest is not safe.
        I thank you for this profit, and from hence   380
        I'll love no friend, sith love breeds such offence.
OTHELLO Nay, stay: thou shouldst be honest.
IAGO I should be wise; for honesty's a fool
                And loses that it works for.
OTHELLO   By the world,
        I think my wife be honest, and think she is not;   385
        I think that thou art just, and think thou art not.

    Wolfit's 'leap at Iago's throat … was a real thrill … suggestive of Kean' (Crosse, *Playgoing*, p. 146). 'He almost strangled Iago in blind rage' (*Scotsman*, 4 April 1959). Olivier 'locks Finlay by the throat and hurls him to the ground threatening him with a trick knife-blade concealed in a bracelet' (Tynan, *National Theatre Production*, p. 8). Anthony Hopkins speaks 'be sure thou prove my love a whore' gently, almost cooingly (Jonathan Miller, BBC). Laurence Fishburne nearly drowns Branagh's Iago in the sea. Similarly, Ray Fearon pushed McCabe's head under in a basin of water (RSC archive film). In Mendes's thirties' or forties' production, David Harewood drew a pistol (*DT*, 18 September 1997).

374 Edwin Booth postponed his moment of violence and greatly softened it: 'I carry no weapon in this scene, but seeing Iago's dagger, I clutch it in frenzy and am about to stab him when the Christian overcomes the Moor, and throwing the dagger from me, I fall upon the seat with a flood of tears. To this weeping Iago may allude in his next speech, where he says contemptuously "Are you a man?"' (*Variorum*).

I'll have some proof. Her name, that was as fresh
As Dian's visage, is now begrimed and black
As mine own face. If there be cords or knives,
Poison or fire or suffocating streams,   390
I'll not endure it. Would I were satisfied!
IAGO I see, sir, you are eaten up with passion.
    I do repent me that I put it to you.
    You would be satisfied?
OTHELLO   Would? Nay, I will.
IAGO And may. But how? How satisfied, my lord?   395
    Would you, the supervisor, grossly gape on?
    Behold her topped?
OTHELLO   Death and damnation! O!
IAGO It were a tedious difficulty, I think,
    To bring them to that prospect. Damn them then,
    If ever mortal eyes do see them bolster   400

387   The second quarto text (1630) has 'Her name', and the Folio has 'My name'. Most
    productions have 'Her' – certainly it was the rule in eighteenth- and early
    nineteenth-century texts – so that when an actor uses 'My' it is a matter for comment.
    Fechter used it (to Ottley's disgust, Ottley, p. 23) and Olivier did, so as 'to hammer home the
    hero's egoism' (Tynan, *National Theatre Production*, p. 9).

89b–91a   Spranger Barry 'bursts out with' these lines 'with the impetuous ferocity natural to one of
    Othello's complexion, still improved with the wildest harmony of voice' *(London Chronicle,*
    7 March 1757). The lines were cut in the early nineteenth century, and Phelps adds them, in
    manuscript (promptbook). John Barton also cut them, at least for the Aldwych season (1972
    promptbook). Parker's film cuts 387–90. Ray Fearon here fell on all fours at 'Would I were
    satisfied' and Iago joined him (RSC archive film).

96–406a   Cut by Oscar Asche (promptbook).

397   'Behold her topped?' Bell records the omission of the word 'topped', and all
    nineteenth-century acting texts leave it discreetly in the air, i.e. 'Behold her . . . ?' Salvini's
    translation avoids the problem with 'Vederli / L'una in braccio dell' altro?' ('To see them /
    One in the arms of the other?')

98–409   Gentleman was offended by this speech (Bell), but it wasn't pruned until Macready set the
    pattern. He crossed out 'bolster' with a thick penstroke, and then in faint pencil (perhaps as
    an afterthought) the whole sentence in which it appears. Lines 404–6a are also struck out
    (promptbook). Phelps followed Macready's example. Fechter cut from 399b to 406a. Both
    Edwin Booth and Irving kept 'bolster', but cut the goats, monkeys and wolves lines. Salvini
    and Ellen Terry cut the whole passage (his printed version; her promptbook). By this speech
    Anthony Hopkins's restraint bursts, and he here howls and growls freely (Jonathan
    Miller, BBC).

More than their own. What then? How then?
What shall I say? Where's satisfaction?
It is impossible you should see this,
Were they as prime as goats, as hot as monkeys,
As salt as wolves in pride, and fools as gross   405
As Ignorance made drunk. But yet, I say,
If imputation and strong circumstances,
Which lead directly to the door of truth,
Will give you satisfaction, you might have't.
OTHELLO Give me a living reason she's disloyal.   410
IAGO I do not like the office;
But sith I am entered in this cause so far –
Pricked to't by foolish honesty and love –
I will go on. I lay with Cassio lately,
And being troubled with a raging tooth   415
I could not sleep.
There are a kind of men so loose of soul
That in their sleeps will mutter their affairs.
One of this kind is Cassio.
In sleep I heard him say, 'Sweet Desdemona,   420
Let us be wary, let us hide our loves.'

411–27   It was probably here that G. F. Cooke as Iago 'grasped Kemble's left hand with his own, and then fixed his right, like a claw, on his shoulder. In this position, drawing himself up to him with his short arm, he breathed his poisonous whispers. Kemble coiled and twisted his hand, writhing to get away – his right hand clasping his brow, and darting his eye back on Iago' (quoted by Sprague, p. 194). Lewes gives us a general picture of Kean, applicable here and up to the end of the scene: 'he represented with incomparable effect the lion-like fury, the deep and haggard pathos, the forlorn sense of desolation alternating with gusts of stormy cries for vengeance, the misgivings and sudden reassurances, the calm and deadly resolution of one not easily moved, but who, being moved, was stirred to the very depths' (Lewes, *Actors*, p. 6). 'Throughout Iago's speech [Salvini] remains seated, holding himself in check with the greatest difficulty, likely at any instant to spring upon Iago and blot him out . . . he grasps the arms of the chair, bracing himself against its back; then he draws the cloth upon the table into a crumpled mass' (Mason, pp. 56–7). Beerbohm Tree listened 'half stopping his ears' (promptbook). Frank Finlay in John Dexter's production 'almost bursts into tears . . . to think of the general so vilely deceived' (Tynan, *National Theatre Production*, p. 9). Olivier, unable to bear any more, claps his hand over Iago's mouth at the end of the speech (film). In Suzman's video, Richard Haines whispers his dream into Kani's ear, holding and rocking him. Kani's eyes close and his breath comes hard. In Nunn's video, McKellen arranges the chairs for them and tells his story in a hushed, embarrassed voice.

And then, sir, he would gripe and wring my hand,
Cry, 'O sweet creature!' and then kiss me hard,
As if he plucked up kisses by the roots
That grew upon my lips; then laid his leg   425
Over my thigh, and sighed, and kissed, and then
Cried, 'Cursèd fate that gave thee to the Moor.'
OTHELLO O monstrous, monstrous!
IAGO   Nay, this was but his dream.
OTHELLO But this denoted a foregone conclusion.
IAGO 'Tis a shrewd doubt, though it be but a dream;   430
And this may help to thicken other proofs
That do demonstrate thinly.
OTHELLO   I'll tear her all to pieces!
IAGO Nay, yet be wise; yet we see nothing done,

422–7   From Bell's edition onwards some or all of these lines were cut. Bell's edition cuts the 'thigh'
         lines, and Kemble follows that text. Macready also omitted the lines immediately before,
         from 423b. Versions of this cut were standard for the rest of the nineteenth and early
         twentieth centuries.

432b   This was Spranger Barry's most famous climax: 'His gradual preparation for the volcanic
         burst of "I'll tear her all to pieces", and the burst itself, in its exquisite agony, as well as
         power, surpassed the grandest of the effects which the stage in those days saw so
         frequently. You could observe the muscles stiffening, the veins distending, and the red blood
         boiling through his dark skin – a mighty flood of passion accumulating for several minutes –
         and at length bearing down its barriers, and sweeping onward in thunder, love, mercy,
         reason, all before it. The females at this point used invariably to shriek, whilst those with
         stouter nerves grew uproarious in admiration . . .' (Bernard, *Retrospections*, I, p. 17). Kean
         here had a 'fiery intensity', said Lewes, which he missed in Salvini's performance (Lewes,
         Actors, p. 269). Edwin Booth allowed 'the *savage*' to 'have vent, – but for a moment only;
         when Othello next speaks he is tame again and speaks sadly'. His next remarks reveal
         contemporary stage practice: 'Iago has caught and held him . . . Do not stoop to the old
         stage trick of displaying Desdemona's handkerchief, as if by accident, while Othello's back is
         turned' (*Variorum*). Beerbohm Tree illustrated the line by tearing up the papers on his desk
         (promptbook). In 1972 John Barton cut Othello's outburst here together with the two
         previous lines (1972 promptbook). Ben Kingsley here clawed 'at the air like a frantic cat' (*L*,
         3 October 1985). Willard White spoke the line 'with chair-bound temperance' (*G*, 26 August
         1989). Parker cuts it.

433–42   In Nunn's production, Iago mentioned the handkerchief casually as he was tidying papers,
         and Othello at 442 broke down completely, flinging himself against the back wall
         (promptbook and video). Parker inserts shots here of Cassio finding the handkerchief and
         leaving it with Bianca – a piece of the story, rather than of Othello's imagination.

> She may be honest yet. Tell me but this:
> Have you not sometimes seen a handkerchief 435
> Spotted with strawberries in your wife's hand?
> OTHELLO I gave her such a one; 'twas my first gift.
> IAGO I know not that; but such a handkerchief –
> I am sure it was your wife's – did I today
> See Cassio wipe his beard with.
> OTHELLO   If it be that – 440
> IAGO If it be that, or any that was hers,
> It speaks against her with the other proofs.
> OTHELLO O that the slave had forty thousand lives!
> One is too poor, too weak, for my revenge.
> Now do I see 'tis true. Look here, Iago, 445
> All my fond love thus do I blow to heaven;
> 'Tis gone.
> Arise, black vengeance, from thy hollow cell!
> Yield up, O love, thy crown and hearted throne
> To tyrannous hate! Swell, bosom, with thy fraught, 450
> For 'tis of aspics' tongues.
>   *He kneels.*
> IAGO   Yet be content.
> OTHELLO O, blood, blood, blood!

435, 438   Some gesture here towards the handkerchief seems appropriate enough. J. B. Booth 'while pretending to lay his hand upon his heart . . . tuck[ed] away more securely in his doublet the very handkerchief which . . . he intended Cassio *should* wipe his beard with' (Gould, *Tragedian*, p. 108). And Michael Bryant in Peter Hall's production was observed by B. A. Young: 'See how his hand steals to the handkerchief concealed under his coat as he turns his back towards Othello' (*FT*, 22 March 1980).

441–2   Barton cut this for the Aldwych season (promptbook).

443–7   Beerbohm Tree here 'picks up rose, tears it up and throws it in front of table' (promptbook). One critic thought the effect too ingenious and calculating for Othello. The actor must be 'more wholly a creature of passion and simplicity than any modern Northerner can imagine. Sir Herbert Tree is too clever for the work' (*O*, 14 April 1912). In Nunn's video, Willard White literally blows here on line 446, as did Ray Fearon (RSC archive film).

448–51a   Barton cut these lines in 1972 (promptbook).

449–50a   Fechter cut this.

452   Keats wrote of Edmund Kean's utterance here that it was 'direful and slaughterous to the deepest degree; the very words appear stained and gory. His nature hangs over them, making a prophetic repast. The voice is loosed on them like the wild dog on the savage relics of an eastern conflict; and we can distinctly hear it "gorging and growling o'er carcase and limb"' (*Champion*, 21 December 1817). 'Before he [Kean] exclaims "Blood!" which he

IAGO Patience, I say; your mind perhaps may change.
OTHELLO Never, Iago. Like to the Pontic Sea,
　　　Whose icy current and compulsive course　　　　　　　455
　　　Ne'er feels retiring ebb but keeps due on
　　　To the Propontic and the Hellespont,
　　　Even so my bloody thoughts with violent pace
　　　Shall ne'er look back, ne'er ebb to humble love,
　　　Till that a capable and wide revenge　　　　　　　　460
　　　Swallow them up. Now by yond marble heaven,

does in a suppressed and muffled voice, he opens and shuts his hands convulsively, as if he had really lost the free use of his bodily and mental powers' (Robinson, *Diary*, I, p. 225). Cut by Parker.

454–61a　Kemble omitted this famous passage, and Gould asserts that Edmund Kean never said it. J. B. Booth only included the speech 'at the urgent solicitation of personal friends'. His delivery, according to Gould's admiring account, was highly illustrative: the words 'came with headlong speed . . . "Hellespont" sounded like a torrent dashed on rocks. "Till that a capable and wide revenge / Swallow them up" gave the sound and figured the very action of engulfing waves' (Gould, *Tragedian*, p. 109). But Hazlitt's making a point of Macready's omission of the passage in 1816 (Hazlitt, V, p. 339) suggests that Kean did at some stage include it. Fechter cut it, and Phelps restored it in manuscript in his promptbook. But when Edwin Booth said it in 1881, Dutton Cook mentions the fact as an example of where 'the text is here and there restored' (Cook, *Nights*, II, p. 301). Salvini included it, impressing Emma Lazarus with his ability to rise, after 'be sure thou prove my love a whore' at 360, to this second 'still grander height' without 'pause or respite' (C, November 1881). According to Ronald Bryden, Olivier broke the long verse paragraph at "Shall ne'er look back": 'he let the memories he was forswearing rush in and stop him, gasping with pain, until he caught breath' (Ronald Bryden, *NS*, 1 May 1964). John Russell Brown remembered it differently: 'there was a long silence after "humble" while Othello forced himself to say the word 'love' that had stuck in his throat; this silence was full with the impression of physical struggle, and when at last the word came it was, convincingly, quiet' (*Sh.S*, 18, p. 155). Parker cuts the whole thing.

461b–3a　Edwin Booth knelt and held 'both hands above the head, with upturned palms and fingers towards the back . . . suggestive of the Orient' (*Variorum*). Beerbohm Tree bowed 'his head to dust in Moorish fashion' (promptbook). Olivier made the idea significant rather than decorative. ' "Now by yond ma-a-a-rble heaven" – [was] a surging atavistic roar' (Tynan, *National Theatre Production*, p. 9), after which 'he tore the crucifix from his neck . . . crouching forehead to ground, [and] made his "sacred vow" in the religion which caked Benin's altars with blood' (*NS*, 1 May 1964). Anthony Hopkins gives himself up to frenzy here, shouting and gabbling the vow of vengeance (Jonathan Miller, BBC).

In the due reverence of a sacred vow
I here engage my words.

IAGO   Do not rise yet.

He kneels.

Witness you ever-burning lights above,
You elements that clip us round about,   465
Witness that here Iago doth give up
The execution of his wit, hands, heart,
To wronged Othello's service. Let him command,
And to obey shall be in me remorse,
What bloody business ever.

[*They rise.*]

OTHELLO   I greet thy love,   470
Not with vain thanks, but with acceptance bounteous;
And will upon the instant put thee to't.
Within these three days let me hear thee say
That Cassio's not alive.

IAGO   My friend is dead;
'Tis done at your request. But let her live.   475

OTHELLO Damn her, lewd minx! O, damn her, damn her!
Come, go with me apart. I will withdraw

463bff. and SD   Gentleman notes that Iago's 'master-stroke of hypocrisy' here 'seldom fails to cause laughter in one, and to draw execrations from another part of the house' (Bell). Edwin Booth said 463b in 'a tone of devotional entreaty' (Winter, *Edwin Booth*, p. 197). In John Barton's production 'Othello and Iago cut their wrists and lay them together' (1972 promptbook); in Parker's film and Attenborough's production they cut palms. Bob Hoskins's Iago has to hold Othello still for his own vow (Jonathan Miller, BBC).

474   G. F. Cooke used to 'start' here, 'and the spectator might plainly read in his expressive face, "What, murder my friend and companion?" – he then covered his face with his hands, and gradually lifting his head, when he withdrew his hands, his face and eyes were turned upward – he then started again, as if remembering the oath he had just taken, and after a second mental struggle said, as if submitting to necessity . . . "My friend is dead" '(Dunlap, *Memoirs*, II, p. 351). Lewes complained that Fechter here '*proposes* instead of ordering Cassio's death' – a murder and not a sentence. He does it 'with a sort of subdued hesitation, as if conscious of the crime'. In this way he belittles Othello and 'bears out Rymer's sarcasm'. Lewes added in a footnote that Rymer 'reads very often like sound criticism when one has just witnessed the performances at the Princess's theatre' (Lewes, *Actors*, pp. 155–6).

476   *The Times* noted that at Damn her, lewd minx! O, damn her, G. V. Brooke 'gave an expression of sorrow to the repetition of the curse' (quoted in Lawrence, *Gustavus Vaughan Brooke*, p. 81). Edwin Booth suggested four 'damn hers': 'say the first savagely, the second time less so, melt with the third and choke with tears at the fourth' (*Variorum*).

> To furnish me with some swift means of death
> For the fair devil. Now art thou my lieutenant.
> IAGO I am your own for ever.   480
>
> > *Exeunt*

479b–80 Edwin Booth 'quickly kneeling . . . kisses Othello's hand, and his face reveals his triumph'
(*Variorum*). Oscar Asche's Othello 'fell senseless at Iago's feet, and the curtain descended.
It was a fine climax, justified by the line in the following act, "this is his second fit; he had
one yesterday"' (Dickins, *Forty Years*, p. 146). Beerbohm Tree and Laurence Irving
embraced here (promptbook). John Barton's Iago saluted (1972 promptbook). David
Suchet made 'I am your own for ever' sound almost as though it were a homosexual
declaration (*S*, 18 January 1986). In Nunn's production, the line was 'not the cry of a
servant, still less (*pace* Olivier) of a man in love with his own master, but the
mephistophelean claim of a succubus bound for the abyss' (*O*, 27 August 1989). But the
video suggests something more personal. During the preceding moments, both have been
breathing hard, Iago appearing to be genuinely overcome – swallowing with emotion at 'I
greet thy love'. Face to face, at close quarters, they clasp hands at 479, and at 480 Iago
bows as if to kiss Othello's hand. In Parker's film, Iago and Othello embrace and we see
Branagh almost glance at the camera in his accustomed manner over Othello's shoulder,
but he quickly shuts his eyes – for once the emotion is too much for him. In Attenborough's
production, Ray Fearon and Richard McCabe knelt forehead to forehead (RSC archive film).
In Mendes's production, Russell Beale's Iago was left alone for a moment after 480, and
retched violently: 'A reaction of delayed shock to Othello's pistol-wielding fury? Or a sudden
awareness of just how vile he is?' (*DT*, 18 September 1997).

Most productions have their interval here.

ACT 3, SCENE 4

Enter DESDEMONA, EMILIA *and* CLOWN.

DESDEMONA Do you know, sirrah, where Lieutenant Cassio lies?
CLOWN I dare not say he lies anywhere.
DESDEMONA Why, man?
CLOWN He's a soldier, and for one to say a soldier lies is
    stabbing. 5
DESDEMONA Go to. Where lodges he?
CLOWN To tell you where he lodges is to tell you where I lie.
DESDEMONA Can anything be made of this?
CLOWN I know not where he lodges, and for me to devise a lodging,
    and say he lies here, or he lies there, were to lie in mine own 10
    throat.
DESDEMONA Can you enquire him out, and be edified by report?
CLOWN I will catechise the world for him: that is, make questions,
    and by them answer.
DESDEMONA Seek him; bid him come hither; tell him I have moved 15
    my lord on his behalf and hope all will be well.
CLOWN To do this is within the compass of man's wit, and therefore
    I will attempt the doing of it. *Exit*
DESDEMONA Where should I lose that handkerchief, Emilia?

The first twenty-odd lines of this scene, until the clown's exit, were 'with strict justice,
banished' from the stage, wrote Gentleman (Bell) and so they remained in most nineteenth-
and twentieth-century productions. Both Peter Hall and John Barton kept this opening, and
Nunn some of it, omitting 6–14 (promptbook). For the settings, Kemble simply indicates
'another apartment in the castle'; Macready made it a shallow scene, in the first groove, the
shutters closing in front of the previous set. He puts a note in for Desdemona – 'no glove' –
a reminder of how constant glove-wearing was (promptbook; see also note at 2.1.163–71).
Oscar Asche's set was 'A hall in castle: rostrum and steps UR; arches, along the side L. Two
couches and palms disposed about' (promptbook).

0 SD   Imogen Stubbs in Nunn's production came on hunting for the handkerchief, even looking in
the wastepaper basket (promptbook). In the video, on line 16 she stresses 'hope' and, like a
schoolgirl, crosses her fingers. At 26–7, as she lies back in a garden chair she laughingly
mimes drawing such humours up out of her stomach.

EMILIA I know not, madam.   20
DESDEMONA Believe me, I had rather lose my purse
    Full of crusadoes; and but my noble Moor
    Is true of mind and made of no such baseness
    As jealous creatures are, it were enough
    To put him to ill thinking.
EMILIA   Is he not jealous?   25
DESDEMONA Who, he? I think the sun where he was born
    Drew all such humours from him.
              Enter OTHELLO.
EMILIA   Look where he comes.
DESDEMONA I will not leave him now; let Cassio
    Be called to him. – How is't with you, my lord?
OTHELLO Well, my good lady. [*Aside*] O hardness to dissemble!   30
    How do you, Desdemona?
DESDEMONA   Well, my good lord.
OTHELLO Give me your hand. This hand is moist, my lady.
DESDEMONA It yet hath felt no age, nor known no sorrow.
OTHELLO This argues fruitfulness and liberal heart.
    Hot, hot, and moist. This hand of yours requires   35
    A sequester from liberty, fasting and prayer,
    Much castigation, exercise devout;
    For here's a young and sweating devil here
    That commonly rebels. 'Tis a good hand,
    A frank one.

31b   Fechter's stage direction is: 'coaxing by placing her hands clasped on the shoulder of
      Othello'. Webster's Desdemona said it 'mimicking his tone of voice' (Carroll).

32   Madge Kendal, Ira Aldridge's Desdemona in 1865, recalled that 'Mr Aldridge opened his
      hand and made me place mine in it to emphasize the difference in their colour . . . the effect
      he produced was so great that the audience always rewarded it with a round of applause'
      (Kendal, *Dame Madge Kendal*, pp. 86–7).

34   Edwin Booth examined her hand 'as in palmistry' (*Variorum*), as did Donald Sindon in
      Ronald Eyre's production (promptbook).

35   In Nunn's production, Othello said the line 'in despair' as he examined her hand, at which
      Desdemona 'blows on it like soup' (*Literary Review*, November 1989).

35–40 Boaden speaks of Sarah Siddons here: 'The surprise arising to astonishment, a sort of *doubt*
      if she heard aright, and that being admitted, what it could *mean*; a hope that it would end in
      nothing so unusual from him as *offensive* meaning; and the slight relief, upon Othello's
      adding – "'Tis a good hand, / A frank one": all this commentary was quite as legible as the
      text' (Boaden, *Kemble*, i, p. 259). Ellen Terry's marginal comment is 'puzzled to follow it'
      (promptbook).

DESDEMONA   You may indeed say so,   40
    For 'twas that hand that gave away my heart.
OTHELLO A liberal hand! The hearts of old gave hands;
    But our new heraldry is hands, not hearts.
DESDEMONA I cannot speak of this. Come now, your promise.
OTHELLO What promise, chuck?   45
DESDEMONA I have sent to bid Cassio come speak with you.
OTHELLO I have a salt and sorry rheum offends me;
    Lend me thy handkerchief.
DESDEMONA   Here, my lord.
OTHELLO That which I gave you.
DESDEMONA   I have it not about me.
OTHELLO Not?   50
DESDEMONA No, faith, my lord.
OTHELLO   That's a fault. That handkerchief
    Did an Egyptian to my mother give:
    She was a charmer and could almost read
    The thoughts of people. She told her, while she kept it,
    'T would make her amiable and subdue my father   55
    Entirely to her love; but if she lost it
    Or made a gift of it, my father's eye
    Should hold her loathèd and his spirits should hunt
    After new fancies. She dying gave it me,
    And bid me when my fate would have me wive,   60
    To give it her. I did so, and take heed on't:
    Make it a darling, like your precious eye.
    To lose't or give't away were such perdition

42   'A liberal hand'. Here Beerbohm Tree interposed Desdemona's words from 4.2 'I hope my
    noble lord esteems me honest' (64) and Othello's rejoinder 'O ay: as summer flies . . .' etc.
    (65–8). He then continued with 3.4 as before, though inevitably with his disgust and her
    despair much further advanced than they are in the original text (promptbook).

48ff.   Here is a rare glimpse of Betterton: 'the wonderful agony he appeared in when he examined
    the circumstances of the handkerchief . . . the mixture of love that intruded upon his mind
    upon the innocent answers Desdemona makes, betrayed in his gestures such passions as
    would admonish a man to be afraid of his own heart' (Steele, *Tatler*, no. 167, 2 May 1710).

51b–71 Forrest 'cut up into little strips the gorgeousness and Eastern amplitude of the Moor's
    description of the handkerchief . . . "take heed on't" he exclaimed in an earnest tone of
    tender entreaty – then, changing to the rigid and fierce – "Make it a darling like your
    precious eye" – and so forth!' (Forster, *Essays*, p. 23). Fechter opened this speech with 'a
    terrific [i.e. terrifying] smile' (his stage direction). He cut 64b–71. Oliver Parker cuts from
    65–71.

As nothing else could match.
DESDEMONA   Is't possible?
OTHELLO 'Tis true. There's magic in the web of it: 65
        A sibyl, that had numbered in the world
        The sun to course two hundred compasses,
        In her prophetic fury sewed the work;
        The worms were hallowed that did breed the silk,
        And it was dyed in mummy, which the skilful   70
        Conserved of maidens' hearts.
DESDEMONA   I'faith, is't true?
OTHELLO Most veritable; therefore look to't well.
DESDEMONA Then would to God that I had never seen't!
OTHELLO Ha? Wherefore?
DESDEMONA Why do you speak so startingly and rash?   75
OTHELLO Is't lost? Is't gone? Speak; is't out of th'way?
DESDEMONA Heaven bless us!
OTHELLO Say you?
DESDEMONA It is not lost, but what and if it were?
OTHELLO How?   80
DESDEMONA I say it is not lost.
OTHELLO   Fetch't, let me see't.
DESDEMONA Why so I can, sir; but I will not now.
        This is a trick to put me from my suit.
        Pray you let Cassio be received again.
OTHELLO Fetch me the handkerchief. My mind misgives.   85
DESDEMONA Come, come;
        You'll never meet a more sufficient man.
OTHELLO The handkerchief!
DESDEMONA   I pray, talk me of Cassio.
OTHELLO The handkerchief!
DESDEMONA   A man that all his time

72–81   Ellen Terry marks 'overlapping' here in her promptbook.
79   Fechter's face was 'averted when she says "It is not lost", and he turns suddenly with all his
        love and trust flowing back to him, to take her to his arms, when she repels him with the
        addition "but what an if it were?"' (Morley, *Journal*, p. 230).
81ff.   Forrest's glare here 'was almost supernatural and a lady who sat in the same box with me
        clutched convulsively at her husband's arm for protection' (Harrison, *Edwin Forrest*, p. 64).
88–93   'The handkerchief!' Olivier said that he intended 'angry insistence' here, 'but it developed
        into angry imploring' (*Life International*, 18 May 1964). He spoke the third iteration
        'whimpering . . . , his hands clasped before him in prayer' (Tynan, *National Theatre
        Production*, p. 9). Anthony Hopkins is playful until the sudden fury of 'Zounds'. Penelope
        Wilton's Desdemona brilliantly catches the mixture of bewilderment, coaxing disbelief and

Hath founded his good fortunes on your love,   90
Shared dangers with you –
OTHELLO The handkerchief!
DESDEMONA   I'faith, you are to blame.
OTHELLO Zounds!   *Exit*
EMILIA Is not this man jealous?
DESDEMONA   I ne'er saw this before.
Sure there's some wonder in this handkerchief;   95
I am most unhappy in the loss of it.
EMILIA 'Tis not a year or two shows us a man.
They are all but stomachs, and we all but food;
They eat us hungerly, and when they are full,
They belch us.

Enter IAGO *and* CASSIO.

Look you, Cassio and my husband.   100
IAGO There is no other way: 'tis she must do't.
And lo, the happiness! Go, and importune her.

nascent no-nonsense matronliness (Jonathan Miller, BBC). Imogen Stubbs's Desdemona
was too young for tact and her 'repeated support for Cassio even as Othello has bellowed
his roar of agony about the handkerchief is very painful' (*S*, 2 September 1989). Laurence
Fishburne raises his hand as if to hit Desdemona on 92, but refrains (Parker's film).

93   Helena Faucit recalled that before Macready exited 'he took my face in both his hands,
looked long into my eyes, and then the old look came back into his, and it spoke as plainly
as possible "My life upon her faith"' (quoted by Sprague, p. 197). Here Beerbohm Tree's
Desdemona (Phyllis Neilson-Terry) came downstage and saw the torn rose petals
(promptbook).

94   Salvini met a common criticism of Emilia here by inventing a speech for her in which she
blames herself for what she has done, determines to tell Iago everything, and hopes that
Othello's rage will not last.

98–100a   The '1755' edition cuts these lines as does Bell's edition and most nineteenth-century acting
texts. Oscar Asche cut the rest of the act from here, and the opening of Act 4, moving
straight into the eavesdropping scene at Iago's 'Stand you awhile apart' (4.1.72).
Desdemona and Emilia exited instead of Othello, who hid behind one of the potted palms.
Parker keeps Emilia's lines, which she speaks looking at Iago, who is lurking at the half-open
door, which he then slams after 'belch us' – as though recognising that she speaks from
experience. Parker cuts the rest of scene and the first nine lines of 4.1.

100 SD   Salvini cut this entrance and the rest of the scene. Beerbohm Tree cut only Cassio out – but
even when Cassio has appeared, he has been much curtailed.

DESDEMONA How now, good Cassio ! What's the news with you?

CASSIO Madam, my former suit. I do beseech you
      That, by your virtuous means, I may again   105
      Exist and be a member of his love,
      Whom I, with all the office of my heart,
      Entirely honour. I would not be delayed.
      If my offence be of such mortal kind
      That nor my service past nor present sorrows,   110
      Nor purposed merit in futurity,
      Can ransom me into his love again,
      But to know so must be my benefit:
      So shall I clothe me in a forced content,
      And shut myself up in some other course   115
      To fortune's alms.

DESDEMONA   Alas, thrice-gentle Cassio,
      My advocation is not now in tune:
      My lord is not my lord; nor should I know him,
      Were he in favour as in humour altered.
      So help me every spirit sanctified,   120
      As I have spoken for you all my best,
      And stood within the blank of his displeasure
      For my free speech! You must awhile be patient.
      What I can do, I will; and more I will
      Than for myself I dare. Let that suffice you.   125

IAGO Is my lord angry?

EMILIA   He went hence but now
      And certainly in strange unquietness.

IAGO Can he be angry? I have seen the cannon
      When it hath blown his ranks into the air,
      And like the devil from his very arm   130
      Puffed his own brother – and is he angry?
      Something of moment then. I will go meet him.
      There's matter in't indeed if he be angry.

03b–16a   All of Cassio's speech, apart from 'Madam, my former suit' was customarily cut from Bell's
          edition onwards, throughout the nineteenth century.

116bff.   Ellen Terry notes in the margin of her promptbook here 'slightly bored' and 'keep voice low'.

120–5   Bell's edition records this cut – Kemble keeps 'You must awhile be patient . . .' to the end.
          Jude Kelly's Cassio sulked in a deckchair while Desdemona tearfully explained her failure
          with Othello (Loehlin, '*Othello*').

131   Edwin Booth told Furness that his father, 'following, I presume, old stage traditions', always
          added '"yet he stood unmoved"' (*Variorum*).

DESDEMONA I prithee do so.

                                              Exit Iago
                    Something sure of state,
          Either from Venice, or some unhatched practice   135
          Made demonstrable here in Cyprus to him,
          Hath puddled his clear spirit; and in such cases
          Men's natures wrangle with inferior things,
          Though great ones are their object. 'Tis even so;
          For let our finger ache, and it endues   140
          Our other healthful members even to a sense
          Of pain. Nay, we must think men are not gods,
          Nor of them look for such observancy
          As fits the bridal. Beshrew me much, Emilia,
          I was – unhandsome warrior as I am –   145
          Arraigning his unkindness with my soul;
          But now I find I had suborned the witness
          And he's indicted falsely.
EMILIA Pray heaven it be state matters, as you think,
          And no conception nor no jealous toy   150
          Concerning you.
DESDEMONA Alas the day, I never gave him cause.
EMILIA But jealous souls will not be answered so.
          They are not ever jealous for the cause,
          But jealous for they're jealous. 'Tis a monster   155
          Begot upon itself, born on itself.
DESDEMONA Heaven keep that monster from Othello's mind.
EMILIA Lady, amen!
DESDEMONA I will go seek him. Cassio, walk here about.
          If I do find him fit, I'll move your suit   160

134–48   The Smock Alley text omits Desdemona's wifely excuses for Othello's behaviour, and her
         self-accusation. Bell's edition cuts all but the first two lines, and with small variations
         nineteenth- and early twentieth-century acting texts followed suit. The 'finger' passage is
         always omitted from these.

   159   From the '1755' edition onwards, throughout the nineteenth century – Fechter excepted –
         the third act ended here, Bianca having been cut entirely from these productions. She was
         erratically restored in the early twentieth century, but only for the eavesdropping scene, not
         here. Fechter, who had kept all the scenes in this act within the first boudoir-cum-study
         setting, offended Ottley's sense of propriety again: 'for a woman of the class of Bianca to
         force herself into the Governor's Castle, and, above all, into his wife's apartment, is
         repugnant to every dictate of reason and propriety' (Ottley, p. 27). Beerbohm Tree, who
         freely rearranged Shakespeare's order, put this episode after 4.3 (promptbook).

And seek to effect it to my uttermost.
CASSIO I humbly thank your ladyship.

Exeunt Desdemona and Emilia

Enter BIANCA.

BIANCA 'Save you, friend Cassio.
CASSIO   What make you from home?
    How is it with you, my most fair Bianca?
    I'faith, sweet love, I was coming to your house.   165
BIANCA And I was going to your lodging, Cassio.
    What! Keep a week away? Seven days and nights?
    Eight score eight hours? And lovers' absent hours
    More tedious than the dial eight score times!
    O weary reckoning!
CASSIO   Pardon me, Bianca.   170
    I have this while with leaden thoughts been pressed;
    But I shall in a more continuate time
    Strike off this score of absence. Sweet Bianca,
    Take me this work out.
BIANCA   O Cassio, whence came this?
    This is some token from a newer friend.   175
    To the felt absence now I feel a cause.
    Is't come to this? Well, well.
CASSIO   Go to, woman!
    Throw your vile guesses in the devil's teeth
    From whence you have them. You are jealous now
    That this is from some mistress, some remembrance.   180
    No, by my faith, Bianca.
BIANCA   Why, whose is it?
CASSIO I know not neither; I found it in my chamber.
    I like the work well. Ere it be demanded –
    As like enough it will – I'd have it copied.

162 SD.2 During the last two decades, alertness to questions of gender and ethnicity (Nunn and Parker both cast black actresses in the part, and in the same spirit, Kelly cast a white actress) has made Bianca's part much more prominent. She has, in effect, joined Emilia and Desdemona to make a trio of used and abused women.

163ff. Suzman's Bianca, though played by a white actress, enters ululating, in the video, and much of her scene with Cassio is spent rolling around with him on the ground. Nunn's Bianca (Marsha Hunt) crept up on Cassio as he sat, feet on table, hat over eyes; she put her hands over his eyes, and as she spoke began to undo his shirt buttons (promptbook and video).

175 Nunn's Bianca sniffed the hankerchief here (promptbook).

Take it and do't, and leave me for this time.   185
BIANCA Leave you? Wherefore?
CASSIO I do attend here on the general;
      And think it no addition, nor my wish,
      To have him see me womaned.
BIANCA   Why, I pray you?
CASSIO Not that I love you not.
BIANCA   But that you do not love me.   190
      I pray you, bring me on the way a little,
      And say if I shall see you soon at night.
CASSIO 'Tis but a little way that I can bring you,
      For I attend here; but I'll see you soon.
BIANCA 'Tis very good; I must be circumstanced.   195

Exeunt

189   Fechter ended the scene here (adding 'but I'll see you soon', line 194) with a tableau: as
      Cassio conducted her to the arcade, embracing her, Iago appeared at the door on the left
      and broke into a loud laugh. Bianca ran off at the noise, Cassio made 'signs to be silent'.
      Then Iago, 'with comical gravity, puts his finger to his lips, stretching out his hand as if to
      make an oath. The curtain falls' (Fechter's stage direction). Ottley describes this as being
      'after the coarsest possible fashion' (Ottley, p. 27).

ACT 4, SCENE I

Enter OTHELLO *and* IAGO.

IAGO Will you think so?
OTHELLO   Think so, Iago?
IAGO   What,
          To kiss in private?
OTHELLO   An unauthorised kiss!
IAGO Or to be naked with her friend in bed
          An hour or more, not meaning any harm?
OTHELLO Naked in bed, Iago, and not mean harm?   5
          It is hypocrisy against the devil.
          They that mean virtuously and yet do so,
          The devil their virtue tempts, and they tempt heaven.
IAGO So they do nothing, 'tis a venial slip;
          But if I give my wife a handkerchief –   10
OTHELLO What then?

From Kemble onwards (except for Irving in 1876, and Salvini) throughout the nineteenth century, and in some twentieth-century productions, this act usually started at line 192 ('Get me some poison, Iago'). Edwin Booth's edition omits the whole scene, and Lena Ashwell, writing in 1926, testifies to its being 'generally not played' – so as to avoid the blow that Othello gives to Desdemona at the end of it (Ashwell, *Reflections*, p. 116). Beerbohm Tree opened the act at scene 3, but redistributed some of the intervening material. Olivier and Frank Finlay made a strong impact here: they 'sway together in a sickening rhythm that suggests a bond uniting them closer than marriage' (Harold Hobson, *ST*, 26 April 1964). In Parker's film, this scene takes place, with appropriate symbolism, in a torture chamber of the castle. In Kelly's production, it was 'rather absurdly played as a military strategy session, with Iago writing phrases like "unauthorised kiss" and "naked in bed" up on a white board' (Loehlin, '*Othello*'), then 'writing Desdemona's name and underlining the "demon" in it' (Potter, *Othello*, p. 183).

3–8   Bell's edition, like the editions before it, preserves the opening of this act, but these lines about being 'naked in bed' went too far, and they are omitted. De Vigny translates them, but loses their erotic edge: 'ou bien s'enfermer dans la nuit / Seule avec un amant, sans péché ni sans bruit'. Willard White, in Nunn's production, made line 5 'the wondering query of a child-like innocent abroad' (*FT*, 26 August 1989).

IAGO Why, then 'tis hers, my lord; and being hers,
        She may, I think, bestow't on any man.
OTHELLO She is protectress of her honour too.
        May she give that?   15
IAGO Her honour is an essence that's not seen:
        They have it very oft that have it not.
        But for the handkerchief –
OTHELLO By heaven, I would most gladly have forgot it.
        Thou said'st – O it comes o'er my memory,   20
        As doth the raven o'er the infected house,
        Boding to all! – he had my handkerchief.
IAGO Ay, what of that?
OTHELLO   That's not so good now.
IAGO   What
        If I had said I had seen him do you wrong?
        Or heard him say – as knaves be such abroad,   25
        Who having by their own importunate suit
        Or voluntary dotage of some mistress
        Convincèd or supplied them, cannot choose
        But they must blab –
OTHELLO   Hath he said anything?
IAGO He hath, my lord; but be you well assured   30
        No more than he'll unswear.
OTHELLO   What hath he said?
IAGO Faith, that he did – I know not what he did.
OTHELLO What, what?
IAGO Lie –
OTHELLO With her?
IAGO   With her, on her, what you will.
OTHELLO Lie with her? Lie on her? We say lie on her when they belie 35
        her. Lie with her! Zounds, that's fulsome! Handkerchief –

33   Parker uses a breathless stillness at 'What, what?', and the faint sound of dripping water, to
     wind up the tension.
35ff. The Smock Alley text cut everything between 'Lie on her' and 'O devil!' The '1755' edition
     goes as far as 'that's fulsome!' which it gives to Iago, and cuts the rest including the fit,
     running straight on to 'I will chop her into messes' at 188. Bell's edition follows suit, but
     delicately avoids 'lie on her'. This cut, which gets rid of both the fit and the eavesdropping
     scene, was made early in the eighteenth century. In a collection of letters 'sent to *The Tatler*
     and *Spectator* during the time those works were publishing', there is one which speaks of
     'whole scenes left out . . . amongst the rest, that which confirms Othello's jealousy, when he
     sees the handkerchief in Cassio's hands, . . . I have likewise a notion that Othello's trance,
     being a thing not strained, but very natural, and which did once give great satisfaction, how

confessions – handkerchief! To confess and be hanged for his
labour. First to be hanged and then to confess. I tremble at it.
Nature would not invest herself in such shadowing passion without
some instruction. It is not words that shakes me thus. Pish! Noses,   40
ears, and lips. Is't possible? – Confess? Handkerchief? O devil!

> [*He*] *falls in a trance.*

that comes to be omitted I know not . . .' (Lillie, *Letters*, I, pp. 255–6). Opinion was divided
when Garrick revived it in 1745–6. Macklin thought it a piece of 'impudence' to restore 'a
passage which . . . must be looked upon as an excrescence of the worst sort' (Kirkman,
Memoirs, II, p. 260). But Benjamin Victor thought 'the trance had a fine effect, your manner
of falling into it, and recovery from it, was amazingly beautiful' (Genest, *Some Account*, IV,
pp. 147–8).

No one else, until Irving in 1876, was to enact the 'trance' itself, though both Forrest and
Fechter opened this act in a prostrate position, it being understood that they had just
suffered an epileptic fit. At least that is the implication in this description of Forrest: 'contrary
to the usual practice he retained the scene in the fourth act in which the racked mind gives
way and epilepsy supervenes, and the spectacle thus presented of a brawny form, clad in a
white tunic, lying flat on a couch with wide-stretched limbs, was, to use the mildest possible
term, revolting' (John Foster Kirk, *Lippincott's Magazine*, June 1884). If the 'spectacle' had
included anything more revolting than that, i.e. his actually falling down in the throes, Kirk
would have said so. Fechter's edition indicates that the act opens here with Othello
discovered, 'stretched unconscious on the divan', Iago 'contemplating him with a diabolic
sneer'. Ottley records that this arrangement, 'sprawling face downwards', was later altered
and he 'now lies on his back on a narrow settee, which is much too short for him, his head
dangling over at one end, his legs at the other . . . without any struggling, he recovers very
suddenly, on hearing the name Cassio' (Ottley, p. 11). Lewes thought he was merely
'*sleeping*; and when he rises . . . he is indeed calm and unaffected by the fit as if he had only
been asleep' (Lewes, *Actors*, p. 154).

What Henry Irving restored in 1876 sounds more like a faint than a fit: 'The signs of
swooning had, obviously, been closely studied, and were faithfully conveyed' (Knight,
Theatrical Notes, p. 103). However, despite the hopes of critics, no one followed Irving, and
even as late as Godfrey Tearle, the cut was still being made (MacCarthy, *Theatre*, p. 72).

Valk included it (Agate, *Chronicles*, p. 304) and Wolfit 'writhed on the ground like a
contortionist and foamed at the mouth' (Charles Graves, *Scotsman*, 4 April 1959). Olivier
gave 'long, shuddering breaths, the head flung back, the jaw thrust out . . . and when he falls
thrashing to the ground . . . Iago shoves the haft of a dagger between his teeth to keep him
from biting off his tongue' (Tynan, *National Theatre Production*, p. 10). As Iago in 1938,
Olivier made cuckold's horns with his fingers on Othello's head (Williamson, *Old Vic Drama*,

IAGO Work on,
      My medicine, work! Thus credulous fools are caught;
      And many worthy and chaste dames even thus,
      All guiltless, meet reproach. What ho, my lord!   45
      My lord, I say! Othello!

              Enter CASSIO.

              How now, Cassio!
CASSIO What's the matter?
IAGO My lord is fallen into an epilepsy.
      This is his second fit; he had one yesterday.
CASSIO Rub him about the temples.
IAGO   No, forbear.   50
      The lethargy must have his quiet course.
      If not, he foams at mouth and by and by
      Breaks out to savage madness. Look, he stirs.
      Do you withdraw yourself a little while;
      He will recover straight. When he is gone,   55
      I would on great occasion speak with you.

                        [*Exit Cassio*]

p. 97), and succumbed to 'a sort of hysterical collapse . . . for which the text gives no warrant' (*NS*, 19 February 1938). David Suchet cradled Othello's head in his lap and stroked his hair – 'a single stunning shaft of sympathetic vulnerability' (*FT*, 8 January 1986). In 1964 Mitchell Ryan's Iago to Earl Jones's Othello was 'directed to do things better left undone such as spitting on Othello while the latter lay writhing on the floor' (*SQ*, 15, Autumn 1964). In Suzman's video, strange nightmare sounds mark Othello's inner disintegration, as they do in Parker's film, where cellos start to drone menacingly at 'Lie with her?'. Fishburne's Othello, his breath short and his head jerking, sits with his arms strung out between a pair of hanging chains, and the sequence then switches to shots of the 'Noses, ears and lips' and other body parts of Cassio and Desdemona love-making. Instead of sound, Mendes's lighting was particularly noted here: 'Iago crouches over the fallen general, feeding Othello's own lines into his ear; the shadow of a fan becomes a huge wheel rolling Othello to his fate' (*Glasgow Herald*, 20 September 1997). Perhaps it was here in Mendes's production that Beale 'tenderly strokes Othello's cheek', which the critic interpreted as buried sexual desire – 'a window' had been 'thrown open on the play' (*DT*, 18 September 1997).

43   In Suzman's video, Richard Haines whoops over Othello here, hitting and kicking him.

50   In Parker's film, Branagh betrays a note of panic on 'No, forbear' – the last thing he wants is for Cassio and Othello to talk and possibly clear things up between them.

52   John Barton cut this reference to foaming at the mouth (promptbook).

     How is it, general? Have you not hurt your head?
OTHELLO Dost thou mock me?
IAGO   I mock you? No, by heaven!
     Would you would bear your fortune like a man!
OTHELLO A hornèd man's a monster and a beast.   60
IAGO There's many a beast then in a populous city,
     And many a civil monster.
OTHELLO Did he confess it?
IAGO   Good sir, be a man:
     Think every bearded fellow that's but yoked
     May draw with you. There's millions now alive   65
     That nightly lie in those unproper beds
     Which they dare swear peculiar. Your case is better.
     O, 'tis the spite of hell, the fiend's arch-mock,
     To lip a wanton in a secure couch
     And to suppose her chaste! No, let me know;   70
     And knowing what I am, I know what she shall be.
OTHELLO O, thou art wise; 'tis certain.
IAGO   Stand you awhile apart,
     Confine yourself but in a patient list.
     Whilst you were here, o'erwhelmèd with your grief –
     A passion most unsuiting such a man –   75
     Cassio came hither. I shifted him away
     And laid good scuse upon your ecstasy;
     Bade him anon return and here speak with me,
     The which he promised. Do but encave yourself,
     And mark the fleers, the gibes, and notable scorns   80
     That dwell in every region of his face;
     For I will make him tell the tale anew,
     Where, how, how oft, how long ago, and when

57   In Parker's film, Othello's line at 63 ('Did he confess it?') is inserted after Iago's 'How is it, general?' Iago's privately startled look at the camera continues the anxious idea started at line 50.

58   Beerbohm Tree included the eavesdropping scene (but not the fit), starting it here and placing it after 4.3 (promptbook).

60   Like the 'monster' and the 'beast' Donald Sinden was on all fours here until Iago's 'Stand you awhile apart' at line 72 (promptbook).

63   McKellen here, as elsewhere, was 'the finicky gentleman's gentleman', dusting Othello down and setting him to rights (*I*, 2 October 1989).

He hath and is again to cope your wife.
I say but mark his gesture. Marry, patience,   85
Or I shall say you're all in all in spleen
And nothing of a man.
OTHELLO   Dost thou hear, Iago?
I will be found most cunning in my patience,
But – dost thou hear – most bloody.
IAGO   That's not amiss.
But yet keep time in all. Will you withdraw?   90
      [*Othello withdraws.*]
Now will I question Cassio of Bianca,
A housewife that by selling her desires
Buys herself bread and clothes. It is a creature

84   Forbes-Robertson, whose edition cuts and dovetails the end of Act 3 and the beginning of
      Act 4, cut the trance but included the eavesdropping scene, just as Beerbohm Tree did. Here
      he altered 'cope' to 'see'. In the film, Olivier screams here in agony, and John Kani roars
      (Suzman video).

92ff. Harley Granville-Barker assumes that Othello's 'dodging in and out of hiding' is all part of
      this episode's deliberate grotesqueness (Granville-Barker, *Prefaces*, p. 54 and footnote 30).
      But at Shakespeare's Globe, the downstage pillars would have obviated the need to dodge.
      As we have seen, this eavesdropping section was omitted in productions from the early
      eighteenth century onwards (see note at 4.1.35ff.). When, in 1773, it was thought that Garrick
      would revive the play, the editor, George Steevens, hoped he would include 'the listening
      scene' so as to avoid Othello's jealousy appearing to be 'unnaturally precipitated' (Boaden,
      Correspondence, I, p. 593). But Garrick never mounted the play again, and that part of the
      scene remained in limbo until Fechter resuscitated it. Granville-Barker, writing in 1948,
      suggested that the omission was still current: 'most actors of Othello, I think, have shirked
      this scene, wholly or in part' believing it to be belittling (*Prefaces*, p. 54, footnote). As
      recently as 1953–4 Earle Hyman, in New York, dropped it (*SQ*, 5, 1954).
          Fechter set it in the same room in which the third act was played, which, of course, gave
      the same offence to Ottley (Ottley p. 28; see note at 3.4.159). However, Bianca, and
      therefore this episode, was still cut from later productions, including Salvini's and the
      Irving–Booth revival in 1881. *Macmillan's Magazine*, like George Steevens in 1773, could still
      complain that without this scene Othello 'is somewhat too easily moved!' (July 1881). In
      Asche's production the scene (much curtailed) had Othello alone onstage (thus avoiding
      Granville-Barker's 'dodging in and out') listening to Iago, Cassio and Bianca in the wings
      (promptbook). John Barton went to the other extreme and cut all of Othello's interjections
      (both promptbooks). Mendes, praised for his 'well-judged nuances', had Othello listening
      'in the same position at the same louvred windows as Brabantio (the jealous husband
      replacing the jealous father)' (*IoS*, 21 September 1997).

That dotes on Cassio; as 'tis the strumpet's plague
To beguile many and be beguiled by one. 95
He, when he hears of her, cannot refrain
From the excess of laughter. Here he comes.

Enter Cassio.

As he shall smile, Othello shall go mad;
And his unbookish jealousy must construe
Poor Cassio's smiles, gestures, and light behaviours 100
Quite in the wrong. How do you now, lieutenant?

CASSIO The worser that you give me the addition
Whose want even kills me.

IAGO Ply Desdemona well and you are sure on't.
Now if this suit lay in Bianca's power, 105
How quickly should you speed!

CASSIO   Alas, poor caitiff!

OTHELLO [*Aside*] Look how he laughs already!

IAGO I never knew a woman love man so.

CASSIO Alas, poor rogue! I think, i'faith, she loves me.

OTHELLO [*Aside*] Now he denies it faintly, and laughs it out. 110

IAGO Do you hear, Cassio?

OTHELLO [*Aside*]   Now he importunes him
To tell it o'er. Go to, well said, well said!

IAGO She gives it out that you shall marry her.
Do you intend it?

CASSIO Ha, ha, ha! 115

OTHELLO [*Aside*] Do you triumph, Roman? Do you triumph?

CASSIO I marry her? What! A customer! I prithee, bear some
charity to my wit. Do not think it so unwholesome. Ha, ha, ha!

OTHELLO [*Aside*] So, so, so, so: they laugh that wins.

IAGO Faith, the cry goes that you shall marry her. 120

CASSIO Prithee, say true.

IAGO I am a very villain else.

OTHELLO [*Aside*] Have you scored me? Well.

CASSIO This is the monkey's own giving out. She is persuaded I will
marry her out of her own love and flattery, not out of my 125
promise.

OTHELLO [*Aside*] Iago beckons me. Now he begins the story.

CASSIO She was here even now. She haunts me in every place. I was
the other day talking on the sea-bank with certain Venetians, and
thither comes this bauble and, by this hand, falls me thus 130
about my neck.

110–26 Fechter cut this section, even he partly shirking the scene.

OTHELLO [*Aside*] Crying 'O dear Cassio!' as it were. His gesture
   imports it.
CASSIO So hangs and lolls and weeps upon me, so hales and pulls me.
   Ha, ha, ha!   135
OTHELLO [*Aside*] Now he tells how she plucked him to my chamber.
   O, I see that nose of yours, but not that dog I shall throw it
   to!
CASSIO Well, I must leave her company.
IAGO Before me, look where she comes!   140
CASSIO 'Tis such another fitchew! Marry, a perfumed one.

                        Enter BIANCA.

   What do you mean by this haunting of me?
BIANCA Let the devil and his dam haunt you! What did you mean
   by that same handkerchief you gave me even now? I was a fine fool
   to take it. I must take out the work? A likely piece of work   145
   that you should find it in your chamber and not know who left
   it there! This is some minx's token, and I must take out the work?
   There, give it your hobby-horse, wheresoever you had it. I'll
   take out no work on't.
CASSIO How now, my sweet Bianca! How now, how now!   150
OTHELLO [*Aside*] By heaven, that should be my handkerchief!
BIANCA If you'll come to supper tonight, you may. If you will not,
   come when you are next prepared for.   *Exit*
IAGO After her, after her!
CASSIO Faith, I must. She'll rail in the streets else.   155
IAGO Will you sup there?
CASSIO Faith, I intend so.
IAGO Well, I may chance to see you; for I would very fain speak with
   you.
CASSIO Prithee, come; will you?   160
IAGO Go to; say no more.
                                             Exit Cassio

132–3   Fechter gave this to Iago, cutting 'His gesture imports it.' His direction is 'putting his arms
        round him in imitation of Bianca' – 'a most unseemly and unjustifiable alteration' (Ottley,
        p. 28).
137–8   Fechter altered 'nose' to 'face', which, Ottley said, 'is nonsense. You cannot throw a man's
        face to the dogs, without throwing the head also; but the nose you may' (Ottley, p. 28).
        Forbes-Robertson cuts this evidence of Othello's barbarity altogether, as do Oscar Asche
        and Webster. It was the only interjection of Olivier's (together with line 136) that was not cut
        (film).

OTHELLO [*Coming forward.*] How shall I murder him, Iago?
IAGO Did you perceive how he laughed at his vice?
OTHELLO O, Iago!
IAGO And did you see the handkerchief?   165
OTHELLO Was that mine?
IAGO Yours, by this hand. And to see how he prizes the foolish woman
  your wife: she gave it him, and he hath given it his whore.
OTHELLO I would have him nine years a-killing. A fine woman, a fair
  woman, a sweet woman!   170
IAGO Nay, you must forget that.
OTHELLO Ay, let her rot and perish, and be damned tonight, for she
  shall not live. No, my heart is turned to stone: I strike it and it
  hurts my hand. O, the world hath not a sweeter creature! She
  might lie by an emperor's side and command him tasks.   175
IAGO Nay, that's not your way.
OTHELLO Hang her, I do but say what she is: so delicate with her
  needle, an admirable musician – O, she will sing the savageness
  out of a bear – of so high and plenteous wit and invention –
IAGO She's the worse for all this.   180
OTHELLO O, a thousand, thousand times – and then of so gentle
  a condition!
IAGO Ay, too gentle.
OTHELLO Nay, that's certain; but yet the pity of it, Iago! O Iago,
  the pity of it, Iago!   185

166   Ellen Terry's promptbook changes this to 'Away, away' and ends the scene there. After a
      scene-change she brought them on again at 192 ('Get me some poison'), presumably
      achieving the effect of lapsed time. Parker's film cuts to the ramparts, Othello and Iago
      continuing the conversation with 'Damn her, lewd minx!' (from 3.3.476) inserted here.
169–87   Some people in the eighteenth century mourned the loss of this section: 'one of those
      soothing passages which show how much against the nature of the hero is the crime he is
      afterwards to commit' (John Hill, *The Actor*, p. 143). Fechter failed to restore this passage.
      Salvini brought back only 'O, the world hath not a sweeter creature!' ('mai piu dolce
      creatura / Non ebbe il mondo') but he cut the needle and the bear and the pity of it, going
      straight to 'Get me some poison.' Tynan reports a remark by Dexter to Finlay in rehearsal:
      'Think of yourself as a ring-master. Just give him an occasional flick of the whip – like "Nay,
      that's not your way" – to keep him in order.' Thus Iago here was immobile, while Olivier
      'circled' the stage (Tynan, *National Theatre Production*, p. 10). Bob Hoskins achieves the
      same effect by turning Othello this way and that in his hands, like a puppet (Jonathan Miller,
      BBC). Parker cuts everything from 'hurts my hand' up to and including 'Nay, that's certain.'
184–5   Since eighteenth- and early nineteenth-century theatre texts only rejoined (or opened) this
      scene at 188 and 192 respectively, this much-quoted line was never said by the actors of the

IAGO If you are so fond over her iniquity, give her patent to offend;
for if it touch not you, it comes near nobody.
OTHELLO I will chop her into messes. Cuckold me!
IAGO O, 'tis foul in her.
OTHELLO With mine officer!   190
IAGO That's fouler.
OTHELLO Get me some poison, Iago, this night. I'll not expostulate
with her, lest her body and beauty unprovide my mind again – this
night, Iago.
IAGO Do it not with poison; strangle her in her bed, even the bed she   195
hath contaminated.
OTHELLO Good, good! The justice of it pleases; very good!
IAGO And for Cassio, let me be his undertaker. You shall hear more
by midnight.
OTHELLO Excellent good!   200
                    A trumpet [sounds within].
What trumpet is that same?
IAGO I warrant something from Venice.

                Enter LODOVICO, DESDEMONA *and* ATTENDANTS.

period before Irving's first production. Kean, according to Genest, probably only ever read
the play in the playhouse version (Genest, *Some Account*, IV, p. 148 footnote), which would
have brought him in at 'Get me some poison.' But he must have restored at least this line,
for Lewes remembers his tone (without, unfortunately, describing it) at 'But oh, the pity of it,
Iago! the pity of it [sic]' (Lewes, *Actors*, p. 152). Tynan describes Valk here, who 'lifted his
great lion's head and sent his poor voice piping into the vaulted roof above him: "Oh the
pity of it Yaggo – the pee-ee-eety of ee-eet!"' (Tynan, *A View*, p. 60). Robert Speaight noted
Olivier's 'piercing "Oh the pity of it, Iago", when he blots himself in agony against the wall'
(Speaight, 'Shakespeare', p. 379). In Nunn's production, Iago crouched beside Othello, his
arms around him, stroking his head. In the video, the camera closes in on them, and Iago's
eyes never leave Othello's face (promptbook and video).

188, 192   When the '1755' edition and Bell's edition brought Othello in at 'I will chop her into messes',
the immediate provocation was Iago's 'With her, on her; what you will' and the mad rage
Othello suffers immediately before the fit. When, on the other hand, Kemble brought
Othello on at 'Get me some poison', the provocation was Desdemona's inability to produce
the handkerchief at 3. 4.

192   Beerbohm Tree, using the omitted 'brothel' section of 4.2 as a quarry, inserted the speech
'Had it pleased heaven / To try me with affliction' (4.6ff.) here, just before 'Get me some
poison' (promptbook).

193   De Vigny does not translate 'body and beauty'; he simply says 'douleur' (sorrow).

'Tis Lodovico. This comes from the duke. See, your wife's with
    him.
LODOVICO God save you, worthy general!
OTHELLO   With all my heart, sir.   205
LODOVICO The duke and Senators of Venice greet you.
                   [*He gives Othello a letter.*]
OTHELLO I kiss the instrument of their pleasures.
                  [*He opens the letter and reads.*]
DESDEMONA And what's the news, good cousin Lodovico?
IAGO I am very glad to see you, signior;
    Welcome to Cyprus.   210
LODOVICO I thank you. How does Lieutenant Cassio?
IAGO Lives, sir.
DESDEMONA Cousin, there's fallen between him and my lord
    An unkind breach; but you shall make all well.
OTHELLO Are you sure of that?   215
DESDEMONA My lord?
OTHELLO 'This fail you not to do, as you will –'
LODOVICO He did not call; he's busy in the paper.
    Is there division 'twixt my lord and Cassio?
DESDEMONA A most unhappy one; I would do much   220
    T'atone them, for the love I bear to Cassio.
OTHELLO Fire and brimstone!
DESDEMONA My lord?
OTHELLO Are you wise?
DESDEMONA What, is he angry?
LODOVICO   Maybe the letter moved him;   225
    For as I think they do command him home,
    Deputing Cassio in his government.
DESDEMONA By my troth, I am glad on't.
OTHELLO   Indeed!
DESDEMONA   My lord?
OTHELLO I am glad to see you mad.
DESDEMONA   Why, sweet Othello?
OTHELLO Devil!   230

224   Fechter gave this to Iago who seizes 'the arm of Othello across the table, . . . stopping him
       violently' (his stage direction).
230 SD   Q and F give no direction here; it was inserted by Theobald (1733) on the grounds provided
       by line 263b. Kemble indicates no more than Theobald's, but de Vigny's (in 1829) is 'Il la
       frappe avec les papiers qu'il tient à la main.' Whether the French were following English
       tradition, or the other way round, this way of giving the blow became customary. Fechter

[*He strikes her.*]

DESDEMONA I have not deserved this.

LODOVICO My lord, this would not be believed in Venice,
    Though I should swear I saw't. 'Tis very much.
    Make her amends; she weeps.

OTHELLO   O devil, devil!
    If that the earth could teem with woman's tears,   235
    Each drop she falls would prove a crocodile.
    Out of my sight!

DESDEMONA   I will not stay to offend you.

LODOVICO Truly, an obedient lady.
    I do beseech your lordship, call her back.

OTHELLO Mistress!   240

DESDEMONA My lord?

did it, and Bradley (in 1904) reports a further softening when he describes the 'tap on the shoulder with a roll of paper, as some actors, feeling the repulsiveness of the passage, have made it' (Bradley, *Tragedy*, p. 149). Salvini shocked Furness with 'the backhanded blow . . . full upon those sweet lips' (*Variorum*), but both Mason and Salvini's stage direction indicate that the letter was his instrument (Mason, p. 74).

By starting the act at 4.2, Edwin Booth avoided not only the fit and the eavesdropping, but the blow as well, and Beerbohm Tree's radical rearrangement of Shakespeare's sequence also avoided the whole of this episode, including Lodovico's entrance and Othello's recall to Venice (promptbook). That arrangement still held in some productions after the First World War (see note on Lena Ashwell's comment at 4.1). In Orson Welles's film, the slap seems to come almost from the camera itself: 'Othello's hand moves across the frame to slap Desdemona's face as she approaches looking directly into the camera. It is ingenious, unexpected and effective. But it does not stop one's breath . . .' (Davies, 'Filming *Othello*', p. 209). Olivier used the rolled-up paper, but it was Maggie Smith's Desdemona who drew Tynan's comments: 'her reaction . . . is not the usual collapse into sobs; it is one of deep shame and embarrassment for Othello's sake . . . she holds herself rigidly upright and expressionless, fighting back her tears. "I have not deserved this" is not an appeal for sympathy but a protest quietly and firmly lodged' (Tynan, *National Theatre Production*, p. 10). In Barton's production, Lisa Harrow's reaction to the slap was one of sheer 'incredulity'. It was 'an emotional high point, one of the most poignantly significant moments of the play' (*Coventry Evening Telegraph*, 10 September 1971). Nunn's production at the Other Place was at such close quarters that 'we can see the deadly blue eyes [of Iago] flicker in surprised satisfaction when Othello strikes his wife, before reverting to their implacable stare' (*L*, 7 September 1989).

238   Parker cuts from here to the end of the scene.

OTHELLO What would you with her, sir?
LODOVICO   Who? I, my lord?
OTHELLO Ay, you did wish that I would make her turn.
          Sir, she can turn, and turn, and yet go on,
          And turn again. And she can weep, sir, weep.   245
          And she's obedient; as you say, obedient,
          Very obedient – proceed you in your tears –
          Concerning this, sir, – O, well-painted passion! –
          I am commanded home – get you away!
          I'll send for you anon. – Sir, I obey the mandate,   250
          And will return to Venice. – Hence, avaunt!
                                      [*Exit Desdemona*]
          Cassio shall have my place. And, sir, tonight
          I do entreat that we may sup together.
          You are welcome, sir, to Cyprus. Goats and monkeys! *Exit*
LODOVICO Is this the noble Moor whom our full senate   255
          Call all-in-all sufficient? Is this the nature
          Whom passion could not shake? Whose solid virtue
          The shot of accident nor dart of chance
          Could neither graze nor pierce?
IAGO   He is much changed.
LODOVICO Are his wits safe? Is he not light of brain?   260
IAGO He's that he is; I may not breathe my censure

244–5 Hopkins literally turns Desdemona round and round, snarling at her with his tongue out (Jonathan Miller, BBC). Willard White's voice here 'rises into a near squeal on the second 'weep', skidding out of control like his thoughts' (*Literary Review*, November 1989). David Harewood, in Mendes's production, also 'spins her round in his hands, as if by illustrating the word literally he can make it real' (*NS*, 19 September 1997).

252 'Olivier turns this line into an ironic *double entendre* – hasn't Cassio already usurped his place in bed?' (Tynan, *National Theatre Production*, p. 10).

254 Benedict Nightingale, describing Scofield's 'operatic and implausible' manner, cited this cry which 'becomes a Verdiesque rumble, prefaced by a great jerk of the pelvis, and followed by a half-stumbling, half-staggering canter offstage. The intention may be to show us Othello the poseur . . . the effect is incongruous, external, and not very moving' (*NS*, 28 March 1980). After Othello's exit, Bob Hoskins's Iago gives a surprised lift of the eyebrows to the camera, as though Othello were performing better than he could have hoped (Jonathan Miller, BBC). Willard White delivered the line 'more in exasperation than hysteria' (*L*, 7 September, 1989). In Suzman's video, strange jangling noises again mark Othello's disintegration.

255–63a Bell's edition records this cut; Kemble's restores Lodovico's first speech, but cuts his second – 'Are his wits safe? Is he not light of brain?'

What he might be. If what he might he is not,
I would to heaven he were.
LODOVICO   What! Strike his wife!
IAGO Faith, that was not so well; yet would I knew
        That stroke would prove the worst.
LODOVICO   Is it his use?   265
        Or did the letters work upon his blood
        And new-create this fault?
IAGO   Alas, alas!
        It is not honesty in me to speak
        What I have seen and known. You shall observe him,
        And his own courses will denote him so,   270
        That I may save my speech. Do but go after,
        And mark how he continues.
LODOVICO I am sorry that I am deceived in him.
                                                Exeunt

ACT 4, SCENE 2

Enter OTHELLO *and* EMILIA.

OTHELLO You have seen nothing then?
EMILIA Nor ever heard, nor ever did suspect.
OTHELLO Yes, you have seen Cassio and she together.
EMILIA But then I saw no harm, and then I heard
        Each syllable that breath made up between them. 5
OTHELLO What! Did they never whisper?
EMILIA   Never, my lord.
OTHELLO Nor send you out o'th'way?
EMILIA   Never.
OTHELLO To fetch her fan, her gloves, her mask, nor nothing?
EMILIA Never, my lord.
OTHELLO That's strange. 10
EMILIA I durst, my lord, to wager she is honest,

Furness quotes Lloyd (*Essays*, 1858) who said that this scene was sometimes omitted, making the Bedchamber scene appear with 'all the shockingness of a contrived, cold blooded murder' (*Variorum*). Beerbohm Tree cut it, but he transposed some of its speeches to 3.4 (as we have seen), to 4.1 (which he placed after Shakespeare's 4.3) and to 4.3 itself. Salvini postponed this 'brothel' episode, putting it immediately after Roderigo's and Iago's dialogue at the end of the present scene. This meant that he could run the 'brothel scene' on into the willow-song scene, thus saving a scene change. It was an arrangement followed as recently as 1953–4 when Earle Hyman played Othello in New York (*SQ*, 5, 1954).

    The manner of Othello's and Emilia's entry has varied. During the nineteenth century it was sedate enough – de Vigny's Othello entered 'sombre, mais calme, et d'un air scrutateur'. But in the twentieth century Othello has been furiously uncontrolled. Harold Hobson thought Olivier 'extraordinarily savage and intense' with Emilia here (*ST*, 26 April 1964). Ronald Eyre's Emilia entered dragging on a laundry basket. Othello ran after her, and at line 3 started pulling the sheets out of the basket and throwing them round the stage (promptbook). Scofield 'manhandles her in' (promptbook).

1ff. In both Nunn's and Mendes's productions Othello ransacked Desdemona's dressing table, Willard White trying in vain to unlock the drawer (promptbook) and David Harewood sniffing the bedsheets as well (*G*, 18 September 1997).

Lay down my soul at stake. If you think other,
Remove your thought; it doth abuse your bosom.
If any wretch have put this in your head,
Let heaven requite it with the serpent's curse!   15
For if she be not honest, chaste, and true,
There's no man happy. The purest of their wives
Is foul as slander.

OTHELLO   Bid her come hither; go!

Exit Emilia

She says enough; yet she's a simple bawd
That cannot say as much. This is a subtle whore,   20
A closet lock and key of villainous secrets;
And yet she'll kneel and pray. I have seen her do't.

Enter DESDEMONA *and Emilia.*

DESDEMONA My lord, what is your will?
OTHELLO   Pray, chuck, come hither.
DESDEMONA What is your pleasure?
OTHELLO   Let me see your eyes.
Look in my face.
DESDEMONA   What horrible fancy's this?   25
OTHELLO [*To Emilia*] Some of your function, mistress:
Leave procreants alone and shut the door;
Cough or cry 'hem' if anybody come.
Your mystery, your mystery! Nay, dispatch!

Exit Emilia

20   Macready crossed out the 'whore' that his Kemble-edition still printed, and substituted 'one'. Edwin Booth favoured 'drab'. Their sexual inhibition was reversed in Ronald Eyre's direction here, that Sinden should sniff the sheet he is holding (promptbook).

23b   In Suzman's video, John Kani clicks his fingers here and hisses 'cssk, cssk', as though picking up a whore in the street. Willard White tossed the keys from hand to hand (promptbook and video). Parker cuts.

25   The Eyre promptbook has: 'flings her on the floor . . . kneels over her, throwing her dress up to her waist'. 'It's as if he wants to próve his love of a whore when he nearly rapes her . . .' (Eric Shorter, *DT*, 9 August 1979).

29 SD   Emilia's departure was made much of in some nineteenth-century performances. Macready 'closes the door after her' (promptbook) and perhaps his manner is reflected in de Vigny's direction: 'Othello reste longtemps, la main sur la clèf, qu'il a tournée deux fois et regarde Desdemona avec des yeux terribles'. In Fechter's edition, Desdemona seems to ask for Emilia's support, and as she goes Emilia kisses her hand 'tenderly to Desdemona, who falls exhausted on her knees as soon as Emilia had disappeared'.

DESDEMONA Upon my knees, what doth your speech import?   30
      I understand a fury in your words,
      But not the words.
OTHELLO   Why? What art thou?
DESDEMONA Your wife, my lord; your true and loyal wife.
OTHELLO Come, swear it; damn thyself;
      Lest, being like one of heaven, the devils themselves   35
      Should fear to seize thee. Therefore be double-damned:
      Swear thou art honest.
DESDEMONA   Heaven doth truly know it.
OTHELLO Heaven truly knows that thou art false as hell.
DESDEMONA To whom, my lord? With whom? How am I false?
OTHELLO Ah, Desdemon, away, away, away!   40
DESDEMONA Alas, the heavy day! Why do you weep?

30–2   This was one of Sarah Siddons's best moments. She showed 'a deep concern that Othello
should so grossly err, a feeling that subdued all petulance at being unjustly accused'
(Boaden, *Kemble*, I, p. 260).

33–8   Fechter's Desdemona raised 'her hand as if to make an oath', and Othello grabbed it,
throwing it back at her at 'thou art false as hell' (his stage direction). Sinden 'rummages
through Desdemona's laundry basket with real passion and appetite, sniffing like a hound at
the sheets'(*DT*, 9 August 1979). Willard White laughed as he talked to her then pushed her
on to the prie-dieu and slammed her hand down on the Bible for line 34 (promptbook and
video).

40   Quin uttered this line 'very affectingly, by a melancholy murmur in his voice, very expressive
of that mixture of love and anguish conflicting in his mind' (Boaden, *Correspondence*, I,
p. 31). John Bernard described Barry here: 'he looked a few seconds in Desdemona's face,
as if to read her feelings and disprove her suspicions; then, turning away, as the adverse
conviction gathered in his heart, he spoke them falteringly, and gushed into tears' (Bernard,
Retrospections, I, pp. 17–18). Fechter made Desdemona arise 'with a cry of joy' at 'O
Desdemona', and throw 'herself on the breast of Othello, who disengages himself, repulses
her, and falls sobbing on the divan' (his stage direction). This moment in the James Earl
Jones–Christopher Plummer *Othello* early in 1982 illuminated the whole play for Walter Kerr:
'Desdemona, body curled double in despair and retreat is already in near-foetal position.
Looking down at her, and possibly seeing her for the bewildered, unformed creature she is,
this Othello slowly lowers himself, stretches out his massive military-man's arms, and draws
the folds of his voluminous cloak over both of them. As his body shelters hers, conforms to
hers, the two seem little more than children lost in a fairy-tale forest and falling asleep
beneath a blanket of snow. Their love for each other, so rapidly being destroyed, is in the
silence. The silence is finally broken with a surprisingly hushed, tender reading of that
line . . ."O Desdemona! Away! away! away!" Secretly, scarcely daring to let himself hear the

      Am I the motive of these tears, my lord?
      If haply you my father do suspect
      An instrument of this your calling back,
      Lay not your blame on me. If you have lost him,   45
      I have lost him too.
OTHELLO   Had it pleased heaven
      To try me with affliction, had they rained
      All kind of sores and shames on my bare head,
      Steeped me in poverty to the very lips,
      Given to captivity me and my utmost hopes,   50
      I should have found in some place of my soul
      A drop of patience. But, alas, to make me
      The fixèd figure for the time of scorn
      To point his slow unmoving finger at!
      Yet could I bear that too, well, very well;   55
      But there where I have garnered up my heart,
      Where either I must live or bear no life,
      The fountain from the which my current runs
      Or else dries up – to be discarded thence

words he is pronouncing, he sounds as though he were toying with the notion of an impossible flight that will bring her to safety, safety from the treacherous world into which he has stumbled, safety from himself' (*NYT*, 14 February 1982). In Suzman's video, John Kani crawls towards her and embraces her, sobbing, while she cradles his face. Both Willard White (promptbook) and Ray Fearon (RSC archive film) embraced Desdemona for the first two 'away's and threw her off on the third.

46–63   Leigh Hunt observed of Kean here: he 'trembles and halts . . . you might fancy you saw the water quivering in his eyes' (Hunt, *Dramatic Criticism*, p. 202). Forster contrasted this favourably with Macready whose tears seemed 'heavily rolling down the face' (Forster, *Essays*, p. 15). By contrast, Olivier, having fallen on the ground in the act of throwing Desdemona off, shouts the speech at her in a fury (film). Barton directed his Othello to pull Desdemona to the ground and at 'there' (line 56) to grab her 'muffin' as the 1972 promptbook puts it. He cut 61b–3. Perhaps the idea had come from the production at the Mermaid (shortly before Barton's 1972 Aldwych season) which, said Robert Cushman, had 'one glory: Othello delivered the speech beginning "Had it pleased heaven . . . " looking Desdemona straight in the crotch, which makes unusual sense of the lines "the fountain from the which my current runs", and particularly of the instruction "Turn thy complexion there." No other Othello I've seen has shown much interest in where *there* might be . . .' (*P and P*, October 1971). In some more recent productions, 'there' was Desdemona's reflection in her hand mirror which Othello thrust in her face (Nunn promptbook and the Attenborough RSC archive film).

> Or keep it as a cistern for foul toads   60
> To knot and gender in! Turn thy complexion there,
> Patience, thou young and rose-lipped cherubin;
> Ay, there look grim as hell!
> DESDEMONA I hope my noble lord esteems me honest.
> OTHELLO O ay: as summer flies are in the shambles,   65
> That quicken even with blowing. O, thou weed,
> Who art so lovely fair and smell'st so sweet
> That the sense aches at thee, would thou hadst ne'er been
>   born!
> DESDEMONA Alas, what ignorant sin have I committed?
> OTHELLO Was this fair paper, this most goodly book,   70
> Made to write 'whore' upon? What committed!
> Committed? O thou public commoner!

66–8 The sensuality of the lines worried Macready, for he crossed them out heavily; but, thinking better of it, wrote 'in' twice in the margin (promptbook). Edwin Booth disappointed the critic of the *Athenaeum* on just this matter. Booth failed to convey that Othello feels here 'with absolute faintness of desire and quintessential agony of passion, the subtle perfume he describes . . .' (7 May 1881). Olivier entered into their spirit: 'he crawls across the stage and lies on top of Desdemona: for a moment desire almost overcomes disgust: or rather, both emotions co-exist' (Tynan, *National Theatre Production*, p. 11). In the film he is kneeling with her clasped to him. In Suzman's video, John Kani, using the quarto text ('O thou black weed . . .') similarly rolls on top of Desdemona, and she on him at 'Alas, what ignorant sin . . .?' Nunn also used the quarto text here, and Willard White clasped Desdemona's neck (promptbook). In the video, the camera lingers on their intermingled black and white hands, heads and necks. Parker cuts the word 'weed' – fearing, perhaps, its modern connotations.

70–1a Macready cut this, thus avoiding the word 'whore' (promptbook). Fechter put 'shame' for 'whore', and Edwin Booth had his usual 'drab': 'not too violently', he warns, 'more of indignation than anger' (*Variorum*). In the film, Olivier, on the contrary, flings her savagely to the floor.

72–80 De Vigny translates 'Heaven stops the nose at it' as 'Le jour en le voyant se détourne de honte' (The day, seeing it, turns away in shame'). Salvini's Italian is equally insipid: 'Copre il cielo la faccia' ('The sky covers its face'). Fechter cut the whole thing after line 74. Willard White lifted Desdemona on to a stool, and in a grotesque parody of his earlier business at his arrival on Cyprus, he circled her, holding his nose and pointing (video and promptbook). In Suzman's video, on each word of 'Impudent strumpet', John Kani pokes a finger into each of her breasts. The gender violence of Kelly's production was horribly pointed here, when 'Othello increasingly enraged flung Desdemona up against the wall of the armoury (where this scene was set), ripped off her skirt and blouse, and seemed to rape her onstage. At

I should make very forges of my cheeks
That would to cinders burn up modesty
Did I but speak thy deeds. What committed!   75
Heaven stops the nose at it, and the moon winks;
The bawdy wind, that kisses all it meets,
Is hushed within the hollow mine of earth
And will not hear it. What committed?
Impudent strumpet!

DESDEMONA   By heaven, you do me wrong.   80
OTHELLO Are not you a strumpet?
DESDEMONA   No, as I am a Christian.
If to preserve this vessel for my lord
From any other foul unlawful touch
Be not to be a strumpet, I am none.
OTHELLO What, not a whore?
DESDEMONA   No, as I shall be saved.   85
OTHELLO Is't possible?
DESDEMONA O, heaven forgive us!
OTHELLO   I cry you mercy then:
I took you for that cunning whore of Venice
That married with Othello. You, mistress,
That have the office opposite to Saint Peter,   90
And keeps the gate of hell! You, you, ay, you!

Enter Emilia.

Desdemona's sobbing scream "By heaven, you do me wrong!" Othello seemed to come to himself. Slowly he dropped to his knees, kissing Desdemona's body as he sank lower, until his face was against her hips, at which point he suddenly pulled back, retching and staggered away' (Johnson-Haddad, 'Shakespeare Theatre *Othello*', p. 10).

81–5   Bell's edition records a cut at Desdemona's speech which leaves her only 'No, as I am a Christian'. In Oxberry's edition (1819) that cut extends as far as 87a ('O, heaven forgive us!'), thus avoiding 'What, not a whore?' Kemble, however, keeps all Othello's 'whores' and 'strumpets', and Macready in his promptbook prefers substitution rather than omission. Phelps's promptbook has 'What! not a . . .!' and this section came to be known in F. R. Benson's company as 'the Notta' (Trewin, *Benson*, p. 137). In Barton's production Brewster Mason 'with superb audacity plays . . ."Are you not a strumpet?" on a hopeful note; reconciliation hovers in the air, to be dashed to the ground on "I cry you mercy then . . ."'. (Cushman, *P and P*, October 1971). Nunn used the same idea, but to indicate Desdemona's hope, not Othello's: 'her face lit up with joy at the prospect that all is to be well between them, only to crease up with anguish as the terrible truth came flooding back with his return to brutal abuse' (Smallwood, 'Shakespeare', p. 112).

We have done our course; there's money for your pains.
I pray you turn the key, and keep our counsel.   *Exit*
EMILIA Alas, what does this gentleman conceive?
How do you, madam? How do you, my good lady?   95
DESDEMONA Faith, half-asleep.
EMILIA Good madam, what's the matter with my lord?
DESDEMONA With who?
EMILIA Why, with my lord, madam.
DESDEMONA Who is thy lord?
EMILIA   He that is yours, sweet lady.   100
DESDEMONA I have none. Do not talk to me, Emilia.
I cannot weep, nor answers have I none
But what should go by water. Prithee tonight
Lay on my bed my wedding sheets, remember;
And call thy husband hither.
EMILIA   Here's a change indeed! *Exit*   105
DESDEMONA 'Tis meet I should be used so, very meet!
How have I been behaved that he might stick
The smallest opinion on my least misuse?

Enter IAGO *and Emilia.*

IAGO What is your pleasure, madam? How is't with you?
DESDEMONA I cannot tell. Those that do teach young babes   110

92ff.   Fechter threw a purse on the table before departing, and Salvini elaborated the business, shaking the purse 'savagely . . . in the ear of Emilia, and departs throwing it at her feet with a fine expression of scorn and indignation' (Knight, *Notes*, p. 23). Oscar Asche's Iago, Alfred Brydone, 'deliberately appropriated the purse Othello had flung to Emilia . . .' (Dickins, *Forty Years*, p. 146). Webster's Emilia, having been given the money, threw it angrily at his feet (promptbook). Olivier flings the loose coins at her (film). Ellen Terry's Desdemona was remarkable here for 'a natural nervous speechlessness and what may be called suppressed hysteria' (*Theatre*, June 1881). For a later production in 1898, she marked in her promptbook 'try new effect. *Standing*', and for the following dialogue she continues: 'stand like a stone' and 'keep from tears'. The numbness of 'Faith, half asleep' lies behind this idea, an inspiration denied to earlier Desdemonas by its omission from Bell's edition onwards. Patrick Stewart delivered line 92b not to Emilia but to Desdemona 'as he tossed her a handful of coins' (Johnson-Haddad, 'Shakespeare Theatre *Othello*', p. 10).
94ff.   In Salvini's rearrangement, this dialogue is made to follow 4.1, as if in response to the blow that Othello would have just given Desdemona.
104   Cumberland's acting edition (1829) and Macready's promptbook cut this reference to sheets. De Vigny turns them into 'la robe que j'avais quand je fus mariée'.

Do it with gentle means and easy tasks.
He might have chid me so; for, in good faith,
I am a child to chiding.

IAGO   What is the matter, lady?

EMILIA Alas, Iago, my lord hath so bewhored her,
    Thrown such despite and heavy terms upon her   115
    As true hearts cannot bear.

DESDEMONA Am I that name, Iago?

IAGO   What name, fair lady?

DESDEMONA Such as she said my lord did say I was.

EMILIA He called her whore. A beggar in his drink
    Could not have laid such terms upon his callet.   120

IAGO Why did he so?

DESDEMONA I do not know; I am sure I am none such.

IAGO Do not weep, do not weep! Alas the day!

EMILIA Hath she forsook so many noble matches,
    Her father, and her country, and her friends,   125
    To be called whore? Would it not make one weep?

DESDEMONA It is my wretched fortune.

IAGO   Beshrew him for't!
How comes this trick upon him?

DESDEMONA   Nay, heaven doth know.

EMILIA I will be hanged if some eternal villain,
    Some busy and insinuating rogue,   130

114, 119, 126   Here again the promptbooks of Macready, Phelps, Fechter, Booth, Asche and Terry all
delete the word 'whore' or substitute 'wanton' and 'drab'. 'Bewhored' is also altered to
'becalled' (Fechter) or 'miscalled' (Terry). By Asche's time this practice was beginning to
irritate the critics. Dickins laments the fact that 'Mrs Grundy' should have played so large a
part in the preparation of Asche's text (Dickins, *Forty Years*, p. 144–5).

117-18   Sarah Siddons's 'delicacy' here 'electrified the house' (Boaden, *Kemble*, I, p. 260).

122   Ellen Terry's promptbook breaks up the line with vertical strokes every two words and in the
margin she writes 'Break down.' She had held back her tears till now.

123   McKellen's Iago gave Desdemona his handkerchief, rocked and hugged and 'encroaches
upon [her], thin fingers stroking her hair' (video and *L*, 7 September 1989).

129-43   Boaden describes the Emilias of his day breaking forth thankfully at this moment, having
waited through four 'tedious acts' for it: 'here taking her ground upon the *virtuous*
indignation of the audience, the actress becomes a perfect fury; and . . . parades herself to
the lamps in a semi-circle, and speaks thunder to the Gods themselves'. Line 143 was cut at
this period, something Boaden abhors since it facilitates Emilia's final flourish (Boaden,
Siddons, I, pp. 73–4 and footnote). Parker's film cuts the whole passage.

> Some cogging, cozening slave, to get some office,
> Have not devised this slander; I'll be hanged else.
> IAGO Fie, there is no such man; it is impossible.
> DESDEMONA If any such there be, heaven pardon him.
> EMILIA A halter pardon him and hell gnaw his bones! 135
>   Why should he call her whore? Who keeps her company?
>   What place, what time, what form, what likelihood?
>   The Moor's abused by some most villainous knave,
>   Some base notorious knave, some scurvy fellow.
>   O heaven, that such companions thou'dst unfold, 140
>   And put in every honest hand a whip
>   To lash the rascals naked through the world,
>   Even from the east to th'west!
> IAGO   Speak within door.
> EMILIA O fie upon them! Some such squire he was
>   That turned your wit the seamy side without 145
>   And made you to suspect me with the Moor.
> IAGO You are a fool, go to.
> DESDEMONA   O good Iago,
>   What shall I do to win my lord again?
>   Good friend, go to him; for, by this light of heaven,
>   I know not how I lost him. Here I kneel: 150

134 Oxberry's edition (1819) gives this little piece of piety to Iago.

135 Edwin Booth cut this and the *Athenaeum* noted that the Americans were 'leagues ahead' of the English in censoring Shakespeare. If such a phrase is ' too "shocking" . . . we care not how soon the attempt to play Shakespeare is abandoned' (22 January 1881).

136 The 'whore' here becomes 'so' in Macready's, and 'that' in Ellen Terry's promptbook. Edwin Booth has his inevitable 'drab'.

144–6 In Webster's production Emilia whispered her lines to Iago so that Desdemona cannot hear, and Iago then kissed her on his line (promptbook).

147a Irving gave the line with 'such an apparent poohpoohing of the absurd suggestion of there being a "cogging knave" somewhere, and at the same time such a hearty intensity of double meaning as to make it admirable' (Saintsbury, *Scrap Book*, p. 115).

148 Ellen Terry said this so pathetically that she once moved Irving's Iago to tears: 'But he knew how to turn it to his purpose: he obtrusively took the tears with his fingers and blew his nose with much feeling, softly and long . . . so that the audience might think his emotion a fresh stroke of hypocrisy' (Terry, *Story*, p. 205). Dutton Cook thought that Terry's Desdemona should remember her husband's rank and not 'fling herself upon the bosom of Iago, and . . . accept the consolation of his embraces and caresses' (Cook, *Nights*, II, p. 320).

150ff. Boaden admired Sarah Siddons's 'kneeling adjuration, the pathos that swelled upward as she uttered the words ". . . Or that I do not YET, and ever *did*, / And ever *will*, though he do

> If e'er my will did trespass 'gainst his love
> Either in discourse of thought or actual deed;
> Or that mine eyes, mine ears, or any sense
> Delighted them in any other form;
> Or that I do not yet, and ever did,   155
> And ever will – though he do shake me off
> To beggarly divorcement – love him dearly,
> Comfort forswear me! Unkindness may do much,
> And his unkindness may defeat my life,
> But never taint my love. I cannot say 'whore':   160
> It does abhor me now I speak the word;
> To do the act that might the addition earn
> Not the world's mass of vanity could make me.
> IAGO I pray you be content; 'tis but his humour.
> The business of the state does him offence,   165
> And he does chide with you.
> DESDEMONA If 'twere no other –
> IAGO   It is but so, I warrant.
>   [*Trumpets sound within.*]
> Hark how these instruments summon to supper!
> The messengers of Venice stay the meat.
> Go in, and weep not; all things shall be well.   170
>   *Exeunt Desdemona and Emilia*

shake me off / To BEGGARLY DIVORCEMENT, love him dearly"' (Boaden, *Kemble*, I,
p. 260). Parker's film makes this a tear-brimming prayer with violins on the soundtrack.

160b–3   From the '1755' edition onwards, eighteenth- and nineteenth-century acting editions have
cut Desdemona's little pun here.

164–70   Bob Hoskins's Iago strokes Desdemona, who weeps on his shoulder, and when the
trumpets sound he imitates them, as though cheering up a child (Jonathan Miller, BBC).
McKellen's and McCabe's Iagos likewise jollied her along – in the video, McKellen tweaks
her nose on ''Tis but so' and wipes it with his handkerchief. McCabe swung her arm in a
pretend march, on 'messengers from Venice stay the meat' (RSC archive film).

171ff.   Edwin Booth's edition marks this as a new scene 'Before the castle', and so does Webster's
promptbook. Earle Hyman coped with the problem of location by shifting this part of the
scene and placing it after 4.3, the willow-song scene, so that Roderigo's fight with Cassio at
5.1 runs straight on from Iago's incitement of Roderigo to kill him ('Shakespeare on the New
York stage', *SQ*, 5, 1954). Bernard Miles's production at the Mermaid in 1971 had set the
'brothel' section of 4.2 in Desdemona's bedroom, making no change for Roderigo's entry:
'Iago and Roderigo are left to argue amongst the discarded bedclothes . . . Where is the
privacy of the bedroom? Othello might as well murder Desdemona on a street corner as in
this public place' (*City Press*, 23 September 1971). Perhaps fixed sets accustom audiences to

Enter RODERIGO.

How now, Roderigo?

RODERIGO I do not find that thou deal'st justly with me.

IAGO What in the contrary?

RODERIGO Every day thou daff'st me with some device, Iago, and
rather, as it seems to me now, keep'st from me all conveniency   175
than suppliest me with the least advantage of hope. I will indeed
no longer endure it. Nor am I yet persuaded to put up in peace
what already I have foolishly suffered.

IAGO Will you hear me, Roderigo?

RODERIGO Faith, I have heard too much; for your words and   180
performances are no kin together.

IAGO You charge me most unjustly.

RODERIGO With naught but truth. I have wasted myself out of my
means. The jewels you have had from me to deliver to Desdemona
would half have corrupted a votarist. You have told me she hath   185
received them, and returned me expectations and comforts of
sudden respect and acquaintance, but I find none.

IAGO Well, go to; very well.

RODERIGO Very well, go to! I cannot go to, man, nor 'tis not very
well. By this hand, I say 'tis very scurvy and begin to find myself   190
fopped in it.

IAGO Very well.

RODERIGO I tell you 'tis not very well. I will make myself known to
Desdemona. If she will return me my jewels, I will give over my
suit and repent my unlawful solicitation; if not, assure yourself I   195
will seek satisfaction of you.

IAGO You have said now?

RODERIGO Ay, and said nothing but what I protest intendment of
doing.

IAGO Why, now I see there's mettle in thee, and even from this instant   200
do build on thee a better opinion than ever before. Give me thy
hand, Roderigo. Thou hast taken against me a most just
exception; but yet I protest I have dealt most directly in thy
affair.

such anomalies: there was no complaint when, at 184–5, Attenborough's Roderigo tried to
find his jewels among Desdemona's things (RSC archive film). Nunn's video shows
Roderigo doing the same.

200ff.   In Webster's production 'the two draw their swords'. Iago laughed and they fought a little as
Iago said 'and even from this instant . . .' They then sheathed their swords, and at 'Give me
thy hand' Roderigo did so, instantly thinking better of it (Carroll).

RODERIGO It hath not appeared.   205

IAGO I grant indeed it hath not appeared; and your suspicion is not
without wit and judgement. But, Roderigo, if thou hast that in
thee indeed, which I have greater reason to believe now than
ever – I mean purpose, courage, and valour – this night show it. If
thou the next night following enjoy not Desdemona, take me from   210
this world with treachery, and devise engines for my life.

RODERIGO Well, what is it? Is it within reason and compass?

IAGO Sir, there is especial commission come from Venice to depute
Cassio in Othello's place.

RODERIGO Is that true? Why, then Othello and Desdemona return   215
again to Venice.

IAGO O no, he goes into Mauritania and takes away with him the
fair Desdemona, unless his abode be lingered here by some
accident; wherein none can be so determinate as the removing of
Cassio.   220

RODERIGO How do you mean 'removing' of him?

IAGO Why, by making him uncapable of Othello's place – knocking
out his brains.

RODERIGO And that you would have me to do?

IAGO Ay, if you dare do yourself a profit and a right. He sups tonight   225
with a harlotry, and thither will I go to him. He knows not yet of
his honourable fortune. If you will watch his going thence – which
I will fashion to fall out between twelve and one – you may take
him at your pleasure. I will be near to second your attempt, and
he shall fall between us. Come, stand not amazed at it, but go along   230
with me. I will show you such a necessity in his death that you shall
think yourself bound to put it on him. It is now high supper-time
and the night grows to waste. About it!

RODERIGO I will hear further reason for this.

IAGO And you shall be satisfied.   235

Exeunt

218 In Webster's production, after 'Desdemona' Roderigo said 'Oh' and turned away,
whereupon Iago turned him back and continued 'unless . . .' (Carroll) – another important
link in the plot underlined.

Salvini ended 4.2 with the 'brothel' section of the scene, which he had omitted from its
usual place after the blow.

In Parker's film, Iago studies a chessboard and as he speaks the transposed words from
5.1.128–9 ('This is the night / That either makes me, or foredoes me quite'), he flips the
pieces into the water.

ACT 4, SCENE 3

Enter OTHELLO, LODOVICO, DESDEMONA, EMILIA *and*
ATTENDANTS.

LODOVICO I do beseech you, sir, trouble yourself no further.
OTHELLO O, pardon me; 'twill do me good to walk.
LODOVICO Madam, good night. I humbly thank your ladyship.
DESDEMONA Your honour is most welcome.
OTHELLO Will you walk, sir? O, Desdemona.   5
DESDEMONA My lord?
OTHELLO Get you to bed on th'instant. I will be returned forthwith.
    Dismiss your attendant there. Look't be done.
DESDEMONA I will, my lord.
              Exeunt [Othello, Lodovico and Attendants]
EMILIA How goes it now? He looks gentler than he did.   10
DESDEMONA He says he will return incontinent;
    He hath commanded me to go to bed
    And bade me to dismiss you.
EMILIA   Dismiss me?
DESDEMONA It was his bidding; therefore, good Emilia,
    Give me my nightly wearing, and adieu.   15
    We must not now displease him.
EMILIA I would you had never seen him.
DESDEMONA So would not I: my love doth so approve him

From the '1755' edition onwards through most of the nineteenth century this scene ended at
line 17, so that almost the whole of Desdemona's and Emilia's dialogue was dropped. We do
not know when the cut was first made. Boaden blamed the English 'rage . . . for action'
(Boaden, *Siddons*, II, p. 156) but it could have been the earlier rage for the heroic. Rymer
calls this episode a 'filthy sort of Pastoral scene' (Rymer, *Short View*, p. 158). Phelps and
Fechter omitted even the first sixteen lines, passing straight on to 5.1, Roderigo's murder.
However, there were some notable exceptions.

18ff.   Possibly because of the continental popularity of Rossini's opera *Otello,* in which the willow
song figures prominently, this scene and the song were performed in nineteenth-century
French and German productions when they were dropped from English and American: 'go
to the Théâtre-Français', wrote de Broglie, 'and you will see Desdemona . . . stopping to take
her ornaments off piece by piece, in the presence of the public, and to talk negligently with

That even his stubbornness, his checks, his frowns –
Prithee, unpin me – have grace and favour in them.   20
EMILIA I have laid those sheets you bade me on the bed.
DESDEMONA All's one. Good faith, how foolish are our minds!
If I do die before thee, prithee shroud me
In one of those same sheets.
EMILIA   Come, come, you talk.
DESDEMONA My mother had a maid called Barbary: 25
She was in love, and he she loved proved mad
And did forsake her. She had a song of willow;
An old thing 'twas but it expressed her fortune,
And she died singing it. That song tonight

her companion: you will see her interrupt her confessions of anxiety, by which she is
devoured . . . then suddenly remembering her childhood, you will hear her sing, 'à demi
voix', an old ballad' – all of which, he says, though it does not advance the plot as French
dramaturgy dictates, nevertheless fascinates the public (Broglie, 'Sur *Othello*', pp. 268–9).

In 1853 G. H. Lewes was taken by surprise by it in a German production where Herr
Dessoir played Othello, and Fraulein Fuhr Desdemona: 'What a scene it is! . . . where she
talks as she undresses, of Lodovico, of reputed false wives etc., one of the most
Shakespearean scenes in the whole drama, and always omitted on our stage' (Lewes,
Essays, p. 260). No mention of Emilia here. Salvini included the scene, though he cut
Emilia's speeches, as did Edwin Booth who (in 1869 at Booth's Theatre, New York) was the
first English-speaking actor–manager to restore the scene. Irving followed in 1876, though
not, strangely, with Ellen Terry in 1881. In 1898, Ellen Terry did a short tour with Frank
Cooper, and the Grand Theatre, Fulham, was the setting for her first rendering of this scene.
Beerbohm Tree restored it for Phyllis Neilson-Terry, who, said his wife, Maud Holt Tree, was
'perfect in poise, in voice, in gentleness, in beauty' (Tree, 'Herbert and I', p. 147).

In Robeson's 1930 production, Peggy Ashcroft played it with a 'grave wistful sweetness'
(*Punch,* 28 May 1930). In Barton's production, Lisa Harrow, with Elizabeth Spriggs as Emilia,
made the scene for B. A. Young, 'the emotional peak of the evening' (*FT,* 13 September 1971).
Felicity Kendal, in Peter Hall's production, was especially noted here: 'when she sits on a
chair, in a simple white shift, with her feet not touching the ground, she becomes a terribly
vulnerable little-girl figure' (*Evening News,* 21 March 1980). In the video, Joanna Weinberg,
Suzman's Desdemona, was very open and serious here – innocent but not childish. In
Nunn's production, Desdemona's bedroom was made intimately real – 'a sepia photograph
of Brabantio stands reproachfully on Desdemona's night-table' (*TLS,* 8 September 1989) –
and within it the intimate relationship between the two women was especially noticed, 'as
they huddle in the lamplight, while the wind howls outside, waiting for the vengeful Moor's
return' (*L,* 7 September 1989).

> Will not go from my mind. I have much to do   30
> But to go hang my head all at one side
> And sing it like poor Barbary – prithee, dispatch.

EMILIA Shall I go fetch your nightgown?

DESDEMONA   No, unpin me here.
> This Lodovico is a proper man.

EMILIA A very handsome man.

DESDEMONA   He speaks well.   35

EMILIA I know a lady in Venice would have walked barefoot to
> Palestine for a touch of his nether lip.

DESDEMONA [*Sings*]
> The poor soul sat sighing by a sycamore tree,
>   Sing all a green willow;
> Her hand on her bosom, her head on her knee,   40

30b–51 This passage which includes the song, is not in the quarto. It remained precarious, for the
Smock Alley text omits it. A beautiful voice is not necessary. One of Webster's cast wrote
'God knows, Uta Hagen [Webster's Desdemona] can't sing', but that it was one of the best
moments of her performance (letter to Carroll). Maggie Smith, in John Dexter's production,
made 'the whole auditorium hold its breath . . . even the most ordinary words such as "Nay,
that's not next" . . . became inexplicably poignant' (*O*, 26 April 1964). Imogen Stubbs sang
the blues which the *Spectator* thought inappropriate to the time and place (2 September
1989), but which the *Listener* thought 'exactly captures the tone of a precocious, fragile
white teenager trying to sing the blues' (7 September 1989). Among Mendes's forties period
details was, 'enchantingly, a portable phonograph from which "Sing willow, willow, willow",
issues forth as a torch song' (*TLS*, 3 October 1997). In Parker's film, Emilia gives Desdemona
a bath here, and during the song there is a cut to Othello, now in full eastern robes, carrying
a sword, and wandering by the moonlit sea.

33–4 Ellen Terry marked 'Hair' in the margin here, so that 'unpin' must refer to that rather than to
her gown. (Bernard Miles made great play with this line in the press, so as to justify his
nude Desdemona, see *T*, 8 September 1971). Beerbohm Tree made a maze of Shakespeare's
text and it is difficult to map his route clearly. At this point in the scene he brought in
Desdemona's dialogue with Emilia in 4.2, starting at 'call thy husband hither', and ending
with Iago's 'weep not; all things shall be well'. Then this scene continued to the end of the
song. In other words the two intimate moments between Emilia and Desdemona were put
together, though the presence of Iago spoiled the special quality of the present scene. In
Nunn's production 'you could hear the rustle of hair and corset as Desdemona is unpinned'
(*FT*, 26 August 1989).

34 In Nunn's video, Zoë Wanamaker and Imogen Stubbs both giggle at the mention of
Lodovico.

          Sing willow, willow, willow;
     The fresh streams ran by her and murmured her moans;
          Sing willow, willow, willow.
     Her salt tears fell from her and softened the stones –
Lay by these.   45
          Sing willow, willow, willow –
Prithee, hie thee; he'll come anon.
          Sing all a green willow must be my garland.
          Let nobody blame him; his scorn I approve –
Nay that's not next. Hark, who is't that knocks?   50
EMILIA It's the wind.
DESDEMONA [*Sings*]
     I called my love false love, but what said he then?
          Sing willow, willow, willow;
     If I court moe women, you'll couch with moe men –
So get thee gone; good night. Mine eyes do itch –   55
Does that bode weeping?
EMILIA   'Tis neither here nor there.
DESDEMONA I have heard it said so. O, these men, these men!
     Dost thou in conscience think – tell me, Emilia –
     That there be women do abuse their husbands
     In such gross kind?
EMILIA   There be some such, no question.   60
DESDEMONA Wouldst thou do such a deed for all the world?
EMILIA Why, would not you?
DESDEMONA   No, by this heavenly light.
EMILIA Nor I neither by this heavenly light;
     I might do't as well i'th'dark.
DESDEMONA Wouldst thou do such a deed for all the world?   65
EMILIA The world's a huge thing; it is a great price
     For a small vice.
DESDEMONA   In troth, I think thou wouldst not.

54   Edwin Booth's edition makes the same sort of patchwork here as Beerbohm Tree's promptbook. He goes back to 4.2. with 'call thy husband hither' (105a) and continues to the end of that scene.

55   Imogen Stubbs's Desdemona hugged Emilia but the hug was not returned (Nunn promptbook).

60   Ellen Terry marks in her promptbook that Emilia says her line 'jollily to cheer her up'. She cuts the rest of this scene, as did all the others in the nineteenth century, even when they restored as far as here. Only Desdemona's pieties at line 79, and the final couplet, escaped.

64   In the video, Imogen Stubbs giggles again.

EMILIA In troth, I think I should, and undo't when I had done it.
Marry, I would not do such a thing for a joint-ring, nor for
measures of lawn, nor for gowns, petticoats, nor caps, nor any   70
petty exhibition. But for all the whole world! Ud's pity,
who would not make her husband a cuckold, to make him a
monarch? I should venture purgatory for't.

DESDEMONA Beshrew me, if I would do such a wrong for the whole
world.   75

EMILIA Why, the wrong is but a wrong i'th'world; and having the world
for your labour, 'tis a wrong in your own world, and you might
quickly make it right.

DESDEMONA I do not think there is any such woman.

EMILIA Yes, a dozen; and as many to th'advantage as would store   80
the world they played for.
    But I do think it is their husbands' faults
If wives do fall. Say that they slack their duties
And pour our treasures into foreign laps,
Or else break out in peevish jealousies,   85
Throwing restraint upon us; or say they strike us,
Or scant our former having in despite –
Why, we have galls, and though we have some grace,
Yet have we some revenge. Let husbands know
Their wives have sense like them: they see, and smell,   90
And have their palates both for sweet and sour
As husbands have. What is it that they do
When they change us for others? Is it sport?
I think it is. And doth affection breed it?

78   In Nunn's production, Desdemona here unlocked her dressing- table drawer (the one
Othello couldn't open, see note at 4.2.1ff) and produced Cassio's chocolates – locked away
'not because she fears sexual misconstruction but because she would like to be thought too
grown-up for frivolous sweet-guzzling by Othello' (*I*, 2 October 1989).

82–99   Most of Emilia's final speech appears only in the Folio. It is an obvious economy, though
later the speech would probably have been thought too ribald anyway. Rosenberg says that
the Smock Alley text cuts 'much' of it (Rosenberg, *Masks*, p. 26). John Dexter's Joyce
Redman 'with Desdemona kneeling at her feet managed brilliantly to speak her polemic
about men's infidelity in such a way as . . . not to break the mood' (*O*, 26 April 1964). In
Nunn's video, Imogen Stubbs and Zoë Wanamaker are close and confiding here, hugging
each other at 92b-93a. In Kelly's production, at Emilia's half-line, 'or say they strike us', 'the
air was heavy with the silence of two abused wives, each too ashamed to confide in the
other' (Potter, *Othello*, pp. 182-3).

I think it doth. Is't frailty that thus errs?   95
It is so too. And have not we affections,
Desires for sport, and frailty, as men have?
Then let them use us well; else let them know
The ills we do, their ills instruct us so.
DESDEMONA Good night, good night. God me such uses send,   100
Not to pick bad from bad, but by bad mend!

Exeunt

101–1   In the Hawkins–Quayle production, Elizabeth Kentish as Desdemona 'knelt to pray. I had
seen this before, but her making the last two lines of the scene the beginning of her prayer
was new to me and ingenious' (Crosse, *Playgoing*, p. 152). The idea of having a prayer at all
might have come from Verdi's 'Ave Maria' here. Suzman's Joanna Weinberg gently touches
Emilia's face here, and goes slowly off (video). In Nunn's production, Zoë Wanamaker leant
over and cuddled Desdemona, then exited on Desdemona's second 'goodnight'.
Desdemona's last words were spoken at the prie-dieu (promptbook).

Enter IAGO *and* RODERIGO.

IAGO Here, stand behind this bulk, straight will he come.
       Wear thy good rapier bare, and put it home.
       Quick, quick, fear nothing; I'll be at thy elbow.
       It makes us or it mars us; think on that,
       And fix most firm thy resolution.   5
RODERIGO Be near at hand; I may miscarry in't.
IAGO Here, at thy hand; be bold, and take thy stand.

The proscenium doors of the Restoration stage, which lasted until the early nineteenth century, would have served for Iago's exit to his house and re-entrance. At those downstage moments, he would have been well placed for the 'corner-looks', as one paper described them, so typical of Iago (*Examiner*, 31 January 1808). The 1766 Drury Lane prompt copy indicates 'Domestic town' opposite prompt, and 'Castle scene' promptside. Kemble has 'a street' to which Macready added a house 'with a door in it' for Iago and Emilia (promptbook). Fechter had 'two streets, which lead off on the right and left . . . at the angle . . . Iago's house; on the left a tree, with a seat made of broken columns, fragments, and cornices etc. On the right, the ruins of a Mosque (Night)' (his stage direction). Webster's designer, Robert Edmund Jones, had a very dark stage (so dark that it was difficult for the actors to find Roderigo's corpse) with a green light spilling diagonally, casting huge shadows, and occasionally catching an actor's face (personal letters from members of the cast to Carroll). John Dexter went further by setting the scene 'in complete darkness, and the lanterns in the hands of the actors cast only a dim light. The confusion of the fight is vividly conveyed by the movement of the lanterns to and fro' (Alexander Anikst, quoted in Tynan, *National Theatre Production*, p. 108).

    During the last quarter of the nineteenth century, this scene was often omitted. Edwin Booth (at the Princess's Theatre 1881, before he joined Irving at the Lyceum) restored it, but the *Athenaeum* felt that it was 'of very little importance' (22 January 1881). Salvini cut the scene entirely, thus making all the big domestic scenes with Desdemona run together: the 'brothel' section of 4.2, 4.3 and 5.2. Oscar Asche also cut 5.1, and Dickins scornfully observed that not one of the next day's reviews noticed its absence (Dickins, *Forty Years*, p. 145). Parker cuts it, transferring a few lines from Iago's closing speech to the end of 4.2, and at 5.2.74.

[He retires.]

RODERIGO I have no great devotion to the deed,
    And yet he hath given me satisfying reasons.
    'Tis but a man gone. Forth my sword! He dies!   10
IAGO *[Aside]* I have rubbed this young quat almost to the sense,
    And he grows angry. Now, whether he kill Cassio,
    Or Cassio him, or each do kill the other,
    Every way makes my gain. Live Roderigo,
    He calls me to a restitution large   15
    Of gold and jewels that I bobbed from him
    As gifts to Desdemona.
    It must not be. If Cassio do remain,
    He hath a daily beauty in his life
    That makes me ugly; and besides, the Moor   20
    May unfold me to him – there stand I in much peril.
    No, he must die. But soft, I hear him coming.

Enter CASSIO.

RODERIGO I know his gait; 'tis he. Villain, thou diest!
                [He lunges at Cassio.]
CASSIO That thrust had been mine enemy indeed

---

8   Fechter's Roderigo said this 'scratching his ear' (his stage direction).

10a   Nunn's Roderigo read this from a letter – the one from Iago that Lodovico produces at
    5.2.305–6 (promptbook).

14   During this speech Fechter's Iago 'goes to his door, which he half opens to facilitate retreat'
    (his stage direction). Webster's Cassio and Bianca are heard offstage laughing from time to
    time and, at the end, calling out 'goodbye' and 'farewell Cassio' (Carroll).

23–65   From the '1755' edition onwards throughout the nineteenth century, this episode – the
    wounding of Cassio and Roderigo, followed by the murder of Roderigo – was greatly
    shortened. Othello's entrance, after line 27, was the first to go, and it has hardly ever been
    played since. (But see note at his entrance below.) Then, from Bell's edition onwards
    Lodovico and Gratiano do not appear before Iago addresses them at 65 ('What may you be?
    are you of good or evil?') This greatly speeds up the action between 37 and 65, so that the
    fight, the departure and return of Iago, and the murder of Roderigo all follow rapidly one
    upon the other. The traditional business indicated in Bell's edition, Kemble's and the other
    early nineteenth-century acting texts, is that Cassio and Roderigo wound each other, Iago
    cuts Cassio in the leg from behind, and then exits. Webster choreographed a fairly elaborate
    and long-drawn-out fight featuring a cloak (Carroll). In Peter Hall's production, Iago trips
    Cassio up, puts his foot on his head, cuts open his leg and makes his exit – whereupon
    Cassio faints (promptbook).

But that my coat is better than thou think'st.   25
I will make proof of thine.
              [*He wounds Roderigo.*]
RODERIGO   O, I am slain!
       [*Iago wounds Cassio in the leg and exit*]
CASSIO I am maimed forever. Help, ho! Murder, murder!

             Enter OTHELLO.

OTHELLO [*Aside*] The voice of Cassio: Iago keeps his word.
RODERIGO O villain that I am!
OTHELLO [*Aside*]   It is even so.
CASSIO O help, ho! Light! A surgeon!   30
OTHELLO [*Aside*] 'Tis he. O brave Iago, honest and just,
    That hast such noble sense of thy friend's wrong!
    Thou teachest me. Minion, your dear lies dead,
    And your unblest fate hies. Strumpet, I come!
    Forth of my heart those charms, thine eyes, are blotted;   35
    Thy bed, lust-stained, shall with lust's blood be spotted.
                        Exit Othello

         Enter LODOVICO *and* GRATIANO.

CASSIO What, ho! No watch? No passage? Murder, murder!
GRATIANO 'Tis some mischance; the cry is very direful.
CASSIO O, help!
LODOVICO Hark!   40
RODERIGO O, wretched villain!
LODOVICO Two or three groan. It is a heavy night.
    These may be counterfeits: let's think't unsafe
    To come in to the cry without more help.
RODERIGO Nobody come? Then I shall bleed to death.   45
LODOVICO Hark!

---

27 SD   Rowe's edition (1709) has Othello enter 'above at a window', presumably the proscenium
        box balcony. Since the mid-eighteenth century this entrance has usually been omitted; even
        Edwin Booth, in whose production the whole scene is restored, dropped it (see Cook,
        Nights, II, p. 301). Peter Hall included it: Scofield appeared crawling towards Cassio (then in
        a faint) and taking him for dead (promptbook). Irving Wardle remarked on the 'very
        peculiar moments' that Hall restored, particularly this one (*T*, 21 March 1980). Nunn nodded
        towards this episode by having Othello appear 'as a massive black shadow during
        Roderigo's murder and Cassio's wounding' (*T*, 26 August 1989).
) and ff.   Iago re-entered 'in his shirt' (Rowe's edition, 1709), 'in his shirt with a light and sword' (Bell's
        edition), or in his 'night-gown' (Kemble). Fechter introduced a new piece of business for

Enter Iago, with a light.

GRATIANO Here's one comes in his shirt, with light and weapons.
IAGO Who's there? Whose noise is this that cries on murder?
LODOVICO We do not know.
IAGO   Did you not hear a cry?
CASSIO Here, here; for heaven's sake, help me!
IAGO   What's the matter?   50
GRATIANO This is Othello's ancient, as I take it.
LODOVICO The same indeed, a very valiant fellow.
IAGO What are you here that cry so grievously?
CASSIO Iago? O, I am spoiled, undone by villains!
        Give me some help.   55
IAGO O me, lieutenant! What villains have done this?
CASSIO I think that one of them is hereabout
        And cannot make away.
IAGO   O, treacherous villains!
        [*To Lodovico and Gratiano*] What are you there? Come in,
            and give some help.
RODERIGO O, help me here!   60
CASSIO That's one of them.
IAGO   O murderous slave! O villain!
            [*He stabs Roderigo.*]
RODERIGO O damned Iago! O inhuman dog!
            [*He faints.*]
IAGO Kill men i'th'dark? Where be these bloody thieves?
        How silent is this town! Ho, murder, murder!

Iago, which Edwin Booth followed: he draws his sword 'with a sudden inspiration to
dispatch [Cassio], but is prevented by the timely entrance of other persons' – i.e. Lodovico
and Gratiano (*A*, 8 March 1862). Modern productions (e.g. Suzman and Nunn) have used
much the same business (Nunn's promptbook, Suzman's video).

61 SD and ff.   Gould remembers the lantern in J. B. Booth's hand shining in his 'pale and fiendish face, as
with a sword-stroke into Roderigo's wounded body he delivers himself of this stroke of
devilish wit – "Kill men i' the dark!"' (Gould, *Tragedian*, p. 90). Hawkins describes actors
before Kean as not remembering 'that the whole fortune of the Ancient hinged upon this
event . . . Not so Kean. He gave and repeated the murderous thrust till no life could be
supposed to remain; . . . he continued to watch and hover . . . his manner perfectly cool,
while his eye expressed the most restless anxiety' (Hawkins, *Edmund Kean*, I, p. 253; quoted
in *Variorum*). Irving was more lighthearted, 'turning over with his foot in indolent and
mocking curiosity, the body of Roderigo to see if life were extinct' (*A*, 7 May 1881). Michael
Bryant, with grotesque cheek, wiped his dagger on Roderigo (promptbook).

[*Lodovico and Gratiano come forward.*]
What may you be? Are you of good or evil? 65
LODOVICO As you shall prove us, praise us.
IAGO Signior Lodovico?
LODOVICO He, sir.
IAGO I cry you mercy. Here's Cassio hurt by villains.
GRATIANO Cassio? 70
IAGO How is't, brother?
CASSIO My leg is cut in two.
IAGO   Marry, heaven forbid!
        Light, gentlemen. I'll bind it with my shirt.

                Enter BIANCA.

BIANCA What is the matter, ho? Who is't that cried?
IAGO Who is't that cried? 75
BIANCA O, my dear Cassio, my sweet Cassio!
        O, Cassio, Cassio, Cassio!
IAGO O notable strumpet! Cassio, may you suspect
        Who they should be that have thus mangled you?
CASSIO No. 80
GRATIANO I am sorry to find you thus; I have been to seek you.
IAGO Lend me a garter: so. O for a chair
        To bear him easily hence!
BIANCA   Alas, he faints!
        O, Cassio, Cassio, Cassio!
IAGO Gentlemen all, I do suspect this trash 85
        To be a party in this injury.
        Patience awhile, good Cassio. Come, come,
        Lend me a light. Know we this face or no?
        Alas, my friend and my dear countryman!
        Roderigo? No – yes, sure – O, heaven, Roderigo! 90
GRATIANO What, of Venice?
IAGO Even he, sir; did you know him?
GRATIANO   Know him? Ay.
IAGO Signior Gratiano! I cry your gentle pardon.
        These bloody accidents must excuse my manners
        That so neglected you.

O and ff.   From the '1755' edition onwards throughout the nineteenth century, Bianca's entrance here
            was of course cut. All that was left before the end of the scene were Iago's innocent 'Know
            we this face or no?' plus the next two lines, and only enough of Emilia for her to be
            informed and sent off to 'tell my lord and lady what hath happed'. Modern productions
            have highlighted Bianca's exploited position here.

GRATIANO   I am glad to see you.   95
IAGO How do you, Cassio? O, a chair, a chair!
GRATIANO Roderigo?
IAGO He, he, 'tis he.
                [*Enter* ATTENDANTS *with a chair.*]
                O, that's well said, the chair!
        Some good men bear him carefully from hence.
        I'll fetch the general's surgeon. [*To Bianca*] For you,
                mistress,   100
        Save you your labour. – He that lies slain here, Cassio,
        Was my dear friend. What malice was between you?
CASSIO None in the world, nor do I know the man.
IAGO [*To Bianca*] What, look you pale? – O, bear him out o'th'air.
        [*Cassio is carried off; Roderigo's body is removed*]
        Stay you, good gentlemen. Look you pale, mistress?   105
        Do you perceive the gastness of her eye?
        [*To Bianca*] Nay, if you stare, we shall hear more anon.
        Behold her well; I pray you, look upon her.
        Do you see, gentlemen? Nay, guiltiness
        Will speak, though tongues were out of use.   110

                Enter EMILIA.

EMILIA 'Las, what's the matter? What's the matter, husband?
IAGO Cassio hath here been set on in the dark
        By Roderigo and fellows that are 'scaped.
        He's almost slain and Roderigo dead.
EMILIA Alas, good gentleman! Alas, good Cassio!   115
IAGO This is the fruits of whoring. Prithee, Emilia,
        Go know of Cassio where he supped tonight.
        [*To Bianca*] What, do you shake at that?
BIANCA He supped at my house, but I therefore shake not.
IAGO O, did he so? I charge you go with me.   120
EMILIA O, fie upon thee, strumpet!
BIANCA I am no strumpet, but of life as honest
        As you that thus abuse me.
EMILIA   As I? Foh! Fie upon thee!
IAGO Kind gentlemen, let's go see poor Cassio dressed.

122ff.   In his video Nunn stressed Bianca's defiance here by bringing the camera close in on her
         lines at 122–3. Suzman's video goes further, stressing the sheer danger she is in. To horrible
         sound effects, a crowd of soldiers and sailors rough Bianca up and carry her off, clearly
         intending a gang rape.

Come, mistress, you must tell's another tale.   125
Emilia, run you to the citadel
And tell my lord and lady what hath happed.
Will you go on afore? [*Aside*] This is the night
That either makes me, or fordoes me quite.

Exeunt

ACT 5, SCENE 2

Enter OTHELLO, *with a light, and* DESDEMONA *in bed.*

Richard Hosley in 'The Staging of Desdemona's Bed' (*SQ*, 14, 1963, pp. 57–65) argues that in the earliest productions the Folio direction, 'Enter Othello, and Desdemona in her bed', means what it says – i.e. that the bed was pushed on, not 'discovered'. Rowe's edition (1709) has 'Desdemona . . . discovered asleep in her bed' – i.e. the shutters of the previous scene drew open. His frontispiece shows a canopied bed set broadside-on across the stage, with its curtains loosely fastened back. The 1766 Drury Lane promptbook has the 'Pearl Chamber – Desdemona's bed, candles, armed chair, toilet [dressing table], two carpets [actors always died, costume-conscious, on carpets on the eighteenth-century stage] a dagger and a sword'. Macready describes 'an arch centre, about seven feet wide – curtains divided in the centre and festooned up, hang from it – the bed is within the recess'. Both he and Phelps show a similar sketch (promptbooks).

But just as with the Senate scene, this arrangement forced Othello to turn away from the audience. Fechter therefore put the bed on one side 'with its back to the audience, so as to conceal the sleeping Desdemona, and raised on a dais with several steps; so that it looks as portentous as a catafalque prepared for a great funeral pomp' (Morley, *Journal*, p. 231). However, Fanny Kemble describes the old 'alcove' arrangement in Salvini's production, and wishes that the bed were at the side 'so that [Desdemona] can remain on it while answering Othello, rather than having to address him standing up . . . to save Othello from having to turn his back' (*TB*, July 1884). But, as we shall see, Desdemona still got out of bed in the new arrangement.

Fechter's bedroom set combined domestic with religiose sentiment: an oratory on one side, with a prie-dieu 'surmounted by a Madonna and lighted by a red lamp', Desdemona's bed with a small 'toilette glass fallen from her hand' and her clothes 'scattered about' (his stage direction). The prie-dieu and Madonna are prominent in Verdi's opera, where Desdemona sings an Ave Maria at the end of the willow-song scene (Verdi, like some Shakespearean producers, ran 4.3 and 5.2 together). The idea appealed to Beerbohm Tree: 'the great bed with its purple hangings, the prie-dieu with a light upon it, and a window opening on a garden where the cypresses stand beneath a southern blue and sparkling stars' (*DT*, 10 April 1912). In modern times sets have been simpler. Valk's production just had bed curtains hanging from the flies, and caught back at the four corners of the stage (*Picture Post*, 8 August 1942).

0 SD The first and second quartos have Othello enter 'with a light', a device on the Globe stage to indicate night. Bell's edition indicates a sword as well, with the direction that he lays it down at line 5. A contemporary engraving of Kean shows him carrying both poignard and lamp. Macready deletes the light (promptbook) and it must have become less common since Winter finds it absurd of Novelli to enter 'carrying a huge silver lamp, lighted' (Winter, *Shakespeare*, p. 300). Fechter, Salvini, Robeson in 1943, Willard White in 1989, all carried swords, sheathing or laying them down as though changing their minds (Fechter's stage direction, Mason, p. 89, and Webster's and Nunn's promptbooks). Ronald Eyre kept the light but gave it to Desdemona, who entered with a candle before getting into bed (promptbook). Scofield came on with a powerful candle, symbol (thought one critic) of the 'purity and brevity of [Desdemona's] life', which was 'timed to burn out as all the murders were over' (*Cahiers Elizabéthains*, October 1980). In Attenborough's production, Ray Fearon carried a lantern and put it down as he began to speak (RSC archive film). In some productions Othello has locked the door behind him – e.g. Fechter (Morley, *Journal*, p. 321) and Nunn (promptbook).

For reasons either of spectacle or symbolism or both, actors have often altered Othello's costume for the last act. Salvini wore a red mantle (Mason, p. 89), Olivier a white tunic where before he had worn black (film). Robeson also had a scarlet cloak like 'a clash of cymbals', which he slipped off to 'reveal the powerful muscles of his arms and shoulders, the very symbol of the irresistible primal passion that has engulfed him' ('Broadway in Review', *Theatre Arts*, 27, New York, 1943); in the video, Suzman's John Kani is naked to the waist, barefoot, and wearing black harem trousers; in Nunn's, Willard White has exchanged his military uniform for a kaftan; in Parker's film Laurence Fishburne is swathed in a white and gold robe which he takes off to reveal a dark tunic.

A rare glimpse of J. P. Kemble shows a distraught rather than a deliberate Othello: 'the glare he threw round the chamber ... his hurried step, his hollow murmurs, his convulsed and shivering frame ... When he drew back the curtain and wildly gazed upon his sleeping victim, compassion seemed for a moment to shake his purpose; but ... [was] instantly lost in the recollection of his dishonour and the desire of revenge' (Cumberland, p. 6). Salvini, by contrast, entered at first 'very slowly ... in deep meditation' (Mason, p. 89); he 'stole towards the sleeping Desdemona ... afraid of the folds of his own cloak, which dragged behind him' (Stanislavski, *My Life*, p. 272). Rossini may have been an influence. Stendhal describes Otello's long-drawn-out tip-toeing entrance in the opera, down a twisting staircase at the back, his light appearing and disappearing, his scimitar glinting (*Rossini*, p. 234). In Suzman's video, John Kani enters from behind a backlit scrim hanging behind Desdemona's bed, his huge shadow cast before him – thus 'making him into the featureless black devil of a colonial fantasy the film imposes only to deconstruct' (Hodgdon, 'Race-ing *Othello*', p. 30).

OTHELLO It is the cause, it is the cause, my soul:
    Let me not name it to you, you chaste stars.
    It is the cause. Yet I'll not shed her blood,
    Nor scar that whiter skin of hers than snow
    And smooth as monumental alabaster –   5
    Yet she must die, else she'll betray more men.
    Put out the light, and then put out the light:

1–2   Fechter here looked at himself in Desdemona's handmirror, rushed to the open window, apostrophised the stars and flung the mirror out – 'the cause' thus being that he is black: 'Can anything be conceived more absurd?', asked Ottley (p. 29). The idea surfaced again in 1964, when James Earl Jones 'puts Desdemona's white hand next to his brown one and then speaks "It is the cause" – a frightful gyp [i.e. mistake] . . . that opportunistically distorts and diminishes this resounding line into a comment on race prejudice' (*New Yorker*, 24 October 1964). Actors have usually been less specific about what 'it' (i.e. 'the cause') is. Salvini spoke the opening lines as though giving voice to his meditation and avoided the problem by speaking 'in a tone so low as to be barely audible' (Mason, p. 89).

7   Henry Fielding, in *A Journey From This World to the Next* (1743), imagines Shakespeare in Elysium listening to Betterton and Barton Booth justifying their emphases in this line. Betterton maintained an equal emphasis throughout, while Booth accented the second 'the' thus: 'Put out the light and then put out *the* light' (quoted in *Variorum*). The Shakespearean editor Theobald (first edition 1733) wrote that 'the players . . . commit the absurdity of making Othello put out the candle' (quoted in *Variorum*). How, he asks, would Desdemona see him to talk of his 'eyes rolling' and his 'gnawing his nether lip'? James R. Siemon mentions the innovation of a window as a light source ('Green medium, or Calcium Light, to strike on Othello's face through window C and R') in one of Kean's touring promptbooks (Siemon, '"Nay, That's Not Next"', p. 42). Harrison, describing Forrest, speaks of moonlight: 'his eyes happened to fall upon the flaming candle, and in a moment he rose, took the candle as if to puff it out, and do the murder by moonlight'. Forrest spoke the second 'put out the light' as a question (presumably following the suggestion of Warburton, the eighteenth-century textual editor), and left the candle lighted (quoted by Sprague, p. 211). Fechter also turned the phrase into a question, making the symbolism plain by looking 'at it [the light] and Desdemona alternately' (his stage direction). Salvini introduced thunder and lightning, which according to Lewes was thought to be melodramatic and which 'had better have been omitted' (Lewes, *Actors*, p. 270). Rossini may have been an influence here: the lantern having been set down, 'a gust of wind blows it out . . . Flashes of lightning chase each other across the sky, in an ever quickening succession . . .' (Stendhal, *Rossini*, p. 235). In Parker's film the scene opens with soft music and a close-up of a lamp, the first in a row, which Othello blows out one by one as he approaches the bed.

If I quench thee, thou flaming minister,
I can again thy former light restore,
Should I repent me; but once put out thy light,   10
Thou cunning'st pattern of excelling nature,
I know not where is that Promethean heat
That can thy light relume. When I have plucked thy rose,
I cannot give it vital growth again;
It needs must wither. I'll smell it on the tree.   15
                    He kisses her.
O balmy breath, that dost almost persuade
Justice to break her sword! One more, one more!
Be thus when thou art dead, and I will kill thee
And love thee after. One more, and this the last.
So sweet was ne'er so fatal. I must weep.   20
But they are cruel tears: this sorrow's heavenly –
It strikes where it doth love. She wakes.
DESDEMONA Who's there? Othello?
OTHELLO   Ay, Desdemona.
DESDEMONA Will you come to bed, my lord?
OTHELLO Have you prayed tonight, Desdemon?
DESDEMONA   Ay, my lord.   25
OTHELLO If you bethink yourself of any crime

8–15   Parker cuts.

13–14 Stanislavski conjures up Salvini: 'how he stood admiring the sleeping woman, how he
       feared and almost ran away from his own prey' (Stanislavski, *My Life*, p. 272).

22   Here Salvini kissed 'his sleeping wife, then goes to the window, and stands with the lightning
       playing on his face' (*A*, 10 April 1875).

24   A correspondent to the *Tatler* or *Spectator* recorded 'a general tittering' here in the
       audience 'that had they all been lechers of sixty odd they could not have given greater
       indications of satisfaction in a brutal way' (Lillie, *Letters*, I, p. 256). From Macready onwards
       (promptbook), nineteenth-century and early twentieth-century acting texts cut this line. In
       Suzman's video, Joanna Weinberg speaks the line movingly, with loving expectation. In
       Kelly's production, Desdemona knelt behind Othello, who was sitting on the edge of the
       bed, and sprinkled rose-petals over him – recalling the rose-petal moment in the first act
       (see Johnson-Haddad, 'Shakespeare Theatre *Othello*', p. 9).

25ff. Ira Aldridge was 'permeated with one thought . . . immediate revenge . . . He cannot stand
       on his feet; he sways to and fro; he sits heavily on a small table at the bedside . . . he does
       not know where to put his hands, which are itching to suffocate Desdemona; he bangs them
       on his knees and feverishly presses them to his side . . .' (A. F. Kon, quoted by Stock and
       Marshall, *Ira Aldridge*, p. 258). Salvini was remarkable for 'his tiger-like pacing at the back
       of the room . . . with his eyes fixed on her and filled with the light of her approaching doom'

        Unreconciled as yet to heaven and grace,
        Solicit for it straight.
DESDEMONA Alack, my lord, what may you mean by that?
OTHELLO Well, do it, and be brief: I will walk by: 30
        I would not kill thy unprepared spirit;
        No – heaven forfend! – I would not kill thy soul.
DESDEMONA Talk you of killing?
OTHELLO   Ay, I do.
DESDEMONA   Then heaven
        Have mercy on me!
OTHELLO   Amen, with all my heart!
DESDEMONA If you say so, I hope you will not kill me.   35
OTHELLO Hum!
DESDEMONA And yet I fear you, for you're fatal then
        When your eyes roll so. Why I should fear I know not,
        Since guiltiness I know not, but yet I feel I fear.
OTHELLO Think on thy sins.
DESDEMONA   They are loves I bear to you.   40
OTHELLO Ay, and for that thou diest.
DESDEMONA That death's unnatural that kills for loving.
        Alas, why gnaw you so your nether lip?
        Some bloody passion shakes your very frame:
        These are portents; but yet I hope, I hope   45
        They do not point on me.
OTHELLO   Peace, and be still!

(James, *Art*, p. 174). Desdemona has also contributed to the power of these moments. One of the only things we know of the first performances is that the boy who played Desdemona in 1610 'pleaded her case very effectively' (see *The Riverside Shakespeare*, p. 1852). Sarah Siddons too 'spoke with such an appeal to the heart that the greatest part of the audience manifested their sympathy in tears' (*London Magazine*, March 1785). Salvini's Mme Piamonti 'was the personification of pitiful protesting love gradually resolving into speechless terror' (Towse, *Sixty Years*, p. 163). Modern feminism has created different expectations. In Mendes's 'modern' production, Claire Skinner's unaggressive manner seemed out of period: 'Wouldn't a modern woman . . . be more forthright, mocking and indignant when stating her innocence?' (*IoS*, 21 September 1997).

34   Kean spoke 'Amen' twice and revealed in that exclamation 'unfathomable depths of love' (Stendhal, *Rossini*, p. 219).

38, 43   These two references to Othello's grimaces have sometimes been cut. Ellen Terry excised them from her promptbook, as have modern productions. Dexter did, and Barton, at least in his Stratford season, though the rolling eyes were restored for the Aldwych season (promptbooks). Nunn included them (promptbook), though in the video we cannot see Willard White's face. Parker cuts both.

DESDEMONA I will so. What's the matter?
OTHELLO That handkerchief which I so loved and gave thee,
      Thou gav'st to Cassio.
DESDEMONA   No, by my life and soul!
      Send for the man and ask him.
OTHELLO   Sweet soul, take heed.   50
      Take heed of perjury: thou art on thy death-bed.
DESDEMONA Ay, but not yet to die.
OTHELLO   Yes, presently.
      Therefore confess thee freely of thy sin;
      For to deny each article with oath
      Cannot remove nor choke the strong conception   55
      That I do groan withal. Thou art to die.
DESDEMONA Then Lord have mercy on me!
OTHELLO   I say, Amen.
DESDEMONA And have you mercy too! I never did
      Offend you in my life; never loved Cassio
      But with such general warranty of heaven   60
      As I might love. I never gave him token.
OTHELLO By heaven, I saw my handkerchief in's hand.
      O perjured woman! Thou dost stone my heart,
      And mak'st me call what I intend to do
      A murder, which I thought a sacrifice.   65
      I saw the handkerchief.
DESDEMONA   He found it then;
      I never gave it him. Send for him hither;
      Let him confess a truth.
OTHELLO   He hath confessed.
DESDEMONA What, my lord?
OTHELLO That he hath used thee.
DESDEMONA   How? Unlawfully?   70
OTHELLO Ay.
DESDEMONA He will not say so.
OTHELLO   No, his mouth is stopped:
      Honest Iago hath tane order for't.
DESDEMONA O, my fear interprets! What, is he dead?
OTHELLO Had all his hairs been lives, my great revenge   75

67   Helena Faucit wrote that 'it was as though I spoke for myself in uttering the swift rejoinder' (Faucit, *Female Characters*, p. 77). In the video, Imogen Stubbs screams this line.
70a–2a   Booth and Irving cut this from their editions. Oscar Asche had 'loved' for 'used'.
74   Parker here interrupts the scene with a flash to the moment in the previous scene (which is thus supposed to be happening simultaneously) in which Iago tells Emilia to 'run you to the citadel / And tell my lord and lady what hath happed' (5.1.126–7).

Had stomach for them all.
DESDEMONA Alas, he is betrayed, and I undone.
OTHELLO Out, strumpet! Weep'st thou for him to my face?
DESDEMONA O banish me, my lord, but kill me not!

78–84   English Desdemonas, according to Fanny Kemble, 'acquiesce with wonderful equanimity in
their assassination'. She, however, was determined to make 'a desperate fight of it'. She
says she 'got up on my knees on my bed and threw my arms tight round Othello's neck
(having previously warned Mr Macready, and begged his pardon for the liberty), that being
my notion of the poor creature's last appeal for mercy' (Kemble, *Records*, III, pp. 368–9).
Helena Faucit was told by Macready that she 'added intensity to the last act by "being very
difficult to kill" . . . I would not die with my honour tarnished . . . I felt for *him* as well as
myself – for I knew what remorse and misery would overwhelm him' (*Female Characters*,
p. 50). Not everyone liked it that way. Gustavus Vaughan Brooke's Desdemona in 1853, Miss
Anderton, 'struggled in almost an erect position', something which 'made it a positive fight.
This was out of character, even in the presence of an extreme so desperate' (*A*, 10
September 1853). By contrast, 'it is an unalloyed delight . . . to see [Charlotte Vandenhoff]
sad, fearful, yet gentle as a bruised dove, bend meekly . . . and receive her death while
kissing the hand which gives it' (*Tallis's Dramatic Magazine*, April 1851).

   Fechter's stage directions, which show that his Desdemona made a run for it, were
probably influenced by Rossini's *Otello.* Dumas described Mme Malibran escaping Otello
and then 'folle, éperdue, elle courait, essayant d'ouvrir les portes, de gravir les murailles'
(quoted by Cook, '*Othello* in Paris', *The Theatre*, 1 October 1880). Fanny Kemble, writing in
1848, said the same for Italy, both in the play and in the opera (Kemble, *Records*, III,
p. 368). According to his directions, Fechter's Othello was to pursue her with his sword, and
whirl it over her head, but Theodore Martin (Helena Faucit's husband) wrote that no English
audience would have tolerated this: 'even now there is too much violence. Why should
Desdemona spring out of bed, to be brutally thrust back into it? Tradition was right in
confining Desdemona to her couch.' He also complained that Fechter brought the bed 'so
far forward that every detail is thrust upon our senses' (quoted by Sprague, p. 214). Modern
Desdemonas are no longer so confined – e.g. Imogen Stubbs, who ran panic-stricken to the
door we know to be locked (promptbook). At the Other Place 'the panic and terror of
impending death was that of a real bedroom in a newspaper story where violence has
unaccountably bubbled up' (*FT*, 26 August 1989).

   Madge Kendal writes of Ira Aldridge: 'in the last act, in which he made me wear toed
stockings with sandals to suggest being undressed, he used to take me out of bed by my
hair and drag me round the stage before he smothered me . . . the audience hissed the
business vociferously' (Kendal, *Dame Madge Kendal*, p. 87). The Italians were equally
brutal. After 'Weep'st thou for him' (78) Salvini 'drags her to her feet, as she kneels facing

OTHELLO Down, strumpet! 80
DESDEMONA Kill me tomorrow; let me live tonight!
OTHELLO Nay, if you strive –
DESDEMONA But half an hour!
OTHELLO   Being done, there is no pause.
DESDEMONA But while I say one prayer!
OTHELLO   It is too late.
DESDEMONA O, Lord, Lord, Lord! 85

him; he then clutches her right arm . . . and grasps her neck and head . . . knotting his fingers in her loose hair, and pulling back her head as if to break her neck. Holding her thus, he swiftly forces her up the stage and through the curtains of the alcove' (Mason, p. 95). This was with an American actress. With his Italian Desdemona, Mme Piamonti, he 'lifted her in the air, dashed with her across the stage . . . You heard a crash as he flung her on the bed and growls as of a wild beast over his prey' (Towse, *Sixty Years*, p. 163). Novelli did much the same, 'degrading that deed of sacrifice to a beastly Bill Sikes murder of Nancy' (Winter, *Shakespeare*, p. 300).

Anglo-Saxon actors inspired much vaguer descriptions. Of Irving, Cook merely said that his 'death scene avoids the conceits of Signor Salvini and Mr Fechter' (Cook, *Nights*, II, p. 108); while of Edwin Booth, Winter wrote simply that his murder was sacrificial, not a 'ferocious slaughter suggestive of the African jungle and redolent of the menagerie' (Winter, *Edwin Booth*, p. 195).

85 SD   This is the original direction, and the method of killing her would scarcely have been specified if the deed was not to be done in full view. Rowe's frontispiece catches Othello red-handed, with Desdemona dead, not asleep, one breast exposed. At some point in the nineteenth century it became usual to drop the bed curtains in front of Desdemona and Othello, leaving the audience to imagine the rest. Macready neatly had it that 'Desdemona shrieks and clutching at the curtains, pulls them down before the bed' (promptbook). Phelps followed this (*DT*, 4 November 1861), and in fact it is the exception which draws comment.

In Melbourne Gustavus Vaughan Brooke was rebuked: 'we suggest, upon the repetition of the tragedy . . . that its consummation should take place behind the curtain and out of sight' (*Argus*, 28 February 1855). Benson reports that his father tearfully upbraided him: '"You promised, Frank, that you would strangle her behind the curtains . . . I cannot bear it on the stage"' (Benson, *Memoirs*, p. 218). Fechter, from Theodore Martin's description (see previous note), seems not to have dropped the curtain, and Ottley complains that after 'every possible circumstance of barbarity . . . he actually kneels upon her body'. The scene was so extravagant that it 'called forth an irreverant titter from the gallery' (Ottley, p. 30). Rossi in 1881 in New York murdered her 'in full view of the audience . . . by strangling her with his hands after twisting her long hair about her neck, as he shook her violently and then dragged her about the bed and finally tossed her down upon the pillows . . . murmurs

> *He smothers her.*
> EMILIA *(Within)* My lord, my lord! What, ho! My lord, my lord!
> OTHELLO What noise is this? Not dead? Not yet quite dead?
>   I that am cruel am yet merciful;

of dissatisfaction were audible in the house' (*New York Herald*, 1 November 1881, quoted in Sprague, p. 212).

This was strangling not suffocating, and it may be that the tradition of closed curtains (though Rossi himself left them open) had led to a noisier murder than suffocating – silence and an 'empty' stage being thought undesirable. Both Salvini and Novelli operated out of sight and we read of 'the most extreme violence of snorting fury' in Salvini and of Novelli's 'snarls, gasps, growls and gurgles' (Winter, *Shakespeare*, pp. 290, 300). Macready, on the contrary, had indicated 'a pause, of about half a minute – count 15', during which, presumably, it was to be imagined that he was smothering her (promptbook).

In modern times some actors have committed the murder by way, partly, of an act of love. Orson Welles, in his film, killed her by stretching a scarf over her face and stopping her mouth with his (though on the stage 'he apparently killed [her] by wrapping her up in the bed clothes', Crosse, *Playgoing*, p. 152). Olivier was more thorough: 'he clasps Desdemona's body, still loved despite his conviction of her guilt, kisses her lips and strangles her, gripping her white neck with his huge black hand. It takes him a long time to strangle her, and all the while he clings to her lips. Then, when all is over, he throws her body on the nuptial bed' (Alexander Anikst, quoted in Tynan, *National Theatre Production*, p. 109). In Nunn's production, Willard White lay on top of Desdemona to stop her breath and then rolled off her almost post-coitally (promptbook and video): 'The murder . . . has the steamy exhalation of both sexual release and death' (*FT*, 26 August 1989).

Suzman's video directs the camera not towards Othello, but to the pillow itself and to Desdemona's faintly heard agony beneath it. In Mendes's production, David Harewood smothered her then 'lifts the pillows from her face and . . . allows a moment of punishing hope, a brief sense that murder might suddenly prove to have been nothing, a pillow fight' (*NS*, 19 September 1997).

86   After his long silence Macready here made a 'thrilling' effect. As Emilia knocked (Kemble's direction calls for knocking) he thrust out 'his dark despairing face through the curtains' forming in its 'contrast with the drapery, a marvellous piece of colour' (Marston, *Recent Actors*, pp. 83–4). Forster tells of a woman in the audience who 'hysterically fainted' here (Forster, *Essays*, p. 24). The business passed into stage practice in the nineteenth century (see Sprague, p. 216) but Salvini prolonged it by then withdrawing his face and remaining hidden. 'The tension was insufferable' (Towse, *Sixty Years*, p. 164).

86–7 In Parker's film, Emilia appears to give Desdemona back her voice for 'Othello thinks [her] "My lord, my lord!" whispered at the door is coming from Desdemona's suffocated corpse and pushes the pillow down harder on her dead face' (Rutter, 'Looking at Shakespeare's Women', p. 256).

I would not have thee linger in thy pain.
So, so.
EMILIA (*Within*) What, ho! My lord, my lord!
OTHELLO   Who's there?   90
EMILIA [*Within*] O, good my lord, I would speak a word with you.
OTHELLO Yes – 'tis Emilia – by and by. – She's dead.
'Tis like she comes to speak of Cassio's death:
The noise was high. Ha! No more moving?
Still as the grave. Shall she come in? Were't good?   95
I think she stirs again. No. What's best to do?
If she come in, she'll sure speak to my wife –
My wife, my wife! What wife? I have no wife.
O insupportable! O heavy hour!
Methinks it should be now a huge eclipse   100
Of sun and moon, and that th'affrighted globe
Should yawn at alteration.
EMILIA [*Within*]   I do beseech you
That I may speak with you. O, good my lord!
OTHELLO I had forgot thee. O, come in, Emilia.

90   Sprague quotes critics and textual editors from Rymer onwards complaining of the
       improbability of Desdemona's returning to speech after the suffocation, and then dying
       without any fresh violence. None of them suggests that the stage offered a remedy for this
       in the form of a dagger at 'So, so', but at some point in the eighteenth century it became the
       custom to finish Desdemona off in that way. The wound served the double purpose:
       'drawing blood accounts naturally for gaining power of speech and yet may be mortal'
       (Gentleman, *Censor*, I, p. 148). The textual editor Steevens incorporated this as a direction
       in his edition (1773) and it was said that both Powell (d. 1769, Garrick's protégé at Drury
       Lane) and Spranger Barry used the dagger (see Sprague, pp. 215–16). The custom
       remained, with the added refinement in de Vigny's edition and in Fechter's, that Othello
       turns away his eyes. Edwin Booth added a 'trembling hand' over his face and a 'groan' at
       'So, so' (*Variorum*). Salvini thought that 'So, so' meant that Othello 'kneels on her breast to
       hasten her end' (quoted in *Variorum*). Modern Othellos have tended to respect Othello's
       intention of not scarring her, and have strangled her at 'So, so'.
98   Edwin Booth describes his acting here: 'at this word [wife] he pauses as if stunned, or rather,
       puzzled . . . then under the full force of the horror, he almost screams, "I have no wife!" and
       falls prostrate on the divan . . . where he writhes' (*Variorum*). In Attenborough's production,
       Ray Fearon wept here and embraced Desdemona (RSC archive film).
104   Here Fechter 'goes to the door, which in his agitation, he tries to open at the hinges, and
       perceiving his mistake, leans against the wall, distracted, wiping the cold damps from his
       forehead' (his stage direction).

Soft, by and by. Let me the curtains draw.   105
Where art thou?

[*He unlocks the door.*]

What's the matter with thee now?

Enter EMILIA.

EMILIA O, my good lord, yonder's foul murders done.
OTHELLO What? Now?
EMILIA But now, my lord.
OTHELLO It is the very error of the moon: 110
        She comes more nearer earth than she was wont
        And makes men mad.
EMILIA Cassio, my lord, hath killed a young Venetian
        Called Roderigo.
OTHELLO   Roderigo killed?
        And Cassio killed?
EMILIA   No, Cassio is not killed.   115
OTHELLO Not Cassio killed! Then murder's out of tune,
        And sweet revenge grows harsh.
DESDEMONA O, falsely, falsely murdered!
EMILIA   O Lord! What cry is that?
OTHELLO That? What?
EMILIA Out and alas, that was my lady's voice!   120
        [*She draws the bed-curtains.*]
        Help, help, ho, help! O, lady, speak again!
        Sweet Desdemona, O sweet mistress, speak!
DESDEMONA A guiltless death I die.
EMILIA O, who hath done this deed?
DESDEMONA Nobody; I myself. Farewell.   125
        Commend me to my kind lord. O farewell!   *She dies.*
OTHELLO Why, how should she be murdered?
EMILIA   Alas, who knows?
OTHELLO You heard her say herself it was not I.
EMILIA She said so; I must needs report the truth.
OTHELLO She's like a liar gone to burning hell: 130

105 In Nunn's production, Willard White 'folds [Desdemona's] hands as if by the gesture he
     could restore life' (*Literary Review*, November 1989).

126 Desdemona can be a powerful presence in the scene, as the first commentator testified
     when he said in 1610 that she 'moved us more after she was dead, when lying on her bed,
     she entreated the pity of the spectators by her very countenance' (see *The Riverside
     Shakespeare*, p. 1852).

'Twas I that killed her.

EMILIA   O, the more angel she,
And you the blacker devil!

OTHELLO She turned to folly, and she was a whore.

EMILIA Thou dost belie her, and thou art a devil.

OTHELLO She was false as water.

EMILIA   Thou art rash as fire to say   135
That she was false. O, she was heavenly true!

OTHELLO Cassio did top her: ask thy husband else.
O, I were damned beneath all depth in hell
But that I did proceed upon just grounds
To this extremity. Thy husband knew it all.   140

EMILIA My husband?

OTHELLO   Thy husband.

EMILIA   That she was false to wedlock?

OTHELLO Ay, with Cassio. Nay, had she been true,
If heaven would make me such another world
Of one entire and perfect chrysolite,
I'd not have sold her for it.

EMILIA   My husband?   145

OTHELLO Ay, 'twas he that told me on her first;
An honest man he is, and hates the slime
That sticks on filthy deeds.

EMILIA   My husband?

OTHELLO What needs this iterance, woman? I say thy husband.

EMILIA O mistress, villainy hath made mocks with love!   150
My husband say that she was false?

OTHELLO   He, woman;
I say thy husband. Dost understand the word?

141ff.   Emilia's incredulous iterations were curtailed from Bell's edition onwards during the
nineteenth century. Fechter cut the whole idea, and had her exclaim 'My husband!' only
once. He excised 142b–53, a passage which includes Othello's image of the 'one entire and
perfect chrysolite'. Parker also cuts the chrysolite. It is from here on that Emilia can come to
dominate the play, sparking dull productions into sudden life. Edith Evans made 'the last
scene the most tragic in the play. That four-times-repeated cry of "My husband!" is a
revelation. When she cries "Help, help, ho, help . . ." [165] . . . It is like a bellow from the
mouth of Melpomene herself' (Farjeon, *Scene*, p. 167). Modern Emilias, however, have
communicated more than strong theatre: 'When, roaring, Wanamaker defies Othello – "Do
thy worst!" [158] – and breaks free of her collusion with Iago's lies – "Perchance, Iago, I will
ne'er go home" [196] – the voice Emilia acquires seems to be the voice of women's history'
(Rutter, 'Looking at Shakespeare's Women', p. 257).

My friend, thy husband, honest, honest Iago.
EMILIA If he say so, may his pernicious soul
   Rot half a grain a day! He lies to th'heart.   155
   She was too fond of her most filthy bargain.
OTHELLO Ha!
EMILIA Do thy worst.
   This deed of thine is no more worthy heaven
   Than thou wast worthy her.
OTHELLO   Peace, you were best.   160
EMILIA Thou has not half that power to do me harm
   As I have to be hurt. O gull! O dolt!
   As ignorant as dirt. Thou hast done a deed –
   I care not for thy sword – I'll make thee known,
   Though I lost twenty lives. Help! help! ho, help!   165
   The Moor hath killed my mistress. Murder, murder!

   Enter MONTANO, GRATIANO *and* IAGO.

MONTANO What is the matter? How now, general?
EMILIA O, are you come, Iago? You have done well,
   That men must lay their murders on your neck.
GRATIANO What is the matter?   170
EMILIA Disprove this villain, if thou be'st a man.
   He says thou told'st him that his wife was false.
   I know thou didst not, thou'rt not such a villain.
   Speak, for my heart is full.
IAGO I told him what I thought, and told no more   175
   Than what he found himself was apt and true.
EMILIA But did you ever tell him she was false?
IAGO I did.
EMILIA You told a lie, an odious damnèd lie:
   Upon my soul, a lie, a wicked lie!   180
   She false with Cassio? Did you say with Cassio?
IAGO With Cassio, mistress. Go to, charm your tongue.

157ff.   In Parker's film, Anna Patrick 'doesn't even flinch when [Othello] puts his sword to her throat but stretches away from the blade as if she were going to spit, then knocks it aside' (Rutter, 'Looking at Shakespeare's Women', p. 256).

162b–3a   Emilia's words have been too close to the bone for some actors. Salvini cut 'As ignorant as dirt', and Beerbohm Tree cut the whole thing (promptbook). In the video, Suzman's Emilia pummels Othello on these lines.

166   Fechter directs Emilia to rush to the door where Othello 'detains her, but she seizes his armed hand and struggles with him crying for help'. Edwin Booth on the other hand has Othello go to the bed and lie 'moaning there, not loudly' (*Variorum*).

EMILIA I will not charm my tongue; I am bound to speak:
My mistress here lies murdered in her bed.
ALL O, heavens forfend! 185
EMILIA And your reports have set the murder on.
OTHELLO Nay, stare not, masters; it is true indeed.
GRATIANO 'Tis a strange truth.
MONTANO O monstrous act!
EMILIA Villainy, villainy, villainy!
I think upon't, I think – I smell't – O villainy! 190
I thought so then; I'll kill myself for grief.
O villainy, villainy!
IAGO What, are you mad? I charge you get you home.
EMILIA Good gentlemen, let me have leave to speak.
'Tis proper I obey him, but not now. 195
Perchance, Iago, I will ne'er go home.
OTHELLO O! O! O!

Othello falls on the bed.

EMILIA Nay, lay thee down and roar,
For thou hast killed the sweetest innocent
That e'er did lift up eye.
OTHELLO [*Standing up.*] O, she was foul!
I scarce did know you, uncle; there lies your niece, 200
Whose breath indeed these hands have newly stopped.
I know this act shows horrible and grim –
GRATIANO Poor Desdemon, I am glad thy father's dead:
Thy match was mortal to him, and pure grief
Shore his old thread in twain. Did he live now, 205
This sight would make him do a desperate turn,
Yea, curse his better angel from his side
And fall to reprobance.
OTHELLO 'Tis pitiful; but yet Iago knows
That she with Cassio hath the act of shame 210
A thousand times committed. Cassio confessed it,
And she did gratify his amorous works
With that recognisance and pledge of love
Which I first gave her. I saw it in his hand:
It was a handkerchief, an antique token 215

192 Here Suzman's video has Emilia strike Iago.
203–8 From Bell's edition onwards this speech was shortened, but Macready cut the reference to Brabantio. Fechter also cut it.
215 In Suzman's video, Emilia and Iago exchange glances here, and when the same thing happens in Parker's film, it was, in Lois Potter's view, 'the most exciting moment of the film':

My father gave my mother.

EMILIA   O God! O heavenly God!

IAGO Zounds, hold your peace!

EMILIA   'Twill out, 'twill out. I peace!
No, I will speak as liberal as the north;
Let heaven, and men, and devils, let them all,
All, all cry shame against me, yet I'll speak.   220

IAGO Be wise and get you home.

EMILIA   I will not.

            [*Iago draws his sword and threatens Emilia.*]

GRATIANO   Fie,
Your sword upon a woman!

EMILIA O thou dull Moor, that handkerchief thou speak'st of
I found by fortune and did give my husband,
For often, with a solemn earnestness –   225
More than indeed belonged to such a trifle –
He begged of me to steal it.

IAGO   Villainous whore!

EMILIA She give it Cassio! No, alas, I found it
And I did give't my husband.

'the camera rapidly cuts between the faces of Emilia (who realizes what this means) and Iago (who realizes, for the first time, what her knowledge means for him)' (Potter, p. 196).

217–30a   Fechter greatly shortens this part of 5.2 throughout, and all this passage goes except the bare minimum – 223b–4 and 227. E. Booth has Iago 'start' here and tremble violently (*Variorum*). Parker cuts 217b–20, and 225–7.

221   Anna Patrick, Parker's Emilia, pauses for split second after Iago orders her home, and 'the true report of Emilia's story hangs in the balance. Emilia in headshot looks into Iago's eyes. "I will not" declares her divorce' (Rutter, 'Looking at Shakespeare's Women', p. 256).

223   This was the moment from *Othello* that Garrick chose for the painter Francis Hayman, who was planning six illustrations from Shakespeare's plays. Garrick's description seems to have been theatrically inspired; he offered to demonstrate his idea of Othello and Iago when they met: 'the background, you know, must be Desdemona murdered in her bed; . . . Othello . . . must be thunderstruck with horror, his whole figure extended with his eyes turned up to heaven and his frame sinking as it were at Emilia's discovery . . . Emilia must appear in the utmost vehemence, with a mixture of sorrow on account of her mistress and . . . should be in the middle. Iago on the left hand should express the greatest perturbation of mind and should shrink up his body at the opening of his villainy, with eyes looking askance . . . on Othello and gnawing his lip in anger at his wife' (Little and Kahrl, *Letters*, I, pp. 82–3).

IAGO   Filth, thou liest!
EMILIA By heaven, I do not, I do not, gentlemen.   230
                O murderous coxcomb, what should such a fool
                Do with so good a wife?
OTHELLO   Are there no stones in heaven
                But what serves for the thunder? Precious villain!
        [*Othello runs at Iago; Montano disarms him; Iago stabs Emilia from
                                behind and exit.*]
GRATIANO The woman falls; sure he hath killed his wife.
EMILIA Ay, ay; O, lay me by my mistress' side.   235
GRATIANO He's gone, but his wife's killed.
MONTANO 'Tis a notorious villain. Take you this weapon,
                Which I have here recovered from the Moor.
                Come guard the door without; let him not pass,
                But kill him rather. I'll after the same villain,   240
                For 'tis a damnèd slave.
                                Exeunt Montano and Gratiano
OTHELLO   I am not valiant neither,
                But every puny whipster gets my sword.
                But why should honour outlive honesty?
                Let it go all.
EMILIA   What did thy song bode, lady?
                Hark, canst thou hear me? I will play the swan   245
                And die in music: [*Sings*] 'Willow, willow, willow.'
                Moor, she was chaste; she loved thee, cruel Moor;

232b–3   Salvini, who (like de Vigny) cut the immediately following murder of Emilia, burst out here
          with 'utter desperation, reckless of heaven and hell' and then crying ' "Ahi! Ahi!", he throws
          himself beside and upon the bed clasping Desdemona's body' (Mason, p. 101).

233 SD   In Parker's film, the camera leaves Othello to follow an elaborate escape bid by Iago.
          Shielding himself with Emilia as he exits, he stabs her, and throws her at his pursuers to
          slow them down: 'a western/ gangster film cliché [which] shows the film at its most obvious'
          (Potter, *Othello*, p. 196). He then hides behind a doorway which turns out to be where
          Roderigo has been laid: 'Here Parker gives us the film's most unusual camera shot as Iago's
          full image is rotated in the frame to mirror Roderigo's perspective' (Samuel Crowl, *SB*,
          Winter 1996, p. 42).

244ff.   Scofield fell on the floor and at 'Let it go all' took off his swordbelt and threw it aside
          (promptbook). John Carey described him: 'he suddenly and rather carefully lies on the floor
          and knocks his head against it – there was laughter in the auditorium' (BBC Radio 3, *Critics'
          Forum*, 29 March 1980).

244–6   This was cut from the quarto and from all the productions which omit the song at 4.3.

So come my soul to bliss, as I speak true;
So speaking as I think, I die, I die.   *She dies*
OTHELLO I have another weapon in this chamber;   250
   It was a sword of Spain, the ice-brook's temper.
   O, here it is. – Uncle, I must come forth.
GRATIANO (*Within*) If thou attempt it, it will cost thee dear;
   Thou hast no weapon, and perforce must suffer.
OTHELLO Look in upon me then, and speak with me,   255
   Or naked as I am, I will assault thee.

                [*Enter Gratiano.*]

GRATIANO What is the matter?
OTHELLO   Behold, I have a weapon:
   A better never did itself sustain
   Upon a soldier's thigh. I have seen the day
   That with this little arm and this good sword   260
   I have made my way through more impediments
   Than twenty times your stop. But, O vain boast!

249 SD   Judging by the 'two carpets' (see note at 5.2 setting) in the 1766 Drury Lane promptbook, Emilia must have remained dead onstage to the end, but not, as she asks, 'by my mistress' side' (see Siemon, '"Nay, That's Not Next"', p. 49). Oxberry's edition (1819) shows a diagram of the final tableau which includes her. But Macready's promptbook has 'two servants catch Emilia and bear her off'. Fechter had an attendant place her 'at the foot of the prie-dieu in the oratory' and then draw the curtain (his stage direction). In Suzman's video, Emilia (Dorothy Gould) 'reaches out her hand towards Othello as she dies, and . . . he himself closes her eyes. In such a race-dominated society, this brief moment of physical contact . . . is . . . weighted with significance . . . Emilia shows that it is possible to fight one's way out of racism, though only at great cost' (Potter, *Othello*, p. 178–9). In Nunn's video, Emilia gropes for Desdemona's hand, and 'the camera allows audiences to see the wedding ring each woman wears' (quoted from Philip McGuire by Potter, *Othello*, p. 191).

250   Forrest 'having provided himself with "a sword of Spain" *loosened in the hilt*, threw himself into an attitude of defiance, and rattled "the ice-brook's temper" above his head' (Forster, *Essays*, p. 24).

250–69   Cut by Fechter. As Ottley says, 'the pruning knife is set aside, and the sickle used instead . . .' (Ottley, p. 29). The same could be said of Parker, who cuts all of Othello's speech (257b–79).

257bff.   Here, in Webster's production, it got as far as drawing on both sides and Gratiano defending himself before Othello subsided (Carroll). Scofield, on the other hand, let the 'exquisite lines slip idly from him' in a 'dreamy, lethargic state' which John Bayley felt corresponded to Desdemona's 'bemused' manner at 'Faith, half-asleep' (4.2.96) (*TLS*, 28 March 1980).

Who can control his fate? 'Tis not so now.
Be not afraid, though you do see me weaponed:
Here is my journey's end, here is my butt   265
And very sea-mark of my utmost sail.
Do you go back dismayed? 'Tis a lost fear:
Man but a rush against Othello's breast,
And he retires. Where should Othello go?
                    [*He goes to the bed.*]
Now, how dost thou look now? O ill-starred wench!   270
Pale as thy smock! When we shall meet at compt
This look of thine will hurl my soul from heaven
And fiends will snatch at it. Cold, cold, my girl,
Even like thy chastity.
O cursèd, cursèd slave! Whip me, ye devils,   275
From the possession of this heavenly sight!

264–7 Bell's edition, and Kemble's puzzlingly cut these three lines.

270–4 This was perhaps the moment at which Aldridge 'lifted the lifeless body of his murdered and wronged wife from the bed as though she had been an infant. There was something terribly touching in this display of physical strength brought to life by mental agony' (*Era*, 12 April 1848). Fechter spoke 'Cold, cold, my girl', having just tried to warm one of her hands between his own (his stage direction). Oscar Asche, like Aldridge, gathered 'the dead Desdemona in his arms'. That, and 'the holding of her body against his heart, was beautifully imagined' (Dickins, *Forty Years*, p. 146).

275–9 The Smock Alley text cut lines 275b–8, and although they are included in eighteenth-century theatre editions, Gentleman is doubtful about them because of their 'horrid ideas' (note in Bell). Helena Faucit recalls Macready: 'he seemed to me to be like a soul in hell . . . there was a piteousness, a pathos, in his reiteration of the loved one's name . . . its penultimate syllable long and not short, as in Italy it is, bringing into it a prolonged moaning sound . . .' (Faucit, *Female Characters*, p. 78). Edwin Booth, reluctant to let Othello forgo even his own sympathy, suggested a gesture towards Iago on 'O cursèd, cursèd slave' (*Variorum*). Perhaps it was here that Salvini so impressed Emma Lazarus: 'the indescribable accent with which he utters the very name of the "divina Desdemona" . . . is in itself a revelation, and after the lurid horror of the final catastrophe the music of that first tone comes back to us with unforgettable pathos!' (*C*, November 1881). This is a Verdian effect, for in the opera the music of their first love-duet does literally return at the end – though there it comes on Otello's dying words which Salvini cut. Agate writing about Robeson in 1930 regretted that the passage was 'sighed' over Desdemona's body (Agate, *Chronicles*, p. 288). In the video, John Kani howls and sobs with Desdemona in his arms – as did Ray Fearon (RSC archive film).

Blow me about in winds! Roast me in sulphur!
Wash me in steep-down gulfs of liquid fire!
O Desdemon! Dead Desdemon! Dead! O! O!

Enter LODOVICO, *Montano*, CASSIO *in a chair, Iago in the charge of* OFFICERS.

LODOVICO Where is this rash and most unfortunate man?   280
OTHELLO That's he that was Othello: here I am.
LODOVICO Where is that viper? Bring the villain forth.
OTHELLO I look down towards his feet; but that's a fable.
    If that thou be'st a devil, I cannot kill thee.
        [*He wounds Iago.*]
LODOVICO Wrench his sword from him.
IAGO   I bleed, sir, but not killed.   285

279 SD   Edwin Booth drew 'the bed-curtains at Iago's entrance that Desdemona's corpse may not be polluted by Iago's gaze' (*Variorum*). Iago is usually brought in as a prisoner here – though the direction does not appear until Bell's and Kemble's editions. Fechter had him followed by a press of threatening 'common people' and curious women. 'At the sight of Iago, Othello involuntarily moves towards him, and is promptly intercepted; Iago looks at him with contemptuous irony' (his stage direction). Webster's José Ferrer entered with a bloody head, hands tied behind him, and jacketless (Carroll). Michael Bryant, in Peter Hall's production, 'grinned unrepentantly' (*Cahiers Elizabéthains*, October 1980). Salvini's Emilia, who was still alive, was made to curse Iago here, calling him a vile tiger, after which she went to the back of the stage and wept.

283–4   Scofield delivered this 'with his back to the audience, and it was very hard to see what could be gained from denying Othello direct communication with the audience' (*Sh.S*, 34, p. 154). Suzman's video has John Kani crouching before Iago, looking for his devil's feet.

284 SD   This moment was one of Salvini's greatest. To Henry James his 'tiger-like spring' was 'ineffaceable': 'He has sighted [Iago], with the intentness of fate, for a terrible moment, while he is still on one knee beside Desdemona; and the manner in which the spectator sees him – or rather feels him – rise to his avenging leap is a sensation. After this frantic dash, the one thing Othello can *do* to relieve himself, . . . he falls into a chair . . . and lies there for some moments . . . convulsed with long inarticulate moans' (James, *Art*, pp. 174–5). In Suzman's video, Richard Haines screams as he is wounded. In Attenborough's production, Ray Fearon unsheathed and cut Iago's neck (RSC archive film).

285b   J. B. Booth spoke the line 'staunching the wound, and mastering the anguish of it, and with a look of steady hatred and defiance . . . As if he would say, "You are right, you cannot kill me. I am a devil"' (Gould, *Tragedian*, p. 91). Macready's utterance was 'like the hiss of a

OTHELLO I am not sorry neither; I'd have thee live,
    For in my sense 'tis happiness to die.
LODOVICO O, thou Othello, that wert once so good,
    Fallen in the practice of a damnèd slave,
    What shall be said to thee?
OTHELLO   Why, anything: 290
    An honourable murderer, if you will;
    For naught did I in hate, but all in honour.
LODOVICO This wretch hath part confessed his villainy.
    Did you and he consent in Cassio's death?
OTHELLO Ay.   295
CASSIO   Dear general, I never gave you cause.
OTHELLO I do believe it, and I ask your pardon.
    Will you, I pray, demand that demi-devil
    Why he hath thus ensnared my soul and body?
IAGO Demand me nothing; what you know, you know.   300
    From this time forth I never will speak word.
LODOVICO What! Not to pray?
GRATIANO Torments will ope your lips.

---

disabled serpent venomous to the last' (*TJ*, 10 October 1840). Fechter cut 283–92. Saintsbury admired Henry Irving here especially: 'stoical composure, outward preservation of respect to the general, and yet a covert suggestion of the same ironic kind as that which Othello himself had made on the futility of his wrath, are all implied in it' (Saintsbury, *Scrap Book*, pp. 115–16). In Parker's film, Branagh smiles conspiratorially at Othello.

289   Salvini cut this unflattering line, as did Barton from the 1972 promptbook, and Parker from his film.

297   Salvini's Italian is more gracious than the original. Perhaps a similar sense of Othello's too cursory apology here made Orson Welles kiss Cassio. But Crosse grumbled that it was 'unnecessary' (Crosse, *Playgoing*, p. 152).

300–1   Henry Irving achieved a remarkable effect here. After saying these lines 'the agony of the wound he had received made him gradually grow . . . the tortured figure with tightly compressed lips appeared to tower into the borders' (Foss, *The Author*, p. 80). José Ferrer in Webster's production spoke this on his knees, but was without fear or regret, the defiant egotist to the end (*New York World Telegram*, 23 May 1945). Suzman's Iago here spat slowly on the ground (video). In Nunn's production, Ian McKellen 'leans across the death-loaded bed and slowly says to Othello "What you know, you know": the implication is that he has simply articulated the Moor's own buried insecurities' (*G*, 26 August 1989). In Parker's film Iago's and Othello's heads are shown together in close-up – a shared, private moment – Branagh maintaining his conspiratorial smile.

OTHELLO　　　　　　　　　　　　　Well, thou dost best.
LODOVICO Sir, you shall understand what hath befallen,
　　　Which, as I think, you know not. Here is a letter　　　　305
　　　Found in the pocket of the slain Roderigo,
　　　And here another: the one of them imports
　　　The death of Cassio, to be undertook
　　　By Roderigo.
OTHELLO　　　　　O villain!
CASSIO　　　　　　　　　Most heathenish and most gross!
LODOVICO Now here's another discontented paper,　　　　310
　　　Found in his pocket too; and this, it seems,
　　　Roderigo meant to have sent this damnèd villain,
　　　But that, belike, Iago, in the nick,
　　　Came in and satisfied him.
OTHELLO　　　　　　　　　　　O the pernicious caitiff!
　　　How came you, Cassio, by that handkerchief　　　　315
　　　That was my wife's?
CASSIO　　　　　　　　　I found it in my chamber;
　　　And he himself confessed but even now
　　　That there he dropped it for a special purpose
　　　Which wrought to his desire.
OTHELLO　　　　　　　　　　O fool, fool, fool!
CASSIO　There is besides in Roderigo's letter　　　　320
　　　How he upbraids Iago, that he made him
　　　Brave me upon the watch, whereon it came

305–14　Some productions have cut this clumsy piece of plotting, e.g. Salvini's, Ellen Terry's, Oscar Asche's, Webster's, John Barton's, and Parker's film.

316　'I found it in my chamber'. Kemble's edition has 'Takes it out of his pocket'. Cumberland's (1829) has Othello ask his question (315–16) 'pointing to the handkerchief found on Cassio's knee'. It must have become the tradition since Macready crosses out Kemble's direction and remarks 'Tied on his L knee' (promptbook).

319b　Here, where most players 'rave and tear their hair and fall into mock agonies', Kean 'repeats the word over quickly, and almost inarticulately, and with a half smile of wonder at his incredible stupidity in having been such a "fool"' (*Blackwood's Magazine*, March 1818). Ottley remembers 'the clasped hands, palm upwards, gathered across the head, as if to crush a fevered brain, which threatened to burst out into a volcano – exclaiming the while with trembling gasping utterance, and in agonised tones – "Fool! fool! fool!"' (Ottley, p. 32). Webster directed Robeson to turn his back here (Carroll). Willard White's deep bass voice rose memorably here, to a 'broken falsetto' (*I*, 26 August 1989). Ray Fearon in Attenborough's production, crouched with his hands (like Kean) over his head (RSC archive film). Parker cuts.

> That I was cast; and even but now he spake –
> After long seeming dead – Iago hurt him,
> Iago set him on.   325
> LODOVICO You must forsake this room and go with us.
> Your power and your command is taken off
> And Cassio rules in Cyprus. For this slave,
> If there be any cunning cruelty
> That can torment him much and hold him long   330
> It shall be his. You shall close prisoner rest
> Till that the nature of your fault be known
> To the Venetian state. Come, bring him away.
> OTHELLO Soft you; a word or two before you go.

331   Bell's edition and Kemble's make Iago exit here, interpolating 'Away with him' and cutting
      Lodovico's line at 359, 'Look on the tragic loading of this bed.' Bell's edition is slightly
      confusing in directing Lodovico to say 'O Spartan dog' to Iago, in spite of Iago's earlier
      departure, but perhaps he gestured in some way in the direction of his exit. Iago's exit makes
      possible a moment of confrontation between him and Othello, which actors have taken
      advantage of. *The Examiner* (31 January 1808), describing G. F. Cooke, said that 'you see his
      irritation through all his firmness' here, and noted 'the malicious gnash of countenance
      which he gives at parting'. Hazlitt complained of 'Mr Kean's pointing to the dead bodies
      after the catastrophe' (Hazlitt, v, p. 221), something J. B. Booth also did with extraordinary
      elaboration: 'he looked at Othello with a significant gaze, then pointed to his own wife, as if
      to express that her violation by the Moor was the cause of all this perfidy. He then struck his
      breast in a triumphant manner meaning that his vindication was complete and gratifying'
      (quoted from the *Morning Post* by Sprague, pp. 222–3). He did this in London in 1836 and
      was laughed at (*Theatrical Observer*, 26 November 1836), which probably accounts for the
      simpler 'Parthian look . . . a Gorgon stare in which hate seemed both petrified and
      petrifying', that Richard Grant White remembered (*Atlantic Monthly*, August 1881).
      Macready's Iago threw a glance round the room and gave a 'demoniacal smile' in which the
      critic read that 'even now . . . his heart is filled with a joy of the blackest dye' (*TJ*, October
      1840). But Lady Pollock remembered something less gleeful: 'at the last his dogged aspect
      was passionate with his frustrated design, when, with his cap plunged over his brow, he
      burst the doors open with clenched fists to make his passage free' (Pollock, *Macready*,
      p. 113). Phelps too, 'glancing round with one look of ineffable scorn . . . reared himself erect
      and strode out of the room, defiant to the last' (quoted by Sprague, p. 223). Later Iagos
      stayed on the stage and made their 'points' after Othello's death.

334ff. The Smock Alley text cut 344b–7a – the reference to Othello's tears. Hazlitt cited line 341 as
      one of the places where Kean's 'lips might be said less to utter words than to bleed drops of
      blood gushing from the heart' (Hazlitt, XVIII, p. 263). Macready gave the speech 'in a calm,

> I have done the state some service and they know't: 335
> No more of that. I pray you, in your letters
> When you shall these unlucky deeds relate,
> Speak of me as I am; nothing extenuate,
> Nor set down aught in malice. Then must you speak
> Of one that loved not wisely, but too well;   340
> Of one not easily jealous but, being wrought,
> Perplexed in the extreme; of one whose hand,
> Like the base Indian, threw a pearl away
> Richer than all his tribe; of one whose subdued eyes,
> Albeit unusèd to the melting mood,   345
> Drops tears as fast as the Arabian trees
> Their medicinable gum. Set you down this;
> And say besides that in Aleppo once

impressive and collected manner; . . . the last request of a man to whom this world was as nothing and whose last resolve nothing could alter . . .' (*TJ*, 22 August 1840). Forrest 'drew his hand along his arm, as if to wipe off the tears that had fallen there!' (Forster, *Essays*, p. 25). Edwin Booth, surprisingly, acted 'with violent gestures and disordered voice, as though the frenzy of passion had still hold of his mind. He who can so misconceive this passage can never truly realize Othello' (*MM*, July 1881). Salvini 'weeps copiously' from 336, 'I pray you, in your letters . . .', to 347, 'medicinable gum' (Mason, p. 105). Lewes objected to Salvini's last act in general, saying that he 'alternately raged and blubbered – and was never pathetic' (Lewes, *Actors*, p. 272).

  Olivier spoke this kneeling on the bed 'hugging Desdemona up to him, her head lolling on his shoulder' wrote Bamber Gascoigne, 'in tragic parody' of the 'passionate link' between them (*O*, 26 April 1964). James Earl Jones, in 1982, according to Kerr, was 'masterly' with his 'simple, factual and desperately honest valedictory "Speak of me as I am"' (*NYT*, 14 February 1980). Scofield, according to one critic, spoke the whole thing 'as if he were reading a company report' (*Evening News*, 21 March 1980). One reviewer felt that Willard White spoke as though trying to restore order, just as earlier he had folded Desdemona's hands (see note at 105 above) (*Literary Review*, November 1989). In Parker's film, Laurence Fishburne's eyes stream with tears on 345–7 without distorting his face.

343   Few actors have said 'Judean' (Folio's reading) instead of 'Indian'. Edwin Booth did, in 1881, and the *Athenaeum* thought it unnecessary and unclear (22 January 1882). James Earl Jones said 'Judas' (in 1982) but Richard Levin (*SQ*, 34 (1983), p. 72) doubted if the audience noticed.

348ff.   The problems of where the weapon is, and how to get hold of it secretly, have occupied actors. J. B. Booth had flung a 'silken robe' over his shoulder earlier in the speech, and had 'possessed himself' of a dagger concealed in his turban (which he then, presumably, hid under the robe) (Gould, *Tragedian*, p. 116). Kean stole to the bed and took the dagger that

Where a malignant and a turbaned Turk
Beat a Venetian and traduced the state,   350
I took by th'throat the circumcisèd dog
And smote him thus.
            He stabs himself.

had dispatched Desdemona (see Sprague, p. 220), and 'to divert all suspicion, . . . simulated
a pride in his punishment of the turbaned Turk . . . his eyes wandered with searching
brilliance from face to face to see whether any suspicion . . . lurked in their minds . . .'
(Hawkins, *Edmund Kean*, 1, p. 231). Fechter played an elaborate trick. He approached Iago
with his dagger 'no one daring to stop him', as though Iago were the 'circumcisèd dog'. He
then seized him, 'forcing him – still bound but smiling with bold effrontery – to kneel before
Desdemona' (his stage direction) and then 'to flash surprise – stabs not Iago but himself'.
Morley felt that this was wrong because by that stage Othello is very far from 'spending
thought' on Iago (Morley, *Journal*, p. 232). Edwin Booth did it by moral power: at some
point 'Othello opens the curtains – pauses – kisses Desdemona – slowly and with deepest
feeling of remorse – turns towards the others who, in respectful sympathy droop their
heads, and therefore do not see his purposed suicide until it is too late' (*Variorum*).
Beerbohm Tree had the notion of 'snatching . . . a dagger from Cassio'. This was 'most
effective' according to the *Morning Leader* (10 April 1912). Similarly Wolfit 'snatched the
sword . . . from one of the soldiers, an effective trick, but not an improvement on the
concealed dagger' (Crosse, *Playgoing*, p. 146). Olivier used the blade concealed in his trick
bracelet with which he had threatened Iago at 'be sure thou prove my love a whore'
(3.3.360). Scofield's knife was hidden in his crucifix (promptbook). With a glance at Olivier,
John Kani uses a knife concealed in his necklet (Suzman's video). Both Willard White
(promptbook) and Ray Fearon (RSC archive film) took daggers previously hidden under the
bed. Parker has Cassio secretly slip a weapon to Othello at the beginning of the speech,
'thus seriously complicating our response to his suicide' (Samuel Crowl, *SB*, Winter 1996,
p. 42).

352 SD   Dumas (père) was intrigued by the different ways in which actors drove the dagger in.
Talma and Joanny raised the dagger and plunged it in with a downward movement. Kean
and Charles Kemble used both hands and pressed it in horizontally. Macready forced it in
below the ribs and directed it upwards (see Cook, *Theatre*, October 1880 and Sprague,
p. 220). Kean's stab was 'stealthy' and he fell backwards (Ottley, p. 32). One biographer
said that this backwards fall happened 'in the attempt to imprint a last kiss' on Desdemona
(Hawkins, *Edmund Kean*, 1, p. 231), but the following close observer did not appear to notice
it: 'he literally dies standing; it is the dead body of Othello that falls, heavily and at once;
there is no *rebound*' (quoted in Sprague, p. 220). Siemon notes that a century of Othellos,
from 1770 to 1870, were almost never allowed to die upon a kiss, and that this was so as to

LODOVICO O bloody period!
GRATIANO   All that's spoke is marred!
OTHELLO I kissed thee ere I killed thee: no way but this,
          Killing myself, to die upon a kiss.   355
                              He [falls on the bed and] dies
CASSIO This did I fear, but thought he had no weapon,

leave Desdemona, 'in lovely, lonely isolation . . . unviolated by Othello's own bleeding corpse' (' "Nay, That's Not Next"', pp. 49–50).

It was Macready who developed the idea of trying and failing to reach Desdemona: after falling 'he motions to be raised, his wish being complied with he hastily staggers towards the bed . . . supporting himself by the walls and furniture of the room, ejaculates faintly her name, just gazes on her face and falls dead upon the floor' (*TJ*, 22 August 1840). According to the Bancrofts, Gustavus Vaughan Brooke seems to have reached the bed, if not Desdemona: 'Acting, although not speaking, the closing words [line 355], he staggered towards the bed, dying as he clutched the heavy curtains of it, which, giving way, fell upon his prostrate body as a kind of pall, disclosing at the same time, the dead form of Desdemona' (*Mr and Mrs Bancroft*, p. 75). It is difficult to be sure, but when they say 'acting but not speaking', the Bancrofts presumably mean, not that he kissed her, but that he attempted to. Fechter, having forced Iago to his knees (see previous note) 'stabs himself and throws the dagger at the feet of Iago, who shrinks in terror, as if struck on the face by the blood of Othello'. He then tried to embrace Desdemona 'but unable to reach her – falls in despair and dies. Cassio kneels before him' (his stage direction). Morley said that 'the audience is deeply stirred', but this sort of thing 'belongs rather to French melodrama than English tragedy' (Morley, *Journal*, p. 233). Edwin Booth returned to the old staggering and curtain-clutching – but 'not much', he says, so perhaps the curtains did not fall (*Variorum*).

The Italians shocked everyone. Salvini did not stab himself, but died 'by hacking open his throat with a curved knife' (Winter, *Shakespeare*, pp. 291–2), 'and imitating the noise that escaping blood and air make together when the windpipe is severed' (Knight, *Notes*, p. 24). Nothing is said of his trying to reach Desdemona. Rossi also emitted 'spasmodic gurgling sounds, as of a person choked by blood' (Winter, *Shakespeare*, p. 269). Grasso 'having bared his throat and gashed it slowly across with his knife, drags himself to the foot of Desdemona's bed and proceeds to "gargle" realistically' (Beerbohm, *Theatres*, p. 575). Winter quotes Novelli on witnessing a public suicide: 'He held his razor – thus: and he bent forward – so . . . I hear the dying man give a gurgle in the throat . . . like this – s.s.s.r.r.r. .R-R-r! And then I say: *That* is the way! *Now* I know how the Moor died' (quoted in Winter, *Shakespeare*, pp. 303–4).

The English never attempted anything very bloody or noisy, though Agate says that Baliol Holloway showed 'considerable virtuosity in the death-scene'. However, he was not

For he was great of heart.
LODOVICO [*To Iago*]   O Spartan dog,
More fell than anguish, hunger, or the sea,
Look on the tragic loading of this bed:
This is thy work. The object poisons sight;   360

'quite sure about that final attitude when he lay prone on the ground with arms outstretched like a Rugby footballer who has just scored a try' (Agate, *Chronicles*, p. 281). Olivier plunging the spike of his bracelet into his neck while holding Desdemona up in his other arm shows considerable virtuosity too; the resulting embrace of their two dead bodies makes a moving spectacle (film).

From Macready onwards, up to the early twentieth century, it was usual to bring the curtain down here, after line 353, omitting Othello's last words at 354–5 – words which had in any case been omitted since Bell's edition. Macready simply directed everybody to advance towards the bodies and stand sorrowfully over them as the curtain falls (promptbook). Phelps did the same, making the final curtain 'slow' (promptbook). Fechter also ended here with a little tableau. Cassio (we have seen) is kneeling before the dead Othello, 'the guards advance towards Iago; and, as they place their hands on his shoulder the curtain falls' (his stage direction). Salvini added only Cassio's lines (356–7) so as to finish on a heroic note ('for he was great of heart') followed by a 'quick curtain' (Mason, p. 107). Edwin Booth, as Iago, finally indulged himself rather in his father's manner, by bringing down 'the final curtain standing over Othello, pointing triumphantly at the dead body and gazing up at the gallery with a malignant smile of satisfied hate'. This, in Irving's production, was 'as though a splash of crimson had been introduced in a delicate nocturne by Whistler' (Dickins, *Forty Years*, p. 40). It is possible that this moment came later, but it is difficult to see how Gratiano, Lodovico or Cassio could have tolerated it, or where it could be fitted in during their dialogue. Oscar Asche finished the play here, and no doubt there were others. Beerbohm Tree actually got as far as lines 354–5, but finished there. In an echo of his murder of Desdemona, Willard White does die upon a kiss – lying on top of her and then falling to one side (Nunn's video).

359–60   Iagos of the late eighteenth, nineteenth and early twentieth centuries either made their exit before Othello's death (see note at 331), or had the curtain lowered on them immediately after it. Olivier, as Iago, continued in his unrepentant scene-stealing spirit here when 'he swaggered across the stage and had a good look at the corpses' (Crosse, *Playgoing*, p. 123). Crosse deeply disapproved, and even the slightest attention to Iago at this stage can jar. In Dexter's production Lodovico spoke 'the object poisons sight' as though the words referred to Iago, and not the bed. Robert Speaight thought this wrong, for 'by now [he] has passed beyond our interest' (Speaight, 'Shakespeare'). David Suchet, however, held his audiences here. Having fallen, distraught upon Othello's corpse he reached out 'yearningly as he is

Let it be hid.
[*The bed-curtains are drawn.*]
Gratiano, keep the house
And seize upon the fortunes of the Moor,
For they succeed on you. To you, lord governor,
Remains the censure of this hellish villain:
The time, the place, the torture, O, enforce it!   365
Myself will straight aboard, and to the state
This heavy act with heavy heart relate.

Exeunt

dragged away', thus making coherent the sometimes puzzling hints of homosexuality earlier on (*NS*, 17 January 1986). In Suzman's video, Richard Haines's bowed head is yanked up and then dropped. In Parker's film Branagh clambers on to the bed and lays his head on Othello's leg, eyes searching the camera once more. In Attenborough's production, Richard McCabe never looked at the bed (RSC archive film).

365   Hall's Iago, Michael Bryant, sustained his smiling to the end, 'never more beamingly amiable than when he is about to be led off to the torture chamber' (*T*, 21 March 1980). James Fenton saw it as an attack of 'tertiary silliness. He is left with lolling head and a pale idiotic smile, as if the badness had exhausted itself, leaving him genial and banal' (*ST*, 23 March 1980). This was one of McKellen's most telling moments, when 'exposed, wounded and cuffed [he] peers with fascinated rapture over the bodies of his victims . . . as chilling as a glimpse into the mind of a Sutcliffe, Christie or Kurten' (*20–20*, October 1989). The *Independent* (26 August 1989) called it McKellen's 'finest moment' and interpreted his gaze as showing him 'still hungry for their secret'.

Perhaps the Victorian instinct to end the play at Othello's death was right, for this play winds itself down more perfunctorily than most. What Ronald Bryden said about Olivier must probably have been felt by many audiences after exceptional performances: 'as he slumped beside her in the sheets, the current stopped. A couple of wigged actors stood awkwardly about' (*NS*, 1 May 1964). All the same, productions less clear about Othello's centrality have given the last flourish to Iago: Jonathan Miller ends with the echoing sound of Bob Hoskins's laughter (BBC TV). Nunn's video closes with McKellen in the frame, his 'dead-eyed gaze' seeming to Hodgdon to 'proclaim his complicity in the colonial project' (Hodgdon, 'Race-ing *Othello*', p. 33).

BIBLIOGRAPHY

Acting editions

Bell's Edition of Shakespeare's Plays, ed. Francis Gentleman, vol. I,
Othello, as Performed at the Theatre Royal Drury Lane. Regulated
from the Prompt-Book . . . by Mr Hopkins, Prompter. London,
1774.

Booth, Edwin, *Shakespeare's Tragedy of Othello* . . . as Produced by Edwin
Booth. Adapted from the Text of the Cambridge Editor with
Introductory Remarks by H. L. Hinton. New York: Hurd and
Houghton, 1869.

Cumberland edition. *Othello, a Tragedy*. Printed from the Acting Copy
with Remarks by D-G [George Daniel]. (Issued as part of
Cumberland's British Theatre, vol. II), 1829.

Fechter, Charles, *Othello* (Charles Fechter's acting edition). London:
W. R. Sams, 1861.

Irving, Henry, *Othello*, in *The Henry Irving Shakespeare* . . . ed. Henry
Irving and F. A. Marshall. London: Blackie, 1888 [1887]–90.

Kemble, J. P., *Shakespeare's Othello* . . . Revised by J. P. Kemble as it is
Performed at the Theatres Royal. London: J. Miller, 1814.

Oxberry's edition. Othello, *a Tragedy*. (Issued as part of *The New English
Drama*, vol. V). London, 1819.

Salvini, Tommaso, *Othello, a Tragedy*, the Italian Version as Performed by
Signor Salvini and his Italian Company at Drury Lane Theatre [with
the English text]. London 1875.

Promptbooks

Asche, Oscar – Lily Brayton promptbook; His Majesty's Theatre, 1908.
The Shakespeare Centre Library.

Attenborough, Michael, The promptbook, Royal Shakespeare Theatre,
Stratford-upon-Avon, 1999 is imperfectly photocopied. The archive
film made of the performance on 22 April 1999 has been used instead.

Barton, John, The Royal Shakespeare Theatre, Stratford-upon-Avon and
the Aldwych Theatre promptbooks, 1971 and 1972. The Shakespeare
Centre Library.

Eyre, Ronald, The Royal Shakespeare Company promptbook,
Stratford-upon-Avon, 1979. The Shakespeare Centre Library.
Hall, Peter, The National Theatre promptbook, 1980. The Royal National
Theatre, London.
Macready, William Charles, promptbook 'used in touring, probably from
1843 on', Forster Collection, Victoria and Albert Museum Library
(see Charles Shattuck in *The Shakespeare Promptbooks*, Urbana:
University of Illinois Press, 1965).
Nunn, Trevor, The Royal Shakespeare Company promptbook,
Stratford-upon-Avon, 1989. The Shakespeare Centre Library.
Phelps, Samuel, Drury Lane promptbook, 1864. The Shakespeare Centre
Library.
Terry, Ellen, two promptbooks for the production at the Grand Theatre,
Fulham, August 1898. The Ellen Terry Memorial Museum,
Tenterden, Kent.
Tree, Herbert Beerbohm, His Majesty's Theatre promptbook, 1912.
HBT/000228. The Bristol Theatre Collection, Bristol University.

Note: The Smock Alley text is described by Marvin Rosenberg in *The
Masks of Othello*, pp. 20–7. All my information comes from these
pages. The original is in the Folger Shakespeare Library, Washington
DC.
The '1755' promptbook is so designated because its cast list fits that of
Covent Garden five years later. The printed date MDCCLV is believed
to be a misprint for MDCCLX. See Marvin Rosenberg, 'The
Refinement of *Othello* in the Eighteenth-century British Theatre',
Studies in Philology, 51 (1954), pp. 75–94. I am indebted to this article
for its information about the acting text of *Othello* at this period.
The 1766 Drury Lane promptbook is described by George Winchester
Stone Jr, in 'Garrick and Othello, *Philological Quarterly*, 45 (January
1966), pp. 304–20. I am indebted to this article for all my references to
this text. The original is in the Folger Shakespeare Library.

OTHER WORKS

Agate, James, *Brief Chronicles: A Survey of the Plays of Shakespeare and the
Elizabethans in Actual Performance*, London: Jonathan Cape, 1943.
Alger, W. R., *The Life of Edwin Forrest*, 2 vols. Philadelphia, 1877.
Ashwell, Lena, *Reflections from Shakespeare*. London: Hutchinson, 1926.
Baldwin, T. W., *Organisation and Personnel of the Shakespearean Company*.
Princeton University Press, 1927.

Bancroft, Squire and Marie, *Mr and Mrs Bancroft On and Off the Stage.* London, 1889.

Barrett, Lawrence, *Edwin Forrest.* Cambridge, MA, 1882.

Beerbohm, Max, *Around Theatres.* London: Rupert Hart-Davis, 1953.

Benson, Frank, *My Memoirs.* London, 1930.

Bernard, John, *Retrospections of the Stage*, 2 vols. (in I). Boston: Carter and Hendee, 1832.

Bishop, George W., *My Betters.* London: Heinemann, 1957.

Bland, Sheila S., 'How I Would Direct *Othello*', in Mythili Kaul, ed., *Othello: New Essays by Black Writers.* Washington DC: Howard University Press, 1997.

Boaden, James, *Memoirs of Mrs Siddons, Interspersed with Anecdotes of Authors and Actors*, 2 vols. London and Philadelphia, 1827.
  The Life of John Philip Kemble, Esq., 2 vols. London, 1825.

Boaden, James, ed., *The Private Correspondence of David Garrick with the Most Celebrated Persons of his Time*, 2 vols. London: H. Colburn and R. Bentley, 1831.

Bradley, A. C., *Shakespearean Tragedy: Lectures on Hamlet, Othello, King Lear, Macbeth*, London: Macmillan, 1966 (first pub. 1904).

Broglie, Achille-Léon-Victor, Duc de, 'Sur *Othello*, traduit en vers français par Monsieur Alfred de Vigny, et sur l'état de l'art dramatique en France en 1830', *La Revue Française*, January 1830, in Francois Guizot, *Notices historiques et critiques sur les principales pièces de Shakespeare*, Paris 1821, reprinted with *Shakespeare et son temps: étude litteraire*, Paris, 1852, pp. 264–343.

Brown, John Russell, 'Three Kinds of Shakespeare', *Shakespeare Survey*, 18 (1965), pp. 147–55.

Budden, Julian, *The Operas of Verdi*, 3 vols. New York: Oxford University Press, 1978–81, vol. III.

Burton, Robert, *The Anatomy of Melancholy.* Oxford: I. Lichfield, 1621.

Busi, Anna, *Otello in Italia, 1777–1972.* Bari: Adriatica, 1973.

Carlin, Murray, *Not Now, Sweet Desdemona: A Duologue for Black and White within the Realm of Shakespeare's 'Othello'.* Nairobi, Lusaka and Addis Ababa: Oxford University Press, 1969.

Carlisle, Carol Jones, *Shakespeare from the Green Room: Actors' Criticisms of Four Major Tragedies.* Chapel Hill: University of North Carolina Press, 1969.

Carroll, Janet Barton, 'A Promptbook Study of Margaret Webster's Production of *Othello*'. PhD dissertation, Louisiana State University, 1977.

Chaudhuri, Sukanta, 'Shakespeare and the Ethnic Question', in Tetsuo Kishi, Roger Pringle and Stanley Wells, eds., *Shakespeare and Cultural Traditions: The Selected Proceedings of the International Shakespeare Association World Congress, Tokyo 1991*, pp. 174–87, Newark and London: Associated University Presses, 1994.

Cibber, Colley, *An Apology for the Life of Colley Cibber*, ed. B. R. S. Fone. Ann Arbor: University of Michigan Press, 1968.

Cibber, Theophilus, 'The Life of Barton Booth, Esq.', in *The Lives and Characters of the most Eminent Actors and Actresses of Great Britain and Ireland from Shakespeare to the Present Time*. London: R. Griffiths, 1753.

Cole, J. W., *The Life and Theatrical Times of Charles Kean*, 2 vols. London, 1860.

Cole, Toby and Helen Krich Chinoy, eds., *Actors on Acting: The Theories, Techniques and Practices of the Great Actors of All Times as Told in their own Words*. New York: Crown Publishers, revised edition 1970, repr. 1978, pp. 410–17.

Coleridge, Samuel Taylor, in *Coleridge on Shakespeare*, ed. Terence Hawkes. Harmondsworth: Penguin, 1969.

Cook, Dutton, *Nights at the Play: A View of the English Stage*, 2 vols. London, 1883.

Cooke, William, *Memoirs of Charles Macklin, Comedian*. London, 1806.

Cowhig, Ruth, 'Blacks in English Renaissance Drama and the Role of Shakespeare's Othello', in David Dabydeen, ed., *The Black Presence in English Literature*. Manchester University Press, 1985, pp. 1–25.

Crosse, Gordon, *Shakespearean Playgoing, 1890–1952*. London: Mowbray, 1953.

Crowl, Samuel, 'Othello', *Shakespeare Bulletin*, vol. 14, no.1 (Winter 1996), pp. 41–2.

Davies, Anthony, 'Filming *Othello*', in Anthony Davies and Stanley Wells, eds., *Shakespeare and the Moving Image: The Plays on Film and Television*. Cambridge University Press, pp. 196–210.

Davies, Thomas, *Dramatic Miscellanies; Critical Observations on Several Plays of Shakespeare*, 3 vols. London, 1784.

Memoirs of the Life of David Garrick, 2 vols. London, 1780.

Dickins, Richard, *Forty Years of Shakespeare on the English Stage, August 1867 to August 1907*. n.d.

Donaldson, Peter S., *Shakespearean Films/Shakespearean Directors*. Boston: Unwin Hyman, 1990.

Dowling, Maurice G., *Othello Travestie: an Operatic Burlesque Burletta*. London, 1834.

Downes, John, *Roscius Anglicanus*, ed. Montague Summers. New York: B. Blom, 1929, re-issued 1968.

Ducis, Jean-Francois, *Othello*, in *Œuvres de J.-F. Ducis.* Paris, 1839.

Dunlap, William, *Memoirs of George Frederick Cooke*, 2 vols. 1813.

Engle, Ron, 'Audience, Style and Language in the Shakespeare of Peter Zadek', in Dennis Kennedy, ed., *Foreign Shakespeare; Contemporary performance.* Cambridge University Press, 1993.

Farjeon, Herbert, *The Shakespearean Scene: Dramatic Criticisms.* London and New York: Hutchinson [1949].

Faucit, Helena, *On Some of Shakespeare's Female Characters.* Edinburgh and London: Blackwood and Sons, 1891.

Fenwick, Henry, 'The Production', introduction to *The BBC TV Shakespeare: Othello.* London, 1981.

Findlater, Richard, *Michael Redgrave, Actor.* London: Heinemann, 1956.

Fisher, H. K., *Life and Letters and the London Mercury*, 54 (July 1947).

Foote, Samuel, *A Treatise on the Passions, so far as they Regard the Stage: with a Critical Enquiry into the Theatrical Merit of Mr G[arrick], Mr Q [uin], and Mr B[arry]. The First considered in the Part of Lear, the Two Last Opposed in Othello.* London, 1747.

Forster, John, and G. H. Lewes, *Dramatic Essays: John Forster and G. H. Lewes*, ed. William Archer and Robert Lowe. London, 1896.

Foss, George, *What the Author Meant.* London: Oxford University Press, 1932.

Furness, Horace Howard, *Othello: A New Variorum Edition of Shakespeare.* Philadelphia, 1886, vol. VI.

Furnivall, Frederick James and others, eds., *The Shakespeare Allusion-Book: A Collection of Allusions to Shakespeare from 1591–1700.* London: Oxford University Press, 1932 re-issue.

Gardner, Helen, 'The Noble Moor', in Kenneth Muir, ed., *Interpretations of Shakespeare: British Academy Lectures.* Oxford: Clarendon Press, 1985; paperback 1986, pp. 161–79.

Genest, John, *Some Account of the English Stage*, 10 vols. Bath, 1830, vol. IV.

Gentleman, Francis, *The Dramatic Censor; or, Critical Companion*, 2 vols. London, 1770.

Gielgud, John, *An Actor and his Time.* Harmondsworth: Penguin, 1981.

Stage Directions. London: Heinemann, 1979.

Gildon, Charles, 'Some Reflections on Mr Rymer's Short View of Tragedy and an Attempt at a Vindication of Shakespeare in an Essay Directed to John Dryden, Esq.', in Brian Vickers, ed., *Shakespeare: The Critical Heritage*, 6 vols. London: Routledge, 1974–81, vol. II.

Gilman, Margaret, *Othello in French.* Paris: E. Champion, 1925.

Gould, T. R., *The Tragedian: An Essay on the Histrionic Genius of Junius Brutus Booth*. New York, 1868.

Granville-Barker, Harley, *Prefaces to Shakespeare 4: Othello [and] Love's Labour's Lost*. London: Batsford, repr. 1977.

Graves, Charles, '*Othello* Recalled', *Scotsman*, 4 April 1959.

Greenblatt, Stephen, *Renaissance Self-Fashioning: From More to Shakespeare*. Chicago and London: Chicago University Press, 1980; paperback 1984.

Gregory, Kenneth, ed., *The First Cuckoo: a Selection of the Most Witty, Amusing and Memorable Letters to 'The Times', 1900–1975*. London: Allen and Unwin, 1976.

Grossman, Edwina Booth, *Edwin Booth: Recollections by his Daughter*. New York, 1894.

Hackett, J. H., *Notes and Comments upon Certain Plays and Actors of Shakespeare*. New York, 1864.

Haig, Stirling, 'Vigny and *Othello*', *Yale French Studies*, 33 (1964).

Harrison, Gabriel, *Edwin Forrest: The Actor and the Man*. New York, 1889.

Hawkins, F. W., *The Life of Edmund Kean*, 2 vols. London, 1869.

Hazlitt, William, *The Complete Works of William Hazlitt*, ed. P. P. Howe, 21 vols., London and Toronto, 1930–4, vols. V and XVIII.

Hedgecock, F. A., *A Cosmopolitan Actor: David Garrick and his French Friends*. London, 1912.

Hill, Aaron, *The Prompter, a Theatrical Paper (1734–36)*, ed. William Appleton and Kalman A. Burnim. New York: B. Blom, 1966.

The Works of the Late Aaron Hill, Esq., 4 vols. London, 1753.

Hill, John, *The Actor: a Treatise on the Art of Playing*. London, 1750.

Hobson, Harold, *Theatre*. London: Longman's, 1948.

Hodgdon, Barbara, 'Race-ing Othello, Re-engendering White-Out II', in Richard Burt and Lynda E. Boose, eds., *Shakespeare the Movie, II: Popularizing the Plays on Film, TV, and Video*. London and New York, Routledge, 2003.

'Race-ing *Othello*, Re-engendering White-Out', in Lynda E. Boose and Richard Burt, eds., *Shakespeare the Movie: Popularizing the Plays on Film, TV, and Video*. London and New York: Routledge, 1997, repr. 2001.

'Kiss me Deadly; or the Des/Demonized Spectacle', in Virginia Vaughan and Kent Cartwright, eds., *Othello: New Perspectives*. London: Associated University Presses, 1991.

Honigmann, E. A. J., *Othello*, The Arden Shakespeare, 3rd edition. London: Thomas Nelson, 1999, reprinted 2002.

Hunt, Leigh, in *Leigh Hunt's Dramatic Criticism, 1808–1831*, ed. L. H. Houtchens and C. W. Houtchens. New York: Columbia University Press, 1949.

Hunter, G. K., 'Othello and Colour Prejudice' and 'Elizabethans and Foreigners', in *Dramatic Identities and Cultural Tradition: Studies in Shakespeare and his Contemporaries*. Liverpool University Press, 1978.

Hyman, Earle, 'Othello: or Ego in Love, Sex and War', in Mythili Kaul, ed., *Othello: New Essays by Black Writers*. Washington DC: Howard University Press, 1997.

J. T., *A Letter of Complaint to the Ingenious Author of a Treatise on the Passions*. 1747.

James, Henry, *The Scenic Art: Notes on Acting and the Drama, 1872–1901*, ed. Allan Wade. New Brunswick: Rutgers University Press, 1949.

Italian Hours. London, 1909.

Jennings, Caleen Sinette, *Casting Othello*, in *Playing Juliet/Casting Othello*, Illinois, London and Melbourne: Dramatic Publishing, 1999.

Johnson, Samuel, in *Dr Johnson on Shakespeare*, ed. W. K. Wimsatt. Harmondsworth: Penguin, 1969.

Johnson-Haddad, Miranda, 'The Shakespeare Theatre *Othello*' and 'Patrick Stewart on Playing Othello', *Shakespeare Bulletin* (Spring 1998), pp. 9–11 and 11–12.

Johnson-Haddad, Miranda, 'The Shakespeare Theatre at the Folger, 1990–91', *Shakespeare Quarterly*, 42 (1992), pp. 472–84.

Jones, Eldred, *The Elizabethan Image of Africa*. Charlottesville: University Press of Virginia, 1971.

Othello's Countrymen: The African in English Renaissance Drama. Oxford University Press, 1965.

Jorgens, Jack J., *Shakespeare on Film*. London: University Press of America, 1991.

Kemble, Frances Anne, *Records of a Later Life*, 3 vols. New York: Henry Holt, 1882.

Temple Bar, July 1884.

Kendal, Madge, *Dame Madge Kendal, by Herself*, London: J. Murray, 1933.

Kingsley, Ben, 'Othello', in Russell Jackson and Robert Smallwood, eds., *Players of Shakespeare 2: Further Essays in Shakespearean Performance by Players with the Royal Shakespeare Company*. Cambridge University Press, 1988.

Kirk, John Forster, 'Shakespeare's Tragedies on the Stage,' *Lippincott's Magazine*, June 1884.

Kirkman, J. T., *Memoirs of the Life of Charles Macklin Esq.*, 2 vols. London, 1799.

Knight, Joseph, *Theatrical Notes*. London, 1893.

Lamb, Charles, in *The Works of Charles and Mary Lamb*, 7 vols., ed. E. V. Lucas. London: Methuen, 1903–5.

Lawrence, W. J., *The Life of Gustavus Vaughan Brooke*. London, 1892.

Lazarus, Emma, 'Tommaso Salvini', *The Century*, November 1881, pp. 110–17.

Leavis, F. R., 'Diabolic Intellect and the Nobel Hero: or the Sentimentalist's Othello', in *The Common Pursuit*. London: 1952; Harmondsworth: Penguin, 1962, pp. 136–59.

Lewes, George Henry, *On Actors and the Art of Acting*. London: Smith, Elder, 1875.

Lillie, Charles, ed., *Original and Genuine Letters sent to the Tatler and the Spectator, During the Time those Works were Publishing*, 2 vols. London, 1725.

Little, David M. and George M. Kahrl, eds., *The Letters of David Garrick*, 3 vols. London: Oxford University Press, 1963, vol. 1.

Loehlin, James, '*Othello* in Washington', unpublished seminar paper. Shakespeare Association of America, 1998.

Lounsbury, Thomas R., *Shakespeare and Voltaire*. [1902], repr. New York, London: Blom, 1968.

MacCarthy, Desmond, *The Theatre*. London: MacGibbon and Kee, 1954.

MacDonald, Joyce Green, 'Acting Black: *Othello, Othello* Burlesques, and the Performance of Blackness', *Theatre Journal*, 46 (May 1994), pp. 231–49.

Macready, William Charles, *Macready's Reminiscences and Selections from his Diaries and Letters*, ed. Sir F. Pollock, 2 vols. London: Macmillan, 1875.

Marowitz, Charles, 'An *Othello*', in *Open Space Plays*, selected by Charles Marowitz. Harmondsworth: Penguin, 1974.

'Charles Marowitz Directs', *Theatre Quarterly*, 8 (October–December 1972).

Marshall, Herbert and Stock, Mildred, *Ira Aldridge, the Negro Tragedian*. London: Rockliff, 1958.

Marston, Westland, *Our Recent Actors: Recollections*, 2 vols. London, 1888.

Martin-Harvey, John, *The Autobiography of Sir John Martin-Harvey*. London: Sampson Low, Marston, 1933.

Mason, E. T., *The Othello of Tommaso Salvini*. New York: Putnam's, 1890.

Merivale, Herman Charles, *Bar, Stage and Platform: Autobiographic Memories.* London: Chatto and Windus, 1902.

Montague, C. E., *Dramatic Values.* London: Chatto and Windus, 1931.

Morley, Henry, *The Journal of a London Playgoer* [London, 1866] ed. M. R. Booth. Leicester University Press, 1974.

Morris, Clara, *Stage Confidences: Talks about Players and Play Acting.* London, 1902.

Murphy, Arthur, *The Life of David Garrick.* Dublin, 1801.

Nagler, A. M., *A Source Book in Theatrical History.* New York: Dover, 1952.

Neill, Michael, 'Unproper Beds: Race, Adultery and the Hideous in *Othello*', *Shakespeare Quarterly*, 40 (1989), pp. 383–412.

Odell, George C. D., *Shakespeare from Betterton to Irving.* 2 vols. New York, [Charles Scribner's, 1920] reprinted by Dover Publications, 1966.

Ogude, S. E., 'Literature and Racism: the Example of Othello', in Mythili Kaul, ed., *Othello: New Essays by Black Writers.* Washington DC: Howard University Press, 1997.

Okri, Ben, 'Meditations on *Othello*', *West Africa*, 23 and 30 March 1987, 562–4, 618–19.

Orkin, Martin, 'Othello and the "Plain Face" of Racism', *Shakespeare Quarterly*, 38 (Summer 1987), pp. 166–88.

Ottley, Henry, *Fechter's Version of Othello Critically Analysed.* London, 1861.

Oulton, W. C., *The History of the Theatres of London, Containing an Annual Register of All the New and Revived Tragedies, Comedies, Operas, Farces, Pantomimes that Have been Performed . . . from the year 1771 to 1795,* 2 vols. London, 1796.

Pechter, Edward, *'Othello' and Interpretive Traditions.* University of Iowa Press: 1999.

Pollock, Lady, *Macready as I Knew Him, 1793–1873.* London: Remington, 1884.

Potter, Lois, *Othello.* Manchester and New York: Manchester University Press, 2002.

Quarshie, Hugh, 'Second Thoughts about Othello', International Shakespeare Association, Occasional Paper no. 7. Chipping Campden: 1999.

Rees, James, *The Life of Edwin Forrest.* Philadelphia, 1874.

Robinson, Henry Crabb, *Diary, Reminiscences and Correspondence,* ed. Thomas Sadler, 2 vols. London, 1872.

Robson, William, *The Old Playgoer*, [London, 1846], Facsim. edn, Intro.
by Robert Gittings. Sussex: Centaur Press, 1969.

Rosenberg, Marvin, *The Masks of Othello: The Search for the Identity of
Othello, Iago and Desdemona by Three Centuries of Actors and Critics*.
Berkeley: University of California Press, 1961.

  'The Refinement of *Othello* in the Eighteenth Century', *Studies in
Philology*, 51 (January 1954), pp. 75–94.

Rothwell, Kenneth S., *A History of Shakespeare on Screen: A Century of
Film and Television*. Cambridge University Press, 1999.

Rutter, Carol Chillington, 'Looking at Shakespeare's Women on Film', in
Russell Jackson, ed., *The Cambridge Companion to Shakespeare on
Film*. Cambridge University Press, 2000.

Rymer, Thomas, *A Short View of Tragedy*, in Curt A. Zimansky, ed., *The
Critical Works of Thomas Rymer*. New Haven: Yale University Press,
1956.

Said, Edward, *Orientalism*. London: Penguin, 1991 (first pub. 1978).

Saintsbury, George, *A Second Scrap Book*. London, 1923.

Salvini, Tommaso, *Leaves from the Autobiography of Tommaso Salvini*. New
York, 1893.

  'Impressions of some Shakespearean Characters', *The Century*,
November 1881, pp. 117–25.

Shattuck, Charles, 'Shakespeare's *Othello* and its Actors', *Player's
Magazine*, vol. 13, pt 6, 1937.

Shaw, Bernard, 'A Dressing-Room Secret', in *Shaw on Shakespeare: An
Anthology of Bernard Shaw's Writings on the Plays and Production
of Shakespeare*, ed. Edwin Wilson. Harmondsworth: Penguin,
1961.

  *London Music in 1888–9, as Heard by Corno di Bassetto . . . with Some
Further Autobiographical Particulars*. London: Constable, 1937.

  Our Theatres in the Nineties, 3 vols. London: Constable, [1932], repr.
1948.

Siemon, James R., ' "Nay, That's Not Next": *Othello*, v.ii in Performance',
Shakespeare Quarterly, 37 (1986), pp. 38–51.

Singh, Jyotsna, 'Othello's Identity, Post-colonial Theory, and
Contemporary African Re-Writings of *Othello*', in Margo Hendricks
and Patricia Parker, eds., *Women, 'Race', and Writing in the Early
Modern Period*. London and New York: Routledge, 1994.

Smallwood, Robert, 'Shakespeare at Stratford-upon-Avon, 1989 (Part I)',
Shakespeare Quarterly, 41 (1990), pp. 101–14.

Speaight, Robert, 'Shakespeare in Britain', *Shakespeare Quarterly*, 15
(Autumn 1964), pp. 377–89.

Spivak, Bernard, *Shakespeare and the Allegory of Evil.* New York: Columbia University Press, 1958.

Sprague, A. C., *Shakespeare and the Actors: The Stage Business in his Plays (1660–1905).* Cambridge, MA: Harvard University Press, 1945.

Stanislavski, Constantin, *My Life in Art.* London: Methuen, 1980.

Stendhal, Henri Beyle, *Life of Rossini,* Paris, 1824; trans. Richard N. Coe. London: Calder, 1956.

Stevenson, Robert Louis, *The Works of Robert Louis Stevenson,* 26 vols. London, 1922–3, vol. XXIV.

St John, Christopher, ed., *Ellen Terry and Bernard Shaw: A Correspondence.* London: Constable, 1931.

Suchet, David, 'Iago in *Othello*', in Russell Jackson and Robert Smallwood, eds., *Players of Shakespeare 2: Further Essays in Shakespearean Performance by Players with the Royal Shakespeare Company.* Cambridge University Press, 1988.

Suzman, Janet, 'Who Needs Parables?', Tanner Lectures on Human Values, 1995, www.tannerlectures.utah.edu/lectures/Suzman96.pdf.

Terry, Ellen, *The Story of my Life.* London: Hutchinson, 1908.

Towse, J. R., *Sixty Years of the Theatre: An old Critic's Memories.* New York, 1916.

Tree, Maud Holt, 'Herbert and I', in Max Beerbohm, *Herbert Beerbohm Tree: Some Memories of Him and his Art.* London, 1920.

Trewin, J. C., *Benson and the Bensonians.* London: Barrie and Rockliff, 1960.

The Theatre since 1900: Illustrated from the Raymond Mander and Joe Mitchenson Theatre Collection. London: A. Dakers, 1951.

Tynan, Kenneth, *A View of the English Stage, 1944–63.* London: Davis-Poynter, 1975.

Othello, [by] William Shakespeare, the National Theatre Production. London: Hart Davis, 1966.

Curtains: Selections from the Drama Criticism and Related Writings. London: Longmans Green, 1961.

Vandenhoff, George, *An Actor's Notebook: Or the Green-Room and Stage.* London: John Camden Hotten, 1865.

Vaughan, Virginia, *Othello: A Contextual History.* Cambridge University Press, 1994.

Vickers, Brian, *Shakespeare: The Critical Heritage,* 6 vols. London: Routledge, 1974–81.

Victor, Benjamin, *The History of the Theatres of London and Dublin, From the Year 1730 to the Present Time,* 2 vols. Dublin: G. Faulkner and J. Exshaw, 1761.

Vigny, Alfred de, *Le More de Venise*, in *Œuvres complètes de Alfred de Vigny*, 5 vols. Paris, 1918, vol. II.

Webster, Margaret, *Don't Put your Daughter on the Stage*. New York: Alfred A. Knopf, 1972.

Shakespeare Today. London: J. M. Dent, 1957.

Shakespeare without Tears. New York: World Publishing, 1955.

Williamson, Audrey, *Old Vic Drama: A Twelve Years' Study of Plays and Players*. London: Theatre Book Club, 1948.

Wilson, John Dover, in *Othello*, ed. John Dover Wilson and Alice Walker, Cambridge University Press, 1957, repr. 1980.

Winter, William, *Shakespeare on the Stage*. London, 1912.

The Life and Art of Edwin Booth. London, 1893.

Wood, William B., *Personal Recollections of the Stage*. Philadelphia, 1855.

Wright, James, *Historia Histrionica* (1699), in W. C. Hazlitt, ed., *A Select Collection of Old English Plays*, 15 vols. London: Reeves and Turner, 1874–6, vol. XV.

Young, Stark, *Immortal Shadows: A Book of Dramatic Criticism*. New York: Scribner's Sons, 1948.

INDEX